BECOMING
POLITICAL

BECOMING

POLITICAL

Readings and

Writings in the

Politics of

Literacy Education

edited by

Patrick Shannon
Penn State University

 Heinemann
Portsmouth, NH

Heinemann Educational Books, Inc.

361 Hanover Street Portsmouth, NH 03801-3959
Offices and agents throughout the world

Library of Congress Cataloging-in-Publication Data

Becoming political: readings and writings in the politics of literacy
  education/edited by Patrick Shannon.
     p.   cm.
  Includes bibliographical references and index.
  ISBN 0-435-08701-0
  1. Teachers — United States — Political activity. 2. Teachers —
Canada — Political activity. 3. Literacy — Political aspects — United
States. 4. Literacy — Political aspects — Canada. 5. Educational
change — United States. 6. Educational change — Canada.
7. Educational equalization — United States. 8. Educational
equalization — Canada. I. Shannon, Patrick, 1951 —
LB2844.1.P6B43   1992
371.1'04 — dc20   91 — 29265
                                                            CIP

Designed by Maria Szmauz.
Printed in the United States of America.
92 93 94 95 96 9 8 7 6 5 4 3 2 1

CONTENTS

SECTION ONE
How is Literacy Defined?

SECTION TWO
What Is Read and Written?

SECTION THREE
Who Is Considered Literate?

SECTION FOUR
How is Literacy Taught?

SECTION FIVE
What Is Possible in Literacy Education?

CONTRIBUTORS

Sue Bietila is a parent from the Riverfront neighborhood in Milwaukee, Wisconsin.

William Bigelow is a high school social studies teacher from Portland, Oregon.

Jeanette L. Bishop is a resource teacher in New Minas, Nova Scotia.

David Bloome is a professor of education at The University of Massachusetts, Amherst.

Linda Brodkey is a professor of English at The University of Texas, Austin.

Susan M. Cameron is an elementary school teacher in Antigonich, Nova Scotia.

Susan M. Church is a school supervisor in Dartmouth, Nova Scotia.

Linda Cook is an elementary school teacher in Dartmouth, Nova Scotia.

James Paul Gee is a professor of linguistics at The University of Southern California.

Perry Gilmore is a professor of education at the University of Alaska, Anchorage.

Henry Giroux is Kenneth B. Waterbury Chair of Secondary Education at The Pennsylvania State University.

Roberta F. Hammett is a secondary English teacher in Kings County, Nova Scotia.

Jill Hartling-Clark is a resource teacher in New Minas, Nova Scotia.

Shirley Brice Heath is a professor of anthropology and education at Stanford University.

David Levine is a secondary social studies teacher in Milwaukee, Wisconsin.

Lynn Moody is a primary teacher in Halifax, Nova Scotia.

Sonia Nieto is a professor of education at The University of Massachusetts, Amherst.

Katherine Paterson is the author of *Bridge to Terabithia, The Great Gilley Hopkins*, *Park's Quest*, and many others.

Bronwyn Norton Peirce is a graduate student at the Ontario Institute for the Study of Education, Toronto.

Patrick Shannon is a professor of education at The Pennsylvania State University, University Park.

Roger I. Simon is a professor of education at The Ontario Institute for the Study of Education, Toronto.

Audrey Sturk is a secondary English teacher in Kings County, Nova Scotia.

Rita Tenorio is a kindergarten teacher in Milwaukee, Wisconsin.

Stephanie S. Tolan is the author of *Grandpa and Me, Pride of the Peacock, The Great Skinner Homestead*, and many others.

Cathy Townsend-Fuller is a special education teacher in Port Williams, Nova Scotia.

John Trimbur is a professor of English at Worcester Polytechnic Institute, Massachusetts.

INTRODUCTION:

Why Become Political?
Patrick Shannon

Literacy is both liberating and dominating. Through it, we can learn to read and write the world to meet our needs and interests, taking from and making of the world what we will. Text is but one way in which we express our literacy. We not only read and write (make sense of and from) the alphabet in connected passages, but we also read other types of symbols embedded in social practice and institutions and write other types of symbols through our social action to define ourselves and affirm our cultural and social histories. Through literacy, we can also learn to read and write the world others prepare for us, taking from it correct thoughts, correct behaviors, and correct lives. In this way, skills to decode, encode, and translate text are all there is to literacy.

Teaching is also liberating and dominating. By teaching, we can learn the connections between our lives and those of others and the relationships between those lives and the world we live in. In this way, we achieve a type of solidarity among teachers and students and a blurring of teacher and taught as we explore and help others to explore what we wish to make of this world. But by teaching, we may also control the lives of others by concentrating on the management of time, students, information, and materials. In the end, we may not realize that by doing this we too are controlled by the maze of organization without real choices about what, how, and why we teach. In this way, teaching continues a set of hierarchies between teacher and student, among students, and within the curriculum, all of which ensure that most participants will find the teaching exchange unsatisfying.

Schooling is also liberating and dominating. It is a process that can help students and teachers develop the liberating sides of literacy and support teachers who develop liberating relationships while they teach, leading all to greater control over their lives and even to self-transformation. Schooling can focus our attention on discussion of how we wish to live together in and out of the classroom. But schooling can be an arena for indoctrination, acculturation,

1

and standardization, an institution designed to reproduce the social and economic status quo.

The literacy, teaching, and schooling dialectics demonstrate that our job as literacy educators is political. Even apparently innocuous decisions about setting goals for programs and lessons, selecting materials, and deciding how to interact with students during lessons are actually negotiations over whose values, interests, and beliefs will be validated at school. Sometimes these negotiations are explicit and loud, as when a parent attempts to remove a book from a class reading list or a library shelf. More often, though, negotiations are implicit and silent, as when textbook authors and publishers make decisions about goals, materials, and instruction and embed them in the language of a teacher's manual and the lesson procedures for teachers and students to follow. The consequences of these negotiations can be seen in the ways in which literacy is defined in school programs, in what is read and written at school, in who is and who is not considered literate, and in how literacy is taught.

Contrary to popular rhetoric, the dominating sides of schooling, teaching, and literacy are most prevalent in North American education from preschool to graduate and professional schools. To date, the politics of this education has marginalized many members of racial and ethnic minorities from even the dominating side of literacy, restricted most females access to certain types of scientific literacy, limited the poor to vocational literacy, alienated teachers from their literacy teaching, and denied both students and teachers sophisticated and liberating literacies. These facts are documented in the statistics of continued enrollments in academic programs; of test scores; of racial, gender, and economic class background of labeled learners at school; of who becomes teachers; and of teachers who burn out in the classroom. Moreover, these facts are the reality of students' and teachers' lives during and after their time in schools.

Despite these alarming consequences, few practicing teachers recognize the political facts about school life and school literacy. Rather, they consider themselves apolitical in their work—lamenting the politics they do recognize in "the system," defining their role as delivering already determined content in traditional ways, and abdicating their rightful place in the decision making that influences their students' and their lives in and out of school. However, teachers' denial does not mean that they stand apart from the politics of literacy education. Their inattention and lack of action perpetuates the status quo: policymakers and educators with vested interest in current practices and programs accept their silence as tacit endorsement of current practice and use it to argue against change. That is, teachers' political naïveté concerning literacy, teaching, and schooling actually contributes to their students' and their own predicament. The title of this book is a misnomer. All teachers are political, whether they are conscious of it or not. Their acts contribute to or challenge the status quo in literacy education, in schools, and in society.

Becoming Political: Readings and Writings in the Politics of Literacy Education is designed to help teachers identify and begin to overcome this false consciousness about themselves and their relationships to schooling and society. This process begins by asking questions: Why are the dominating sides of literacy, teaching, and schooling more often practiced than the liberating sides? Why is it that despite the rhetoric that education is the backbone of democracy the participants in schooling have so little voice in matters of consequence in the classroom? Why are they so unfree? Who really is served by the current organization and practice of schools? How can the liberating sides of literacy, teaching, and schooling be realized? However, educators with a questioning attitude are not business as usual in schools. Some may find it insubordinate and overly negative even to ask such questions. This is a conditioned response that comes from years of accepting what's given as what must be. Teachers without these questions are the result of teachers' colleges that focus on instructional methods and management strategies without investigating their historical and philosophical underpinnings, of schools with too many students for teachers to have time to consider the meaning of their work, and of the victory of the process—product metaphor from business and experimental science over the morality of teaching (Luke 1988; Shannon 1989).

To seek changes in literacy, teaching, and schooling—and you wouldn't be reading this book if you weren't interested in change—the nature of literacy, teaching, and schooling must be seen as problematic. That is, we must look beyond recent attention to test scores in order to recognize that literacy education is not a system in and of itself. Rather, it is a historically constructed entity that can only be understood in its close and intricate interplay with social life and social structure. As a constructed rather than a naturally given entity, literacy education represents the moral, social, political, and even economic values of those who struggled to bring it to its present form and of those who struggle still to maintain that form. In short, literacy educators must say, "It doesn't have to be this way. Together, we can change it." Asking questions is a constructive act because it makes change possible.

Educators who begin to ask questions about pedagogy, about subjective and institutional barriers to teachers' and students' autonomy, and about the necessary conditions to promote the liberating sides of literacy, teaching, and schooling join a distinguished tradition within North American schools (Shannon 1990; Willensky 1990). Over a century ago Francis Parker (1884) argued that traditional schooling served "the aristocracy" rather than the masses. "The methods of the few, in their control of the many, still govern our public schools, and to a great degree determine their management," he wrote (p. 436). "The problem for the aristocrats is how to give the people education and keep them from exercising the divine gift of choice; to make them believe that they are educated and at the same time to prevent free action of mind. The problem was solved by quantity teaching" (p. 408).

During the 1920s, 1930s, and 1940s at the Little Red Schoolhouse in New York City, Elizabeth Irwin asked questions that led her students and teachers to use literacy to understand themselves and their times more fully. In her history of the school, DeLima (1942) shares several examples of students' poignant writing about hopelessness, greed, and war. Septima Clark (1962; 1990) relates her questions about literacy and the enfranchisement of African Americans in the 1950s and 1960s. Her questions involved her as director of the citizenship schools movement, in which adults learned to write an end to apartheid in the United States. Today in Portland, Oregon, Bill Bigelow asks his high school students what it means that Columbus discovered America (1989) and why labor history is excluded from history textbooks (1988).

Marietta Johnson's questions about teaching led her to establish the Organic School in Fairhope, Alabama, in 1907. At this school, "there is no fixed curriculum, but the teachers keep a simple record of work done as a guide to the next teacher" (Johnson 1938, p. 70). Johnson's intention was to help students and teachers develop "the ability to wait for data, to hold the mind open and ready, to receive new facts, to delay decisions and opinions" (Johnson 1929, p. 128). In 1940, Natalie Cole, a teacher in an economically poor section of Los Angeles, asked questions: "the child had sincerity, directness and rhythm in his art — delight and unexpectedness. Why not take those as my criteria for writing?" (p. 98). Carole Edelsky (1989) questions the purposes of teaching and its relationship to helping students and teachers become educated people. She argues that a questioning stance on life, an enthusiasm for equality and justice, and an extensive repertoire of formal ways of knowing the world can be developed under teaching conditions that develop from a whole language perspective.

John Dewey's questions about schooling and his belief that philosophy is made up of hypotheses that are testable against everyday social events required that he open an elementary school. According to Dewey (1936), this "laboratory school" was community centered rather than child centered through its eight-year history (1896–1904). Students, teachers, and parents were all considered community members. They planned the programs and curriculum together in order to harmonize the children's interests and lives with adult ends and values. Different questions about the ability of traditional schools to help poor and minority populations challenged Myles Horton to found the Highlander Folk School, a school designed to help adults realize that the solutions to their social problems could be found in their collective intelligence and social action in their community, once community members believed themselves capable masters of their own fate (Adams 1975; Horton 1990). William Tierney (1989) asks questions about the curriculum and practice in colleges and universities across North America. Central to his concerns are the contradictions among universities' organizational structures, the ideologies that inform the various competing departments and programs, and the rhetorical goal of preparing liberated, educated citizens.

My sense of this tradition and my questions about literacy, teaching, and schooling drive my efforts to become political. I began by reconsidering my experience as a primary-grade teacher in an attempt to discover why I felt so uncomfortable during lessons, while I felt so at home with children. This self-examination led me to acknowledge my duplicity in my own discomfort because I left my history as a student, my philosophy of community life, and my politics at the classroom door when I accepted the dominant tradition of literacy, teaching, and schooling. At home and during "off task" time with students I was Pat Shannon, but during lessons I was a teacher. These two personae rarely met.

My subsequent attempts to see if others shared this frustration (e.g., 1982; 1983; 1984; 1985; 1986; 1987; 1988; 1989; 1990; 1991) forced me to see connections among my life in the classroom, the organization of schools, the rationalization of everyday life, and societal structure. My (our) frustration and my forced schizophrenia was, and is, endemic to my life — forced gently, firmly, and continuously by the way in which our lives are organized for us in schools. However, my discomfort showed me that this forced life is not natural to our internal system, and my studies taught me that it is not natural to a social life.

With these realizations came the need and the right to struggle against the subjective and objective circumstances that make traditional literacy, teaching, and schooling so dissatisfying for me, many of my colleagues, and so many students.

My writing, speaking at conferences, working in professional organizations, and teaching at college express my pain and attempt to make literacy, teaching, and schooling seem problematic for literacy educators and researchers. This book is the result of another form of action, my participation in and leadership of a group of educators endeavoring to become political during a two-and-a-half-week Summer Institute at Mount Saint Vincent University in Halifax, Nova Scotia, during 1990. I accepted the University's invitation to participate upon the presupposition that discussion of literacy, teaching, and schooling would prompt Institute participants' action to reestablish themselves in the political negotiations in their school systems and to improve policies and practices in their learning and teaching environments. I sought to help participants to add explicitly political questions to the pedagogical questions that they were already asking while they developed critical theories of literacy education. I considered my participation in the Institute an expression of my ongoing political development.

When I accepted the invitation, I had no knowledge of how the Institute operated or the teaching conditions in Nova Scotia, although I had been to Halifax once before briefly, and I had taught college in Ontario for two years. My lack of knowledge was exacerbated by the Institute directors' request for a syllabus and a list of readings before my arrival. Moreover, they asked if I had any preliminary assignments for participants to do before they attended the Institute. Hoping to ground our work in participants' school lives but having only a slight idea of what those lives might be, I suggested an observational exercise, set criteria for and selected readings, and outlined loose parameters for our work.

I wrote a letter to the participants requesting that they do the following:

[E]ngage in a bit of observation, thinking, and writing before we gather in July. Pick an issue (a rule, an activity, an object, an attitude, etc.) from your workplace that you consider political. Write a description of it. Who's involved? What's the immediate context? Is language involved? Is literacy? After you have a description of the issue, on another sheet of paper consider how the issue relates to other aspects of social life: Why does the issue exist, who is served by it, and who is not? Now and only now, start to examine your connection with the issue. Are you involved directly? When did the issue become political for you? Did the issue have an antecedent? Were you involved in it? What might the issue become in the future? Finally, is change in this issue necessary? Can literacy play a role in that change? What's your role in changing it? I hope we can start our work together with a discussion of these issues in order to explore ourselves and our definitions of politics and literacy. I'll bring an issue too.

When we met we exchanged descriptions of the issues (but not the analyses) and wrote about what we thought was political about someone else's issue. Later we returned our responses and analyses and talked in pairs about the similarities and differences between our definitions of politics, our interpretations of the issues, and our school experiences. Our issues ranged from school rules for adolescent petting to feminist concerns for voice in union matters, to teacher–parent relations, to alienation among teachers, to drastic cuts in educational budgets. Participants marveled at the differences in interpretation and remarked upon the value of looking at their issues through another's eyes. No one questioned the political relevance of anyone else's issue or denied the possibility that others could be correct in their interpretation. By the end of the first day, although we had not defined politics explicitly (we never did), we had affirmed the importance of our study together regardless of the differences among our experience and working conditions.

For the reading to direct our talk, I selected seventeen previously published articles in order to address what I consider to be categories for understanding the consequences of the imbalance of the dialectics in literacy education:

- How is literacy defined?
- What is read and written?
- Who is considered literate?
- How is literacy taught?

In addition to addressing these questions, I selected reading that would:

- schools in order to broaden participants' perspectives as they developed schools in order to broaden participants' perspective as they developed deeper insights into their immediate circumstances.
- Achieve a balance between explicit and implicit political issues and provide new ways to look at the familiar as well as consider the issues that often escape teachers' notice.
- Provide elaborate critiques of current definitions, policy, and practices as well as make suggestions for constructive change in order to develop participants' abilities to analyze their practice while engendering a sense of hope that literacy education can be changed.
- Offer theoretical and practical perspectives on similar issues in order to develop a sense of praxis among teachers.
- Come from familiar sources in order to make participants' consideration of the politics of literacy education seem less exotic and more accessible, and to demonstrate that seemingly apolitical journals do address political issues.

The selected readings were arranged so that themes could be reconsidered across categories.

Literacy	Reading and Writing	Literate	Taught
Giroux	Paterson	Brodkey	Peirce
	Tolan		
Gee	Shannon	Gilmore	Bietila and Levine
Heath	Bigelow	Shannon	Shannon
Shannon	Bloome and Nieto	Simon	Trimbur

During the Institute, our mornings were spent discussing these articles. We considered all the readings in a category over two mornings. During the afternoons participants conducted self-directed research about the politics and role of literacy in their working situation. Although Institute participants found several of the readings challenging, they reported in their evaluations that the grouping of the readings into categories helped them make connections among issues that they had previously considered separate and that the different perspectives from which the recurring themes were seen enabled them to develop sophisticated responses to the questions that formed the categories.

Moreover, they found that the large- and small-group discussions of their interpretations of the readings encouraged them to look critically at their own, their school's, and their government's stance toward literacy education. According to participants' comments, political consciousness raising for teachers cannot be an isolated or individual activity. Rather, their formal and informal talk validated, yet interrogated, their individual and collective concerns and caused them to develop a solidarity that continued after the Institute.

Early in our discussions, the participants complained about the vocabulary used in several of the readings: discourse; language of critique, language of possibility, and projects of possibility; covert censorship; true consensus; and marginalized groups. They wondered aloud whether the concepts behind the vocabulary were worth the struggle to read the articles. Our talk about their experiences and our experience with other groups and leaders from the Institute proved the worth of the concepts, if not the terminology.

Comments about the term *discourse* soon led participants to explore connections between the readings and their lives (see Gee). One suggested that the discourse of teachers—the ways they use language, think, and act—makes them a distinct group from the parents and students they serve. Others suggested that discourse differences were the basis for the feelings of alienation whole language teachers felt in their schools when they are all but shunned by traditional teachers (see Shannon, chapter 4). When coupled with other readings, the selections on discourse became a way for participants to understand why standard school practices systematically disadvantage students who are from neither the middle nor the upper class. (see Gilmore; Heath; Peirce).

During the Institute, the participants' attempts to develop a language of critique, a systematic analysis that becomes part of an everyday consideration of work and life, began with a discussion of recent budget cuts for education in Nova Scotia (see Giroux; Shannon, chapter 12). Their initial talk about the discourse of government officials directed them toward the language of the cuts. "Curriculum reorganization" meant that entire programs were eliminated from the curriculum and school. "Unit reassignment" translated into teachers with as many as ten years of service being fired and class sizes raised to unspecified levels. Participants quickly began to attribute intent to governmental doublespeak and to address issues of censorship in terms of the government's failure to disclose important information on this and other matters. The discussion was broadened when one participant argued that teachers fail to disclose all types of vital information to students and parents. Participants acknowledged that teachers fail to make explicit their own questions about testing, tracking, and curriculum, and that this failure is an explicit example of censorship (see Paterson; Tolan). Slowly, we began to consider personal and institutional assumptions about race, class, gender, social organization, authority, and control as cases of covert censorship wherein teachers don't think to raise questions because "everyone thinks that way" (see Bigelow; Brodkey; Shannon, chapter 7).

Once started, the participants' language of critique became part of the group's discourse, and they found themselves estranged from other groups at the Institute. Other groups were less than generous when members of our section used their language of critique to discuss the interactions and hierarchical relationships among Institute participants. When they spoke about the politics of the Institute, their concerns were generally ignored by other participants. In short, they suffered the pain of separation that often comes when individuals attempt to acquire an additional discourse that allows critique of a former discourse community. In fact, they became a marginalized group within the Institute (see Bloome and Nieto).

Discussion of true consensus began with my comment that many U.S. teachers believe that Nova Scotia teachers work under the best possible conditions for literacy education because the Nova Scotia Ministry of Education has set policy that requires teachers to follow whole language or learner-centered philosophy. Their perception is that there is consensus among Nova Scotia teachers concerning how to teach (see Trimbur). The participants were quick to dispel this myth of consensus. They spoke of the many sub-discourse communities within schools and how the government's attempt to override these differences with policy instead of negotiations led to the estrangement from their fellow teachers that many of them felt. According to participants, schools were not forums in which teachers could define and openly discuss their differences in order to devise ways in which they could work together in schools. With this acknowledgment of false consensus came talk about what ought to be done to better the conditions for teachers and students at any level of schooling. During these discussions, participants' language of critique met a language of possibility and hope (see Peirce; Shannon, chapter 17; Simon).

Afternoons were left open to allow participants to research political issues and actions that individuals and groups might undertake when schools reopened in the fall. Most of this research concerned plans for projects to promote the liberating sides of literacy, teaching, and schooling in the participants' immediate settings (see Bietila and Levine; Tenorio). Some of those plans are to be found in the final section of this book. Although each participant produced an interesting writing, I limited the selection to those that met certain criteria. Selected writings were:

- Representative of the background of the participants in the Institute: elementary and secondary school teachers, special educators, and administrators.
- Demonstrative of the variety of genres that participants used for their plans: retrospectives, reanalyses of data, essays, curriculum proposals, narratives of classroom events, a game, pamphlets, and a song.
- Challenging in the contexts in which they consider the themes that developed during our discussions.
- Likely to make a difference in the participants' work.

The authors of the seven examples of writings included in this book recognize that change starts with individuals who ask questions about their own practice, needs, and hopes for students. Lynn Moody wonders about her relationships with parents. Cathy Townsend-Fuller and Jill Hartling-Clark reconsider the use of tests in their special education programs. Susan Church reexamines her role as an advocate for whole language. Roberta Hammett searches for meaning in the AIDS education portion of her English teaching. Audrey Sturk seeks connections between literature and community life. Jeanette Bishop and Susan Cameron muse about why their talk rarely considered politics. And Linda Cook reconsiders her advice to a student. Each acknowledges that our discussions and the themes from the readings jar even the experimental attitudes they brought with them to the Institute.

Yet none see themselves as solely responsible for their attitude and the way they conduct themselves at work. They do not believe they are in total control of their lives at school or that they can bring about the changes they seek by themselves. All see connections between their work, the organization of schools, and the structure of society. Moody places parent−teacher relationships in the context of social class and racial realities in cities. Townsend-Fuller and Hartling-Clark recognize the symbiotic relationship between testing, tracking, and schooling even in a province that calls itself "learner-centered." Church acknowledges the contradictions between bureaucratic policymaking and whole language and within the whole language movement. Hammett situates AIDS education within the knowledge of gay and lesbian culture and both within a homophobic society. Sturk forges links between adolescent and elderly lives in her community through novel study and community projects. Bishop and Cameron demonstrate how events and issues in schools affect the lives of students, teachers, parents, and administrators. Cook directs our attention to the prospects of liberatory practice at school in a racist, sexist, and classist society. In the end, each challenges the dominating sides of literacy, teaching, and schooling and offers bold plans for changing themselves, their work, their schools, and their communities.

By their own accounts, the participants who contributed to this book found the enactment of their projects of possibility more difficult than the planning of them. During the Institute, our group developed a political discourse that enabled individuals to identify, define, and analyze barriers to the liberatory sides of literacy, teaching, and schooling and to articulate rationales for the end to those barriers. They found sympathetic and questioning peers who were willing and able to help them address their concerns. However, in September, participants returned to a variety of discourse communities (e.g., traditional teachers, whole language teachers who think only about pedagogy, administrators, students and parents, and others) with varying amounts of interest in discussion of making changes in the politics of literacy education. They found themselves marginalized individuals at school, and they remain a marginalized group among all Institute participants. (The Institute directors dropped the Institute's explicit political strand from the options for the next year's offerings.) Yet as those writers report in their updates six months after their original plans, they are optimistic about the prospects for their plans; they are refining their languages of critique and possibility to reveal the myths of consensus among school personnel and to build coalitions; and they are committed to action in the promotion of the liberatory sides of literacy, teaching, and schooling.

I offer *Becoming Political* as a project of possibility. This introduction, these readings, and these writings are artifacts of one group's effort to become political. They comprise an impressionistic study of our development and demonstrate our individual and collective theories of critical literacy. The readings helped us to understand ourselves as literacy educators: the readings validated teachers' concerns and extended their abilities to analyze their circumstances in schools and their connections to the social structure. The writings tell of our plans and actions to make literacy, teaching, and schooling problematic and to make literacy education better for students *and* teachers. My hope is that, taken together, these three types of writing will serve as a catalyst for other groups of educators who wish to become political by questioning, discussing, reading, writing, and acting to change literacy education to make it more equal and just.

In a very real sense, such *action* may be the best expression of the liberatory sides of literacy and teaching because its consequences cannot be contained within academic circles. Rather, it will necessarily spill over to students, other teachers, administrators, parents, and the community. Our work during and after the Institute suggests the heady benefits of immersion in the politics of literacy education with a like-minded, diverse group. However, our work also demonstrates the need for something we could not achieve—continuous contact over time. Just as pedagogically progressive educators need ongoing support from their peers to understand and take risks during their teaching, political progressives need to know that they are not alone, that others will no longer remain silent, and that we are in it together for the long haul.

Literacy education in its current form is not a natural product of evolution, and it need not continue to provide unjust services that benefit different social groups so unequally. Although it may not be easy, through our thoughts, dreams, and actions we can make of literacy education what we will. So what shall we make of it?

References

Adams, F. 1975. *Unearthing Seeds of Fire: The Highlander Folk School*. Winston-Salem, NC: John F. Blair.

Bigelow, W. 1988. *The Power in Our Hands: A Curriculum on the History of Work and Workers in the United States*. New York: Monthly Review Press.

———. 1989. "Discovering Columbus: Rereading the Past." *Language Arts* 66: 635–43.

Clark, S. 1962. *Echo in My Soul*. New York: Dutton.

———. 1990. *Ready from Within*. Trenton, NJ: Africa World Press.

Cole, N. 1940. *The Arts in The Classroom*. New York: John Day.

DeLima, A. 1942. *The Little Red Schoolhouse*. New York: Macmillan.

Dewey, J. 1936. "The Theory of the Chicago Experiment." In K. Mayhew and A. Edwards (eds.), *The Dewey School*. New York: Appleton-Century.

Edelsky, C. 1989. "Challenge to Educators: The Development of Educated Persons." Paper presented at the Appalachian State University's Distinguished Scholars' Colloquium.

Horton, M. 1990. *The Long Haul*. New York: Anchor.

Johnson, M. 1929. *Youth in a World of Men*. New York: John Day.

———. 1938 [1974]. *Thirty Years with an Idea*. University, AL: University of Alabama Press.

Luke, A. 1988. *Literacy, Textbooks, and Ideology*. Philadelphia, PA: Fulmer.

Parker, F. 1884. *Talks on Pedagogies*. New York: Kellog.

Shannon, P. 1982. "Some Subjective Reasons for Teachers' Reliance on Commercial Reading Materials." *Reading Teacher* 35: 884–89.

———. 1983. "The Use of Commercial Reading Materials in American Elementary Schools." *Reading Research Quarterly* 19: 68–85.

———. 1984. "Mastery Learning in Reading and the Control of Teachers and Students." *Language Arts* 61: 484–93.

———. 1985. "Reading Instruction and Social Class." *Language Arts* 62: 604–13.

———. 1986. "Merit Pay, Formal Rationality, and the Teacher's Role During Reading Instruction." *Reading Research Quarterly* 21: 20–35.

———. 1987. "Commercial Reading Materials, Technological Ideology and the Deskilling of Teachers." *Elementary School Journal* 87: 307–29.

———. 1988. "Point/Counterpoint: Direct Instruction." In J. Readence and S. Baldwin (eds.), *37th Yearbook of The National Reading Conference*. Chicago, IL: National Reading Conference.

———. 1989. *Broken Promises: Reading Instruction in 20th Century America*. Greenwich, CT: Bergin & Garvey.

———. 1990. *The Struggle to Continue: Progressive Reading Instruction in the United States*. Portsmouth, NH: Heinemann.

———. 1991. "Politics, Policy, and Reading Research." In R. Barr, M. Kamil, P. Mosenthal, and D. Pearson (eds.), *Handbook in Reading Research*, Vol. II. New York: Longman.

Tierney, W. 1989. "Cultural Politics and the Curriculum in Post Secondary Education." *Journal of Education* 171: 72–88.

Willensky, J. 1990. *The New Literacy: Redefining Reading and Writing in the Schools*. New York: Routledge.

How
Is
Literacy
Defined?

O N E

Critical Literacy and Student Experience: Donald Graves' Approach to Literacy

Henry A. Giroux

How does the "writing and reading approach" developed by Donald Graves imply a view of curriculum organized around a central pedagogical question: how can we as educators make learning meaningful in order to make it critical and how can we make it critical in order to make it emancipatory? Professor Graves' approach to critical literacy is important in this regard because it contains elements of a language of critique and a language of possibility, both of which are essential to the development of a critical theory of curriculum and pedagogy in which hope becomes practical and despair unconvincing.

A language of critique and of possibility

As a language of *critique*, Graves' approach throws into high relief the theoretical and practical flaws of mainstream curriculum theory in the United States. Whereas mainstream or dominant curriculum theory treats knowledge as something to be managed and consumed, Professor Graves sees knowledge as something to be understood and analyzed within the forms of experience that students bring to schools. Whereas mainstream curriculum theory appeals to accountability schemes and sterile, ever-growing forms of quantification to legitimate a particular view of learning, Graves raises questions about how learning can provide the grounds for students to be critical and self-determined

Source: Henry A. Giroux, "Critical Literacy and Student Experience: Donald Graves' Approach to Literacy," *Language Arts* 64 (February 1987): 175–81. Copyright 1987 by the National Council of Teachers of English. Reprinted with permission.

thinkers. Whereas mainstream curriculum theory frequently ignores the issue of student experience by arguing for classroom methods that can be generalized across student populations, Professor Graves argues that student experience is a central aspect of teaching and learning and has to be dealt with in its particular context and specificity. In mainstream curriculum theory, teachers are increasingly reduced to the status of clerks carrying out the mandates of the state or merely implementing the management schemes of administrators who have graduated from schools of education that have supplied them with the newest schemes for testing and measuring knowledge, but rarely with any sense of understanding how school knowledge is produced, where it comes from, whose interest it serves, or how it might function to privilege some groups over others. For Professor Graves, as for myself, this approach to curriculum is in itself part of what I call the new illiteracy, characteristic of the ever-falling rate of critical literacy embedded in the educational management schemes that have proliferated in the age of Reagan.

As a language of *possibility*, Professor Graves' approach to critical literacy provides a crucial insight into the learning process by linking the nature of learning itself with the dreams, experiences, histories, and languages that students bring to the schools. For Graves, it is important that teachers learn to confirm student experiences so that students are legitimated and supported as people who matter, who can participate in their learning, and who in doing so can speak with a voice that is rooted in their sense of history and place.

Student experience and curriculum theory

I want to take the notion of voice and extend its implications to curriculum development by arguing that if we, as educators, are going to give student experience a central place in our school curricula and classroom practices, we have to redefine curriculum not as a warehouse of knowledge merely to be passed on to waiting customers but, more importantly, as a configuration of knowledge, social relations, and values that represents an introduction to and legitimation of a particular way of life. This means that the issue of student experience will have to be analyzed as part of a wider relationship between culture and power. Let me be more specific. As Paulo Freire and others have pointed out, schools are not merely instructional sites designed to transmit knowledge; they are also cultural sites. As cultural sites, they generate and embody support for particular forms of culture as is evident in the school's support for specific ways of speaking, the legitimating of distinct forms of knowledge, the privileging of certain histories and patterns of authority, and the confirmation of particular ways of experiencing and seeing the world. Schools often give the appearance of transmitting a common culture, but they, in fact, more often than not, legitimate what can be called a dominant culture. Moreover, schools are not uniform places simply catering democratically to the needs of different students; they are characterized by the presence of students from both dominant and subordinate cultures, with the dominant culture often sanctioning the voices of white, middle-class students, while simultaneously disconfirming or ignoring the voices of students from subordinate groups, whether they be black, working-class, Hispanic, or other minority groups.

Crucial to this argument is the recognition that it is not enough for teachers to merely dignify the grounds on which students learn to speak, imagine, and give meaning to their world. This is important but it is also crucial for teachers to understand how schools, as part of the wider dominant culture, often function to marginalize, disconfirm, and delegitimate the experiences, histories, and categories that students use in mediating their lives. This means understanding how texts, classroom relations, teacher talk, and other aspects of the formal and hidden curricula of schooling often function to actively silence students.

At issue here is understanding that student experience has to be understood as part of an interlocking web of power relations in which some groups of students are often privileged over others. But if we are to view this insight in an important way, we must understand that it is imperative for teachers to critically examine the cultural backgrounds and social formations out of which their students produce the categories they use to give meaning to the world. For teachers are not merely dealing with students who have individual interests, they are dealing primarily with individuals whose stories, memories, narratives, and readings of the world are inextricably related to wider social and cultural formations and categories. The issue here is not merely one of relevance but one of power. Schools produce not only subjects but also subjectivities and in doing so often function to disempower students by tracking them into classes with lowered expectations, or by refusing to provide them with knowledge that is relevant and speaks to the context of their everyday lives. We know, for example, that many educators view different languages and backgrounds in students as deficits to be corrected, rather than as strengths to build upon. We also know that black, working-class, and other minority children are vastly overrepresented in special education classes and that they make up a large share of the dropout statistics in our nation's schools. I believe that Professor Graves' approach to literacy gains an important theoretical dimension when it incorporates a more critical understanding of how experience is named, produced, sustained, and rewarded in schools. That is, teachers need a critical language that allows them to understand how school knowledge and classroom social relations are constructed, disseminated, and legitimated in everyday instruction and how the underlying interests embodied in them function so as to enable or disable student learning.

I also believe that developing a pedagogy that takes the notion of student experience seriously means developing a critically affirmative language that works both *with* and *on* the experiences that students bring to the classroom. This means not only taking seriously and confirming the language forms, modes of reasoning, dispositions, and histories that give students an active voice in defining the world, it also means working on the experiences of such students in order for them to examine both their strengths and weaknesses. Student experience, like the culture and society of which it is a part, is not all of one piece, and it is important to sort through its contradictions and to give students the chance to not only confirm themselves but also to raise the question: *what is it this society has made of me that I no longer want to be?* Similarly, this means teaching students how to critically appropriate the codes and vocabularies of different cultural experiences so as to provide them with the skills they will need in order to define and shape, rather than simply serve, in the modern world. In other words, students need to understand the richness and strengths of other cultural traditions, other voices, particularly as these point to forms of self-empowerment and social empowerment.

Student experience and a critical pedagogy

Developing a critical pedagogy that takes the notion of student experience seriously also involves rethinking the very nature of curriculum discourse. At the outset this demands understanding curriculum as representative of a set of underlying interests that structure how a particular story is told through the organization of knowledge, social relations, values, and forms of assessment. In short, curriculum itself represents a narrative or voice, one that is multilayered and often contradictory but also situated within relations of power that more often than not favor white, middle-class, English-speaking students. What this suggests for a critical theory of literacy and pedagogy is that curriculum must be seen in the most fundamental sense as a battle-ground over whose forms of knowledge, history, visions, language, culture, and authority will prevail as a legitimate object of learning and analysis. In short, curriculum must be under-stood as a form of cultural politics that embodies the basic elements of a critical pedagogy that is both empowering and transformative. Some of the basic elements of such a pedagogy might include the following.

First, in addition to legitimating student experiences and treating curriculum as a narrative whose interests must be uncovered and critically interrogated, progressive teachers must develop conditions in their classrooms that allow different student voices to be heard and legitimated. In other words, teachers must create classroom social relations that allow students to speak and to appreciate the nature of difference as both a basis for democratic tolerance and as a fundamental condition for critical dialogue and the development of forms of solidarity rooted in the principles of trust, sharing, and a commitment to improving the quality of human life. In this case, the notion of voice is developed around a politics of difference and community that is not rooted in simply a celebration of plurality, but in a particular form of human community that allows and dignifies plurality as part of an ongoing effort to develop social relations in which all voices in their differences become unified in their efforts to identify and recall moments of human suffering and the need for the conditions that perpetuate such suffering to be overcome.

Second, teachers should provide students with the opportunity to interrogate different languages or ideological discourses as they are developed in an assort-ment of texts and curriculum materials. This is important because it provides the basis for students to critically analyze the forms of intelligibility, interests, and moral and political considerations that different voices embody. Examining such discourses must be done not only as a form of ideology-critique intended to uncover and demystify how knowledge claims distort reality, but also as an attempt to recover and reconstruct knowledge which allows students to more fully understand their own histories in order to be able to analyze and interrogate the dominant forms of history with which they are presented. In this case, all aspects of curriculum knowledge and pedagogy can be examined as historical constructions embodying particular interests that not only shape the content and forms of curriculum knowledge, but also produce and legitimate particular forms of subjectivity.

Third, a critical pedagogy must take seriously the articulation of a morality that posits a language of public life, emancipatory community, and individual and social commitment. In other words, students need to be introduced to a language of morality that allows them to think about how community life should be constructed. Fundamental here is what it means to be human and to recognize those ideological and material constraints that restrict human possibilities, especially those possibilities that function to improve the quality of human life for all. A discourse of morality is important both because it points to the need to educate students to fight and struggle in order to advance the discourse and principles of a critical democracy, and because it provides a referent against which students can decide what forms of life and conduct are most appropriate morally amid the welter of knowledge claims and interests they confront in making choices in a world of competing and diverse ideologies.

Fourth, essential to the development of a critical pedagogy is what my colleague Roger Simon has called the moment of transformation. That is, progressive educators need to educate students not only to make choices and to think critically but also to believe that they can make a difference in the world. We might call this a project of possibility, one that can be developed around forms of community work, through curriculum projects that address concrete instances of suffering, or through school projects aimed at addressing public issues with which students are familiar.

Empowering teachers

I want to conclude by pointing out that Professor Graves' approach to learning is not simply about empowering students, it is also about empowering teachers, which in my mind is the precondition for the success of any learning process.

If teachers are to take an active role in raising serious questions about what they teach, how they are to teach, and the larger goals for which they are striving, it means they must take a more critical role in defining the nature of their work as well as in shaping the conditions under which they work. In my mind, teachers need to view themselves as intellectuals who combine conception and implementation, thinking and practice. The category of intellectual is important here for analyzing the particular practices in which teachers engage. For it provides a referent for criticizing those forms of management pedagogies, accountability schemes, and teacher-proof curricula that would define teachers merely as technicians. Moreover, it provides the theoretical and political basis for teachers to engage in a critical dialogue among themselves and others in order to fight for the conditions they need that will allow them to reflect, read, share their work with others, and to produce curriculum materials. At the present time teachers in the United States generally labor under organizational constraints and ideological conditions that leave them little room for collective work and critical pursuits. Their teaching hours are too long; they are generally isolated in cellular structures and have few opportunities to work with their peers; moreover, they generally have little to say over the selection, organization, and distribution of teaching materials. Furthermore, they operate under class loads and within an industrial timetable that is oppressive. Their salaries are a scandal and only now is this situation being recognized by the American public.

The issue is, of course, that intellectual work that operates in the interest of critical pedagogies needs to be supported by practical conditions, and that by fighting for conditions that support joint teaching, collective writing and research, and democratic planning, teachers will make inroads into opening new spaces for creative and reflective discourse and action. The importance of such a discourse cannot be overemphasized. For within such a discourse teachers can develop an emancipatory pedagogy that relates language and power, takes popular experiences seriously as part of the learning process, combats mystification and helps students to reorder the raw experiences of their lives through the perspectives opened up by approaches to learning such as those suggested by Donald Graves.

I want to end by arguing that all those concerned with the issue of how schools can empower both teachers and students need to reestablish a concern for the purpose of education. We need to fight against those who would simply make schools an adjunct of the corporation or the workplace. Schools, after all, are more than "company stores" and need to be seen as vital sites for the development of democracy. Schools need to be defended as an important public service that educates students to be critical citizens capable of exhibiting civic courage. Donald Graves has repeatedly emphasized that in a democracy educators have to be concerned with the way in which students respond. Democracy requires citizens who can think, challenge, and exhibit long-term thought. This means that public schools need to become places that provide the opportunity for literate occasions, that is, opportunities for students to share their experiences, work in social relations that emphasize care and concern for others, and be introduced to forms of knowledge that provide them with the opportunity to take risks and fight for a quality of life in which all human beings benefit. It is to our benefit that Donald Graves not only writes and talks about these issues, but also works with other teachers in implementing them.

TWO

What Is Literacy?
James Paul Gee

t is a piece of folk wisdom that part of what linguists do is define words. In over a decade as a linguist, however, no one, until now, has asked me to define a word. So my first try: what does "literacy" mean? It won't surprise you that we have to define some other words first. So let me begin by giving a technical meaning to an old term which, unfortunately, already has a variety of other meanings. The term is "discourse." I will use the word as a count term ("a discourse," "discourses," "many discourses"), not as a mass term ("discourse," "much discourse"). By "a discourse" I will mean:

> a socially accepted association among ways of using language, of thinking, and of acting that can be used to identify oneself as a member of a socially meaningful group or "social network."

Think of discourse as an "identity kit" which comes complete with the appropriate costume and instructions on how to act and talk so as to take on a particular role that others will recognize. Let me give an example: Being "trained" as a linguist meant that I learned to speak, think and act like a linguist, and to recognize others when they do so. Now actually matters are not that simple: the larger discourse of linguistics contains many subdiscourses, different socially accepted ways of being a linguist. But the master discourse is not just the sum of its parts, it is something also over and above them. Every act of speaking, writing and behaving a linguist does as a linguist is meaningful only against the background of the whole social institution of linguistics, and that institution is made up of concrete things like people, books and buildings; abstract things like bodies of knowledge, values, norms and beliefs; mixtures of concrete and abstract things like universities, journals and publishers; as well as a shared

Source: James Paul Gee, "What Is Literacy?", *TEACHING & LEARNING: The Journal of Natural Inquiry* 2 (1) (Fall 1987): 3−11. Reprinted with permission.

history and shared stories. Some other examples of discourses: being an American or a Russian, being a man or a woman, being a member of a certain socio-economic class, being a factory worker or a boardroom executive, being a doctor or a hospital patient, being a teacher, an administrator, or a student, being a member of a sewing circle, a club, a street gang, a lunchtime social gathering, or a regular at a local watering hole.

There are a number of important points that one can make about discourses, none of which, for some reason, are very popular to Americans, though they seem to be commonplace in European social theory (Belsey 1980; Eagleton 1983; Jameson 1981; Macdonell 1986; Thompson 1984):

1. Discourses are inherently "ideological." They crucially involve a set of values and viewpoints in terms of which one must speak and act, at least while being in the discourse; otherwise one doesn't count as being in it.
2. Discourses are resistant to internal criticism and self-scrutiny since uttering viewpoints that seriously undermine them defines one as being outside them. The discourse itself defines what counts as acceptable criticism. Of course, one can criticize a particular discourse from the viewpoint of another one (e.g., psychology criticizing linguistics). But what one cannot do is stand outside all discourse and criticize any one or all of them—that would be like trying to repair a jet in flight by stepping outside it.
3. Discourse-defined positions from which to speak and behave are not, however, just defined internal to a discourse, but also as standpoints taken up by the discourse in its relation to other, ultimately opposing, discourses. The discourse of managers in an industry is partly defined as a set of views, norms and standpoints defined by their opposition to analogous points in the discourse of workers (Macdonell 1986: 1−7). The discourse we identify with being a feminist is radically changed if all male discourses disappear.
4. Any discourse concerns itself with certain objects and puts forward certain concepts, viewpoints and values at the expense of others. In doing so it will marginalize viewpoints and values central to other discourses (Macdonell, 1986: 1−7). In fact, a discourse can call for one to accept values in conflict with other discourses one is a member of—for example, the discourse used in literature departments used to marginalize popular literature and women's writings. Further, women readers of Hemingway, for instance, when acting as "acceptable readers" by the standards of the discourse of literary criticism, might find themselves complicit with values which conflict with those of various other discourses they belong to as women (Culler 1982: 43−64).
5. Finally, discourses are intimately related to the distribution of social power and hierarchical structure in society. Control over certain discourses can lead to the acquisition of social goods (money, power, status) in a society. These discourses empower those groups who have the least conflicts with their other discourses when they use them. For example, many academic, legalistic and bureaucratic discourses in our society contain a moral subdiscourse that sees "right" as what is derivable from general abstract principles. This can conflict to a degree with a discourse about morality that appears to be more often associated with women than men in terms of

which "wrong" is seen as the disruption of social networks, and "right" as the repair of those networks (Gilligan 1982). Or, to take another example, the discourse of literary criticism was a standard route to success as a professor of literature. Since it conflicted less with the other discourses of white, middle class men than it did with those of women, men were empowered by it. Women were not, as they were often at cross-purposes when engaging in it. Let us call discourses that lead to social goods in a society "dominant discourses" and let us refer to those groups that have the fewest conflicts when using them as "dominant groups." Obviously these are both matters of degree and change to a certain extent in different contexts.

It is sometimes helpful to say that it is not individuals who speak and act, but rather historically and socially defined discourses speak to each other through individuals. The individual instantiates, gives body to, a discourse every time he acts or speaks and thus carries it, and ultimately changes it, through time. Americans tend to be very focused on the individual, and thus often miss the fact that the individual is simply the meeting point of many, sometimes conflicting, socially and historically defined discourses.

The crucial questions is: how does one come by the discourses that he controls? And here it is necessary, before answering the question, to make an important distinction, a distinction that does not exist in non-technical parlance, but one which is important to a linguist: a distinction between "acquisition" and "learning" (Krashen 1982, 1985; Krashen & Terrell 1983). I will distinguish these two as follows:

> Acquisition is a process of acquiring something subconsciously by exposure to models and a process of trial and error, without a process of formal teaching. It happens in natural settings which are meaningful and functional in the sense that the acquirer knows that he needs to acquire the thing he is exposed to in order to function and the acquirer in fact wants to so function. This is how most people come to control their first language.

> Learning is a process that involves conscious knowledge gained through teaching, though not necessarily from someone officially designated a teacher. This teaching involves explanation and analysis, that is, breaking down the thing to be learned into its analytic parts. It inherently involves attaining, along with the matter being taught, some degree of meta-knowledge about the matter.

Much of what we come by in life, after our initial enculturation, involves a mixture of acquisition and learning. However, the balance between the two can be quite different in different cases and different at different stages in the process. For instance, I initially learned to drive a car by instruction, but thereafter acquired, rather than learned, most of what I know. Some cultures highly value acquisition and so tend simply to expose children to adults modeling some activity and eventually the child picks it up, picks it up as a gestalt, rather than as a series of analytic bits (Scollon & Scollon 1981; Heath 1983). Other cultural groups highly value teaching and thus break down what is to be mastered into sequential steps and analytic parts and engage in explicit explanation. There is an up side and a down side to both that can be expressed as follows: "we are better at what we acquire, but we consciously know more about what we have learned." For most of us, playing a musical instrument, or dancing, or using a second language are skills we attained by some mixture of acquisition and learning. But it is a safe bet that, over the same amount of time, people are better at these activities if acquisition predominated during that time. The point can be made using second language as the example: most people aren't very good at attaining a second language in any very functional way through formal instruction in a classroom. That's why teaching grammar is not a very good way of getting people to control a language. However, people who have acquired a second language in a natural setting don't thereby make good linguists, and some good linguists can't speak the languages they learned in a classroom. What is said here about second languages is true, I believe, of all of what I will later refer to as "secondary discourses": acquisition is good for performance, learning is good for meta-level knowledge (cf. Scribner & Cole, 1981). Acquisition and learning are thus, too, differential sources of power: acquirers usually beat learners at performance, learners usually beat acquirers at talking about it, that is, at explication, explanation, analysis and criticism.

Now what has this got to do with literacy? First, let me point out that it renders the common sense understanding of literacy very problematic. Take the notion of a "reading class." I don't know if they are still prevalent, but when I was in grammar school we had a special time set aside each day for "reading class" where we would learn to read. Reading is at the very least the ability to interpret print (surely not just the ability to call out the names of letters), but an interpretation of print is just a viewpoint on a set of symbols, and viewpoints are always embedded in a discourse. Thus, while many different discourses use reading, even in opposing ways, and while there could well be classes devoted to these discourses, reading outside such a discourse or class would be truly "in a vacuum," much like our repairman above trying to repair the jet in flight by jumping out the door. Learning to read is always learning some aspect of some discourse. One can trivialize this insight to a certain degree by trivializing the notion of interpretation (of printed words), until one gets to reading as calling out the names of letters. Analogously, one can deepen the insight by taking successively deeper views of what interpretation means. But, there is also the problem with "reading class" that it stresses learning and not acquisition. To the extent that reading as both decoding and interpretation is a performance, learning stresses the production of poor per-formers. If we wanted to stress acquisition we would have to expose children to reading and this would always be to expose them to a discourse whose name would never be "Reading" (at least until the student went to the university and earned a degree called "Reading"). To the extent that it is important to have meta-level skills in regard to language, reading class as a place of learning rather than of acquisition might facilitate this, but it is arguable that a reading class would hardly be the best place to do this. While reading classes like mine might not be around any more, it encapsulated the common sense notion of literacy as "the ability to read and write" (intransitively), a notion that is nowhere near as coherent as it at first sounds.

Now I will approach a more positive connection between a viable notion of literacy and the concepts we have dealt with above. All humans, barring serious disorder, get one form of discourse free, so to speak, and this through acquisition. This is our socio-culturally determined ways of using our native language in face-to-face communication with intimates (intimates are people with whom we share a great deal of knowledge because of a great deal of contact and similar experiences). This is sometimes referred to as "the oral mode" (Gee 1986b) — it is the birth right of every human and comes through the process of primary socialization within the family as this is defined within a given culture. Some small, so-called "primitive," cultures function almost like extended families (though never completely so) in that this type of discourse is usable in a very wide array of social contacts. This is due to the fact that these cultures are small enough to function as a "society of intimates" (Givon 1979). In modern technological and urban societies which function as a "society of strangers," the oral mode is more narrowly useful. Let us refer then to this oral mode, developed in the primary process of enculturation, as the "primary discourse." It is important to realize that even among speakers of English there are socio-culturally different primary discourses. For example, lower socio-economic black children use English to make sense of their experience differently than do middle class children; they have a different primary discourse (Gee 1985; 1986a; Michaels 1981; 1985). And this is not due merely to the fact that they have a different dialect of English. So-called "Black Vernacular English" is, on structural grounds, only trivially different from standard English by the norms of linguists accustomed to dialect differences around the world (Labov 1972). Rather, these children use language, behavior, values and beliefs to give a different shape to their experience.

Beyond the primary discourse, however, are other discourses which crucially involve social institutions beyond the family (or the primary socialization group as defined by the culture), no matter how much they also involve the family. These institutions all share the factor that they require one to communicate with non-intimates (or to treat intimates as if they were not intimates). Let us refer to these as "secondary institutions" (such as schools, workplaces, stores, government offices, businesses, churches, etc.). Discourses beyond the primary discourse are developed in association with and by having access to and practice with these secondary institutions. Thus, we will refer to them as "secondary discourses." These secondary discourses all build on, and extend, the uses of language we acquired as part of our primary discourse, and they [are] more or less compatible with the primary discourses of different social groups. It is, of course, a great advantage when the secondary discourse is compatible with your primary one. But all these secondary discourses involve uses of language, either written or oral, or both, that go beyond our primary discourse no matter what group we belong to. Let's call those uses of language in secondary discourses which go beyond the uses of language stemming from our primary discourse "secondary uses of language." Telling your mother you love her is a primary use of language, telling your teacher you don't have your homework is a secondary use. It can be noted, however, that sometimes people must fall back on their primary uses of language in inappropriate circumstances when they fail to control the requisite secondary use.

Now we can get to what I believe is a useful definition of literacy:

> literacy is control of secondary uses of language (i.e., uses of language in secondary discourses)

Thus, there are as many applications of the word "literacy" as there are secondary discourses, which is many. We can define various types of literacy as follows:

> dominant literacy is control of a secondary use of language used in what I called above a "dominant discourse"

> powerful literacy is control of a secondary use of language used in a secondary discourse that can serve as a meta-discourse to critique the primary discourse or other secondary discourses, including dominant discourses

What do I mean by "control" in the above definitions? I mean some degree of being able to "use," to "function" with, so "control" is a matter of degree. "Mastery" I define as "full and effortless control." In these terms I will state a principle having to do with acquisition which I believe is true:

> Any discourse (primary or secondary) is for most people most of the time only mastered through acquisition, not learning. Thus, literacy is mastered through acquisition, not learning, that is, it requires exposure to models in natural, meaningful, and functional settings, and teaching is not liable to be very successful—it may even initially get in the way. Time spent on learning and not acquisition is time not well spent if the goal is mastery in performance.

There is also a principle having to do with learning that I think true:

> One cannot critique one discourse with another one (which is the only way to seriously criticize and thus change a discourse) unless one has meta-level knowledge in both discourses. And this meta-knowledge is best developed through learning, though often learning applied to a discourse one has to a certain extent already acquired. Thus, powerful literacy, as defined above, almost always involves learning, and not just acquisition.

The point is that acquisition and learning are means to quite different goals, though in our culture we very often confuse these means and thus don't get what we thought and hoped we would.

Let me just briefly mention some practical connections of the above remarks. Mainstream middle class children often look like they are learning literacy (of various sorts) in school. But, in fact, I believe much research shows they are acquiring these literacies through experiences in the home both before and during school, as well as by the opportunities school gives them to practice what they are acquiring (Wells 1985; 1986a, b). The learning they are doing, provided it is tied to good teaching, is giving them not the literacies, but meta-level cognitive and linguistic skills that they can use to critique various discourses throughout their lives. However, we all know that teaching is not by any means always that good—though it should be one of our goals to see to it that it is. Children from non-mainstream homes often do not get the opportunities to acquire dominant secondary discourses, for example those connected with the school, prior to school in their homes, due to the lack of access their parents have to these secondary discourses. Thus, when coming to school they cannot practice what they haven't yet got and they are exposed mostly to a process of learning and not acquisition. Since little acquisition thereby goes on, they often cannot use this learning-teaching to develop meta-level skills since this requires some degree of acquisition of secondary discourses to use in the critical process. Further, research pretty clearly shows that many school-based secondary discourses conflict with the values and viewpoints in some non-mainstream children's primary discourses and other community-based secondary discourses (e.g., stemming from religious institutions) (Heath 1983; Cook-Gumperz 1986; Gumperz 1982).

While the above remarks may all seem rather theoretical, they do in fact lead to some obvious practical suggestions for directions future research and intervention efforts ought to take. As far as I can see some of these are as follows:

1.　Settings which focus on acquisition, not learning, should be stressed if the goal is to help non-mainstream children attain mastery of literacies. This is certainly not liable to be a traditional classroom setting (let alone my "reading class"), but rather natural and functional environments, which may or may not happen to be inside a school.

2.　We should realize that teaching and learning are connected with the development of meta-level cognitive and linguistic skills. They will work better if we explicitly realize this and build this realization into our curricula. Further, they must be ordered and integrated with acquisition in viable ways if they are to have any effect other than obstruction.

3.　Mainstream children are actually using much of the teaching-learning they get not to learn but to acquire, by practicing developing skills. We should thus honor this practice effect directly and build on it, rather than leave it as a surreptitious and indirect by-product of teaching-learning.

4.　Learning should lead to the ability for all children—mainstream and non-mainstream—to critique their primary discourses and secondary discourses, including dominant secondary discourses. This requires exposing children to a variety of alternative primary discourses and secondary ones (not necessarily so that they acquire them, but so that they learn about them). It also requires realizing explicitly that this is what good teaching and learning is good at. We rarely realize that this is where we fail mainstream children just as much as non-mainstream ones.

5.　We must take seriously that no matter how good our schools become, both as environments where acquisition can go on (so involving meaningful and functional settings) and where learning can go on, the non-mainstream child will always have more conflicts in using and thus mastering dominant secondary discourses, since they conflict more seriously with his primary discourse and community-based secondary ones. This is precisely what it means (by my definitions above) to be "non-mainstream." This does not mean we should give up. It also does not mean merely that research and intervention efforts must have sensitivity to these conflicts built into them, though it certainly does mean this. It also requires, I believe, that we must also stress research and intervention efforts that facilitate the development of wider and more humane concepts of mastery and its connections to gate-keeping. We must remember that conflicts, while they do very often detract from standard sorts of full mastery, can give rise to new sorts of mastery. This is commonplace in the realm of art. We must make it commonplace in society at large.

References

Belsey, C. (1980). *Critical Practice*. London: Methuen.

Cook-Gumperz, J., Ed. (1986). *The Social Construction of Literacy*. Cambridge: Cambridge University Press.

Culler, J. (1982). *On Deconstruction: Theory and Criticism after Structuralism*. Ithaca, NY: Cornell University Press.

Eagleton, T. (1983). *Literary Theory: An Introduction*. Minneapolis: University of Minnesota Press.

Gee, J.P. (1985). The narrativization of experience in the oral mode, *Journal of Education*, *167*, 9−35.

Gee, J.P. (1986a). Units in the production of discourse, *Discourse Processes*, *9*, 391−422.

Gee, J.P. (1986b). Orality and literacy: From the *Savage Mind* to *Ways with Words*, *TESOL Quarterly*, *20*, 719−746.

Gilligan, C. (1982). *In a Different Voice*. Cambridge: Harvard University Press.

Givon, T. (1979). *On Understanding Grammar*. New York: Academic Press.

Gumperz, J.J., Ed. (1982). *Language and Social Identity*. Cambridge: Cambridge University Press.

Heath, S.B. (1983). *Ways with Words: Language, Life, and Work in Communities and Classrooms*. Cambridge: Cambridge University Press.

Jameson, F. (1981). *The Political Unconscious: Narrative as a Socially Symbolic Act*. Ithaca, NY: Cornell University Press.

Krashen, S. (1982). *Principles and Practice in Second Language Acquisition*. Hayward, CA: Alemany Press.

Krashen, S. (1985). *Inquiries and Insights*. Hayward, CA: Alemany Press.

Krashen, S. & Terrell, T. (1983). *The Natural Approach: Language Acquisition in the Classroom*. Hayward, CA: Alemany Press.

Labov, W. (1972). *Language in the Inner City*. Philadelphia: University of Pennsylvania Press.

Macdonell, D. (1986). *Theories of Discourse: An Introduction*. Oxford: Basil Blackwell.

Michaels, S. (1981). "Sharing time": Children's narrative styles and differential access to literacy, *Language in Society*, *10*, 423−442.

Michaels, S. (1985). Hearing the connections in children's oral and written discourse, *Journal of Education*, *167*, 36−56.

Scollon, R. & Scollon, S.B.K. (1981). *Narrative, Literacy, and Face in Interethnic Communication*. Norwood, NJ: Ablex.

Scribner, S. & Cole, M. (1981). *The Psychology of Literacy*. Cambridge: Harvard University Press.

Thompson, J.B. (1984). *Studies in the Theory of Ideology*. Berkeley and Los Angeles: University of California Press.

Wells, G. (1985). "Preschool literacy-related activities and success in school," in D.R. Olson, N. Torrance, & A. Hildyard, eds. *Literacy, Language, and Learning*. Cambridge: Cambridge University Press.

Wells, G. (1986a). "The language experience of five-year-old children at home and at school" in J. Cook-Gumperz, ed. *The Social Construction of Literacy*. Cambridge: Cambridge University Press.

Wells, G. (1986b). *The Meaning Makers: Children Learning Language and Using Language to Learn*. Portsmouth, NH: Heinemann.

THREE

Oral and Literate Traditions Among Black Americans Living in Poverty

Shirley Brice Heath

Within the past decade, scholars from a wide variety of disciplines have given considerable attention to the oral and literate traditions of Black Americans, especially in an attempt to compare their family and community patterns with those of the school and other mainstream institutions. Anthropologists, social historians, and folklorists have detailed the long-standing rich verbal forms of Afro-American rhymes, stories, music, sermons, and joking and their interdependence with Black–White relations as well as male–female and cross-age interactions within Black communities (Folb 1980; Hannerz 1969; Levine 1977; Smitherman 1977; Whitten & Szwed 1970). Yet schools and employers have repeatedly pictured a majority of Black students and workers as victims of language poverty and called for increased emphasis on literacy skills for Black Americans—young and old.

It is important to bring together these divergent views about language abilities, especially as they relate to oral and written language uses, and to compare family and community language socialization, on the one hand, with the expectations and practices of schools and workplaces, on the other. When children learn language, they take in more than forms of grammar: They learn to make sense of the social world in which they live and how to adapt to its dynamic social interactions and role relations. Through the reciprocal processes of family and community life that flow through communication, children develop a system of cognitive structures as interpretive frameworks and come to share to greater or lesser degrees the common value system and sets of behavioral norms of their sociocultural group (Schieffelin & Ochs 1986). These frameworks and ways of expressing knowledge in a variety of styles and through different

Source: Shirley Brice Heath, "Oral and Literate Traditions Amongs Black Americans Living in Poverty," *American Psychologist* 44 (1989): 367–73. Copyright © 1989. Reprinted with permission.

symbolic systems will vary in their congruence with those of the school and other mainstream institutions. Similarly, those of the school may differ from those of employers. It is important, therefore, to consider the actual—as opposed to the idealized—degrees of congruence from home and community to school and workplace.

In all these settings, judgments about language use extend to evaluations of character, intelligence, and ways of thinking; thus, negative assessments of language abilities often underlie expressions of sweeping prejudicial characterizations of Black Americans, especially those living in poverty. We consider first the primary uses of language in family and community life of poor and Black Americans, rural and urban, and then those of the school and the workplace, taking a comparative view across these varied contexts.

Family and community language socialization

Families socialize their children so that they will learn the forms and functions of language that will help them achieve some self-identity as group members and also meet the needs of everyday interactions. American Black families during slavery and subsequently in the often tumultuous and ever-changing circumstances of their daily lives socialized their young to respond to change, to adapt their communicative behaviors, and to define family in terms that extended beyond kin to neighbor, church, and community (Sobel 1988; Wood 1974). In response to the perils and pressures of White society, Black, communities formed independent organizations—from schools and churches to mutual aid societies—that embodied their sense of being "a people within a people," capable of relying on their own resources and responding to the ever-shifting circumstances of their society (Nash 1988). Children had to learn from an ever-shifting network, continuously adapting through considering when to apply, discard, reform, and supplement facts and skills that others transmitted to them. Standing behind this self-reliance were an array of literate behaviors— interpreting oral and written texts, preparing and practicing oral performances and written summations of them, feeding texts through the tests of individual experience, and remaking texts conceived by other groups in other times and places into confirmations of current group identities and purpose.

In traditional patterns of rural life, especially in the southeastern part of the United States, open spaces and climatic conditions have favored a considerable amount of outdoor public life that, in turn, ensured that youngsters heard and participated in a great variety of oral language performances (Levine 1977). Children inherited an ethos of group involvement in oral decision making. These public occasions for oral performances helped sustain certain other characteristics such as persistence, assertive problem-solving, and adaptability in role-playing (Spencer, Brookins, & Allen 1985). Family members and trusted community members assumed child-rearing responsibilities and demanded numerous kinds of role-playing from the young apparently in the belief that children learn best that which is not directly taught (Barnes 1972; Hill 1972; Stack 1970; Ward 1971; Wilson 1987; Young 1970). Looking, playing imitating, listening, and learning when to be silent complemented children's learning of oral language skills for negotiating, interpreting, and adapting information. These abilities transferred well into individual and group survival in adult life.

Since the 1960s, numerous demographic and socio-economic changes have affected Black Americans. Many have entered the middle and upper classes; yet many remain in poverty, primarily in the rural Southeast or in the inner cities of many parts of the country where their parents or grandparents migrated in the early decades of the 20th century. Then ghettos consisted primarily of two-family dwellings or small apartment houses; with the 1960s came high-rise, high-density projects, where people took residence not through individual and free choice of neighbor and community, but through bureaucratic placement.

In the late 1980s, nearly half of all Black children live in poverty, and most of these, especially in urban areas, grow up in households headed by a mother under 25 years of age who is a school dropout. Between 1970 and 1980, the proportion of young Black families with fathers fell drastically; the Children's Defense Fund estimates that approximately 210,000 Black men in their 20s are not accounted for in the 1980 census (Edelman 1987, p. 11). Multiple explanations are offered to account for the "hidden" Black men and the relatively low Black marital rates for men in their 20s (Wilson 1987). However, in over half of the states, children — regardless of how low the family's income is — are not eligible for Aid for Families with Dependent Children if an unemployed father resides in the household (Edelman 1987). Furthermore, housing rules restrict the number of occupants of a single apartment, and assignments of apartments can rarely take into account the needs or expressed desires of members of extended families to live close to each other. Regardless of the theories — economic and social — for these changed family circumstances, the effects on language socialization of the young are undeniable.

Differences in the space and time of social interactions in rural and urban Black communities of poverty greatly influence both the degree of their divergence from earlier patterns of language socialization and the increased extent of disparity between rural and urban child-rearing patterns. The picture that most closely resembles that of earlier years comes from those areas in which either agricultural or mill work remain viable options and a majority of families still live in single or dual-family dwellings.[1] Much of the social life is out-of-doors, and times of employment, especially for men, vary with seasonal and daily shift patterns. Both male and female adults of several ages are often available in the neighborhood to watch over children who play outside and to supplement the parenting role of young mothers.

Older adults do not simplify or mediate the world for children of the community, but they expect the young to adapt to changing contexts, speakers, and caregivers. They say of the young: "Children have to make their own way in this world" and "have their own heads." Speakers neither censor nor simplify their talk around children, and when they want children to hear them, they often do not address children directly, assuming they are active listeners to the multiparty talk that swirls around them in everyday life (Heath 1983, in press; Ward 1971; Young 1970).

Caregivers ask children only "real" questions — those to which the adults do not know the answers. They accept from children and issue to them direct commands and reprimands. To the grandmother who has just started to iron, the toddler says "Stop that now; stop it," or "Ma, sit down." To the toddler who has removed the top from a perfume bottle, the grandmother says "Put that top back on and come on" as she starts out the door.

Adults tease children, asking them questions and often threatening to take away their possessions, getting them to show their ready wits in front of an audience (Ward 1971; cf. Miller 1986). In the following interaction between two-year old Tyrone and his grandmother, his biological mother and an aunt and uncle sit on the porch talking. Several conversations take place at the same time, but all participants are mindful of the drama between younger and older combatants.

Grandmother: "That your hat? Can I have it?" [she is sitting on the porch in a low chair with a lap full of beans to shell, and Tyrone plays nearby with an old hat]
Tyrone: "Huh?"
Grandmother: "Can I have it?"
Tyrone: "Yea."
Grandmother: "Give it here then."
Tyrone: "Huh?"
Grandmother: "Let me have it."
Tyrone: "NO!" [in a loud voice]
Grandmother: "I buy me one."
Tyrone: "Huh?"
Grandmother: "I buy one."
Tyrone: "Buy one then."
Grandmother: "I buy one this big. I buy one that big." [stretching out her hands]
Tyrone: "That more big." [stretching out his arms]
Grandmother: "You get one bigger than that?"
Tyrone: "Yea."
Grandmother: "I don't care, I get one bigger than that. I get one this big." [stretching out her arms].
Tyrone: "Huh?"
Grandmother: "I get one this big." (repeating her arm stretch]
Tyrone: "I get big." [standing up and stretching out his arms and one leg]
Grandmother: "So." [with an air of resignation to the fact that she can neither stand nor stretch out either leg]
Tyrone: "Yea."
Grandmother: "Yea." (see footnote 1)

Tyrone's requests for repetition by which he builds on his grandmother's sentences illustrate just one kind of challenge game that fills long hours of interactions between youngsters and available older family and community members. Children take adult roles, issue commands and counterstatements, and win arguments by negotiating nuances of meaning verbally and nonverbally. Adults goad children into taking several roles and learning to respond quickly to shifts in mood, expectations, and degrees of jest. Adults expect children *to show* what they know rather than *to tell* what they know (Heath 1983, 1986, in press).

Numerous forms of written language enter these communities through either bureaucratic or commercial transactions, as well as from the school and church. Adults make public the most significant of these written messages, in order to debate their meanings, offer judgments, and negotiate appropriate actions. For those who participate in the many organizations surrounding the church, there are many occasions for both writing long texts (such as public prayers) and reading Biblical and Sunday School materials, as well as legal records of property and church management matters. Through all of these activities based on written materials, oral negotiation in groups makes the writing matter. The spoken word carries behind it personal relations, institutional affiliations, and common goals and ideals (Rosenberg 1970). The community values access to written sources and acknowledges the need to produce written materials of a variety of types for their own purposes, as well as for successful interactions with mainstream institutions. Yet they do not necessarily value the accumulation of all skills within every individual; instead, different levels and types of talent within the community provide a range of varied resources for the community. Thus, some members become valued as the best story-tellers, others as mediators or peacemakers, others as invaluable sources of underground information, and still others as careful record-keepers and schedulers. For example, within Black churches, members acknowledge some members as appropriate treasurers, others as secretaries, and others as brokers who interpret documents from city and state bureaucracies (Bethel 1979). Within families, members ideally distribute and alternate among many roles, especially those related to caregiving for children and the elderly or infirm (Slaughter in press; Slaughter & Epps 1987).

Within these communities, members maintain interpersonal stability by challenging individuals to try to outwit or outdisplay others, while at the same time members expect, and indeed depend on, having a range of sources of knowledge, degrees of expertise, and access to power within the group. The community regards as accomplished, smart, and literate those who have the ability to change forms of interactions, to gather and use information from a variety of sources outside their personal experience, to adjust knowledge to fit different interpretations, and to act on information in individual ways.

The picture of family and community life given above differs radically from that of blighted urban areas of high-rise housing projects. There, spatial and interpersonal boundaries, as well as time constraints of the dominant 8 a.m. to 5 p.m. time frame of employment, and the prevalence of young single mothers contribute to socialization patterns that contrast sharply with those of rural or small-town residents. Small apartments and public housing rules discourage extended families; high-rise buildings often eliminate the possibility of free play outside by very young children.

Young mothers, isolated in small apartments with their children, and often separated by the expense and trouble of cross-town public transportation from family members, watch television, talk on the phone, or carry out household and caregiving chores with few opportunities to tease or challenge their young-sters verbally. No caring, familiar, and ready audience of young and old is there to appreciate the negotiated performance. Playmates and spectators are scarce, as are toys and scenes for play. The mother's girlfriends, the older children of neighbors, visits to the grocery store, welfare office, and laundromat, and the usually traumatic visits to the health clinic may represent the only breaks in daily life in the apartment.

One mother agreed to tape-record her interactions with her children over a two-year period and to write notes about her activities with them (for a full discussion of these data, see Heath, in press; for an explanation of this partici-patory data collection technique used with another dropout mother, see Heath & Branscombe 1984, 1985; Heath & Thomas 1984). Within approximately 500 hours of tape and over 1,000 lines of notes, she initiated talk to one of her three preschool children (other than to give them a brief directive or query their actions or intentions) in only 18 instances. On 12 occasions, she talked to the children as a result of introducing some written artifact to them. In the 14 exchanges that contained more than four turns between mother and child, 12 took place when someone else was in the room. Written artifacts, as well as friends or family members anxious to listen to talk about the children's antics, stimulated the mother's talk to her preschoolers.

The spatial—and resultant social—isolation of urban project life often forces such young mothers into dyadic rather than multi-party interactions with their children. Even for those mothers who were themselves socialized through multi-party teasing and rich community and church life, their childhood playful and teasing exchanges drop away when there is no audience of new potential challengers. Cut off from the family and communal activities of rural life, these young mothers find it difficult to arrange tasks on which to collaborate with their children. Thus, little of their talk surrounds either planning or executing actions with or for the young. Few allegiances, such as church life, provide a sustaining ideology of cultural membership, pride in being Black, or guidance in collecting, assessing, and interpreting information. Instead these young mothers depend in large part on each other, with only infrequent contact with older members of their own families, or they acquiesce to the advice and interpretations of bureaucratic and educational representatives, such as social workers.

Institutional supports of language learning

The implications of this shift from association with family and community alliances are wide-ranging. For example, in a comparative study of Black dropouts and high school graduates in Chicago, those who graduated had found support in school and community associations, as well as church attend-ance; 72% of the graduates reported regular church attendance whereas only 14% of the dropouts did. Alienation from family and community, and subse-quently school, seems to play a more critical role in determining whether a student finishes high school than the socioeconomic markers of family income or education level (Williams 1987). In a study carried out in innercity Boston, positive effects on the academic success of children came with the association of their mothers with organizational ties beyond the family (and with friends who had such ties) and with nondenominational religious affiliations, as well as with stability in the labor force over a number of years (Blau 1981).

In many housing developments, the diversity of languages, ethnic groups, and regional and religious backgrounds punctuate young mothers' isolation. These strange and unfamiliar surroundings cut sharply into possibilities of building mutual trust and shared responsibilities for childcare. Poverty and the stretch for more than the wages can meet erode family bonds, as do the ever-accessible alcohol and drugs of inner-city life. Once children are old enough to leave the isolation of their apartments, they join life on the street, where linguistic and cognitive stimulation abound, often inviting role-switching in language and demeanor (Lefkowitz 1987; Lipsitz 1977; Rappaport 1985). However, the potential of older peers to channel the energies and goals of the younger in societally beneficial directions is often overcome by the environmentally harmful conditions that surround youth in the inner city: malnutrition, child abuse, substance-related damage, and criminal activities. Those who manage to transform these street experiences into success in mainstream academic life may suffer considerably from the sociocultural schizophrenia of being both Black and mainstream American (Anson 1988). They may live (often with devastating outcomes) with the ringing questions that surrounded W.E. DuBois's (1961/1903) analysis of double-consciousness in *The Souls of Black Folk*.

The school's view of spoken and written language

The school has seemed unable to recognize and take up the potentially positive interactive and adaptive verbal and interpretive habits learned by Black American children (as well as other nonmainstream groups), rural and urban, within their families and on the streets. These uses of language—spoken and written—are wide ranging, and many represent skills that would benefit all youngsters: keen listening and observational skills, quick recognition of nuanced roles, rapid-fire dialogue, hard-driving argumentation, succinct recapitulation of an event, striking metaphors, and comparative analyses based on unexpected analogies (Baugh 1983).

Many educators tend to deny the fundamental contribution of these verbal abilities to being literate in the broadest sense. Rather, schools tend to deal with literacy skills as mechanistic abilities that separate out and manipulate discrete elements of a written text, such as spelling, vocabulary, grammar, topic sentences, and outlines, apart from the meaning and interpretation of a text as a whole. Being literate often means having a labeling familiarity with the content of specific written texts (Hirsch 1987).

The insistent focus in school on learning to read and write as the natural forerunner of reading and writing to learn creates innumerable classroom scenes of individuals reading aloud and responding to teacher and test questions about the content of reading materials. After the solo writing of short-phrase answers in the early school years come the short essays and research papers of the secondary school. Teachers usually constrain time and task so that these longer pieces of writing are first drafts only, and they too are solo pieces written without opportunities to shape and test ideas by talking with others. These expectations stand in sharp contrast to those of family and street associates of children from Black and other nonmainstream communities.

The majority of teachers and a major portion of commercial language arts materials stress that children (as well as adults) must learn to read and write as individuals and display their skills and knowledge in the pre-specified and limited forms of work-sheets, standardized tests, brief academic essays, and

answers to teacher and textbook questions. Inner-city schools and those peren-
nially at the bottom of educational profiles receive the most intense pressure to
improve the verbal scores of their students; thus, they tend to rely more on
teaching materials of the above sort than other districts.

Thus, for the majority of students that score poorly on standardized tests,
the school offers little practice and reward in open-ended, wide-ranging uses of
oral and written language (such as giving and reinterpreting directions or
creating and debating alternative plans of action). Occasions for extended
reading, writing, or talking on a sustained topic are relatively few and far
between (Applebee 1981, 1984; Goodlad 1984). Yet such occasions lie at the
very heart of being literate: sharing knowledge and skills from multiple sources,
building collaborative activities from and with written materials, and switching
roles and trading expertise and skills in reading, writing, and speaking.

Language in the workplace: changing needs

Across almost the entire first century of industrialization and urbanization in
the United States, the image of the isolated factory worker carrying out
directions given from superiors stood behind many school activities: Good
students who followed directions and predictably worked on their own made
good workers (Graff 1979, 1987). But during this century of industrial growth,
governmental and human service agencies increased their influence over individual lives by generating more and more documents that needed interpretation —
generally negotiated orally and with several interchanges with both individuals
and groups. To take action on matters ranging from childcare to insurance
choices and appliance warranties, all Americans came increasingly to need oral
negotiation skills and practice in interpreting written documents.

Yet ironically, schools offered little practice or instruction in those language
uses related to negotiation and collaboration in groups. In schools direct and
single "right" answers given by individuals predominate over group interpretations of written texts. The underlying basis of group work — that most "real"
questions have no direct or right answers — is that no single individual is likely
to have the range of information or technical skills needed for most of the
decisions we must make. In most interactions with bureaucracies and other
institutions beyond the family, adults — young and old — depend on distributed
cognition or the construction of knowledge that is possible through talk that
compares, questions, and assesses a wide range of forms of written and spoken
language (Rogoff & Lave 1984; Wertsch 1985).

Similarly, in a rapidly growing percentage of current employment settings,
employers rely less on individuals acting to follow directions and more on
individuals collaborating and negotiating under conditions of almost constant
flux. From jobs paying minimum wage to professional and executive positions,
workers must be able to draw inferences from a variety of types of information,
understand and transmit instructions, develop alternatives, reach conclusions,
and express their decisions effectively. For example, in fast-food restaurants,
cashiers, cooks, and dishwashers negotiate orally with each other and interpret
written directions and numerous highly technical and legal specifications that
abound in commercial establishments and public agencies (e.g., health inspec-

tions and building codes). In the mid-1980s, American manufacturers and service sector employers consistently began to call for workers who were "well-grounded in fundamental knowledge and who have mastered concepts and skills that create an intellectual framework to which new knowledge can be added" (National Academy of Sciences, 1984, p. 17). Increasingly, even the first jobs of young adults assume collaborative work settings and occasions for sharing orally the group's knowledge about ways to solve problems in the workplace. Earlier single-task factory jobs or apprenticed craft positions demanded very different types of language skills. But in the 1980s, advancement depends increasingly on the ability to compose and read graphic and text information about real-world decisions, consult source materials, handle and explain mathematical concepts, control and take responsibility for complex equipment, and transmit information to those both above and below in the work hierarchy (Carnegie Forum on Education and the Economy, 1986; Gainer 1988).

Institutions — from governmental bureaucracies to commercial workplaces — acknowledge that information and contexts of work now change constantly. These institutions require collaboration and shared knowledge building, as well as individual responsibility and commitment. Most of their members, as well as the citizens and workers who come in contact with them, operate primarily and most effectively through a wide range of types of oral language uses as well as an awareness of the power and purposes of written documents. The most valued oral language habits include giving directions, asking clarification questions, offering rapid and on-the-spot summaries, laying out short-term as well as long-range plans, and giving effective and nonthreatening assessments or recommendations to fellow workers. Rarely is any single individual entrusted with writing a document of any significance and for a wide audience: Drafts, multiple readers, and several editions intervene before any final written version. Even more rarely is the reading of a document of any importance given over to a single individual; instead several read the document and meet to discuss its meaning and relevance for action (Barbee 1986; Mikulecky 1982; Mikulecky & Ehlinger 1986; Mikulecky & Winchester 1983).

In the valuation of collaboration and numerous verbal forms of displaying knowledge, as well as taking multiple approaches to interpreting a wide variety of types of texts, formal schooling does not mesh well with either nonmainstream communities or workplaces. Schooling pursues actions and evaluations of students that validate answers instead of questions, fixed knowledge accumulated by individuals reading in isolation, an assumption that learning once acquired need not change in relation to context, and individual performance of one-time-only writing of a very narrow range of genres.

Reexamining what it means to be literate

The insistence of the school on individualizing literacy and separating it from its social and oral roots has ignored traditional oral and literate habits of Black Americans. Yet, ironically these traditional habits match the demands and needs of employers in the late 20th century far better than those of most classrooms. The workplace of the late 20th century demands language skills far beyond those identified as important and taught in schools. Classrooms' narrow focus on only certain kinds of literate behaviors typically discourages Black children's positive transfer of adaptability, keen interpretive talents, and group collaboration to either academic life or employment. Too often Black students, worn down by the effects of poverty and/or the realities of inner-city life, lose hope in themselves. Furthermore, current changes in Black family and community structures of inner-city life are rapidly eroding earlier socialization patterns that offered adaptability, persistence, and strong self-identification within a group. In schools, teachers identify the subject matter and skills to be taught and determine as well the path of development along which the learner *should* move to reach certain prespecified goals. Repeated denial, punishment, and truncation of family and community language socialization patterns minimize the chances that students will manage to transfer these profitably to either the classroom or workplace.

In contrast to Black American family and community life, as well as to new demands of the workplace, in school the competitive display of knowledge by individuals breaks apart the communal acceptance of differential levels of talent and expertise. The focus on general and leveled knowledge across all individuals and the movement of learning along a path prespecified by scope and sequence isolate the learner from the learning group and privatizes knowledge and skills. The school generally insists that adults must always be the teachers, that the verbal display of knowledge is central, and that individual demonstration of literacy prowess is both valued and valuable.

The descriptions given in this article have been of how Black Americans in rural and urban poverty have tried to sustain traditional patterns of learning and roles for spoken and written language. Other nonmainstream sociocultural groups also hold expectations of language and learning that differ markedly from the school's majority premises about literacy. Studies of different groups of Native Americans, as well as those from communities of any one of the several different Hispanic groups (e.g., Puerto Rican, Chicano, recent Mexican-origin, Dominican Republican, Cuban), also document the varieties of ways that young children learn to use oral and written language.

Group sharing, down-playing individual achievement, and remaining available as a resource to members of one's family and primary community have supported language uses and have been among the ideals of many nonmainstream cultural groups throughout American history. Most certainly, numerous exceptions to these ideals have come in recent decades. Individual minority members have left their family connections and communities to join the mainstream and operate ostensibly apart from their cultural and linguistic roots. In addition, environmental and economic forces have cut deeply into traditional community-sustaining patterns of oral and written language use. For Afro-Americans and Native Americans — and increasingly for Hispanic groups — many economic and social policy forces have eroded family and community-based efforts to sustain group cohesion, shared goals, and negotiated intentions.

The majority of the American population wants to hang onto their folk theories about literacy and continue their faith in school as the place where individuals learn to read and write in order to get good jobs. A major function of research in the social sciences is to offer evidence that such premises do not apply universally across cultures or periods of history. Moreover, basing norms and practices of formal schooling on such folk theories may diminish the larger society's ability for self-assessment and adaptation. In the late 1980s, multi-disciplinary investigations of language in the life of minority communities and workplaces strongly suggest that the public adopt a radically different conception of literacy than that which drives formal schooling. These studies (Schieffelin & Ochs 1986) find within families and communities a wide variety of ways that oral and written language can sustain the adaptive and innovative strategies of problem solving that American employers and public service proponents see as rich human resource investments. If, as our folk theories maintain, schools are in the business of improving benefits for society, they have much to learn from the oral and literate traditions of Black American family and community life.

Note

1. I have detailed (Heath 1983, 1986) language socialization in the Black working-class community of Trackton in the piedmont Carolinas between 1960 and 1977. I have also (Heath, in press) described the language socialization of Black children in both a small-town neighborhood and in a high-rise, inner-city project and contrasted the patterns of the current generation with those of their parents not quite two decades ago. Data and generalizations that follow in this section come from unpublished transcripts and field-notes of language interactions in the homes of four preschoolers who are the children of two young women who were children at the time of the original Trackton study.

References

Anson, R.S. (1988). *Best intentions*. New York: Random House.

Applebee, A. (1981). *Writing in the secondary school: English and the content areas*. Urbana, IL: National Council of Teachers of English.

Applebee, A. (1984). *Contexts for learning to write: Studies of secondary school instruction*. Norwood, NJ: Ablex.

Barbee, D.E. (1986). *Methods of providing vocational skills to individuals with low literacy levels: The U.S. experience*. Geneva: International Labour Office.

Barnes, E. (1972). The black community as the source of positive self-concept for black children: A theoretical perspective. In R. Jones (Ed.), *Black psychology*. New York: Harper.

Baugh, J. (1983). *Black street speech: Its history, structure, and survival*. Austin: University of Texas Press.

Bethel, E. (1979). *Social and linguistic trends in a black community*. Greenwood, SC: Lander College, Department of Sociology.

Blau, Z.S. (1981). *Black children/white children: Competence, socialization, and social structure*. New York: Free Press.

Carnegie Forum on Education and the Economy (1986). *A nation prepared: Teachers for the 21st century*. New York: Author.

DuBois, W.E. (1961). *The souls of black folk*. New York: Fawcett (Original work published 1903).

Edelman, M.W. (1987). *Families in peril*. Cambridge, MA: Harvard University Press.

Folb, E.A. (1980). *Runnin' down some lines: The language and culture of Black teenagers*. Cambridge, MA: Harvard University Press.

Gainer, L. (1988). *Best practices: What works in training and development*. Alexandria, VA: American Society for Training and Development.

Goodlad, J.I. (1984). *A place called school: Prospects for the future*. New York: McGraw-Hill.

Graff, H. (1979). *The literacy myth: Literacy and social structure in the nineteenth-century city*. New York: Academic Press.

Graff, H. (1987). *The labyrinths of literacy: Reflections on literacy past and present*. London: Falmer Press.

Hannerz, U. (1969). *Soulside: Inquiries into ghetto culture and community*. New York: Columbia University Press.

Heath, S.B. (1983). *Ways with words: Language, life, and work in communities and classrooms*. Cambridge, England: Cambridge University Press.

Heath, S.B. (1986). Separating "things of the imagination" from life: Learning to read and write. In W. Teale & E. Sulzby (Eds.), *Emergent literacy* (pp. 156–172). Norwood, NJ: Ablex.

Heath, S.B. (in press). The children of Trackton's children: Spoken and written language in social change. In J. Stigler, G. Herdt, & R.A. Shweder (Eds.), *Cultural psychology: The Chicago symposia*. New York: Cambridge University Press.

Heath, S.B., & Branscombe, A. (1984). Intelligent writing in an audience community. In S.W. Freedman (Ed.), *The acquisition of written language: Revision and response* (pp. 31–32). Norwood, NJ: Ablex.

Heath, S.B., & Branscombe, A. (1985). The book as narrative prop in language acquisition. In B. Schieffelin & P. Gilmore (Eds.), *The acquisition of literacy: Ethnographic perspectives* (pp. 16–34). Norwood, NJ: Ablex.

Heath, S.B., & Thomas, C. (1984). The achievement of preschool literacy for mother and child. In H. Goelman, A. Obert, & F. Smith (Eds.), *Awakening to literacy* (pp. 51–72). Portsmouth, NH: Heinemann.

Hill, R. (1972). *The strengths of black families*. New York: Emerson-Hall.

Hirsch, E.D. (1987). *Cultural literacy*. Boston: Houghton Mifflin.

Lefkowitz, B. (1987). *Tough change: Growing up on your own in America*. New York: Free Press.

Levine, L.W. (1977). *Black culture and Black consciousness: Afro-American folk thought from slavery to freedom*. New York: Oxford University Press.

Lipsitz, J. (1977). *Growing up forgotten*. Lexington, MA: D.C. Heath.

Mikulecky, L. (1982). Job literacy: The relationship between school preparation and workplace actuality. *Reading Research Quarterly*, *17*, 400–419.

Mikulecky, L., & Ehlinger, J. (1986). The influence of metacognitive aspects of literacy on job performance of electronics technicians. *Journal of Reading Behavior*, *18*, 41–62.

Mikulecky, L., & Winchester, D. (1983). Job literacy and job performance among nurses at varying employment levels. *Adult Education Quarterly*, *34*, 1–15.

Miller, P. (1986). Teasing as language socialization and verbal play in a White working-class community. In Schieffelin, B. & Ochs, E. (Eds.), *Language socialization across cultures* (pp. 199–212). New York: Cambridge University Press.

Nash, G.B. (1988). *Forging freedom: The formation of Philadelphia's black community, 1720–1840*. Cambridge, MA: Harvard University Press.

National Academy of Sciences (1984). *High Schools and the changing workplace: The employers' view*. Washington, DC: National Academy Press.

Rappaport, R.N. (1985). *Children, youth, and families: The action-research relationship*. Cambridge, MA: Harvard University Press.

Rogoff, B., & Lave, J. (Eds.). (1984). *Everyday cognition*. Cambridge, MA: Harvard University Press.

Rosenberg, B.A. (1970). *The art of the American folk preacher*. New York: Basic Books.

Schieffelin, B., & Ochs, E. (1986). Language socialization. *Annual Review of Anthropology* (Vol. 15). Palo Alto, CA: Annual Reviews.

Slaughter, D.T. (Ed.) (in press). *Black children and poverty*. San Francisco, CA: Jossey-Bass.

Slaughter, D.T., & Epps, E.G. (1987). The home environment and academic achievement of Black American children and youth: An overview: *Journal of Negro Education, 56*(1), 3–20.

Smitherman, G. (1977). *Talkin' and testifyin': The language of Black America*. Boston: Houghton Mifflin.

Sobel, M. (1988). *The world they made together: Black and white values in eighteenth-century Virginia*. Princeton: Princeton University Press.

Spencer, M., Brookins, G., & Allen, W. (Eds.) (1985). *The social and affective development of Black children*. Hillsdale, NJ: Erlbaum.

Stack, C.B. (1970). *All our kin: Strategies for survival in a Black community*. New York: Harper & Row.

Ward, M. (1971). *Them children: A study in language learning*. New York: Holt, Rinehart & Winston.

Wertsch, J.V. (Ed.). (1985). *Culture, communication, and cognition: Vygotskian perspectives*. Cambridge, England: Cambridge University Press.

Whitten, N.E. Jr., & Szwed, J.F. (Eds.). (1970). *Afro-American anthropology: Contemporary perspectives*. New York: Free Press.

Williams, S.B. (1987). A comparative study of black dropouts and black high school graduates in an urban public school system. *Education and Urban Society, 19*, 311–319.

Wilson, W. (1987). *The truly disadvantaged*. Chicago: University of Chicago Press.

Wood, P. (1974). *Black majority*. New York: W.H. Norton.

Young, V.H. (1970). Family and childhood in a southern negro community. *American Anthropologist, 72*, 169–288.

FOUR

Choosing Our Own Way: Subjectivity in the Literacy Classroom

Patrick Shannon

Promoting student choices is an interesting and dangerous concept. It's interesting because it means that literacy programs could be based on students' interests and their ownership of ideas. Students could pursue topics that they find fascinating, broadening the curriculum in too many ways to count or even imagine. Of course, promoting student choices is dangerous for that very same reason. Can we let students from preschool to graduate school follow their subjectivity concerning literature? Don't we need to be objective and prescriptive about the choice of literature in our classrooms?

In order to address these questions, we must examine the ideology which underlies reading instruction in American schools and the ideology which provides the foundation for literature study at school. Although these ideologies are not identical, they both place little faith in either teachers' or students' judgement. Rather they seek an external, objective method of teaching students how to and what to read, and they have influenced elementary and secondary school literacy education throughout this century.

Scientific management in reading education

Scientific management became popular in industry and society at the turn of the century because of the public's fascination with businessmen and their great wealth, science and technological advancement, and a new psychological discipline, psychology, all of which seemed to foster rapid economic growth.(1)

Source: Patrick Shannon, "Choosing Our Own Way: Subjectivity in the Literacy Classroom." In P. Dreyer and M. Poplin (eds.), *Claremont Reading Conference 54th Yearbook*. Claremont, CA: Claremont Reading Conference, 1990. Copyright © 1990. Reprinted with permission.

The fortunes amassed by the Rockefellers, the Morgans, and the like drew public attention to the way businessmen ran their lives and their industries. Efficiency of effort and expense, calculated investment, and attention to profit and production were offered as the principles of business and a productive society. Schools were unfavorably compared to successful businesses and calls for schools to become more business-like began to surface in newspapers and professional journals.

Science influenced public institutions in two ways. First, people were convinced that science could solve all social problems just as it had unlocked the mysteries of evolution and the universe. Science became the most objective and important method of knowing and of deciding any issue from poverty, to crime, to parenting. Second, people generally understood science as technology rather than as an inquiry process. That is, people recognized the advances in technology and attributed industrial growth and relative prosperity to these scientific inventions. Together, these two influences combined to become the popular notion that technology solved problems without creating new ones.

At that time, the scientists of the mind, psychologists, boasted that human behavior could be explained according to the laws of learning in which external stimuli controlled people's internal reactions and outward actions. That is, learning was orderly and sequential; it required considerable practice at each step in the sequence; and it was externally motivated through rewards. Moreover, most psychologists believed that the amount of learning could only be determined through tests which closely resembled the learning activity.

Scientific management resulted from the combination of these three influences in efforts to develop the most efficient means to produce commodities. First, the most productive worker was identified and studied to determine what he or she did to accomplish his or her tasks. Second, the worker's routine was analyzed to its parts and extraneous movements or elements (e.g., ones that took inordinate amounts of time without significant benefit to the product) were removed from the routine. Third, the streamlined parts were reassembled into a series of activities which were to be taught to all employees to be performed according to plan. Finally, more supervisors were appointed to ensure that all workers were following the prescribed procedures.

In education, test results substituted for time and productivity as the hone for sharpening efficient instructional methods. Through this type of research, algorithms of instruction were identified and developed and then were encoded into teacher's manuals and basal readers. When school districts became too large for superintendents and curricular supervisors to exert simple control of instruction through observation, district and state policies concerning proper instruction and the scope and sequence of skills provided bureaucratic control over literacy lessons. When these bureaucratic measures failed to ensure compliance with tested procedures, basal book and chapter tests, yearly standardized achievement tests, and minimum competency tests enforced a technical control through the mechanical use of the basal materials. Note that teachers' and students' subjectivity is disregarded, even suppressed, in this sequence of events.

For the last sixty years teachers and students have been confronted with so called objective procedures, materials, and evaluation which they were to follow. The rationality of teachers' work was to figure out just how quickly or slowly to move students through the materials, and even there, teachers' rationality was to be guided by tests, district policy, and state competence tests. Methods textbooks, teachers colleges, and journals promoted (and still promote) teachers' use of basal materials in preparation for tests of many types.

Over time, skills which used to be in teachers' instructional repertoires slowly atrophied as the scientific, objective materials supplied the goals, instruction, practice, timetable, and evaluation for reading lessons, and finally teachers' skills have disappeared to the point where teachers believe themselves dependent on both the basal materials and reading professors in order to "choose" what to do during their lessons and in their programs. The apparent dependence becomes the self-fulfilling prophecy that enables current reading professors, state officials, and district administrators to echo the same concern about teachers' subjectivity as the educational experts at the turn of the century— teachers can't teach reading on their own unless we want a nation of illiterates. Perhaps this modern refrain for scientific management is best captured in *Becoming a Nation of Readers*, "America will become a nation of readers only when the verified practice of the best teachers in the best schools can be introduced throughout the country."(2) And if the public can't trust teachers, certainly they shouldn't trust students to choose the most efficient way to learn exactly what the experts want them to learn.

Traditional literature study

Prior to scientific management, most schools employed a curriculum based on the best of the past, a curriculum based on the traditions of Western Civilization.(3) In literature and social sciences, these traditions were expected both to civilize children and to prepare them to live cultivated lives by developing within them academic knowledge and high moral character. Of course, many educators (e.g., William Bennett, Mortimer Adler, Allan Bloom, E.D. Hirsch, and at times William Honig) seek to reintroduce this traditional curriculum back into elementary schools.

From the high school perspective, the traditional curriculum was to prepare students to go on to college. For elementary grades, it was to prepare them to do well in high school. Traditional education, then, was always preparing students for something else. College requirements directed high school curricula, which in turn directed elementary school curricula. For literature, the traditional curriculum meant the use of "good" literature, defined as those books which have withstood the tests of time. Within this logic, literature was not a way for students to learn about themselves, their lives, their culture, or their history. Rather, it was and is a way to learn about Western Civilization and its great moral lessons which should direct students' current understanding and development.

Even today, literature experts doubt teachers' capacity to judge the value of good literature and prepare lists of good books from which teachers can choose. Certainly, the best seller list represents the rejection of "good" literature and serves as the justification for the federal government, state governments, and educational entrepreneurs to make available approved book lists, and even teachers' guides for the selection and use of this literature. The illusion of teacher and student choice is stronger in some situations than others, but teachers' and students' use of their subjectivity in the selection of the literature for their classrooms is indeed illusory, if they must pick from someone else's choices.

The combination of scientific management and the traditional curriculum taking place in the new commercially prepared literature based reading programs makes teachers' subjectivity seem an impediment to children's development of literacy. Basal readers, approved lists, response guides, tests, literature sets, and packaged anthologies of cultural literacy send a loud and clear message that others must make the choices for both teachers and students in order to become a nation of readers who have an appreciation for our European heritage.

This would be acceptable to me if the two ideologies delivered on their promises. But they haven't. America has only a 70 percent literacy rate and graduates only 75 percent of those who enter high school. Those statistics are much lower for some groups in society. Only 17 percent of the seventeen year olds who took the last NAEP literacy test demonstrated that they could write in a sophisticated manner about an author's tone, intent, and style. It seems to me that scientific management and traditional approaches to literacy are to blame because they alienate teachers from their instruction and alienate students from their literacy. They deny teachers' and students' subjectivity and make illiteracy an objective fact of American social life.

A child-centered approach

For as long as 100 years, there have been movements in American education which have challenged the domination of the objective over the subjective in classrooms. Child-centered approaches have their roots in the challenge to traditional education before the turn of the century.(4) Instead of traditional curricula civilizing children, child-centered advocates claimed that schools thwarted children's basic need for activity by treating them as passive receptacles and by using repressive methods of instruction. According to child-centered advocates, educators should proceed according to the child's nature. The role of science was to understand children's interests through observation and systematic analysis in order to help children progress through the natural stages of their development. That is, child-centered advocates challenged traditionalists at the foundation of their position — their view of human nature. According to child-centered advocates, children didn't have to be civilized by schools because children are naturally good. Schools were to protect them from corruption, while they helped students learn about themselves as preparation for the perils of society. Additionally, child-centered advocates challenged scientific management for dehumanizing science as it applies to education. That is, they argued that to deny human subjectivity as fundamental to human social relations was to ignore the essence of social reality for the sake of calculability and efficiency in the educational system.

For these reasons, child-centered advocates attempted to supplant the objectivity of tradition and scientific management with a curriculum designed to understand and to cultivate students' subjectivity. Because students' interests differed individually, child-centered education depended to a considerable extent on teachers' subjective understanding of educative processes and their individual students. Both teachers and students had choices to make in a child-centered program.

Of course, this child-centered philosophy flourished under the guidance of Francis Parker and John Dewey in schools connected with the University of Chicago and later with Hughes Mearns, Caroline Pratt, and Margaret Naumburg in New York City private schools. However, it also was applied successfully in rural Alabama, Arkansas, and Missouri, in public schools in Minneapolis, Indianapolis, and Laporte, and in the thirty high schools of the Eight Year Study. Currently, whole language and process teachers attempt to blend some of the child-centered philosophy concerning human nature, social reality, and learning with language principles of psycholinguistics, functional linguistics, and sociolinguistics in order to mount a challenge to current literacy education programs in public and private schools.

Unlike the traditional and scientific management schools, child-centered programs look remarkably different from district to district, school to school, and classroom to classroom because they are based on the premise that teacher control and student choice are necessary for success in developing both students' and teachers' knowledge and use of literacy. For instance, teachers must control the goals, means, and assessment in their programs, and they must construct their personal models of literacy and learning. Of course, many theorists (e.g., Burke, Goodman, Graves, Meek) and practitioners (e.g., Atwell, Calkins, Romano, Smith) offer guidance and experience, but child-centered teachers must remake these theories and suggestions into their own work.

Foremost among the choices in child-centered programs, teachers must choose to trust their students and students must choose to trust their teachers. Both must choose to control their own time and learning. Students must choose what topics they would like to read and write about and teachers must choose how to respond to their efforts. Through suggestion and demonstration, by making resources available and allowing time, and with advocacy of students' efforts and critiques of their progress, teachers play an important role in students' choices.

Social reconstructionist education

Child-centered advocates imply that student and teacher choice is just a state of mind. It's not that simple. Teachers who choose to promote choice must disavow their history as students, finesse state regulations, and withstand the federal government's bullying. The community, school, district, and state have a hand in deciding what should go on in the classroom. That is, the educational choices are not just pedagogical; they are political as well, and the negotiations concerning what will take place in classrooms are not conducted among parties with equal power.

The social reconstructionists also challenged the traditional and scientific management ideologies within American schooling.(5) However, social reconstructionists began with the acknowledgement of differential power within society and within schools. They suggested that teachers are not free in schools to make their own choices, and often the alternatives which are offered them benefit those individuals and groups with power more than they do the rest of society. According to social reconstructionists, the economic, intellectual, and social distinctions among peoples are artificial; that is, they are the result of unequal and unearned power. Under these unequal and unjust conditions, the schools' and teachers' job is to intervene—not just to allow nature to run its course within the context of unequal social forces as the child-centered advocates seemed to permit, not simply to perpetuate the myths of our European heritage and the glories of Western Civilization as the traditionalists suggested, and not to grind out the most production, most efficiently as the scientific managers advocated. Rather, social reconstructionists talked of intervention to bring about social justice and equality of opportunity and benefit. They believed the role of schooling in a democracy should be to redistribute useful social and academic knowledge equally among all citizens in order to prepare students to make the substantial choices of their lives in and out of schools.

In a way, students' choices can become the curriculum for current social reconstructionists (e.g., Apple, Giroux, Greene, Weis). For example, students might study the consequences of their choices, whether or not they serve students' social, economic, intellectual, and political interests. Ask students to consider: whose values they are promoting by their fascination with TV wrestling, MTV, Nintendo, or GI Joes, Ghostbusters and Barbies? Who benefits? Does their pursuit and purchase of those sexist, classist, racist, and materialist products further social justice and individuals' right to choice? Social reconstructionist teachers attempt to help students face the process of choice and the consequences of their choices head on, and from this self-analysis comes the social analysis necessary for both teachers and students to become active citizens capable of protecting and enhancing their rights.

This outwardly political interpretation of the role of teachers and schools has also been part of American education, although not always in public schools. From the Little Red Schoolhouse in New York City, to the Highlander Folk School in Tennessee, to the citizenship schools across the deep south, to Bill Bigelow's classroom in Portland, Oregon to the Work People's College in Duluth, Minnesota, social reconstructionists have sought to extend the choices of the less powerful through a literacy which stressed self-knowledge, social critique, and action based on that new knowledge. All of their efforts depend on teachers' and students' subjectivity and consciously choosing democracy, freedom, and equality as the primary American ideal to reproduce at school and in society through schooling.

Common ground

Separately, child-centered philosophy and social reconstructionism have enjoyed some success in the past and enjoy an increase in popularity at present. Both feature teacher and student choice prominently in their curricula and organizations. Child-centered advocates stress the pedagogical benefits of choice and social reconstructionists demonstrate the political necessity of choice in a democracy. Yet, neither seems adequate to ensure that teachers and students will be able to choose their own ways at school. Child-centered approaches neglect the political reality of the forces which are opposed to their efforts and why those forces are so opposed. Social reconstructionism, which had developed an analysis of that reality, is not able to penetrate the classroom door because of underdeveloped pedagogical theory and method. If teachers are to promote students' choice and to enable themselves to choose their own way, they should consider the potential benefits of a reciprocal dialogue between child-centered advocates (whole languagers and process teachers) and social reconstructionists (critical educators and radicals).

Despite their different goals and ideas concerning teacher intervention, child-centered advocates and social reconstructionists have a common ground. First, both see social reality as a human artifact which is full of unrealized possibilities because the current reality is always subject to change through variation in human intention and actions. For both, the status quo is not natural, sacrosanct or permanent. We can choose to change it with our head, our hearts, and our hands.

Second, both agree on how people learn — that the production of knowledge and the process of coming to know are dialectically related. Both place students' and teachers' curiosity, risk taking, action, and reflection at the center of education. We can choose to make depth of analyses, the questions asked, and the actions taken the criteria by which the value of what is learned is determined.

Third, both are interested in self-actualization through education. Both groups seek to foster individualism, but not individualistic interest and behavior. We can choose to work for individual development restrained only when it comes at the expense of another.

Fourth, both agree that language plays an important role in how people learn and in self-actualization. Language mediates knowing and it is also knowledge. We can choose to treat language in all its forms as potentially liberating.

Finally, both agree that education must be based on students' experience. We can choose to ground students' efforts to construct reality, to come to know the world and themselves, and to develop active voice in the concrete experience of their daily life.

With all this common ground, there is much to be gained from talk between advocates of child-centered approaches and social reconstructionism. Unification of these ideologies would give new meaning and substance to the idea of choice, making teachers' and students' choices at once a pedagogical and an explicitly political act — an act meant to strike at the center of the ideologies which attempt to control teaching and learning for the sake of science, business, and tradition. A unification of child-centered approaches and social reconstructionism would turn teachers and students choosing their own way into a fundamental right of literacy educators in America.

Notes

1. See Calahan, R. *Education and the cult of efficiency* (Chicago: University of Chicago, 1962) and Herbert Kliebard's *The struggle for the American curriculum* (Boston: Routledge, 1986) for a review of scientific management in American schools and my *Broken promises: Reading instruction in 20th century America* (New York: Bergin & Garvey, 1989) for its application to reading instruction.

2. Anderson, R. et al. *Becoming a nation of readers* (Washington, DC: National Institute for Education, 1985), p. 120.

3. See Applebee, A. *Tradition and reform in the teaching of English* (Urbana, IL: National Council of Teachers of English, 1974) and Kliebard's *The struggle for the American curriculum* for reviews of traditional approaches to literature and Neil Postman's *Teaching as a conserving activity* (NY: Delacourt, 1987) for a modern interpretation of traditional curriculum.

4. See Cremin, L. *The transformation of the school* (NY: Vintage, 1961) and Kliebard's *The struggle for American curriculum* for reviews of child-centered positions and my *The struggle to continue: Progressive reading instruction in the United States* (Portsmouth, NH: Heinemann, 1990) for a translation for reading instruction.

5. See Kilpatrick, W. *The educational frontier* (NY: Appleton, 1935) and Kliebard's *The struggle for the American curriculum* for reviews of social reconstructionism in schools and my *The struggle to continue* for a translation for reading instruction.

What
Is
Read
And
Written?

FIVE

Tale of a Reluctant Dragon
Katherine Paterson

"**C**aution!" cried the sign in the bookstore window, "Some people consider these books dangerous." I stopped to stare. Ranged below the screaming sign were at least three dozen books, but my eye zoomed immediately to the most familiar jacket, *Bridge to Terabithia* by Katherine Paterson. There it lay, flanked on the left by *Mary Poppins* and on the right by the Holy Bible.[1]

Well, I thought, not without a smack of pride, at least I'm in good company. The longer I studied the window, the taller I stood. Just look at the other authors represented in the display for Banned Books Week—Maya Angelou, Alexander Solzhenitsyn, J.D. Salinger, Boris Pasternak, Ursula Le Guin, Gustave Flaubert, M.E. Kerr, Anne Frank, Aristophanes, James Baldwin, Leo Tolstoy, Harriet Beecher Stowe, Kurt Vonnegut, and the other writer in the family connection, my old cousin Samuel Clemens.

Someone asked me later if I had been shocked to find my book there. "Mercy!" I said, "I was honored." And, indeed, these days, when a writer looks at any list of banned or challenged books, she has the feeling she's reading a list of Who's Who in literary history. Any writer is honored in the abstract to make such a list. However, when we move from the abstract to the concrete, that is, when one's book is under actual attack, the writer is more inclined to sympathize with the man who in the old story was tarred, feathered, and ridden out of town on a rail. When asked how he felt about his experience, he replied that if it hadn't been for the honor he'd just have soon have walked.

I do not laugh when I get an angry letter which quotes Matthew 18:6, making it very clear whose neck is being referred to. In case your King James is not at your elbow, the verse reads: "But whoso shall offend one of these

---

Source: Katherine Paterson, "Tale of a Reluctant Dragon," *The New Advocate* 2 (1989): 1–7. Reprinted with permission.

little ones which believe in me, it were better for him that a millstone were hanged about his neck, and that he were drowned in the depth of the sea." As a person who has always taken the Gospels seriously (and this chilling dictum occurs in Mark and Luke as well as Matthew) I cannot dismiss lightly the charge that what I have written is an offense to the very children I claim to care for. Those of us who have spent out lives identifying with St. George, are shocked to find ourselves suddenly become the dragon.

Since a basic task of the novelist is to understand human nature, I have tried over the course of the last ten years to understand those who have attacked my books. This has not been easy for me because, frankly, I am often frightened by anger. In analyzing myself (a favorite occupation with writers) I realize that I was born with (or came quite early into) a ferocious temper that I was warned as a child would probably do me or some innocent soul in if I didn't get it under control. The lesson I learned from this was that anger was a very scary thing. I have managed to channel my frightful temper, along with other less than admirable character traits, into fiction where they have been very useful, but there is something about an extremely angry person which still makes me want to run for cover.

In my more mature years, however, I have come to recognize anger as a dressing gown for some other emotion. And very often what is under the robe is fear. Certainly for me it often was and is. This does not mean that the dragon calls out to St. George. "Say, there, old boy, just what is it you're scared of?" In the first place, George probably hasn't thought it out in just that way, and in the second, he's the one with the fiery sword.

Actually, as a parent, I understand all too well what parents are afraid of. I do not despise these fears. Parents who have no fear of this world in which their children must grow up are either simple-minded or crazy. Of course we fear for our children, and of course those of us who care about our children want to protect them as best we can.

I examine my own reaction to the threat of nuclear war. If a person is not frightened by the specter of nuclear war, she is, I believe, either simple-minded, crazy, or so paralyzed by denial that she is hardly alive. I emerged from this denial into conscious fright, then anger, then joined with people around the world in active protest. Those on the sidelines saw our actions as quixotic, if not positively anti-American, but joining the endeavor was vital to my mental health, and I dare to say, having just watched as President Reagan and General Secretary Gorbachev sign the first treaty to mandate the destruction of a whole class of nuclear weapons, more effective than even the noisiest of us dared hope.

Still the threats to our children remain, and they are overwhelming — nuclear holocaust, drugs, AIDS, organized crime, corruption in high places, terrorism, pollution of the air, water, food, and obscene assaults upon the mind and spirit. Faces of missing children smile out from the breakfast milk carton and the morning paper tells of a load of happy youngsters homeward bound from a church outing, only to have their young bodies shattered and burned by one drunken turn of a wheel.

A wise parent is frightened, a caring parent is desperate to protect. But how to begin? And how to endure?

Then someone, a trusted friend or a respected public figure, says a very sensible thing to you. Begin where you are. Evil is very subtle and persons are often duped. But you must ferret it out in its apparently innocent manifestations, recognize it for what it is, and get rid of it. You must do this not only for your own children, but for all children, for they are not wise enough to do this for themselves.

You are not powerless, this someone assures you. You are a parent and a taxpayer. You not only have the right, you have the obligation to know what goes on in the public schools and libraries of your community. Besides, you are not alone. There are many caring adults who will support you and examples everywhere around the country as to how these battles can be fought and won. The battle may seem insignificant, but it is not. All evil begins in the human heart, so it is up to you to keep from taking root in young lives those ideas which as time goes on will have the power to twist and destroy.

But you must be vigilant and bold, this someone warns. Examine the textbooks and reading materials which your children bring home from school, question them about what their teachers say, visit the school often, and look at the books and magazines in the library.

It is easy to caricature parents whose opinions differ from our own. I try to imagine myself a parent in Germany in the thirties. At what point would I have become alarmed at what was being taught to my children? Would I have dared protest? I hope I would have, but many good, well-meaning people remained silent.

Now having said all this trying to understand my St. Georges and why they might be on the attack, I need to say from the point of view of the dragon why I and my fellows should be spared the sword.

Let me begin with a word spoken more than 300 years ago by that quintessential Puritan, Oliver Cromwell. "I beseech you, in the bowels of Christ," Cromwell pled with his adversaries, "think it possible you may be mistaken." What wars have been waged, inquisitions launched, prisons filled, children maimed and killed by those who knew they were right? We must all have for each other a certain tolerance for each others' ideas and beliefs, if simply because, as right as we truly know ourselves to be, there is that sliver of a possibility that we may be wrong. If I believe that only my ideas are right and that anyone who opposes my ideas is therefore wrong, haven't I by so doing made myself equal with God? Haven't I quite literally taken the name, the position, of God in vain? For God obviously allows a wide variety of convictions to flourish, otherwise most of us would have been struck of dumb or dead long ago.

And if our ideas are right, we do not have to fear opposing ideas. Our arguments may momentarily fail, but time will reveal untruth. Perhaps the worst way to oppose an idea is to seek to suppress it. Banished ideas, like martyrs, have a way of coming back to haunt you. Remember Galileo?

Our democratic system, which I happen to think one of the better political ideas to come along in human history, is founded on the notion that ideas are to be argued openly and freely. We do not believe persons should be gagged, imprisoned, and certainly not killed for what they think. Nor do we believe books should be banned or burned for what they espouse.

In the fall of 1984 I was one of eight writers and illustrators who sent a formal protest to the Board of Education on Peoria, Illinois on behalf of Judy Blume. The ban on several of her books occurred, according to the Assistant Superintendent, from the board's decision to "rid the public schools of Peoria of any material that might be considered offensive by any one religious or ethnic group."

Think about that for a minute. If any materials which might offend any group were to be removed from the schools, what on earth would be left? Certainly the Bible would be one of the first books to go, almost any novel, all of the dictionaries, encyclopedias, and don't count on those "wholesome" teen romances making the cut. There are a lot of us mightily offended by that kind of literary toxic waste.

In a thank you letter to those of us who supported her, Ms. Blume made an observation which I have often quoted since. "What bothers me most," she said, "is the statement that the censors in Peoria and in other communities around the country are making to children—if you don't agree with an idea, stamp it out!"

I was in the Soviet Union a year ago, just after the miniseries *Amerika* was shown on ABC. The Soviets who were trying to move toward better relations with the United States could not understand how we could have allowed the network to show such an anti-Soviet production. "What did you think of this film *Amerika*?" an angry *Pravda* reporter asked me. Well, I said, I was sorry that ABC chose to show it, but when you have freedom of speech and of the press, you must accept the fact that books, articles, even movies that you do not personally approve of will be produced.

"So everything is free?" he snapped back. "There are no rules?" I tried to explain to him the kind of responsibility that citizens in a free society must learn to bear. I'm not sure I convinced him, but I do believe myself that democracy shows enormous respect for the judgment of ordinary human beings. There are few of us, indeed, up to the mark that such a system demands, and so democracy works imperfectly because we are imperfect. Winston Churchill said that it was the worst system of government in the world except for all the others. I am of the many who believes that, despite the inevitable imperfections, democracy is worth defending, which means that I must allow others the same freedoms I ask for myself.

The simple truth that we parents who care about our children must face is that we cannot protect them from all harm, nor can we keep them from exposure to ideas we oppose. We only can hope to help them develop by example and precept an inner strength with which to withstand evil and to recognize and embrace the good. Many of us know sad stories of children who were so protected at home that they were totally unprepared for life at the university or in the workplace. Somehow we have to help them look at the world as it is, at ideas, even at behavior that we do not approve of, so that they may be equipped to live in an unfriendly world. I realize, as the mother of four young adults, that it is easier to pretend that something like AIDS does not exist than to talk with your children about it. To help your children grow strong enough for life is like teaching them how to walk through a forest strewn with land mines. But in the words of the old cliché, no one ever promised us it would be easy.

At the height of the McCarthy era, when our country was gripped by paranoia, President Eisenhower dared to tell the Dartmouth class of 1953:

> Don't join the book-burners. Don't think you're going to conceal faults by concealing evidence that they ever existed. Don't be afraid to go into your library and read every book...We have got to fight it with something better, not try to conceal the thinking of our own people. They are a part of America. And if they think ideas that are contrary to ours, their right to say them, their right to record them, and their right to have them where they're accessible to others is unquestioned, or it's not America.

This is the kind of wise and caring advice we need to give our children and to those who would try to vainly protect them.

There is another matter which some of us dragons wish St. George would ponder before he plunges in the sword. This has to do with the nature and uses of fiction. More often than not when a work of fiction for children is attacked, the fear is that it will set a bad example for children and therefore have a deleterious effect on their behavior.

In Kansas a few years ago parents protested the presence of *The Great Gilly Hopkins* in their school library because of its offensive language. Gilly, the angry foster child who lies, steals, fights, bullies the weak and handicapped, and displays a particularly tasteless variety of racial prejudice, is also caught with the occasional profanity upon her lips. It has always disturbed me that as often as the book has been challenged, not once has anyone objected to the rest of Gilly's rather awful behavior, only to her language.

A child, whether prompted by an adult or not, I do not know, asked me once why Gilly had to cuss. "Well," I said in an often repeated explanation, "a child who lies, steals, fights, bullies, and ferociously acts out her racial prejudice, is not usually a child who says 'fiddlesticks' when frustrated."

The child admitted that she knew a number of people rather like Gilly, and I was right. All of them had considerably fouler mouths than Gilly. "But," she said, "if you put it into a book, we might think it's okay of us kids to talk like that."

"Then, of course," I countered, "you would also think it's okay to lie, steal, fight, bully emotionally disturbed children, and make ugly racist remarks."

The child recoiled in shock. "Oh, no," she said, "of course not."

The whole point of the book is that Gilly's inappropriate behavior, including her language, is an angry defense against the world which has labeled her disposable. A novel, as the French philosopher Jacques Maritain reminds us, is different from all other forms of art in that it concerns itself directly with the conduct of life itself. A novel cannot, therefore, set examples, it must reflect life as it is. And if the writer tells her story truly, then readers may find in her novel something of value for their lives.

After I had spoken at a convention in Philadelphia, a woman came up to me. "I work in a detention center for hard-core delinquents," she said. "That doesn't mean shop lifters and runaways, it means murderers — children who have committed violent crimes. I need to tell you how much your books mean to our kids," she continued. "The other day a girl brought back to the library a copy of *Gilly Hopkins*. 'This is me,' she said."

I hope you can understand from that story why I never would clean up *Gilly Hopkins*. If a child in a detention center can find herself in Gilly, then there is hope that she may find someone who will be Trotter for her. Isn't it far more important for this child to see herself in Gilly, than for the book to receive a seal of approval from polite adult society? I have to believe it is. For the sake of this one child I would gladly remain a dragon.

As I say these words, however, I am reminded once again that in this contemporary battle, it is not just me and George toe to toe. Unlike the legendary monster, I am a protected dragon. St. George may come calling with his sword drawn, but before he gets to me, he must pass through those who protect me. I do not forget that there are people standing between me and the challenger's threats, real people who have time and time again put their own reputations and livelihoods on the line to defend what I and others like me have written. These are the people who stand to lose the most in this often unequal and lonely struggle. For these true heroes, "Thank you" is pitifully inadequate; so is an article in a journal, but we who write are grateful for your willingness not only to defend our books, but to do battle for the right of all Americans of whatever age to choose what we shall read.

I cannot call all these defenders by name. Unfortunately, the battles have raged over countless books in nearly every state. Many have lamented bannings and burnings elsewhere thinking "It can't happen here," only to find to their sorrow that it can.

In Silana, Kansas, a challenge hadn't reached the school board in five years when the parents asked that *Gilly Hopkins* be removed from the library of the elementary school their child attended. They followed the proper procedure; a six-person review committee was appointed. Three members of the committee voted for the book to be removed from the library, two voted to restrict its accessibility to school staff. Only one, the school librarian, voted to keep it available to all students.

But Liz Wilson, the librarian, was undaunted. With the support of the media director, and other librarians in the district, the decision was appealed to the school board. "We think the board will overturn the decision," Rubye Downs, the Director of Media Services said to me in [a] phone call, "but if not, we're ready to go to court."

I apologized to her for all the trouble my book was causing them. "Oh, no," she said, "We all agreed. It couldn't happen to a better book. As librarians we would have had to fight on principle whether we loved the book or not, but all of us love *Gilly*."

And fight they did. They mustered state and national library support. They got the local paper involved which ran long feature stories, even an editorial. And when the board voted unanimously to return *Gilly* to the elementary school library the front page headlines were nearly an inch high: "Gilly survives board test on unanimous vote" they bannered, beside a three-column-wide, eight-inch-high picture of board member Steve Ascher holding up two fingers to count the two risks the board must consider in its decision.

The first risk Ascher pointed out was that of someone's being offended by the language in a book, but the second, the greater risk which the board must avoid, was that of "eroding the freedom that we all believe in." And then this school board member in a small mid-western town went on to present an eloquent plea for the constitutional rights of elementary school children. "The First Amendment is [first] for a special reason," he concluded. "To me, that's what this country is all about."

With bold and eloquent defenders like Liz Wilson, Rubye Downs, and Steve Ascher, I am proud to be a dragon.

Note

1. I have never been able to determine exactly why *Bridge to Terabithia* was included in that particular display. In every other instance of challenge the basic cause has been profanity in the book, although Jesse's crush on Miss Edmonds and praying to the spirits have also been cited.

SIX

Happily Ever After
Stephanie S. Tolan

She was a sixth grade teacher who'd begun using novels instead of the basal reader in her reading class, and she was thanking me for the talk I'd just given at a language arts conference. She beamed as she enthusiastically shook my hand. "My students just love books," she said. "They read and read." As I nodded, her smile faded and she added in sombre tones, "Of course, I couldn't use *your* books in my class. My students want only happy endings."

Another teacher reached for my hand just then, so I turned away for a moment. When I turned back, the woman had gone, and I was left to think about her words with no way to respond. Her students love books but want only happy endings.

Thinking back on my visits to schools over the years, I remembered one student who'd actually said she preferred sad endings because she liked to "cry over a book." Many others had taken me to task for not providing them with what they considered *endings* at all—leaving questions unanswered at the ends of my books: Would Kerry win the swim meet? Would Amanda's father go to jail? Would Josh ever go back to school? Few had complained specifically that my endings weren't happy enough. On the other hand, when I asked how they would answer those unanswered questions, most of them had come up with clearly "happy" answers. I supposed the teacher was basically right. Her students *do* want happy endings.

But she'd gone on to say that books with happy endings are the only ones she assigns. It seems to me that there is something very wrong in this practice. Common, perhaps, but very wrong.

I can also close my eyes and hear memory's echo—"and they lived happily ever after." As always there is a fleeting sense of comfort. Who wouldn't want a story to end that way?

Source: Stephanie Tolan, "Happily Ever After," *The New Advocate* 2 (1989): 9–14. Reprinted with permission.

Those are the words that ended the stories of my own childhood. They ended the fairy tales, of course. And in a slightly different form they ended the many volumes of the Bobbsey Twins and Nancy Drew series, the British mysteries, pirate books, survival books, adventures, romances, and science fiction stories I read. Even the animal stories, after reducing me to tears again and again, assured me, as Black Beauty did on the last page, "My ladies have promised that I shall never be sold, and so I have nothing to fear. And here my story ends. My troubles are all over, and I am at home." (Sewell 1965, p. 256).

That teacher made it quite clear that because my books don't end that way, they will never appear on the assigned reading list in her classroom. I'm sorry about that, not just because I hope my books will be read, but because her rule means that her sixth graders will not encounter in that classroom many other fine books by many other authors, books those children would enjoy and books that, perhaps, they need. I would like to have told that teacher what I find troublesome about an exclusive literary diet of "happily ever afters."

I grew up in the forties and fifties surrounded by happy ending stories; they filled the big screen at home as certainly as they filled the books I read.

Those stories appeared to fit the comfortable world I lived in as well. When the Salk polio vaccine was developed, it conquered what was thought to be the last of the monster childhood diseases. Pestilence was not a threat. My family ate three meals a day and usually had meat at two of them — a fact my mother often marveled at, but we children took for granted. Famine was not a threat. The Second World War that had affected our parents was past tense for us, and while some of us were touched in some way by the Korean Conflict, we knew no immediate danger of invasion, of bombs, of bullets. War was not a threat.

We were guaranteed an education. We were freed by law from the possibility of child labor. We were warm in winter except when we chose to visit the cold, bundled carefully against it. We were middle-class Americans. And when we listened to the old fairy tales, when we read our books and went to our movies and watched our TV programs, we believed.

Perhaps when fairy tales were first told, even children were aware, through their own experience, that the world was a difficult, dangerous place. Perhaps the stories were seen then as pleasant fantasies, diversions, offers of hope. But many children of my generation heard in those stories *promises*. There would be a happily ever after. We had only to grow up to find it. If you were a girl, a handsome prince would come; if you were a boy, you would be that prince; the giants and dragons would be conquered; the fairy godmother could be counted on to come through in the end, no matter how many witches got their hooks into you. Even in stories without the trappings of magic we were assured that good would triumph and evil would either die or be transformed. We had only to look around us to believe.

Our parents were busy protecting us, giving us "childhood." We heard nothing of the pressures of adult life, of mortgage payments, marriages in trouble, unreasonable bosses, devious co-workers or powerlessness. In our world adults were different from ourselves and looked it — women wore high-heeled shoes; men wore hats. Between them they knew the answers to all the questions, solved any problems that came up, and were always right, whether we happened to agree with them or not. If we suspected darker realities, we were assured either that we were imagining things or that "everything will turn out all right."

We believed. And year by year we got older, until finally we became the adults. In the process, we walked out of childhood fantasy into the brick wall of grownup reality. It took some of us longer than others (some are still watching and waiting) to learn the truth. There is not a "happily ever after." Even two paychecks aren't always enough to buy the castle. Handsome princes run off with other women. Knights don't show up in singles bars. And nobody can find the fairy godmothers.

Many members of my generation feel cheated, lied to, and betrayed. "Why didn't they tell us it would be like this?" a woman asked at her twenty-fifth high school reunion. "All that talk about preparing us—why didn't they say life would *stay* so hard?

That sense of betrayal is what leads me to write books for young readers that are different from the ones I used to read. I do believe in happiness. But happiness doesn't suddenly appear in one's life, banishing pain and difficulty forever after.

In *The Uses of Enchantment* Bruno Bettelheim (1977, p. 36) advocates sharing traditional fairy tales with children. "The fairy tale," he says, "not only offers ways to solve problems but promises that a 'happy' solution will be found."

Exactly. But reality breaks that promise. In life there are dilemmas as well as problems. Choices sometimes must be made not between good and evil but between evils. Actions have consequences, and the consequences are not always what we expect, not always what we want.

I try to write realistic fiction, and by that term I don't mean merely fiction that omits magic and involves contemporary characters in recognizable life styles and patterns, but real people living in the real world. In this world there are villains, but they may be hard to recognize because they wear neither black hats nor the scales of a dragon. In this world, though, there are decent, caring people; there are no flawless heroes who can invariably be counted upon to come to a child's rescue. And death doesn't go away.

In my first book, *Grandpa—and Me*, the grandfather, faced with the reality of approaching senility, chooses to end his life on his own terms. There is no "solution" to Alzheimer's disease, let alone a happy one. When a child asked me once why I didn't give that book a happy ending, I laid out for her the only possible endings Grandpa's story could have, given the reality of Alzheimer's. She thought for a moment and said, "I guess that ending is as happy as it gets."

Though there can be no happy ending with Alzheimer's disease, the family of an Alzheimer's patient can have happy moments, love, laughter, caring, and eventually happy memories. If we encourage children to think that these aren't enough, what can we offer them instead?

Recently, I was taken to task by a parent for writing *Pride of the Peacock*, a book in which the main character becomes obsessed by a fear of nuclear war. "You don't tell the readers at the end that if we all work for peace there won't be a war," she said. "What about the INF treaty? What about continuing arms talks? You're frightening our children."

Who is frightening our children? Bombs and missiles are real. Real! The INF treaty does not change that, though it offers one more thread of hope that we can avoid using them. Continuing arms talks do not allow me to promise my readers that there will be no war. While we talk, we go on building weapons. Nor can I promise that working for peace will end the threat of nuclear destruction. I can, however, help them remember that human beings are complex creatures. There may be violence in us, but there is also love and art, literature and music. We can destroy, but we can also create, and every act of creation, every act of reaching out, one person to another, is an affirmation of humanity, of life, joy, happiness, and hope.

In a story, when I offer children hope it is *hope*, not a promise that life will be what they want it to be. No one who believes in honesty can promise a child that. In my books the characters may encounter pain, but they also learn that pain can be survived. It doesn't have to be — cannot be — eradicated, but neither is it all-consuming and everlasting.

Most of my readers are American kids who learn about pestilence, famine, and war primarily through images on their television screens. Few have yet been touched by such horrors in their own lives. But they do know the pain of divorce, loneliness, pressure to succeed, and fear of the future. Should we tell them their pain isn't real? Or that when they grow up it will all go away? Should we tell them they have an inalienable right never to hurt and that there is a "right" answer, a solution that will stop all pain? The truth is that pain and happiness exist together and that the greatest pain is suffered by those who cannot perceive the moments of happiness life offers because they are waiting for a happily ever after that will never be.

The sixth grade teacher and the mother I've mentioned want to protect their children. It's an instinctive stance, but when it leads us to dishonesty, it backfires. That old dishonesty is almost as pervasive today as it was in my own childhood. While today's television programs provide visions of violence unheard of in the fifties, it's a violence without reality, without the consequences of pain and death and destruction. As in the fairy tales, or the Saturday cowboy matinees, there are good guys and bad guys (easily identified), and the good guys still win, however questionable their tactics. Wars are won by the right side — ours (represented by super heroes, G.I. Joe, or virtuous robots). Hunger is what someone feels while deciding whether to have a flame-broiled burger or a fried one, chicken nuggets or pizza.

We have been bombarded lately with reports that the teenage suicide rate is escalating and that drug and alcohol abuse are epidemic among our children, even the very young. Frightened of this phenomenon, we are tempted to work even harder to protect them from dark realities, to give them reassurance. "Don't worry," we want to say. "Everything will be all right." We ask, as they do, for happy endings.

But our children cannot be helped by false reassurances that there are no monsters under the bed. Pain, fear and loneliness, like toxic waste and nuclear warheads, are real. Nor are children helped by being led to believe that a knight will ride in to their rescue or a fairy godmother will wave a magic wand. Those may be comforting fantasies. Understood as fantasies, they may offer temporary solace and escape. But when they are believed, when life without pain is the expectation, the demand, when "happily ever after" is what our children seek, they might well look for it in a bottle, a needle, some white powder, or in the final security of death. One thing we know for sure, they won't find it in their lives.

I would not banish fairy tales, fantasies, stories with happy endings any more than I would banish parties and ice cream and cake. But life is not an unending party and ice cream and cake do not nourish growing bodies. Literature with happy endings should be available to our children, but it should be only a part of the literature they encounter. Responsible adults should no more encourage children to choose only stories with happy endings than they would encourage them to choose only Twinkies™ in the cafeteria. Not all American children are equally privileged, but all are in danger of believing what so much of their culture tells them—that they *ought* to be comfortable, secure and happy—all the time.

Our responsibility to our children does not end when they leave childhood. The literature we offer them should not merely entertain them and shelter them today. It should provide nourishment for their growing minds and spirits and help give them the strength to meet their future. The only certainty in that future is that it won't always be exactly what they want it to be. They sometimes need to see characters who, instead of being eventually freed from their problems and saved from future pain, gain lasting strength from confronting problems and surviving pain. They need to encounter stories in which laughter co-exists with tears, so they do not believe that one eliminates the other. They need to learn the truth that existed before the fairy tales. Life is both difficult and joyful.

References

Bettelheim, B. (1977). *The Uses of enchantment*. New York: Random House.

Sewell, A. (1965). *Black Beauty*. Racine, WI: Whitman Publishing.

SEVEN

Overt and Covert Censorship of Children's Books

Patrick Shannon

The history of the struggle over the content of children's and adolescents' reading materials is nearly as long as the history of schooling in America. An argument concerning which version of the Bible would be read at school resulted in the burning of Quaker books and the refusal to publish Papal doctrines in the Massachusetts Bay Colony during the mid-nineteenth century (Bryson & Delty 1982). Until recently, it seemed fairly easy to distinguish the sides in any censorship dispute — the more politically conservative the group, the more stridently intolerant they were likely to be; the more liberal the group, the more likely to oppose any form of censorship. Life was simple then, but now life is complex because the typical responses of the past no longer can be anticipated in the debate over whose definition of appropriate knowledge will be validated in the library books and textbooks at school. Today, you need a scorecard to determine who's who and what's what, and, even then, you may not always be accurate.

In what follows, I attempt to demonstrate through five examples that censorship is an act of both negation and affirmation because at the same time that censors are removing information, values, and language from children's consideration, they are confirming what knowledge they think is valid, valuable, and virtuous for school curricula and library shelves. In a similar way, those who oppose censorship negate the removal of information and affirm what they think is important for children to know. As I hope to show, censorship is not always a unified, singular act with clear-cut consequences. In the first four examples, censorship can be seen as an opportunity in which we can glimpse what various groups think our society should become, what they think we should know and do, and how they think we should live together. In the fifth example, I suggest that my four-group scorecard will assist you when you

Source: Patrick Shannon, "Overt and Covert Censorship of Children's Books," *The New Advocate* 2 (1989): 97–104. Reprinted with permission.

consider overt acts of censorship, but that it will not equip you to deal with "covert" instances of censorship wherein our collective biases prevent us from considering alternative futures.

A traditional, conservative position on censorship, the first to be considered, is found in Mel and Norma Gabler's *What Are They Teaching Our Children?* (1985), a mixture of homilies, careful text analyses, research reports, law citations, and Bible quotations. Through their corporation, Educational Research Analysts, the Gablers exhort parents in their state of Texas and across the country to read their children's school and library books carefully, to identify materials that they consider anti-family, anti-Christian, or anti-American, and then to band together in order to force school and library officials to remove objectionable materials from the shelves. They do not mince words concerning the importance of this work.

> We can avert the disaster that surely awaits us if humanistic educators win. We must reverse these trends. We must restore schools and textbooks to sanity. We must save our children. Not all at once. Not all in one place. Not by denying our differences, but by working for common goals in our communities and states. (p. 160)

Beyond calling for overt censorship of the books children read at school, the Gablers work toward the prior restraint of "dangerous topics" through the Texas textbook selection process. Because the Texas State Department of Education purchases large quantities of any textbook it approves for school use, the opinions Texans express concerning the content of textbooks is weighed unduly by publishers when they produce a new or revised textbook (Muther 1985). The "Texas effect" influences the scope of the content, the format, the wording, and the illustrations included in most textbooks produced in America. Although the full extent of their influence has not been studied, the Gablers have successfully changed the Texas textbooks committee's approved list on several occasions (Piasecki 1982). Thus, the Texas effect also includes a Gabler effect, and the traditional conservative position impacts all school children in America in this way.

A second, neo-conservative position is offered in Cal Thomas' *Book Burning* (1983). Written when he was vice president of the Moral Majority, Inc., Thomas uses the First Amendment to accuse school officials, establishment publishers, and librarians of censoring Christian and traditional content from school curricula and library shelves. Evoking what has traditionally been thought of as a liberal position—the right of all sides to be heard on any issue— Thomas documents the contradiction between librarians' and school officials' recent liberal rhetoric on the importance of balanced treatment for all issues and their systematic rejection of pro-life, pro-family, pro-Christian, and pro-American information to promote their own humanistic agendas. He cites the unbalanced ratio of pro-choice to pro-life books concerning abortion on library shelves and questions the sincerity and accuracy of librarians' claims that the imbalance is due solely to the literary merit of the books on this topic. Moreover, Thomas discusses the hypocrisy of the American Civil Liberty Union's (ACLU) current position on teaching only one theory of origins (evolution), when Clarence Darrow, representing the ACLU at the Scopes

Trial in 1925, argued the "bigotry" of teaching only one theory (creationism) when others existed.

To complete the role reversal, Thomas (1983, p. xi) argues that the Moral Majority (often labeled "censors for conservatism") could not possibly act as censors in public school classrooms and libraries because "censorship by definition is an act of suppression carried out from a position of power," and Christian America currently is separated from power by a "misinterpretation" of the U.S. Constitution. Make no mistake, here. Thomas and other neoconservatives are not liberals; they clearly would be happy with what Thomas considers a return to Fundamentalist control of schools and other public institutions. However, under the current circumstances, they want unrestricted access to America's youth in order to present their position, just as the liberal rhetoric promises. We can expect more First Amendment challenges to schools' denial of student access to Christian fundamentalist information from the neoconservatives (e.g., *Mozart* v. *the Hawkins County Public Schools*, 1986).

The third position, the liberal one, is the one most familiar to the readers of *The New Advocate*, and it is represented in the work of the American Library Association (ALA). Before 1939, ironically, the ALA's position statements promoted librarians' neutrality concerning controversial issues, and it endorsed librarians as moral censors in order to redirect the interests of the "masses" during their role as general public educators. "There is a vast range of ephemeral literature, exciting and fascinating, apologetic of vice, confusing distinctions between plain right and wrong. . .which it is not the business of a town library to supply" (an 1875 position statement of the Board of Examiners for the Boston Public Library as quoted in Geller 1984, p. 23). Official ALA policy on censorship did not change until 1939, when direct reaction to European fascism led to the acceptance of the Library Bill of Rights to combat "indications in many parts of the world of growing intolerance, suppression of speech and censorship affecting the rights to minorities and individuals" (ALA, 1939, p. 60).

For the last fifty years, the ALA has argued forcefully for the end of all censorship of books, for the reader's right to choose, and for the selection of books for schools and libraries based solely on their literary merit (See Oboler 1981, for a history of this period). The ALA's Intellectual Freedom Committee and its legal defense arm, the Freedom to Read Foundation, offer a censorship hotline, position packets for school and community use, legal and economic support for those in trouble, and the *Newsletter on Intellectual Freedom*. The *Newsletter* provides information concerning censorship in schools across the United States, celebrating victories when censorship is defeated (see Success Stories, *Newsletter on Intellectual Freedom*, Jan. 1988: 32−33), and offers help in plotting strategies for a continued struggle when censorship is upheld (see Tinkering with Tinker, *Newsletter on Intellectual Freedom*, March 1988: 1, 49−52).

A socialist position on censorship, the fourth under consideration, is offered by the Council on Interracial Books for Children (CIBC) with its strident objections to the biases of school textbooks in favor of the status quo — "the myth that the U.S. is all white, all Christian, all middle class, who all live in nuclear, suburban families" (CIBC, 1979, p. 43). Using the "equal protection under the law" clause from the Fourteenth Amendment, the CIBC calls for the demographics of textbook characters to reflect the actual demographics of the current United States (e.g., 50% female, over 20% minority, 10% disabled, etc.). The CIBC recognizes that its suggestion requires considerable change in textbooks, with some current information being eliminated in order to provide space for the new, "anti-biased" information. However, it maintains that these acts do not constitute censorship because the changes only make the textbooks for a public institution comply with federal law and because the CIBC does not recommend that all the currently biased information be cut—what remains can serve as fodder for teaching students to detect bias as they read. "We have no desire to see children's books that would solely help the dominated get a bigger piece of the pie. We don't like the pie, period" (CIBC, 1976, p. 2). Rather than censorship, the CIBC suggests that its concerns for school textbooks are really just "public interest criticisms."

The CIBC stands by its 1976 *Guidelines for Parents, Educators, and Librarians*, which suggests that

> The value system that dominates in [children's] books is very white, very contemptuous of females except in traditional roles, and very oriented to the needs of the upper classes. It is a value system that can serve only to keep people of color, poor people, women, and other dominated groups in their places because directly or indirectly it makes children—our future adults— think that this is the way it should be (CIBC, 1976, p. 2).

It recommends that the selection of library books (and textbooks) be based on social concerns for justice and equality as well as upon literary merit. In its updates (published in *The Bulletin* eight times a year), the CIBC includes reviews of literature for children and adolescents that characterize each book as anti-biased, non-biased, or biased concerning race, gender, age, and class. Because it has championed the rights of oppressed groups since 1966, it has recommended only anti-biased books, and it has maintained a list of objectionable books since 1976, the CIBC may promote self-censorship among teachers, librarians, and publishers during their selection of texts for schools in order to avoid charges of bias (Donaldson 1981).

Of course, there are others who offer modestly different arguments from the above examples while remaining within these four political positions. I chose to personalize the scorecard in order to make it more easily understood. Clearly, the argument over whose definition of knowledge will be validated in school and library books has been expanded. Thirty years ago, who would have anticipated conservatives using the First Amendment against liberals in order to bolster their position on school curricula and library collections; or who would have bet that the left would argue that anything (in this case the Fourteenth Amendment rights of children) would supersede the First Amendment rights of other American citizens? A life around books is complex indeed.

But the CIBC complicates life even further in reference to a social phenomenon it calls "covert censorship": the unconscious presentation of just one side of an issue which distorts reality by making it seem that the one position is all there is worth considering about the issue. Let me be clear here. Excluding alternative points of view is not an overt act of censorship; it is that the alternatives do not occur to the authors, publishers, or the teachers and librarians who select books. Multiply this unconscious bias by the thousands of books published for the young audience, and see the enormous proportions of this type of censorship. To consider covert censorship, for which our scorecard is of no use, we must consider what is left unsaid in children's and adolescent literature rather than engage in the typical practice of literary criticism, analyzing an author's words (Taxel 1979). Perhaps an extended personal example will make this point clearer.

While helping with a study concerning the genre types among children's favorite books (Abrahamson & Shannon 1983), I was struck by the singular social message that each of the books I read seemed to present to its readers. Regardless of the genre type — whether it was about an individual or a group, about animals or people, about the city or the country, about males or females — the authors of these books promoted concern for self-development, personal emotions, self-reliance, privacy, and competition rather than concern for social development, service to community, cooperation toward shared goals, community, and mutual prosperity or even a balance among these social attributes. It disturbed me because I believe that books are an important part of the moral and social development of youth and these books seemed to present but one option available to the children who read them.

In order to determine whether it was just a particular set of books (although I read more than 100 books from the 1982 list) or another example of just one man's opinion, I asked two other adults to look at a random sample of the International Reading Association's Children's Choice books from 1978, 1980, 1982 (Shannon 1986). I picked the recipients of the Children's Choice Award as the book population for two reasons. First, all books published by major houses are submitted to the program, which solicits over 10,000 opinions on the books from school children around the United States concerning which among them are their favorites. Thus, the books we read were selected from a broad list, and they are books that children read. Second, I was told by school and public librarians that Children's Choice lists, published in the *Reading Teacher* each October, served often as a primary source concerning decisions about book purchasing. We chose the lists from those years to be sure that they were available on library shelves.

Two teachers and I read thirty books that were randomly selected from the "young beginning readers" and "young readers" categories (ten from each year) to see if they presented individualist, collectivist, or balanced perspectives. We found that twenty-nine of these books presented an individualist message and that one offered a balanced perspective, in which a boy pursued self-development but not at the expense of his responsibilities to his family and his immediate community. Although many of the books were about groups and group activities, none of the readers considered any of the books to present characters who defined themselves through a collective group identity. Later, I found that Wendy Saul (1983) had difficulty locating collectivist books for adolescents during an extended search. Why are there so few books with a balanced or collectivist theme?

If you accept the CIBC's concept of covert censorship, you must consider that something causes students, Children's Choice coordinators, book editors and publishers, or authors to reject collectivist or balanced social and political views in favor of an individualist perspective. Although this has the makings of a conspiracy for the paranoid among us, I do not think these participants in the

Children's Choice Project (including the publishers, editors, and authors) made a conscious decision to exclude alternative views. Rather, it is more likely that belief in individualism may be so deeply rooted in the American psyche that most participants value personal concerns more highly than social concerns, and their choices in children's literature reflect their viewpoint. That is, few balanced or collectivist books are written, fewer are published, fewer still are selected for the project, and so forth. Indeed, American historian Richard Hofstader (1954) explained that Americans "have shared a belief in the rights of property, the philosophy of economic individualism, the value of competition: they have accepted the economic virtues of capitalist culture as necessary qualities of Man" (p. viii). More recently, after hundreds of interviews, Robert Bellah et al. (1985) suggested that Americans have learned Hofstader's "shared beliefs" all too well because most Americans search for individual comfort and profits and consciously avoid civic and social responsibilities.

If this is the case, then any group of American students, editors, and the like would make the same judgments as those made by the participants in these particular Children's Choice projects. In all honesty, none of the three readers for the study had noticed this bias until they consciously took a step back from the plots and illustrations of children's books and considered what the authors could have said, but did not. The unconscious censorship, then, is hidden in the consensus of opinion that holds, in this case, that individualism provides a better social arrangement than either of the other perspectives. The opinion is so strong that it appears as an objective fact for all Americans (rather than the subjective opinion that it really is), which sets the "natural" boundaries for appropriate social and political thought and action in the United States. Here no one appears to be the censor because everyone has censored his or her own thoughts.

Although it may not seem like censorship at all, covert censorship contains the same elements of negation and affirmation as overt censorship. Overt forms appear only to be negation, but, as I suggested in the examples above, they actually contain an affirmation of what censors or their opponents think is appropriate knowledge for children. For covert censorship, there only seems to be an affirmation of an apparent consensus belief with which no one seems to disagree, but beyond that façade is the negation of all alternatives to that "fact." In my example above, covert censorship affirms self-involvement and competition and negates service to community or a balance between self and society. Is this really a consensus opinion? But covert censorship does much more than that: it actually strips us of our abilities to reason and to act because it makes us behave as if the world is static and that we are powerless to change it. Covert censorship tells us that we can know only what others accept as fact, that we should accept our present circumstances, and that we must live without hope.

There is much to understand and act upon within the overt debate concerning whether a conservative, liberal, or a socialist definition of appropriate knowledge will be validated in the books for children and adolescents. However, I believe it is the covert nondebate of such issues as the individual versus community, the lives of women, minority cultures, the environment, and social organizations that presents a greater danger — not because it is any more insidious but simply because it is so much harder to detect in others and ourselves, and perhaps because it is even more difficult to combat. To remain silent on covert censorship in children's and adolescent literature is to rob American youth of their rightful place in the debate about our future. Without questioning, even challenging, the covert censorship of alternatives to the ideas that we accept as facts, we lock our children and ourselves in the illusion that the past and future will be just the same as things appear to us today. Moreover, by default we all will become trapped in the reality that others will make the decisions about how we are going to live together without allowing us to discuss how we wish to live together. These are the high stakes with which we play if we ignore overt and covert censorship in children's books.

References

Abrahamson, R., & Shannon, P. (1983). A plot structure analysis of favorite picture books. *The Reading Teacher, 37,* 44–48.

American Library Association. (1939). Library's bill of rights. *Library Association Bulletin, 33,* 60–61.

Bellah, R., Madsen, R., Sullivan, W., Swidler, A., & Tipton, S. (1985). *Habits of the heart: Individualism and commitment in American life.* Berkeley: University of California.

Bryson, J., & Delty, E. (1982). *The legal aspects of censorship of public school libraries and instructional materials.* Charlottesville, Va: Michie.

Council on Interracial Books for Children. (1976). *Human (and anti-human) values in children's books.* New York: CIBC.

Council on Interracial Books for Children. (1979). Textbooks: A social responsibility. *Publishers Weekly, 216,* 43–44.

Donaldson, K. (1981). Shoddy and pernicious books and youthful parity: Literacy and moral censorship, then and now. *The Library Quarterly, 51,* 4–19.

Gabler, M., & Gabler, N. (1985). *What are they teaching our children?* Wheaton, Ill.: Victor.

Geller, E. (1984). *Forbidden books in American public libraries, 1876–1939.* Westport, Conn.: Greenwood.

Hofstader, R. (1954). *The American political tradition.* New York: Vintage.

Mozart v. Hawkins County Public Schools, et al, 647 F. Supp. 1194 (E.D. Tenn. 1986).

Muther, C. (1985). What every textbook evaluator should know. *Educational Leadership, 42,* 4–8.

Oboler, E. (1981). *Defending intellectual freedom: The library and the censor.* New York: Wilson.

Piasecki, F. (1982). *Norma and Mel Gabler: The development and cause of their involvement concerning the curricular appropriateness of school textbook content.* Unpublished doctoral dissertation. North Texas State University, Denton.

Saul, E.W. (1983). We gather together: Collectivism in children's books. *School Library Journal, 29,* 30–31.

Shannon, P. (1986). Hidden within the pages: A study of social perspective in young children's favorite books. *The Reading Teacher, 39,* 656–663.

Taxel, J. (1979). Justice and cultural conflict: Racism, sexism, and instructional materials. *Interchange, 9,* 56–84.

Thomas, C. (1983). *Book burning.* Westchester, Ill.: Crossways.

EIGHT

Inside the Classroom: Social Vision and Critical Pedagogy
William Bigelow

There is a quotation from Paulo Freire that I like; he writes that teachers should attempt to "live part of their dreams within their educational space."[1] The implication is that teaching should be partisan. I agree. As a teacher I want to be an agent of transformation, with my classroom as a center of equality and democracy—an ongoing, if small, critique of the repressive social relations of the larger society. That does not mean holding a plebiscite on every homework assignment, or pretending I do not have any expertise, but I hope my classroom can become part of a protracted argument for the viability of a critical and participatory democracy.

I think this vision of teaching flies in the face of what has been and continues to be the primary function of public shooling in the United States: to reproduce a class society, where the benefits and sufferings are shared incredibly unequally. As much as possible I refuse to play my part in that process. This is easier said than done. How *can* classroom teachers move decisively away from a model of teaching that merely reproduces and legitimates inequality? I think Freire is on the right track when he calls for a "dialogical education."[2] To me, this is not just a plea for more classroom conversation. In my construction, a dialogical classroom means inviting students to critique the larger society through sharing their lives. As a teacher I help students locate their experiences socially; I involve students in probing the social factors that make and limit who they are and I try to help them reflect on who they *could* be.

Source: William Bigelow, "Inside the Classroom: Social Vision and Critical Pedagogy," *Teachers College Record* 91 (1990): 437–48. Reprinted with permission.

Students' lives as classroom text

In my Literature in U.S. History course, which I co-teach in Portland, Oregon, with Linda Christensen, we use historical concepts as points of departure to explore themes in students' lives and then, in turn, use students' lives to explore history and our society today. Earlier this year, for instance, we studied the Cherokee Indian Removal through role play. Students portrayed the Indians, plantation owners, bankers, and the Andrew Jackson administration and saw the forces that combined to push the Cherokees west of the Mississippi against their will. Following a discussion of how and why this happened, Linda and I asked students to write about a time when they had their rights violated. We asked students to write from inside these experiences and to recapture how they felt and what, if anything, they did about the injustice.

Seated in a circle, students shared their stories with one another in a "read-around" format. (To fracture the student/teacher dichotomy a bit, Linda and I also complete each assignment and take our turns reading.) Before we began, we suggested they listen for what we call the "collective text"—the group portrait that emerges from the read-around.[3] Specifically, we asked them to take notes on the kinds of rights people felt they possessed; what action they took after having their rights violated; and whatever other generalizations they could draw from the collective text. Here are a few examples: Rachel wrote on wetting her pants because a teacher would not let her go to the bathroom; Christie, on a lecherous teacher at a middle school; Rebecca, on a teacher who enclosed her in a solitary confinement cell; Gina, who is black, on a theater worker not believing that her mother, who is white, actually was her mother; Maryanne, on being sexually harassed while walking to school and her subsequent mistreatment by the school administration when she reported the incident; Clayton, on the dean's treatment when Clayton wore an anarchy symbol on his jacket; Bobby, on convenience store clerks who watched him more closely because he is black. Those are fewer than a quarter of the stories we heard.

To help students study this social text more carefully, we asked them to review their notes from the read-around and write about their discoveries. We then spent over a class period interpreting our experiences. Almost half the instances of rights violations took place in school. Christy said, "I thought about the school thing. The real point [of school] is to learn one concept: to be trained and obedient. That's what high school is. A diploma says this person came every day, sat in their seat. It's like going to dog school." A number of people, myself included, expressed surprise that so many of the stories involved sexual harassment. To most of the students with experiences of harassment, it had always seemed a very private oppression, but hearing how common this kind of abuse is allowed the young women to feel a new connection among themselves—and they said so. A number of white students were surprised at the varieties of subtle racism black students experienced.

We talked about the character of students' resistance to rights violations. From the collective text we saw that most people did not resist at all. What little resistance occurred was individual; there was not a single instance of collective resistance. Christie complained to a counselor, Rebecca told her mother, many complained to friends. This provoked a discussion about what in their lives and, in particular, in the school system encouraged looking for individual solutions to problems that are shared collectively. They identified competition for grades and for positions in sought-after classes as factors. They also criticized the fake democracy of student government for discouraging activism. No one shared a single experience of schools' encouraging groups of students to confront injustice. Moreover, students also listed ways—from advertising messages to television sitcoms—through which people are conditioned by the larger society to think in terms of individual problems requiring individual solutions.

The stories students wrote were moving, sometimes poetic, and later opportunities to rewrite allowed us to help sharpen their writing skills, but we wanted to do more than just encourage students to stage a literary show-and-tell. Our larger objective was to find social meaning in individual experience—to push students to use their stories as windows not only on their lives, but on society.

There were other objectives. We hoped that through building a collective text, our students—particularly working-class and minority students—would discover that their lives are important sources of learning, no less important than the lives of the generals and presidents, the Rockefellers and Carnegies, who inhabit their textbooks. One function of the school curriculum is to celebrate the culture of the dominant and to ignore or scorn the culture of subordinate groups. The personal writing, collective texts, and discussion circles in Linda's and my classes are an attempt to challenge students not to accept these judgments. We wanted students to grasp that they can *create* knowledge, not simply absorb it from higher authorities.[4]

All of this sounds a little neater than what actually occurs in a classroom. Some students rebel at taking their own lives seriously. A student in one of my classes said to me recently, "Why do we have to do all this personal stuff? Can't you just give us a book or a worksheet and leave us alone?" Another student says regularly, "This isn't an English class, ya know." Part of this resistance may come from not wanting to resurface or expose painful experiences; part may come from not feeling capable as writers; but I think the biggest factor is that they simply do not feel that their lives have anything *important* to teach them. Their lives are just their lives. Abraham Lincoln and Hitler are important. Students have internalized self-contempt from years of official neglect and denigration of their culture. When for example, African-American or working-class history *is* taught it is generally as hero worship: extolling the accomplishments of a Martin Luther King, Jr., or a John L. Lewis, while ignoring the social movements that made their work possible. The message given is that great people make change, individual high school students do not. So it is not surprising that some students wonder what in the world they have to learn from each other's stories.

Apart from drawing on students' own lives as sources of knowledge and insight, an alternative curriculum also needs to focus on the struggle of oppressed groups for social justice. In my history classes, for example, we study Shay's Rebellion, the abolition movement, and alliances between blacks and poor whites during Reconstruction. In one lesson, students role-play Industrial

Workers of the World organizers in the 1912 Lawrence, Massachusetts, textile strike as they try to overcome divisions between men and women and between workers speaking over a dozen different languages.

Studying the hidden curriculum

In my experience as a teacher, whether students write about inequality, resistance, or collective work, school is *the* most prominent setting. Therefore, in our effort to have the curriculum respond to students' real concerns, we enlist them as social researchers, investigating their own school lives. My co-teacher and I began one unit by reading an excerpt from the novel *Radcliffe*, by David Storey.[5] In the selection, a young boy, Leonard Radcliffe, arrives at a predominately working-class British school. The teacher prods Leonard, who is from an aristocratic background, to become her reluctant know-it-all — the better to reveal to others their own ignorance. The explicit curriculum appears to concern urban geography: "Why are roofs pointed and not flat like in the Bible?" the teacher asks. She humiliates a working-class youth, Victor, by demanding that he stand and listen to her harangue: "Well, come on then, Victor. Let us all hear." As he stands mute and helpless, she chides: "Perhaps there's no reason for Victor to think at all. We already know where he's going to end up, don't we?" She points to the factory chimneys outside. "There are places waiting for him out there already." No one says a word. She finally calls on little Leonard to give the correct answer, which he does.

Students in our class readily see that these British schoolchildren are learning much more than why roofs are pointed. They are being drilled to accept their lot at the bottom of a hierarchy with a boss on top. The teacher's successful effort to humiliate Victor, while the others sit watching, undercuts any sense the students might have of their power to act in solidarity with one another. A peer is left hanging in the wind and they do nothing about it. The teacher's tacit alliance with Leonard and her abuse of Victor legitimate class inequalities outside the classroom.[6]

We use this excerpt and the follow-up discussion as a preparatory exercise for students to research the curriculum — both explicit and "hidden"[7] — at their own school (Jefferson High School). The student body is mostly African-American and predominately working class. Linda and I assign students to observe their classes as if they were attending for the first time. We ask them to notice the design of the classroom, the teaching methodology, the class content, and the grading procedures. In their logs, we ask them to reflect on the character of thinking demanded and the classroom relationships: Does the teacher promote questioning and critique or obedience and conformity? What kind of knowledge and understandings are valued in the class? What relationships between students are encouraged?

In her log, Elan focused on sexism in the hidden curriculum:

In both biology and government, I noticed that not only do boys get more complete explanations to questions, they get asked more questions by the teacher than girls do. In government, even though our teacher is a feminist, boys are asked to define a word or to list the different parts of the legislative branch more often than the girls are....I sat in on an advanced sophomore English class that was doing research in the library. The teacher, a male, was teaching the boys how to find research on their topic, while he was finding the research himself for the girls. Now, I know chivalry isn't dead, but we are competent of finding a book.

Linda and I were pleased as we watched students begin to gain a critical distance from their own schooling experiences. Unfortunately, Elan did not speculate much on the social outcomes of the unequal treatment she encountered, or on what it is in society that produces this kind of teaching. She did offer the observation that "boys are given much more freedom in the classroom than girls, and therefore the boys are used to getting power before the girls."

Here is an excerpt from Connie's log:

It always amazed me how teachers automatically assume that where you sit will determine your grade. It's funny how you can get an A in a class you don't even understand. As long as you follow the rules and play the game, you seem to get by....On this particular day we happen to be taking a test on chapters 16 and 17. I've always liked classes such as algebra that you didn't have to think. You're given the facts, shown how to do it, and you do it. No questions, no theories, it's the solid, correct way to do it.

We asked students to reflect on who in our society they thought benefited from the methods of education to which they were subjected. Connie wrote:

I think that not only is it the teacher, but more importantly, it's the system. They purposely teach you using the "boring method." Just accept what they tell you, learn it and go on, no questions asked. It seems to me that the rich, powerful people benefit from it, because we don't want to think, we're kept ignorant, keeping them rich.

Connie's hunch that her classes benefit the rich and powerful is obviously incomplete, but it does put her on the road to understanding that the degrading character of her education is not simply accidental. She is positioned to explore the myriad ways schooling is shaped by the imperatives of a capitalist economy. Instead of being just more of the "boring method," as Connie puts it, this social and historical study would be a personal search for her, rooted in her desire to understand the nature of her *own* school experience.

In class, students struggled through a several-page excerpt from *Schooling in Capitalist America* by Samuel Bowles and Herbert Gintis. They read the Bowles and Gintis assertion that

major aspects of educational organization replicate the relationships of dominance and subordinancy in the economic sphere. The correspondence between the social relation of schooling and work accounts for the ability of the educational system to produce an amenable and fragmented labor force. The experience of schooling, and not merely the content of formal learning, is central to this process.[8]

If they are right, we should expect to find different hidden curricula at schools enrolling students of different social classes. We wanted our students to test this notion for themselves.[9] A friend who teaches at a suburban high school south of Portland, serving a relatively wealthy community, enlisted volunteers in her classes to host our students for a day. My students logged comparisons of Jefferson and the elite school, which I will call Ridgewood. Trisa wrote:

> Now, we're both supposed to be publicly funded, equally funded, but not so. At Jefferson, the average class size is 20–25 students, at Ridgewood—15, Jefferson's cafeteria food is half-cooked, stale and processed. Ridgewood—fresh food, wide variety, and no mile-long lines to wait in. Students are allowed to eat anywhere in the building as well as outside, and wear hats and listen to walkmen [both rule violations at Jefferson].

About teachers' attitudes at Ridgewood, Trisa noted: "Someone said, 'We don't ask if you're going to college, but what college are you going to.'"

In general, I was disappointed that students' observations tended to be more on atmosphere than on classroom dynamics. Still, what they noticed seemed to confirm the fact that their own school, serving a black and working-class community, was a much more rule-governed, closely supervised environment. The experience added evidence to the Bowles and Gintis contention that my students were being trained to occupy lower positions in an occupational hierarchy.

Students were excited by this sociological detective work, but intuitively they were uneasy with the determinism of Bowles and Gintis's correspondence theory. It was not enough to discover that the relations of schooling mirrored the relations of work. They demanded to know exactly who designed a curriculum that taught them subservience. Was there a committee somewhere, sitting around plotting to keep them poor and passive? "We're always saying 'they' want us to do this, and 'they' want us to do that," one student said angrily. "Who is this 'they'?" Students wanted villains with faces and we were urging that they find systemic explanations.

Omar's anger exploded after one discussion. He picked up his desk and threw it against the wall, yelling: "How much more of this shit do I have to put up with?" "This shit" was his entire educational experience, and while the outburst was not directed at our class in particular—thank heavens—we understood our culpability in his frustration.

We had made two important and related errors in our teaching. Implicitly, our search had encouraged students to see themselves as victims—powerless little cogs in a machine daily reproducing the inequities of the larger society. Though the correspondence theory was an analytical framework with a greater power to interpret their school lives than any other they had encountered, ultimately it was a model suggesting endless oppression and hopelessness. If schooling is always responsive to the needs of capitalism, then what point did our search have? Our observations seemed merely to underscore students' powerlessness.

I think the major problem was that although our class did discuss resistance by students, it was anecdotal and unsystematic, thereby depriving students of the opportunity to question their own roles in maintaining the status quo. The effect of this omission, entirely unintentional on our part, was to deny students the chance to see schools as sites of struggle and social change—places where they could have a role in determining the character of their own education.

Unwittingly, the realizations students were drawing from our study of schools fueled a world view rooted in cynicism; they might learn about the nature and causes for their subordination, but they could have no role in resisting it.

The "organic goodie simulation"

Still stinging from my own pedagogical carelessness, I have made efforts this year to draw students into a dialogue about the dynamics of power and resistance. One of the most effective means to carry on this dialogue is metaphorically, through role play and simulation.[10]

In one exercise, called the "Organic Goodie Simulation," I create a three-tiered society. Half the students are workers, half are unemployed,[11] and I am the third tier—the owner of a machine that produces organic goodies. I tell students that we will be in this classroom for the rest of our lives and that the machine produces the only sustenance. Workers can buy adequate goodies with their wages, but the unemployed will slowly starve to death on their meager dole of welfare-goodies. Everything proceeds smoothly until I begin to drive wages down by offering jobs to the unemployed at slightly less than what the workers earn. It is an auction, with jobs going to the lowest bidder. Eventually, all classes organize some kind of opposition, and usually try to take away my machine. One year, a group of students arrested me, took me to a jail in the corner of the room, put a squirt gun to my head, and threatened to "kill" me if I said another word. This year, before students took over the machine, I backed off, called a meeting to which only my workers were invited, raised their wages, and stressed to them how important it was that we stick together to resist the jealous unemployed people who wanted to drag all of us into the welfare hole they are in. Some workers defected to the unemployed, some vigorously defended my right to manage the machine, but most bought my plea that we had to talk it all out and reach unanimous agreement before any changes could be made. For an hour and a half they argued among themselves, egged on by me, without taking any effective action.

The simulation provided a common metaphor from which students could examine firsthand what we had not adequately addressed the previous year: To what extent are we complicit in our own oppression? Before we began our follow-up discussion, I asked students to write on who or what was to blame for the conflict and disruption of the previous day. In the discussion some students singled me out as the culprit. Stefani said, "I thought Bill was evil. I didn't know what he wanted." Rebecca concurred: "I don't agree with people who say Bill was not the root of the problem. Bill was management, and he made workers feel insecure that the unemployed were trying to take their jobs." Others agreed with Rebecca that it was a divisive structure that had been created, but saw how their own responses to that structure perpetuated the divisions and poverty. Christie said: "We were so divided that nothing got decided. It kept going back and forth. Our discouragement was the root of the problem." A number of people saw how their own attitudes kept them from acting decisively. Mira said: "I think that there was this large fear: We have to follow the law. And Sonia kept saying we weren't supposed to take over the machine. But if the law and property hurt people why should we go along with it?" Gina said: "I think Bill looked like the problem, but underneath it all was us. Look at when Bill hired unemployed and fired some workers. I was doin' it too. We can say it's role play, but you have to look at how everything ended up feeling and learn something about ourselves, about how we handled it."

From our discussion students could see that their make-believe misery was indeed caused by the structure of the society: The number of jobs was held at an artificially low level, and workers and unemployed were pitted against each other for scarce goodies. As the owner I tried every trick I knew to drive wedges between workers and the unemployed, to encourage loyalty in my workers, and to promote uncertainty and bickering among the unemployed. However, by analyzing the experience, students could see that the system worked only because they let it work — they were much more than victims of my greed; they were my accomplices.

I should hasten to add — and emphasize — that it is not inherently empowering to understand one's own complicity in oppression. I think it is a start, because this understanding suggests that we can do something about it. A critical pedagogy, however, needs to do much more: It should highlight times, past and present, when people built alliances to challenge injustice. Students also need to encounter individuals and organizations active in working for a more egalitarian society, and students need to be encouraged to see themselves as capable of joining together with others, in and out of school, to make needed changes. I think that all of these are mandatory components of the curriculum. The danger of students' becoming terribly cynical as they come to understand the enormity of injustice in this society and in the world is just too great. They have to know that it is possible — even joyous, if I dare say so — to work toward a more humane society.

Teachers and teacher educators as political agents

At the outset I said that all teaching should be partisan. In fact, I think that all teaching *is* partisan. Whether or not we want to be, all teachers are political agents because we help shape students' understandings of the larger society. That is why it is so important for teachers to be clear about our social visions. Toward what kind of society are we aiming? Unless teachers answer this question with clarity we are reduced to performing as technicians, unwittingly participating in a political project but with no comprehension of its objectives or consequences. Hence teachers who claim "no politics" are inherently authoritarian because their pedagogical choices act on students, but students are denied a structured opportunity to critique or act on their teachers' choices. Nor are students equipped to reflect on the effectiveness of whatever resistance they may put up.

For a number of reasons, I do not think that our classrooms can ever be exact models of the kind of participatory democracy we would like to have characterize the larger society. If teachers' only power were to grade students, that would be sufficient to sabotage classroom democracy. However, as I have suggested, classrooms can offer students experiences and understandings that counter, and critique, the lack of democracy in the rest of their lives. In the character of student interactions the classroom can offer a glimpse of certain features of an egalitarian society. We can begin to encourage students to learn the analytic and strategic skills to help bring this new society into existence. As I indicated, by creating a collective text of student experience we can offer students practice in understanding personal problems in their social contexts. Instead of resorting to consumption, despair, or other forms of self-abuse, they can ask why these circumstances exist and what can they do about it. In this limited arena, students can begin to become the subjects of their lives.

When Steve Tozer of the University of Illinois asked me to prepare this article, he said I should discuss the implications of my classroom practice for people in social foundations of education programs. First, I would urge you who are teacher educators to model the participatory and exploratory pedagogy that you hope your students will employ as classroom teachers. Teachers-to-be should interrogate their own educational experiences as a basis for understanding the relationship between school and society. They need to be members of a dialogical community in which they can experience themselves as subjects and can learn the validity of critical pedagogy by doing it. If the primary aim of social foundations of education coursework is to equip teachers-to-be to understand and critically evaluate the origins of school content and processes in social context, then the foundations classroom should be a place for students to discuss how their own experiences as students are grounded in the larger society, with its assumptions, its inequities, its limits and possibilities.

As you know, a teacher's first job in a public school can be frightening. That fear mixed with the conservative pressures of the institution can overwhelm the liberatory inclinations of a new teacher. Having *experienced*, and not merely having read about, an alternative pedagogy can help new teachers preserve their democratic ideals. Part of this, I think, means inviting your students to join you in critiquing *your* pedagogy. You need to be a model of rigorous self-evaluation.

The kind of teaching I have been describing is demanding. The beginning teacher may be tempted to respond. "Sure, sure, I'll try all that when I've been in the classroom five or six years and when I've got a file cabinet full of lessons." I think you should encourage new teachers to overcome their isolation by linking up with colleagues to reflect on teaching problems and to share pedagogical aims and successes. I participated in a support group like this my first year as a teacher and our meetings helped maintain my courage and morale. After a long hiatus, two years ago I joined another group that meets bi-weekly to talk about everything from educational theory to confrontations with administrators to union organizing.[12] In groups such as this your students can come to see themselves as creators and evaluators of curriculum and not simply as executors of corporate- or administrative-packaged lesson plans.

It is also in groups like this that teachers can come to see themselves as activists in a broader struggle for social justice. The fact is that education will not be *the* engine of social change. No matter how successful we are as critical teachers in the classroom, our students' ability to use and extend the analytic skills they have acquired depends on the character of the society that confronts them. Until the economic system requires workers who are critical, cooperative, and deeply democratic, teachers' classroom efforts amount to a kind of low-intensity pedagogical war. Unfortunately, it is easy to cut ourselves off from outside movements for social change—and this is especially true for new teachers. As critical teachers, however, we depend on these movements to provide our students with living proof that fundamental change is both possible and desirable. It seems to me you cannot emphasize too strongly how teachers' attempts to teach humane and democratic values in the classroom should not be isolated from the social context in which schooling occurs.

In closing, let me return to Freire's encouragement that we live part of our dreams within our educational space. Teachers-to-be should not be ashamed or frightened of taking sides in favor of democracy and social justice. I hope *your* students learn to speak to *their* students in the language of possibility and hope and not of conformity and "realism." In sum, your students ought to learn that teaching is, in the best sense of the term, a subversive activity—and to be proud of it.

Notes

1. Paulo Freire and Donaldo Macedo, *Literacy: Reading the Word and the World* (South Hadley, Mass.: Bergin and Garvey, 1987), p. 127.

2. See especially Ira Shor and Paulo Freire, *A Pedagogy for Liberation* (South Hadley, Mass.: Bergin and Garvey, 1983.).

3. See Linda Christensen, "Writing the Word and the World," *English Journal* 78, no. 2 (February 1989): 14—18.

4. See William Bigelow and Norman Diamond, *The Power in Our Hands: A Curriculum on the History of Work and Workers in the United States* (New York: Monthly Review Press, 1988), pp. 15—23.

5. David Storey, *Radcliffe* (New York: Avon, 1963), pp. 9—12. I am grateful to Doug Sherman for alerting me to this excerpt.

6. While most students are critical of the teacher, they should always be allowed an independent judgment. Recently, a boy in one of my classes who is severely hard of hearing defended the teacher's actions. He argued that because the students laughed at Leonard when he first entered the class they deserved whatever humiliation the teacher could dish out. He said the offending students ought to be taught not to make fun of people who are different.

7. See Henry Giroux, *Theory and Resistance in Education: A Pedagogy for the Opposition* (South Hadley, Mass.: Bergin and Garvey, 1983). See especially Chapter 2, "Schooling and the Politics of the Hidden Curriculum," pp. 42—71. Giroux defines the hidden curriculum as "those unstated norms, values, and beliefs embedded in and transmitted to students through the underlying rules that structure the routines and social relationships in school and classroom life" and points out that the objective of critical theory is not merely to describe aspects of the hidden curriculum, but to analyze how it "functions to provide differential forms of schooling to different classes of students" (p. 47).

8. Samuel Bowles and Herbert Gintis, *Schooling in Capitalist America* (New York: Basic Books, 1976), p. 125.

9. See Jean Anyon, "Social Class and the Hidden Curriculum of Work," *Journal of Education* 162 (Winter 1980): 67—92, for a more systematic comparison of hidden curricula in schools serving students of different social classes.

10. There is an implication in many of the theoretical discussions defining critical pedagogy that the proper role of the teacher is to initiate group reflection on students'

outside-of-class experiences. Critics consistently neglect to suggest that the teacher can also be initiator of powerful in-class experiences, which can then serve as objects of student analysis.

11. Bigelow and Diamond, *The Power in Our Hands*, pp. 27–30 and pp. 92–94. See also Mike Messner, "Bubblegum and Surplus Value," *The Insurgent Sociologist* 6, no. 4 (Summer 1976): 51–56.

12. My study group gave valuable feedback on this article. Thanks to Linda Christensen, Jeff Edmundson, Tom McKenna, Karen Miller, Michele Miller, Doug Sherman, and Kent Spring.

NINE

Children's Understandings of Basal Readers
David Bloome   Sonia Nieto

'd rather just read stories and tell her about them.

(Do you like to read?) Un poco los libros de la escuela, los de la biblioteca me gustan mas. [A little the books in school, the books from the library I like more.]

There's nothing to remember.

(Students talking about basals and reading[1])

It is an often cited statistic that basal readers are found in over 90 percent of United States elementary school classrooms (Goodman, Shannon, Freeman and Murphy 1988). Of question in recent reports such as the *Report Card on Basal Readers* (Goodman et al. 1988) is whether basal readers provide effective reading instruction. As part of the concern with effective reading instruction are questions about how children respond to basals and what they think about them (Cairney 1988). Also of concern have been the images and knowledge presented about women, people of color, and disabled people (Britton and Lumpkin 1983).

Although the issues and findings raised in recent reports and studies are sufficient to call for a critical reevaluation of reading curriculum and materials, yet another set of issues needs to be raised. These issues do not concern basal readers per se, but rather their use and the consequences of their use. After all, basal readers are given meaning and function by how people use them and for what they use them.

In this article, we raise a series of questions about children's understandings of basal readers. By the term understanding we do not mean children's compre-

Source: D. Bloome and S. Nieto, "Children's Understandings of Basal Readers," *Theory Into Practice*, 28(4) (1989), 258–264. (Theme issue on "Perspectives on Basal Readers".) Copyright 1989 College of Education, The Ohio State University. Reprinted with permission.

hension of basal stories and workbook passages or a simplistic understanding that basal readers are for learning to read. We have a broader definition of understanding. We mean children's understandings of the social and academic significance, meaning, and consequence of the use of basal readers. As children interact with each other, their teacher, and the basal readers, they understand what kinds of behavior and communication are appropriate, how they are expected to use a written text, what counts as reading and reading progress, and where they stand in status in relation to other students and to the school. Such understandings are not always articulated, but they are present and form the basis on which students act.

It is not easy to explore children's understandings of basal readers. One cannot simply ask children what they think (although that is a good place to start). One must explore the various contexts within which children understand what is occurring around them. Further, children are not a homogeneous group. They are vastly diverse developmentally, culturally, physically, and linguistically, among other ways. It is unreasonable to expect that all children, even within the same situation, will hold the same view and react in the same way. However, the context in which they find themselves defines the "landscape" against which they can react. The task, then, for those interested in children's understandings of basal readers, or any other instructional phenomena, is first to explicate the contexts in which children must act.

The issues we raise about children's understandings of basal readers are explicitly directed at provoking a reexamination of school curriculum, especially with regard to students who tend to get marginalized. Ghory, Sinclair, and Robinson (1988, p. 25) define marginality as a "disconnection between students and the conditions designed for learning." They elaborate:

> Various types of students become marginal, such as the learner not working up to potential, the understimulated exceptional learner, the one with a long history of academic failure or substandard achievement, and the one suddenly performing poorly despite previous success. Students can become marginal regardless of sex, race, family structure, or economic background, although these variables do seem to influence the likelihood of problems with school. Marginal learners can include "children at risk" from low income or minority homes as well as youth from well-to-do families who face less-than-constructive circumstances in the school setting. (p. 25)

The argument we make is this: How children understand basal reading instruction depends on how the use and meaning of basal readers marginalizes them.

We begin by exploring how differences in the use of basals may influence children's understandings of basals, reading, and themselves. We argue that basal reading instruction is a pervasive context within which school reading is defined, even when students do not use basal readers. We then examine "basal" language, meaning not the text of basal stories but the language of basal reading instruction. We argue that "basalese" tends to marginalize some students. We then examine the influence of basal reading instruction on life in classrooms, with particular attention to student resistance. We argue that standard uses of basal systems constitutes a moral rationale (e.g., for ability grouping) that marginalizes some students.

Basals as context

[Me gustan] los de segundo grado porque tienen "cartón duro." [I like the second grade basals because they are hard cardboard.]

When you mess up a story you have to read it again.

You got to stand and hold the place.

Consider the use and meaning of basal readers in three different classrooms. In one, the basal readers are displayed but primarily used to prop open malfunctioning windows during the hot weather of early fall and late spring. The basal reader's skill management system (essentially a sheet on which teachers check off student acquisition of specific reading skills) is surreptitiously filled out to placate the school district's reader supervisor. In the second classroom, students are placed in hierarchical reading groups based on a place-ment test accompanying the basal system. The name of each reading group is the title of the basal book they are reading. In the third, the basal readers used by the school system are neither used nor displayed. The class has no reading groups and none of the materials or recordkeeping associated with the basal system are used.

The use and meaning of basal readers differs greatly in these three class-rooms. In the first, the use of basal readers for reading instruction is overtly undermined and ridiculed. In the second, reading instruction follows the basal system's teacher manual and standard basal reading instructional patterns. Reading instruction is the use of the basal system and reading development is progress through the basal system. In the third classroom, basals do not exist.

In each of these classrooms, children's understanding of basal readers and what importance they attach to them is influenced by how the use of basal readers differs. Each classroom may have children who think completing a workbook page is fun or a pain. However, the issue is not whether a child enjoys or hates workbooks or basal stories. Rather, the issue is what children understand about what reading is and who they are as readers and students (Boljonis and Hinchman 1988).

Interestingly, although the three classrooms described above differ greatly in their use of basal readers, they have in common a need to respond to basal systems, even if that response is to reject them. In many school districts, teachers are mandated both to use basal readers and to use them in particular ways (Goodman et al. 1988). In other districts, basal readers are provided for teachers although teachers may choose an alternative. Regardless, because basal readers are used and have been used traditionally in an overwhelming number of elementary classrooms, reading instruction is defined in terms of basal readers even in those classes where they are not used. Teachers who use a basal reading system need not justify their reading program. Teachers who are allowed to do otherwise and choose to do so often need to justify their reading program as being equivalent to or better than the basal system (Goodman et al. 1988).

Similarly, children's understandings of reading and the reading instruction they receive is also defined by basal readers, even when no basal readers are present in their classroom. In a classroom where a basal reading system is being used in a standard manner, students may understand the significance of what reading group they are in, what basal reader they are reading, what workbook page they are on, as defining how good a reader they are and where they stand in comparison to other students. In a classroom where basal readers are not used, students may still define reading in their classroom in terms of basal readers. Students may say, "We don't have a reading book, we have a novel instead" or they may even say, "We don't have reading." Some students may even think they are not learning because they are having fun and they had previously learned that reading is hard work and bureaucratic.

The use of basal readers as context may extend beyond the basals themselves. For example, consider a classroom where the teacher has substituted children's literature for the basal system. Such a substitution may, by itself, be a minimal change in the substance of instruction. That is, the teacher may use trade books in the same way that the basal readers were used. Instead of round-robin oral recitation and sounding out words from a basal reader, children do the same with a trade book. Therefore, children's understanding of basal readers must be explored within the context of the use and meaning given to basal readers and other instructional texts within their classroom and school.

The language of basal instruction

Reading all you gotta do is blah blah blah

(What do you have to know to do well in reading?) You have to know how to answer questions.

Researchers have analyzed the language of the reading selections in basal readers and found important differences from children's literature and other print materials found in children's lives (e.g., Crismore and Hunter 1986; Goodman et al. 1988; Gourley 1984; Simons and Ammon 1988) as well as differences from the language of parent-child interaction (DeStefano and Kantor 1988). The instructional effectiveness of the tasks found in the teacher manuals and workbooks have also been questioned and found lacking (e.g., Durkin 1981; Goodman et al. 1988). Keller-Cohen and Heineken (1987) found that the language tasks of basal workbooks were good preparation for filling out forms, such as applications for social welfare benefits. Their findings suggest that workbooks and basals may be less about learning to read and write and more about adapting to a bureaucratic society.

But the language of basal reading instruction is not just that printed in the basal readers, teacher manuals, and workbooks. It is also the language that occurs among teacher and students. In some teacher manuals, teachers are directed what to say to students. In a few others, what students are supposed to say in response is also given. However, even if the conversation between teacher and students is not scripted word by word, basal reading instruction has a language that may be found in many classrooms. For convenience, we have labeled the language of basal reading instruction "basalese."[2]

Basalese can be considered a kind of register. A register refers to variation in language according to social situation. After describing some of the characteristics of basalese, we discuss the kind of social situation to which basalese refers.

One characteristic of basalese is its prosodic form (the way in which rhythm, stress, and pitch are used). For example, consider the instructional conversation from a first grade classroom:[3]

Teachers: Okay.	01
Let's begin with Robin.	02
Read the first sentence, hon.	03
Robin: It′ is′	04
It′ is′ a′ cat′.	05
Teacher: Very good.	06
Show′ me′	07
Ann	08
Which one of those pictures is′ the′ cat′?	09
Ann: the first′ one′	10

When Robin is asked to read, she renders the text in a halting, monotone, word-by-word manner, stressing each word in a steady, timed rhythm (stress marks are indicated by ′). That prosodic style is repeated throughout the lesson by both the teacher and students, even when the students are not rendering the printed text. For example, when the teacher says "Show′ me′" (line 07) and "is′ the′ cat′" (line 09) the prosody of those lines clearly mimics that used when Robin rendered the text. When Ann responds to the teacher's question (line 10), she also employs that specific prosodic form. The same prosodic style is used in the next conversation as well.

Teacher: O.K. Let's look at the picture.	21
Where′ is′ the′ cat′?	22
Ahhhh Henry.	23
Henry: On the on the truck	24
Teacher: Complete sentence.	25
Henry: It′ is′ on′ the′ truck′.	26
Teacher: O.K. Good.	27
Is that a complete sentence children?	28
All: Yessss.	29
Teacher: Wasn't that nice.	30

The teacher asks the question (line 22) using the prosody of basalese. When Henry responds (line 24), he first does so with a short phrase that, although correct in content, is not accepted because it is not in the correct form (line 25). When he does make the needed response he does so using the prosodic style of basalese (line 26).

Heather's response to a question later in the lesson shows another characteristic of basalese.

Teacher: What does David ask Andy to′ do′?	41
Heather.	42
Heather [mumbles something undecipherable]	43
Teacher: David′ ask′ Andy′ to′ do′	44
Heather: he ask Andy	45
go′ and′ get′ Beck′ y′ she′ can′ help′ you′.	46
Teacher: Alright.	47

What Heather provides is an exact rendering of what is written in the basal reader. If this were a conversation between two people any place other than a reading group, Heather's response would have been viewed as inappropriate. Although she did provide the information requested (What did David ask Andy to do? go and get Becky) she violates one of the norms of conversation, that people will respond to each other without adding information that is not relevant (see Grice 1975, on cooperative principles of conversation). Heather adds "She' can' help' you.'" The information is irrelevant to the question. Further, it makes it unclear whether Heather really knew what David asked Andy to do or whether she merely knew what lines to recite.

But in basalese, Heather's response is acceptable. First, she has used the prosodic style associated with basalese. Second, and most important, she has reproduced the written text. That is, in basalese, the content of what is said in response to a question must be text reproductive. Although there may be variation in the degree to which the text reproduced must address the question asked, the content of the response must be the reproduction of the basal text.

There is consistency between the prosodic style of basalese and its text reproductive content. In many beginning reading programs, especially those heavily based on phonics or whole word strategies, children's attention is focused on decoding words one by one (Goodman et al. 1988). Letters, letter combinations, and words may be presented in isolation. Children are taught to focus their attention on word-by-word decoding, producing a word-calling style similar to the prosody of basalese.

The prosody of basalese signals a particular history in beginning reading as well as the centrality of text reproduction. Children who do not share that particular history (e.g., children who have learned to read before coming to school) or children who do not hold text reproduction as central to reading (e.g., children who attend to the meaning of what they are reading and may therefore miscue in reading a text) may find themselves marginalized. They may find themselves disconnected from learning in school.

Since both the form and content of basalese emphasize text reproduction, the authority for interpretation is placed in the basal text. Students must ignore any knowledge they may have of their own that could be used to respond to a question or interpret a text and limit themselves to what is given in the basal text. While such a limitation is a problem for all students and can result in marginalizing any student, those students whose background knowledge, experiences, and values are concomitant with the basal may be at less risk than others since the authority of the text validates them.

Basals and life in classrooms

Me gustan algunos cuentos el "workbook" es bien facil.
[I like some stories, the workbook is very easy.]
The reading test is like the workbook but thinner.
The thing about reading is you have to learn.

When Joshua, a first grader, says, "The thing about reading is you have to learn," he emphasizes "have to." Learning is not fun, it is not knowledge acquisition, it is not developing an increasing ability to control the world around one, nor is it membership in a community of authors and readers. Learning is the work of school; it is the labor Joshua exchanges for the social rewards school offers. However, in addition to social rewards, there are also social consequences that can be unpleasant. One may be embarrassed or denied access to activities that are fun (e.g., by being held in during recess, given after-school detention, demoted to a lower reading group, or even held back a grade). Thus, Joshua and other students labor not only for social rewards but also to avoid negative consequences.

At least two questions need to be asked about reading in classrooms as labor. First, what is the role of basal reading instruction with regard to classroom work? And second, how do students respond to the labor they are assigned?

Basal instruction and classroom work

Basal reading systems present themselves as organized in a hierarchical manner, proceeding from basic and prerequisite skills to more advanced skills, and from easy reading passages to harder ones. Learning to read is presented as the accumulation of skills. The organization of basal systems—as a progression from easy to hard, prerequisite to advanced—provides a moral justification for the hierarchical social organization of instruction. More simply, basal systems provide a moral rationale for grouping students according to ability. It is a moral rationale because an inherent moral principle is implied: Students who have already acquired certain skills should proceed to acquire the next set of skills and not be held back by other students.

The basis on which the rationale is made is, at best, questionable. The thesis that reading is a set of discrete skills that can be learned in isolation has been questioned by many reading and language researchers (e.g., Goodman and Goodman 1979; Harste, Woodward and Burke 1984). Reading development does not appear to be reducible to discrete, well-defined, and universal stages and sequences. The nature of reading and of reading development does not provide a justification for a hierarchy of reading groups or for enacting instruction in any other hierarchical social organization (such as an individualized mastery learning program).

Perhaps what is most pernicious about the moral rationale provided by basal reading systems is that it hides linguistic and cultural instructional biases that assign minority students to inferior status and opportunities for instruction. Students whose linguistic and cultural background are not valued by the teacher or school are more frequently placed in lower reading groups, remedial instruction, and special education classes. While such placements may be based on implicit rather than explicit biases (Collins 1987) the effect can nonetheless be devastating (Eder 1983), especially since moving from lower to higher groups may be extremely difficult and not based primarily on ability to read (Borko and Eisenhart 1989). Some children may begin to see themselves as unable to learn. As Corno (1989), building on work by Rohrkemper and Bershon (1984), Nicholls (1983) and Seligman (1975), writes:

> Destructive patterns of academic motivation [can be traced] to negative inter-
> pretations of classroom performance and a general perception of powerless-
> ness. . . . When students feel that classroom learning is beyond their capabilities,

something that results from a lack of personal ability that will never improve, they can fall into a downward spiral with schoolwork from which they may never recover. (pp. 34–35)

Put simply, some students become marginalized, with linguistic and cultural minority students at special risk of being marginalized. What basal reading instruction does is provide a moral rationale that allows students to be marginalized and then hides it.

Responding to basal instruction

It is not unusual to hear children say they find reading and workbooks boring, but it is also not unusual to hear children say that basals and workbooks are fun. Indeed, for some students the basal reading system works well, not necessarily in teaching them to read (which they may do in spite of rather than because of a basal system), but rather in placing them at the head of the class. As they complete workbook pages, make progress through various basal levels, receive stars for doing well on tests, and appropriately answer teacher questions, they see themselves as learners and most importantly as students on the fast track.

Goulder (1978), in a study of Black children in elementary schools, describes students as teachers' pets, troublemakers, and nobodies. The few teacher's pets matched the teachers' and schools' expectations for a "good" student. They received a disproportionate amount of attention and instruction, as well as social status within the classroom and school. The few troublemakers also received a lot of attention, but negative attention directed at discipline. The nobodies received little attention and instruction.

It is reasonable to expect that teachers' pets, troublemakers, and nobodies will respond to basal readers differently because they have different social significance for each group. Whether students in classrooms are divided in distinct social groups, as described by Goulder (1978), or whether the social distinctions among them are less well defined, those social distinctions can be expected to influence their understanding and response to basal reading instruction.

Another factor also mediates how children will respond to basal reading instruction. Children do not always passively accept what is given to them. Corno (1989) makes clear that knowledge about how classrooms work can help students overcome classroom difficulties and problems. Corno states that students may:

1. Make changes in themselves appropriate to the situation at hand,
2. Make changes in the task at hand, and/or
3. Make changes in the larger instructional situation.

Each of these strategies constitutes a kind of resistance to what schooling gives to students. Changes in oneself can range from changing one's effort level to presenting oneself differently in particular classroom situations. Borko and Eisenhart (1989) suggest that the movement from a lower to a higher reading group may require students to make a change in how they interact with the teacher, other students, and the text. One may be the top student in a lower reading group but if one's style of interaction is different from that of the higher reading group, one may not be moved, be moved only temporarily, or continue to be viewed as a lower group reader while attending the higher reading group.

Tasks can be transformed to be less difficult or more difficult. One can cheat and get the answers from other students. One can reduce the cognitive demands of a task by copying from authoritative texts, such as writing a report by copying from an encyclopedia. But one can also make tasks more difficult and cognitively complex in order to make the task more interesting. A boring fill-in-the-blank worksheet can be made more interesting by a student adding a surreptitious demand that the added words read alone will make an off-color sentence. A student can transform the reading of a boring story into a more interesting activity by imagining how it should be revised. Indeed, some students may surreptitiously take control of their own education by transforming the tasks they are given into more cognitively complex ones.

The third type of change noted by Corno (1989), change in the large instructional situation, is more difficult to accomplish by students alone. Nonetheless, students do attempt to change the instructional situation. They complain to the teacher and suggest a change. They write and pass notes both to avoid boredom and to reconstitute the social structure. They disrupt the classroom. Depending on whether and how students resist the social organization and definitions given them in the classroom, they will understand and respond to basal readers differently.

With regard to life in classrooms, basal readers provide a moral rationale for the social organization of students and an interpretation of student behavior that hides what is actually occurring in a classroom and children's understanding. The moral rationale provided by basal readers is, at best, of questionable foundation. The social organization basal reading instruction promotes tends to marginalize at least some students, if not many. Whatever learning does occur is credited to the basal reader while the strategies actually employed by students in response to their use is obfuscated.

Final remarks

You have to do comprehension check and skills check and summary and then you have to do the workbook. (You sound like it's a real hassle to do it.) I know I don't even do those comprehension and summary. Well, she don't get on our nerves if we don't do them so...I guess I'll do them. She didn't write anything on my report [card] so they're optional I guess.

(What do you most like about the basal?) Que es facil, pero es "boring." [That it's easy, but it's boring.]

Me gustan mas los de Puerto Rico. Son mejores, más fácil, los de aquí no me gustan, son una porquería. [I like the ones from Puerto Rico. They are better, easier, the ones from here I don't like, they are a piece of junk.]

How children understand basal readers seems to be mediated by at least three factors: (a) the extent to which the children are familiar and comfortable with "school culture," (b) whether they see themselves as successful or on shaky ground in their own academic progress, and (c) the closeness with which their cultural, linguistic, and class backgrounds approximate those of the characters, settings, values, and language represented in basals and in the way basals are used. Our purpose in presenting children's understanding of basals is to suggest that children have a role to play in selecting materials and how they will be used — a role that can empower them as readers.

When children understand the purposes of reading to be getting better grades, getting through workbooks, perfecting discrete skills, or simply being assigned a standing in the social order, then it is time to question the uses of basals and their consequences. Basal reading instruction tends to marginalize some, if not many students, and to disconnect them from the conditions for learning and intellectual and personal growth and development.

The helplessness often displayed by students subjected to basals gives some indication of the marginalizing effect they may have on children. However, children are not simply the recipients of basal instruction, they are also active and passive resisters of basals and how they are used. From the plaintive pleas, "I'd rather just read stories and tell her what the story is about" to the more militant, "No ne gustan, son una porqueria" [I don't like them, they're a piece of junk], children in different settings are eloquent in their resistance to basals and to being marginalized. It is time they were heard.

Notes

1. The quotations at the beginning of each segment are taken from videotaped interviews of first grade children conducted by undergraduate students at The University of Michigan in 1986 and from interviews conducted in 1988 by a Spanish-English bilingual teacher of her second grade students. We want to acknowledge their efforts and especially thank Rosemary Hiller and Linda Velazquez. We also want to thank the students and parents who participated.

2. The term "primerese" has been used to describe the written discourse of basal stories. We use the term "basalese" because of our focus on the interaction between teacher and student rather than student and written text. Obviously, the two are related.

3. The transcripts all come from videotapes of a single reading group lesson in a first grade classroom from a mid-sized industrial city in the Midwest. The videotapes were made as part of an ethnographic study of reading and writing across grades kindergarten through 8. The lesson was selected for transcription and analysis because many of its discourse features were recurrent in other lessons in that classroom and in other classrooms. The study was funded by a Spencer Seed Grant and is reported in Bloome (1984). We want to thank the teachers and students who participated in the study. The opinions expressed in this article do not necessarily reflect those of the funding agency.

References

Bloome, D. (1984). *Gaining access to and control of reading and writing resources: K-8* (Final report submitted to the National Council of Teachers of English Research Foundation). Urbana, IL: National Council of Teachers of English.

Boljonis, A., & Hinchman, K. (1988). First graders' perceptions of reading and writing. In J. Readence & R.S. Baldwin (Eds.), *Dialogues in literacy research: Thirty-seventh yearbook of the National Reading Conference* (pp. 107–114). Chicago: National Reading Conference.

Borko, H., & Eisenhart, M. (1989). Reading ability groups as literacy communities. In D. Bloome (Ed.), *Classrooms and literacy* (pp. 107–134). Norwood, NJ: Ablex.

Britton, G., & Lumpkin, M. (1983). Basal readers: Paultry progress pervades. *Bulletin of the Council on Interracial Books for Children*, *14*(6), 4–7.

Cairney, T.H. (1988). The purpose of basals: What children think. *The Reading Teacher*, *41*, 420–428.

Collins, J. (1987). Using cohesion analysis to understand access to knowledge. In D. Bloome (Ed.), *Literacy and schooling* (pp. 67–97). Norwood, NJ: Ablex.

Corno, L. (1989). What it means to be literate about classrooms. In D. Bloome (Ed.), *Classrooms and literacy* (pp. 29–52). Norwood, NJ: Ablex.

Crismore, A.G., & Hunter, B.M. (1986). Investigating visual displays in basal reading textbooks. In J.A. Niles & R.V. Lalik (Eds.), *Solving problems in literacy: Learners, teachers and researchers. Thirty-fifth yearbook of the National Reading Conference* (pp. 326–333). Rochester, NY: National Reading Conference.

DeStefano, J., & Kantor, R. (1988). Cohesion in spoken and written dialogue: An investigation of cultural and textual constraints. *Linguistics and Education*, *1*(2), 105–124.

Durkin, D. (1981). Reading comprehension instruction in five basal reading series. *Reading Research Quarterly*, *16*, 515–544.

Eder, D. (1983). Ability grouping and students' academic self-concepts: A case study. *Elementary School Journal*, *84*, 149–161.

Ghory, W.J., Sinclair, R.L., & Robinson, B. (1988). Considering marginal students. In R.L. Sinclair & S.M. Nieto (Eds.), *Renewing school curriculum: Concerns for equal and quality education* (pp. 25–36). Amherst, MA: Coalition for School Improvement.

Goodman, K.S., & Goodman, Y. (1979). Learning to read is natural. In L.B. Resnick & P.A. Weaver (Eds.), *Theory and practice of early reading* (Vol. 1) (pp. 137–154). Hillsdale, NJ: Erlbaum.

Goodman, K.S., Shannon, P., Freeman, Y., & Murphy, S. (1988). *Report card on basal readers*. Katonah, NY: Richard C. Owen.

Goulder, H. (1978). *Teachers' pets, troublemakers, and nobodies: Black children in elementary school*. Westport, CT: Greenwood Press.

Gourley, J. (1984). Discourse structure: Expectations of beginning readers and readability of text. *Journal of Reading Behavior*, *14*, 169–188.

Grice, H.P. (1975). Logic and conversation. In P. Cole & J. Morgan (Eds.), *Syntax and semantics 3: Speech acts* (pp. 41–58). New York: Academic Press.

Harste, J., Woodward, V., & Burke, C. (1984). *Language stories and literacy lessons*. Portsmouth, NH: Heinemann.

Keller-Cohen, D., & Heineken, J. (1987). Workbooks: What they can teach children about forms. In D. Bloome (Ed.), *Literacy and schooling* (pp. 258–288). Norwood, NJ: Ablex.

Nicholls, J.G. (1983). Conceptions of ability and achievement motivation: A theory and its implications for education. In S. Paris, G. Olson, & H. Stevenson (Eds.), *Learning and motivation in the classroom* (pp. 211–237). Hillsdale, NJ: Erlbaum.

Rohrkemper, M.M., & Bershon, B.L. (1984). Elementary school students' reports of the causes and effects of problem difficulty in mathematics. *The Elementary School Journal*, *85*, 127–147.

Seligman, M.E.P. (1975). *Helplessness: On depression, development, and death*. San Francisco: Freeman.

Simons, H.D., & Ammon, P. (1988). Primerese miscues. In J. Readence & R.S. Baldwin (Eds.), *Dialogues in literacy research: Thirty-seventh yearbook of the National Reading Conference* (pp. 115–121). Chicago: National Reading Conference.

Who
Is
Considered
Literate?

TEN

On the Subjects of Class and Gender in "The Literacy Letters"
Linda Brodkey

n "The Discourse on Language," Michel Foucault dramatizes the desire to be "on the other side of discourse, without having to stand outside it, pondering its particular, fearsome, and even devilish features" (215) in this whimsical colloquy between the individual and the institution.

> Inclination speaks out: "I don't want to have to enter this risky world of discourse: I want nothing to do with it insofar as it is decisive and final; I would like to feel it all around me, calm and transparent, profound, infinitely open, with others responding to my expectations, and truth emerging, one by one. All I want is to allow myself to be borne along, within it, and by it, a happy wreck." Institutions reply: "But you have nothing to fear from launching out: we're here to show you discourse is within the established order of things, that we've waited a long time for its arrival, that a place has been set aside for it—a place that both honours and disarms it; and if it should have a certain power, then it is we, and we alone, who give it that power." (215–16)

What Foucault and other poststructuralists have been arguing the last fifteen or twenty years is considerably easier to state than act on: we are at once constituted and unified as subjects in language and discourse. The discursive subject is of particular interest to those of us who teach writing because language and discourse are understood to be complicit in the representation of self and others, rather than the neutral or arbitrary tools of thought and expression that they are in other modern theories, not to mention handbooks and rhetorics. Among other things, this means that since writers cannot avoid constructing a social and political reality in their texts, as teachers we need to

---

Source: Linda Brodkey, "On the Subjects of Class and Gender in 'The Literacy Letters,'" *College English*, February 1989. Copyright 1989 by the National Council of Teachers of English. Reprinted with permission.

learn how to "read" the various relationships between writer, reader, and reality that language and discourse supposedly produce.

New theories of textuality are inevitably new theories of reading. And in the field of writing, those who teach basic writers and welcome new ways to read their texts are perhaps the most likely to recognize the possibilities of discursive subjectivity. The poststructural David Bartholomae of "Inventing the University," for example, writes less confidently but more astutely of what student errors may signify than the Bartholomae of "The Study of Error," published some years earlier at the height of the field's enthusiasm for empirical research and error analysis. For the startling power of a discourse to confer authority, name errors, and rank order student texts speaks more readily to the experience of reading basic writing than promises of improved reliability or validity in the empirical study of errors. While empiricality is far from moot, it makes little difference if one is right if one is not talking about that which most concerns writing and the teaching of writing. Or, as Sharon Crowley has put it, "the quality of the power that is associated with writing varies with the degree of author-ity granted by a culture to its texts" (96). In this society the authority that teachers are empowered to grant to or withhold from student texts derives from the theory of textuality governing their reading.

The question then is how to read what students write. And at issue is the unquestioned power of a pedagogical authority that insists that teachers concentrate on form at the expense of content.

> I'm siting at home now when I have more time to write to you I enjoyed rending your letters. I under stand reading them one word I had a little trouble with the word virginia but know about me well that is hard but I will try.

The errors in spelling and punctuation in this passage are serious, but not nearly as egregious, I suspect, as the tradition that warrants reducing a text to its errors. Remember the anger you feel when someone corrects your pronunciation or grammar while you are in the throes of an argument, and you can recover the traces of the betrayal students must experience when a writing assignment promises them seemingly unlimited possibilities for expression, and the response or evaluation notes only their limitations. The errors are there, and the passage is hard to read. Yet to see only the errors strikes me as an unwarranted refusal to cede even the possibility of discursive subjectivity and authority to the woman who wrote this passage, barring of course that of basic writer which an error analysis would without question grant her.

Changing the subject

This is an essay about the ways discourses construct our teaching. In postmodern theories of subjectivity:

1. all subjects are the joint creations of language and discourse;
2. all subjects produced are ideological;
3. all subject positions are vulnerable to the extent that individuals do not or will not identify themselves as the subjects (i.e., the effects) of a discourse.

Those who occupy the best subject positions a discourse has to offer would have a vested interest in maintaining the illusion of speaking rather than being spoken by discourse. Postmodern rhetoric would begin by assuming that all discourses warrant variable subject positions ranging from mostly satisfying to mostly unsatisfying for those individuals named by them. Each institutionalized discourse privileges some people and not others by generating uneven and unequal subject positions as various as stereotypes and agents. Hence, it is at least plausible to expect most, though not all, of those individuals whose subjectivity is the most positively produced by a discourse to defend its discursive practices against change. And it is equally plausible to expect some, though again not all, of those individuals whose subjectivity is the most negatively produced to resist its discursive practices. Feminists, for example, regularly resist discursive practices that represent female subjectivity solely in terms of reproductive biology. Of course, neither verbal resistance nor other material forms of protest to such reduced subject positions are universal among women.

Discursive resistance requires opportunities for resistance. Altering an institutionalized discourse probably requires an unremitting negative critique of its ideology, a critique that is most often carried out in the academy by attempting to replace a particular theory (e.g., of science or art or education or law) with another. Recently, theoretical battles have proliferated to such an extent that a cover term, *critical theory*, has come to refer to a variety of ideological critiques of theory, research, and practice across the academy: critical legal studies, critical practice, critical anthropology, critical pedagogy, and so on.

Discursive resistance, however, need not be conducted in such abstract terms as we have recently witnessed in the academy. The more usual practice would be for those individuals who are ambivalent or threatened by their subject positions in a given discourse to interrupt the very notion of the unified self — the traditional Cartesian notion that the self is a transcendent and absolute entity rather than a creation of language and ideology — in their spoken and written texts. Such interruptions are likely to take one of two forms: reversing the negative and positive subject positions in a given discourse — as Carol Gilligan does in her feminist revision of the research on the development of moral reasoning among adolescent girls; or re-presenting a stereotype as an agent in a discourse the least committed to the preservation of the stereotype — as Toni Morrison does when representing Afro-American women and men as the agents rather than the victims of events in her novels.

Studies of these and other interruptive practices, rhetorics of resistance in which individuals shift subject positions from one discourse to another or within a discourse in their speaking and writing, would constitute empirical inquiry into the postmodern speculation that language and discourse are material to the construction of reality, not simply by-products reflecting or reproducing a set of non-discursive, material social structures and political formations. Knowledge of multiple subject positions makes possible both the practical and the theoretical critiques that interrupt the assumption of unchanging, irreversible, and asymmetrical social and political relations between the privileged and unprivileged subjects represented in a particular discourse (see Williams, esp. 75 – 141).

What is needed is research that addresses what Stuart Hall has recently called "a theory of articulation," which he describes as "a way of understanding how ideological elements come, under certain conditions, to cohere together within a discourse, and a way of asking how they do or do not become articulated, at specific junctures, to certain political subjects" (53). Since articulation separates intentions from effects, or production from reception, Hall has reinserted the possibility of human agency into poststructural theory. More specifically, articulation distinguishes between the desire to be unified in a discourse and what happens in practice, namely, what individuals do in and with the unified subject positions offered them by such recognizable institutional discourses as, say, science, art, education, law, and religion or ethics.

"The Literacy Letters"

What I mean by research on the rhetorics of discursive practice and attendant practices of resistance is amply illustrated in a curriculum project I have referred to elsewhere as "the Literacy Letters" (see Brodkey). The letters were generated in the discourse of education, since they were initiated by six white middle-class teachers (four women and two men) taking my graduate course on teaching basic writing and sustained by six white working-class women enrolled in an Adult Basic Education (ABE) class. The woman who was teaching the ABE class and taking my course hoped that corresponding would provide the students in her class with what she called an authentic reason to write—on the order of a pen-pal experience for adults. The experienced English teachers from my class, most of whom had not taught basic writing, set out to learn more about the reading and writing concerns of their adult correspondents. As for me, I welcomed the chance to study correspondence itself, which seemed to me a remarkable opportunity to examine both the production and reception of self and other in the writing and reading of personal letters.

Permission to photocopy the letters as data for research was granted by all correspondents before the first exchange. For the two months that they wrote, the correspondents agreed not to meet or talk on the phone. The data, then, are the letters written by the six pairs who wrote regularly: one pair exchanged letters eight times; one pair seven times; two pairs six times; and two pairs five times.

When the teachers first reported that they found writing the letters stressful, I attributed their anxiety to the fact that I would be reading and evaluating their letters as well as those written by the students in the ABE class. But their uneasiness persisted despite repeated assurances that I couldn't look at or read the letters until the semester's end, a standard procedure meant to protect the educational rights of those who agree to participate in classroom research. After reading and thinking about the letters, however, I am no longer so inclined to assume that my presence as such was as threatening or intrusive as I first thought, though doubtless it contributed some to their anxiety.

Learning to read "The Literacy Letters"

Research on basic writers as well as my own experience teaching amply prepared me for the ungainly prose produced by the women in the ABE class (e.g., Bartholomae, Perl, Shaughnessy). But nothing I had read or remembered from my own teaching prepared me for occasional moments of linguistic as well as discursive awkwardness from the teachers. I am not referring to the necessary clumsiness with which the teachers sought their footing before they knew anything about their correspondents, but to intermittent improprieties that occurred once several letters had been exchanged. In fact, I found these occasional lapses so perplexing that it's fair to say that the teachers' unexpected errors, rather than the students' expected ones, led me to think about the literacy letters in terms of the poststructural discursive practices of reproduction and resistance. Only discourse, more specifically the power of a discourse over even its fluent writers, I decided, could begin to explain the errors of these otherwise literate individuals.

That educational discourse grants teachers authority over the organization of language in the classroom, which includes such commonplace privileges as allocating turns, setting topics, and asking questions, is clear from sociolinguistic studies of classroom language interaction (e.g., Stubbs). Many teachers, including those in this study, attempt to relinquish their control by staging opportunities for students to take the privileged subject position of teacher in, say, group discussions or collaborative assignments that grant them, at least temporarily, a measure of control over educational discursive practice. Attempts to transform classroom discussions into conversations between peers are thwarted to the extent that teachers fail to realize that their interpersonal relationships with students, as well as their institutional ones, are constituted by educational discourse. While the power of a discourse is not absolute, neither is it vulnerable to change by individuals who ignore its power, only by those who interrupt or resist or challenge the seemingly immutable reality of unified subjectivity. In much the same way that you don't resist racism by denying that racism exists, but by confronting it in yourself and others, teachers cannot divest themselves of those vestiges of authority that strike them as unproductive by ignoring the institutional arrangements that unequally empower teachers and students.

At the outset, the teachers in this study attempted to mitigate the power of educational discourse over themselves and their correspondents by "playing" student. Their letters are replete with the desire to represent themselves as students of writing pedagogy and their correspondents as their teachers. The longest running correspondence, for instance, was initiated by a teacher who wrote: "I think that some of the things you could tell me might help me to understand what I can do better when I try to help my students learn to improve thier (sic) writing." Since none of the students made suggestions about either curriculum or instruction, roles were not reversed. But making the requests seems to have mooted the possibility of the teachers practicing the most authoritarian "dialect" of educational discourse in their correspondence. To wit, no teacher reduced personal correspondence to spelling or grammar lessons; nor, for that matter, did any of the students from the ABE class ask to be taught or corrected.

Bear in mind that the writers of the literacy letters are not held by the usual arrangements between teachers and students. To be sure, the teachers are teachers and the students are students. But theirs is what might be called an extracurricular relationship, arranged by the authorized teacher. While the teachers assiduously avoided lessons and hence avoided even the possibility of displacing the classroom teacher's authority, there are nevertheless times in the letters when it certainly looks as if by ignoring rather than contesting the authority of educational discourse, they retained control over such discursive privileges as determining what is and what is not an appropriate topic. The teachers exercise their authority infrequently, but decisively, whenever one of their correspondents interrupts, however incidentally, the educational discursive practice that treats class as irrelevant to the subjectivity of teachers and students. Telegraphed by linguistic and/or discursive lapses, the refusal that signals the teachers' unspoken commitment to a classless discourse provokes additional and more pronounced discursive resistance from the ABE writers.

Personal narratives in "The Literacy Letters"

Discursive hegemony on the part of the teachers is most obvious and discursive resistance on the part of the students is most dramatic during storytelling episodes. Personal correspondence evokes personal narratives. The teachers tell a variety of stories in which they represent themselves as busy professionals trying to resolve conflicts among work, family, and school. Social research on storytelling suggests that in exchange for being granted the time it takes to tell a story, the teller is expected to make it worth the listener's while by raising for evaluation or contemplation that which is problematic or unusual about the narrative conflict and its resolution (see Labov, Pratt). That the teachers tell stories representing themselves as guilty about their inability to find enough time is not surprising, since their busy lives have been made all the more complicated by recently adding course work to schedules already overburdened by responsibilities at work and home. Nor are the responses to their stress stories unexpected, for the women from the Adult Basic Education class console and commiserate with the teachers in much the way that research suggests interlocutors ordinarily do. The teachers, however, occasionally respond in extraordinary ways when their correspondents reciprocate with stories about their lives.

The ABE students do not tell narratives about not having the time to fulfill their obligations to the three spheres of work, school, and family. Nor are their stories about internal conflicts like guilt. Instead, they write most frequently about external threats to the well-being of themselves and their families or their neighbors. While work and education often figure in their stories, they are important only insofar as they materially affect their lives: a family is besieged by the threat of layoffs; lack of educational credentials means the low paychecks and the moonlighting that robs families of time with the overworked wage earner.

Clearly teachers and students alike told class-based narratives. Yet the teachers' markedly inept responses to their correspondents' narratives suggest that the hegemony of educational discourse warrants teachers not only to represent themselves as subjects unified by the internal conflicts like guilt that preoccupy professionals, but to disclaim narratives that represent a subject alternatively unified in its conflicts with an external material reality. This refusal to acknowledge the content of their correspondents' narratives, most explicable as a professional class narcissism that sees itself everywhere it looks, alienates the ABE writers from educational discourse and, more importantly, from the teachers it ostensibly authorizes.

Don and Dora. The seven-letter exchange between the teacher and student I'll call Don and Dora is disarming. Frequency alone suggests that both teacher and student found corresponding satisfying. For some weeks they wrote about movies, food, and their families, all topics introduced by Don who represented himself in his initial letter as a complex subject, specifically, as a young man beset by personal failings his correspondent would find amusing.

> I won't tell you how long I like to stay in bed in the morning — though I do stay up very late at night (watching old movies) — but let's just say that it's past 11 AM. Oh well, we all have to have at least one vice. Unfortunately, I have more than one. One of my others is Chinese food. There's a Chinese food cart parked right outside the window of the library where I work, so every afternoon I dash out when the line slacks off...I usually try to get some vegetable dishes, even though I most always end up getting the most highly caloric item on the menu.

His comedic self-presentation is amplied by this final request: "Please let me know what you're doing: do you like Chinese food (and if so, what kind?), do you like old movies (and if so, which ones?), do you think I'm too weird to write back to? I'll look forward to your responses, comments, complaints, etc." In her response letter, Dora picks up the topics of movies and food. "I to enjoy the old movies and (love Chinese food)," she writes, but then goes on to conclude about them both, "so [I] guess that make two of us that are (weird)." Notice that while she responds to his question, "do you think I'm too weird to write back to?", writing back is itself material evidence that Dora doesn't find Don's tastes *too* weird. Dora is, as she puts it, "looking forward to writing back this is my first letter I ever wrote."

Over the next few weeks, their letters follow this pattern. Don writes extended and humorous anecdotes that portray him as a man at odds with himself at work, school, and home, and Dora offers consolation by letting him know how amusing she and the other women in her class find his stories: "Rachel [her teacher] ask me to read your letter to the class we all though that your grandmother and father was funning about the candy." After dutifully playing audience for some weeks, however, Dora dramatically reverses the pattern when she not only asserts herself as a narrator, but as the narrator of tragic rather than comedic events, in this letter which in its entirety reads as follows:

> I don't have must to siad this week a good frineds husband was kill satday at 3:15 the man who kill him is a good man he would give you the shirt off of his back it is really self-defense but anyway I see police academy three it was funny but not is good as the first two

Dora's narrative limns as stark a reality as any represented in the literacy letters. However, the abrupt shift from herself as a narrator who reflects on the aftermath of violence to herself as the student who answers a teacher's questions — "but anyway I see police academy three it was funny but not is good as the first two" — is, for me, one of those moments when the power of discourse seems the most absolute.

It's not implausible to imagine that in telling a narrative Dora is trying out the more positive subject position afforded narrators by the discourse of art, and that Don has held throughout their correspondence. But art is only a respite, it seems, for Dora shifts quickly from narrator back to student. Yet in that brief moment when she inserts herself as the narrator, Dora takes on the more complex subjectivity afforded by the discourse of art to narrators. Though short, the story she tells is one in which the narrator's sympathies are clearly divided between the survivors — the friend and the murderer — a narrative position that Dora grounds in the extenuating circumstances of moral character (a good man "would give you the shirt off of his back") and law ("it is really self-defense"). Her narrative point of view considers not the grisly fact of murder and not even what motivated the murder, but the notion that murder is a consequence of circumstances rather than character.

Narrative strikes me as a potentially effective mode of resistance, for the rules governing storytelling more or less require Don to respond to the content of Dora's narrative. Since Dora attentuated the full interruptive force of the discourse of art on educational discourse, however, by interjecting the comment about the movie, she effectively lost her hold on the rhetorical practice in which the narrative critiques a teacher's exclusive right to initiate topics. The abrupt shift from narrator back to audience returns, or offers to return, teacher and student alike to the already established subject positions of teacher/narrator and student/audience.

Even if Dora's interjection is understood as hesitation, Don might have assisted her by simply responding to the content of her story. He might have asked about motive or even asked why she says nothing about the victim. But Don's response suggests only that he is nonplussed:

> I'm sorry to hear about the problem that you wrote about last week. It's always hard to know what to say when the situation is as unusual as that one. I hope that everything is getting a little better, at least for you trying to know what to say and do in the situation.

Several issues about the fragility of the unity that even the most privileged subjects are able to achieve in language and discourse come immediately to mind. Most obvious, perhaps, is the syntactic lapse in the final sentence ("I hope that everything is getting a little better, at least for *you* trying to know what to say and do in that situation"). Less obvious, though equally to the point, is the way that Don's linguistic facility, under the circumstances, only amplifies the discursive inadequacy of this passage as a response to the content of her narrative.

Bearing in mind that she has just told a story in which the "problem" is the aftermath of murder — her friend's husband is dead and the good man who killed him presumably faces prison — the assertion that this is a matter of manners — "It's always hard to know what to say when the situation is as unusual as that one" — is not simply inappropriate. It constitutes a discursive retreat that threatens to reconstitute Don and Dora in the most profoundly alienated subject relationship of all — self and other — and to give over their more or less satisfying discursive relationship as narrator and audience. Even the demonstrative adjective, *that*, underscores the distance Don places between himself and the world in which he resides and the other and the world in which she resides. The contrast between this awkward first paragraph and the plans to

ON THE SUBJECTS OF CLASS AND GENDER

visit his grandmother on Mother's Day that complete his letter effectively reiterates the terms of their continued correspondence.

In her next letter, Dora again responds to the content of Don's letter, "I am glad to hear that you are going to see your grandmother." And though she makes no further mention in this or any letter of the murder, she writes "I hope you get more energy about work," which remark is followed by:

> I wouldn't want to see you living in Kensington with the rest of us bums. ha ha

It certainly looks as if she has acknowledged the threat of othering by noting that his self-proclaimed and amply documented laziness throughout their correspondence would, in the eyes of many, make him one of the others — "the rest of us bums" — whose subjectivity he's denying. That her class antagonism increases after the next letter, in which he narrates in the usual humorous detail his visit with his grandmother, is evident in the fact that for first time she makes no reference to his anecdote and ends a brief account of her own Mother's Day with, "I got call back to work today. I am very nervous about it. it like started a new job." In his next letter, in which he makes no mention of her job, Don follows yet another extended narrative about a day at the beach with "Keep cool and write soon!" But this time Dora ignores both the narrative and the imperatives and does not write again.

Don's response is characteristic of the kind of discursive uneasiness that arises whenever one of the students interrupts the educational practice that deems such working-class concerns as neighborhood violence irrelevant. And while this is admittedly one of the more dramatic examples, it suggests the extent to which unacknowledged tension over the control of subject positions contributes to rather than alleviates class antagonism, for we see that the teacher's desire to be preserved as the unified subject of an educational discursive practice that transcends class overrides the student's desire to narrate herself as a subject unified in relation to the violence that visited her working-class neighborhood.

Rita and Esther. The second example comes from the six-letter exchange between an experienced secondary English teacher I'll call Rita and the most fluent and prolific writer from the ABE class, a student I'll call Esther. The set itself is unusual, since these are the only correspondents whose letters are often of similar length. From the outset, it's easy to see that Esther is not only actively resisting playing "student" but sometimes even tries to play "teacher." In response to Rita's initial letter, for instance, Esther first compliments her — "My classmates and I read your wonderful letter" — but then faults her for what she neglected to mention: "you never stated your age or your country in the letter. And also where your Grandmother's home was." And unlike the other ABE writers, in her first and subsequent letters, Esther asks for information that Rita has neither offered nor alluded to:

> What is it like where you live and what are the shopping areas like. How is the transportation and the Climate there. What kind of food do you like to eat. You didn't say if you were married, or if you have children. Please write back and let me know.

Though this is admittedly an insight considerably improved by hindsight, the class antagonism that erupts later can probably be traced to Rita's ambivalance about their relationship, for she seems unable either to accept Esther's assumption that they are peers or to assert herself as a teacher. Rita's reluctance to declare herself as either a teacher or a peer may explain her refusal to do more than name the suburb she lives in or the nearby mall in answer to questions like "What is it like where you live and what are the shopping areas like." In short, Rita replies but does not answer Esther's questions.

In a letter near the end of their correspondence, following yet one more futile effort to establish what Rita's life is like—"Do you live near a beach or the shore? Are you going anywhere special this Summer?"—Esther writes this explanation in response to Rita's comment that she sounded "a little discouraged" in her last letter:

> I'm going to have to look for another house because, the Restate is Selling the house unless somebody invests in it and wants me to stay his or her tennant. That is why I was a little discourage because I didn't have a chance to save any money. I'll still answer your letters. Thank you for writing back.

This is a remarkable passage if only because it is one of the few times in the literacy letters when anyone mentions money by name. There are plenty of coded references to money: vacations taken or not taken, the buying of gifts, the cost of public transportation and food. But this particular statement is about money, about the simple economic fact that changing housing requires capital. And given what Esther has written, Rita's response strikes me as a perverse misreading:

> It is difficult to save money. Do you have any idea where you will move? What kind of home are you planning to buy? Interest rates are low now.

The peculiarity arises in the increasing unconnectedness of Rita's sentences to Esther's assertions. The first sentence is a response to Esther's assertion that she hasn't "had a chance to save any money." And the second sentence relates to Esther's claim that she will probably have to move. But in light of what Esther wrote, the assumption that Esther is planning to buy a house or that interest rates are of any consequence to her is, to say the least, surprising. That the question confounds Esther is evident in her next letter, which begins with a passing reference to Rita's sister, whose illness Rita mentioned in her last letter, followed by a brief but pointed attempt to correct the misunderstanding:

> I'm very sorry to hear about your sister. I hope she gets better. About the house. The only way I could buy a house is by hitting a number in the Lotto.

As lessons in elementary economics go this is about as clear as any I know. Yet Rita's response to this assertion is, on the face of it, even more bizarre than her statement that "Interest rates are low now." To wit, she ignores Esther's topic, which is housing, and reintroduces gambling, Lotto, as a topic they might discuss:

> Do you play Lotto frequently? I never think that I can ever win one of those lotteries. Did you ever know anyone who won? Some people play faithfully.

This is a near perfect example of cross-talk, for two conversations are now in play—one about housing and another about gambling. And were this a conversation between peers, Rita would be charged with illicitly changing the topic, since it is she who played the conversational gambit in which Esther's instructive hyperbole—"the only way I could buy a house is if I win the Lotto"—is taken at its face value, and Lotto, which is not the topic but the comment, is tranformed into the topic, now in the form of questions about gambling. It's a familiar teacher's gambit for controlling what does and does not count as knowledge, a remnant, perhaps, of the institutionalized silencing that Michelle Fine suggests "more intimately informs low-income, public schooling than relatively privileged situations" (158).

The salient fact here is that educational discourse empowers teachers to determine what is worthwhile in a student's contributions, presumably even if that judgment has little or no linguistic basis and even if a teacher–student relationship is not entirely warranted. Remember that Esther has been representing herself as an adult whose financial status is precarious and that she has gone to some pains not to occupy the student position that Rita has finally assigned her. It is in Esther's final letter, in which she makes one last attempt to establish subjective parity between herself and Rita, that we see the devastating pedagogical consequences of preserving this particular privilege of educational discursive practice.

> I don't play the Lotto everyday except on my birthday when it July 11 (7/11). I'm really messing up this letter. I'm going to an award dinner on May 30th at 7 p.m. And when I get a lucky number. I don't know anyone that ever won. Thank you for your nice letter. Bye for now.

Esther wrote better letters at the beginning than at the end of the semester. The disintegration of syntax in this her last letter ("when it" for "which is") augurs the disappearance of the working-class adult subject she has been representing and the articulation of the Adult Basic Writer, a subject unified by its errors, its sentence fragments ("And when I get a lucky number") and its rhetorical disjunctures (the sentences and phrases whose meanings are recoverable only by association). That Esther sees the failure as her own. "I'm really messing up this letter," echoes Foucault's assertion that it is the power of discourse to create the illusion that "it is we, and we alone, who give it that power." Finally overwhelmed by educational discourse, the adult subject retreats into silence.

Ellen and Pat. The eight-letter exchange between the student and teacher I'll call Pat and Ellen is by many standards, including my own, the most successful not simply because they wrote the most often, but because Pat's letters grew longer and her errors fewer over the two months she corresponded with Ellen. While she shares the other teachers' aversion to class, Ellen differs considerably from them in her initial and repeated representation of herself as unified in relation to family: "I have been married for 21 years," "[I am] the mother of two teenagers," "I'm a very family-centered person." Ellen's representation of her familial self is often completed or articulated by Pat, when, for example, she writes "I'm all so marry for 22 1/2 year. I have 4 kids." The self unified in relation to family is reminiscent of that represented in many of the working-class narratives, except that the self articulated in their letters is decidedly female.

That gender is a crucial dimension of their subjectivity first becomes apparent when Ellen responds to Pat's physical description of herself with this measured assertion of identification: "It sounds as though you and I look somewhat alike." In this instance, it is Ellen who articulates or completes a representation of self initiated by Pat and hence Ellen who identifies herself as the embodied female subject represented in Pat's physical description. This particular articulation stands out because it is the only corporeal representation of self in the letters and because it is also the only self-representation offered by one of the students with which a teacher identifies or articulates. To be sure, Ellen's articulation is tenuous, qualified immediately by "somewhat," and later by assertions such as "I'm trying to lose some weight before the summer season comes so I won't be so embarrassed in my bathing suit" that suggest the middle-class woman's all too familiar and uneasy relationship to her body.

In the course of their reciprocal articulation, and the co-construction of themselves as gendered subjects, Pat and Ellen tell and respond to stories that narrate their shared concerns as mothers. And it is as mother-women that they ignore the class differences that overwhelm the correspondents in the other two examples. Their mutual concern for their children's education, for instance, overrides material differences between their children's actual access to education. Ellen writes that she and her husband will be traveling to Williamsburg to bring their daughter home from college for the summer: "So far, each year that we've gone we've had to move her in the rain. It would be nice to be able to keep dry for once during all of the trips back and forth to the car." Pat advises Ellen to "think positive," attending not to the fact that Ellen's daughter attends a private college while her son goes to a local community college, but to the prediction that it will probably rain. In what appears to be yet another attempt to lift Ellen's spirits, Pat then recalls that she, her husband, and three children took a trip to Williamsburg eight years earlier, about which she has only this to say: "Williamsburg is a beautiful place."

Toward the end of their correspondence, Ellen and Pat recount their Mother's Days. Ellen's story is short:

> I hope you had an enjoyable Mother's Day. Did your family treat you to dinner? B [Ellen's daughter] cooked the meal and we had a combination Mother's Day and birthday celebration. My husband was one of those Mother's Day presents when he was born so every eighth year his birthday and Mother's Day fall on the same weekend so it was quite a festive time with lots going on.

Pat responds with an elaborate narrative, at least four times longer than any letter she has written, in the course of which she introduces class concerns that unify her identity as the mother and hence differentiate her experience as a mother from Ellen's. In other words, Pat's narrative interrupts their mutually constructed gender identity with a representation of herself as a subject unified in relation to Mother's Day that differs considerably from the self represented in Ellen's narrative.

In the first of five episodes, Pat establishes mood, explaining that on the Thursday evening before Mother's Day, after finally succeeding in bathing and putting the younger children to bed, she found herself "down hartit" and worrying about how hard her husband works at his two jobs and how his not being at home much means that she feels "like a mom and a dad." She follows this orientation to her state of mind with a second episode in which her two older children ask what she wants for Mother's Day. She reports telling her son that "a card will do" but confiding to her daughter that "what I want you can't afford-it." Pressed by the daughter to tell, she admits to wanting "a ciling fane for my dinning room." Pat indicates that a ceiling fan is out of the question by writing "she laugh and so did I laugh." The third episode, which opens with an account of the complicated childcare arrangements made in order for her son to take her window shopping for ceiling fans that Friday evening, includes: a brief description of the shopping spree ("there are lots of fanes to look at but I like this one fane a lots"); a scene in which the son surprises her by giving her the money to buy the fan; and an account of what happens when they return home where the children are waiting ("They all where happy for mom but not as thrill as I was inside of me"). On Saturday, the fourth episode begins with a gift of flowers from her son and his "girl friend" and concludes with dinner with the younger children at McDonald's, where a young woman at the counter tells Pat that her son "is an inspiration to the young people here" who "miss he but there is hope for the future." (In a previous letter Pat has explained that her son worked at McDonald's for a year and a half while attending a local community college, but had since taken a job at a hospital where, after three promotions, he was making 10% more than he had as manager of the night shift at McDonald's.) She concludes the fourth episode with "I was so proud of him. Went I was told this." The fifth and final episode begins on Mother's Day morning with her husband making breakfast, after which she receives a box of candy from the smaller children, a card containing ten dollars from all the children, two "shorts sets" from her grandson, and yet another box of candy from the son's "girl friend." Reflecting on events in the conclusion of her letter, Pat writes: "I was surprize it was a beautiful motherday weekend. I feel like I writing a book so I am lifeing now."

The demonstrations of familial affection in Pat's narrative apparently resolve her internal conflict (discouragement). In a family where money is scarce — the husband works two jobs, the son holds a full-time job while attending community college, and the daughter is employed — the members shower the mother with cash and commodities. Rather than confine their celebration of the mother to service — cooking for her or dining out — the family extends it to include both the material tokens — the flowers, the fan, the clothes, and the candy — and the thrill of consumption — the material event of shopping and paying for the fan. The ritual acts of consumption and service that dramatize the mother's value in this working-class family temporarily align all its members with the economy. In other words, the economic realities that are continually threatening its unity are replaced by a four-day fantasy in which the family compensates the mother for her emotional and physical labor.

Middle-class families do not ordinarily celebrate motherhood with consumption rituals. What Ellen has described is the familiar middle-class service ritual in which the mother is released from the specific task of cooking, a symbol of the domestic responsibilities that threaten to alienate those mothers who also work outside the home from their families. In response to Pat's narrative, Ellen writes, "I enjoyed hearing about all your very nice Mother's Day surprises. It sounds as though you have a very loving and considerate family. They must really appreciate how hard you work and all of the many things you do for them." Ellen's is a gracious comment that fully acknowledges their shared understanding of mothers' work and once again articulates their mutual identity as gendered subjects. But Ellen's response fails to articulate Pat's representation of her own and, by extension, Ellen's subjectivity as contingent on class. It's not just that their families understand the mother differently. I suspect that the working-class celebration of the mother would strike Ellen as too much and that the middle-class celebration would strike Pat as too little. Differences in their material circumstances separate them as mothers (neither Ellen nor her middle-class family need ritual relief from economic hardships), and Ellen's comment fails to acknowledge that Pat's class-based narrative places them in distinct rather than the same subject positions as women.

Ellen concludes her letter with a suggestion that draws Pat's attention to what is not said. "Since this is the last week of your classes you can wrtie (sic) me at my home address if you think that you will have the time and would like to continue writing. I know that I would enjoy hearing from you." Pat understands the absence of any expressed desire to write as well as read her letters to mean that Ellen has lost the enthusiasm for writing she expressed in earlier correspondence: "At first I was nervous about writing to someone I didn't know, but now I enjoy writing them and look forward to your letter each week." By invoking the institutional auspices under which they have been corresponding—"this is the last week of your classes"—Ellen effectively shifts from the discourse of art in which they have both been representing and articulating their subjectivity as mothers in personal narratives to the educational discourse in which Pat would presumably be a student writing for a teacher.

Pat interrupts the shift in discourse and subject positions that Ellen has suggested when she writes: "I would like to know, if you would still wiriting me, or not if not it has been nice writing to you. I don't know if it help you are not, I know it has help me a lot. Thank you very must." Pat offers yet another version of their educational relationship in which she and Ellen would continue to learn from one another by corresponding, but she makes it clear, I think, that the decision to write as well as read is Ellen's. And Ellen chooses not to write back.

Conclusion

Since the late 1970s, that is, since the publication of Pierre Bourdieu and Jean-Claude Passeron's *Reproduction in Education, Society and Culture*, many teachers and parents, and some administrators and social theorists and social scientists, have been concerned about the extent to which schools not only tolerate but legitimate the very forms of classism, racism, and sexism that American education is publicly charged with eliminating. I mention this by way of pointing out that law provides educational opportunity for those it designates as the subjects of social and economic discrimination. Indeed, it is the state that provides a good deal of the funding for the Adult Basic Education program that the working-class students in the study were attending. Yet the data remind us that law does not protect these students from the dialect of educational discourse in which a teacher's control over discursive practice is contingent on the ideology that classroom language transcends class, race, and gender.

The teachers in this study are not ogres — far from it. They are energetic and inventive practitioners committed to universal education. In their writing, however, that commitment manifests itself in an approach to teaching and learning that many educators share in this country, a view that insists that the classroom is a separate world of its own, in which teachers and students relate to one another undistracted by the classism, racism, and sexism that rage outside the classroom. Discursive hegemony of teachers over students is usually posed and justified in developmental terms — as cognitive deficits, emotional or intellectual immaturity, ignorance, and most recently, cultural literacy — any one of which would legitimate asymmetrical relationships between its knowing subjects, teachers, and its unknowing subjects, students. To the credit of the teachers who participated in this study, none took the usual recourse of justifying their discursive control by focusing on errors in spelling, grammar, and mechanics that are indubitably there and that make reading the literacy letters as difficult as reading Lacan, Derrida, Foucault, or Althusser. Yet the teachers frenetically protected educational discourse from class, and in their respective refusals to admit class concerns into the letters, they first distanced and then alienated themselves from their correspondents.

While educational discourse defends its privileged subjects against resistance, against the violence that Dora narrates, against Esther's lesson in economics, and even against Pat's much celebrated mother, the linguistic and rhetorical uneasiness with which these attempts to articulate working-class subjectivity were met suggests that the class-free discourse that seems immutable in theory is, in practice, a source of some ambivalence for the teachers in this study. What is immediately challenged by the narratives is the rhetorical practice in which the privileges of one subject — to tell stories or decide what the topic is — materially diminish the rights of other subjects. What is ultimately challenged is the ideology that class, and by extension race and gender differences, are present in American society but absent from American classrooms. If that's true, it is only true because the representation by students of those concerns inside educational discourse goes unarticulated by teachers.

To teach is to authorize the subjects of educational discourse. We have all been faced with the choice that Pat gave Ellen. To say no to writing is to say no to differences that matter to those students who live on the margins of an educational discourse that insists that they articulate themselves as the subjects teachers represent, or not at all. To say yes to writing is to say yes to those alternative subjectivities that Dora, Esther, and Pat represent in their writing and that are left unchallenged when unarticulated by Don, Rita, and Ellen. In this instance, teachers and students alike lose the opportunity to question the extent to which class figures in any individual's rendering of a unified self. Resistance inside educational discourse is then a practice in cooperative articulation on the part of students and teachers who actively seek to construct and understand the differences as well as similarities between their respective subject positions.

Works cited

Bartholomae, David. "Inventing the University." *When a Writer Can't Write*. Ed. Mike Rose. New York: Guilford P, 1985, 134−65.

———. "The Study of Error." *College Composition and Communication* 31 (1980): 253−69.

Bourdieu, Pierre, and Jean-Claude Passeron. *Reproduction in Education, Society and Culture*. Beverly Hills: Sage, 1977.

Brodkey, Linda. "Tropics of Literacy." *Journal of Education* 168 (1986): 47−54.

Crowley, Sharon. "writing and Writing." *Writing and Reading Differently: Deconstruction and the Teaching of Composition and Literature*. Ed. Douglas Atkins and Michael L. Johnson. Lawrence: UP of Kansas, 1985, 93−100.

Fine, Michelle. "Silencing in the Public Schools." *Language Arts* 64 (1987): 157−74.

Foucault, Michel. "The Discourse on Language." *The Archeology of Knowledge*. New York: Harper & Row, 1976. 215−37.

Hall, Stuart. "On Postmodernism and Articulation: An Interview with Stuart Hall." Ed. Larry Grossberg. *Journal of Communication Inquiry* 10 (1986): 45−60.

Labov, William. *Language in the Inner City: Studies in the Black English Vernacular*. Philadelphia: U of Pennsylvania P, 1972.

Perl, Sandra. "The Composing Processes of Unskilled College Writers." *Research in the Teaching of English* 13 (1979): 317−36.

Pratt, Mary Louise. *Toward a Speech Act Theory of Literary Discourse*. Bloomington: Indiana UP, 1977.

Shaughnessy, Mina. *Errors and Expectations: A Guide for the Teacher of Basic Writing*. New York: Oxford UP, 1977.

Stubbs, Michael. *Language, Schools and Classrooms*. London: Methuen, 1976.

Williams, Raymond. *Marxism and Literature*. New York: Oxford UP, 1977.

ELEVEN

"Gimme Room": School Resistance, Attitude, and Access to Literacy
Perry Gilmore

This paper is based on a three-year study which was conducted in a predominantly low-income black urban community and its elementary school [grades 4−6]. A central focus in the initial phase of the research was to identify school- and community-perceived problems concerning literacy achievement. The problems seen as important by the participants and voiced within the setting then guided the direction of the subsequent investigation (for fuller discussion of this research, see Gilmore 1982, 1985a, b).

The major concerns expressed by the administrators, faculty, parents, and students were much less focused on reading and writing skills per se than might have been expected. Instead, the community members' most frequently articulated concerns about literacy achievement were focused on *social* rather than cognitive dimensions of behavior. Thus a study begun with a direct focus on literacy skill achievement took a slight detour.

The major literacy achievement problem identified and voiced repeatedly by teachers, parents, administrators, and even the children was "attitude." A "good attitude" seemed to be the central and significant factor in students' general academic success and literacy achievement in school. Indeed, in this particular setting, talk about "attitude" was dramatically more prominent than talk about intelligence or reading and writing ability. It was clear to staff and parents as well as students, that in cases of tracking and/or selection for honors or special academic preference, "attitude" outweighed academic achievement or IQ test performance. In particular, a "good attitude" appeared to be central to inclusion in special high-track classes referred to as the Academics Plus Program.

Source: Perry Gilmore, "'Gimme Room': School Resistance, Attitude, and Access to Literacy," *Journal of Education* 167 (1985): 111−28. © 1985 by the Trustees of Boston University. Reprinted with permission.

The Academics Plus Program is described by staff as a rigorous "back to basics" curriculum in which academic achievement is the primary goal. To qualify, a student not only has to be working at a certain grade level, but also to display a "cooperative attitude." The program is in effect a tracking procedure for attitude as well as academic achievement. Teachers sometimes talk about the process as one of "weeding out bad attitudes." A student working at a relatively low grade level might be admitted to the program if his or her behavior indicated a desire to work and be cooperative. In such a case, a "good attitude" outweighs limited academic achievement. In other reported instances, a bright child who might be achieving academically, but whose behavior is characteristic of a "bad attitude," would not be admitted. In such a case, "attitude" again outweighs academic achievement.

The staff often expressed pride and identification when talking about the school and its students, especially the Academics Plus students, referring to "our kids" in a proud and affectionate tone. One teacher, attempting to illustrate the exceptional attitude and reputation of the students, asked, "Have you seen our sixth-grade Academics Plus students? They're cultured. They're not street kids. Have you seen the way they carry themselves?" The reference to the way the students "carry themselves" suggests demeanor and propriety. In this particular urban black low-income community and school, where upward mobility and success in middle-class society are expressed goals, "attitude" rather than reading ability or intelligence is the means for assigning stable stratified social ranks among students.

Less than a third of the population in each intermediate grade level (3−6) was selected for the special academic program. It was clear to the staff, the children, and the parents that although the participation in the Academics Plus Program did not guarantee literacy success and general academic achievement, it certainly maximized the chances for it. It created an elite. It stratified the students. It made mothers cry with their children when they were rejected. And the key factor for admission was something everyone called a "good attitude."

In order to unravel the meaning of "attitude" in this school community, the study focused on discrete social and linguistic behaviors. The object was to discover how attitudes were communicated, understood, and interpreted. The functions and uses of the concept as it was constructed in this particular context were considered.

Two key behavioral events were observed which provided data for the analysis of the enactment of attitude. Correspondences and contrasts in the way people *talked* about attitude and the way people actually *behaved* with regard to attitude were detailed. Both behavioral events stood out as behaviors that were readily noticed, controversial, and problematic for the teachers at school. Both key behaviors were counted as inappropriate, as representative of bad or deteriorating attitudes. Both were performances that stood out and received attention from the staff.

The first key behavioral event is a characteristic response in face-to-face clashes of will between student and teacher. These were conventional displays of emotion that appeared regularly in my field notes and were prominent and noticeable in classroom interactions. These displays of *stylized sulking* were usually nonverbal and often highly choreographed performances which seemed, in the teachers' words, to convey "rebellion," "anger," and a stance of "un-cooperativeness." The displays were themselves discrete pieces of behavior which conveyed information. They were dramatic portrayals of an attitude. They were postures that told a story to the teacher and to onlooking peers. They were portraits of resistance. They were face-saving dances. And they were black: they were regularly interpreted as part of black communicative repertoire and style. Students who frequently used the displays were also students who were identified as having bad attitudes. (See Gilmore, 1984 for fuller discussion of this event.)

The second key behavioral event that will be analyzed is the performance of a distinctive genre of street rhymes which seems to have grown out of the tradition of drills and cheers. The genre is locally referred to as "steps" (or "doin' steps") and it involves chorally chanted rhymes punctuated with foot steps and hand claps which set up a background of rhythm. It is performed by groups of girls and, consistent with tradition in children's folklore (Bauman 1982), it is full of taboo breaking and sexual innuendo in both the verbal and nonverbal modes of its performance. The dances were striking, the chants full of verbal virtuosity. They turned passersby into audiences. They were polished. But they were also "nasty," seen as representing defiance and "deteriorating attitudes." They were seen as black. They were banned from the school. (See Gilmore 1983, for fuller discussion of this event.)

The two behavioral events, stylized sulking and doing steps, provide windows through which we can look at underlying cultural themes. Both communicative events detail concrete and specific aspects of behavior that can be analyzed as to their relation to attitude. Both events were seen as part of black communicative style and both were interpreted as conveying "bad attitudes." It was no surprise that students who were viewed as having good attitudes were also viewed as being good kids. The label became a part of the constitution and indicative of one's worth. Yet when the behaviors subsumed under the "attitude" were examined they consisted largely of a set of linguistic, paralinguistic, and kinesic communicative adornments which are associated with a particular ethnic style and socio-economic class rather than a set of character traits reflecting the nature of individuals. Both key behaviors communicated resistance to the school's carefully articulated rules for proper demeanor.

In the following two sections a brief analysis of each of the key behavioral events will be presented. Stylized sulking and doing steps will be considered in terms of the immediate shape of their performances, their functions and uses, the metaphoric nature they suggested, and the social meanings they held for the participants. The final section of this paper will discuss the data as they relate to attitude assessment and its effects on literacy achievement.

Stylized sulking

Although recent years have witnessed a steadily growing body of ethnographic data concerning classrooms, the realm of emotions has largely been ignored. The sociolinguistic emphasis in classroom research has been primarily focused on verbal aspects of communicative (Hymes 1962) or interactional (Mehan et al. 1976) competence (see, for example, Cazden, John and Hymes 1972;

Edwards and Furlong 1978; Gilmore and Glatthorn 1982; McDermott 1976; Mehan 1979). This body of ethnographic literature illustrates that beyond academic competence students need to demonstrate interactional competence in social settings in order to do well in school. These studies have primarily demonstrated that a student must not only possess academic knowledge, but must also know when and how to display it according to socially acceptable rules of classroom interaction.

Though this sociolinguistic research has certainly enriched the study of schooling and expanded our awareness of important dimensions of the inter-actions surrounding learning events in school, it has somehow failed to address some of the most essential aspects of classroom life. One frequently overlooked aspect is that urban classrooms are often scenes of clashes of will. Many of the most crucial social interactions in school settings are highly charged with emotion and regularly interpreted with regard to "attitude." The ways in which these confrontations are interpreted and treated by teachers and students will strongly affect the nature of the attitudes conveyed as well as any learning which takes place in classrooms.

All situations carry with them a sense of what feelings are appropriate to have. Hochschild (1979) addresses this issue when she discusses *emotion work*, which she describes as "the act of evoking or shaping as well as suppressing feeling in oneself" (p. 552). Hochschild suggests that there are *feeling rules* which are learned and used as baselines in social exchanges. Classrooms provide an excellent setting in which to capture the pedagogy involved in emotion work and the teaching and learning discourse that surrounds feeling rules. In class-rooms such rules are frequently articulated.

Consider the emotion work embedded in the brief classroom interaction taken from my field notes:

> There is a loud chatting and calling out and several students are out of their seats while the teacher is trying to explain how to do the assignment. The teacher suddenly shouts in a loud and angry voice, "Sit down, sit up...(more softly) and don't look surprised or hurt cause we've gone over this before."

The teacher first shows anger, shouting at the class to "sit down" and "sit up" (i.e., get in your seats and sit tall at attention). When several students portray looks of "hurt" or "surprise," she tells them it is not acceptable to feel or, more accurately, to look as if they feel that way. In this particular instance the teacher may have been mediating her expression of emotion by telling the class that it wasn't a serious enough emotion to be hurt by. The teacher reminds the students that they know the rules they were breaking (e.g., calling out, walking around the room while she was talking to them as a class, side-chatting loudly). This reminder is conveyed in the phrase "we've gone over this before." Therefore she is able to justify her own angry response while instructing the class on the appropriate emotional response she expects them to *have* and—even more significant—to *show*.

Thus a three-part lesson is being learned by the students: (a) there is an appropriate set of feelings to have in a given context; (b) there are conventional ways (e.g., postures, facial expressions, and the like) that are used to express your feelings to the other participants in the setting; and (c) even if you are *not* actually feeling the appropriate feelings in a given situation, you can, and are in fact expected to, enact the conventionally accepted bodily and facial configurations that correspond with the approved emotion. *Emotional masquerading*, knowing when and how to disguise inappropriate feelings, is an essential aspect of classroom survival.

Silence and nonverbal behavior are particularly important in classroom interactions because much of student emotional communications must take place without talk. The traditional classrooms I observed support the generalization that most of the talk is by the teacher (Anderson 1977) and that "children's time is spent overwhelmingly in listening and reading" (Cazden 1979a). "Silent communication" was frequent between students and teachers. My classroom observation specifically focused on interactional silences, that is, the features and boundaries of silence in face-to-face interactions other than pauses for thought. (This excluded, for example, the silence which may have occurred while doing independent assigned seatwork such as reading or writing exercises.)

In the following two examples from my field notes each student replies to the teacher's question with silence. In one case the silence is acceptable, in the other it is not.

Example 1 (Acceptable Silence)

Speaker	Utterance	Gestural Adornment
Teacher:	What were you doing?	
Student No. 1:	(silence)	Looks up at teacher with slightly bowed head, eyebrows turned up with slightly quizzical look, shrugs shoulders, raising arms with elbows bent and palms up
Teacher:	Okay. But don't do it again.	

Example 2 (Unacceptable Silence)

Speaker	Utterance	Gestural Adornment
Teacher:	What were you doing?	
Student No. 2:	(silence)	Chin up, lower lip pushed forward, eyebrows in a tight scowl, downward side glance to teacher, left hand on her hip which is thrust slightly forward
Teacher:	Answer me.	
Student No. 2:	(silence)	same
Teacher:	I asked you a question...Answer me.... I said answer me!	walks toward student

These two examples suggest that it is not merely the silence that is or is not appropriate, but the way in which the silent performance is adorned with bodily configuration and gestures. In the first example the gestural adornment was interpreted by the teacher, and by the student's peers, as both a public confession and a public apology. The teacher was allowed to remain in authority and the social structure was not disrupted. In the second example, however, the nonverbal postures and facial expressions were interpreted quite differently. This assorted package of bodily signals was seen as defiant, a public resistance and challenge to the teacher's authority. The child was sent to the principal's office a few minutes later.

Ritual displays have been described as behaviors which provide a "readily readable expression of [an individual's] situation, specifically his intent" as well as "evidence of the actor's alignment in the situation" (Goffman 1976, p. 69). It seems reasonable then to view as *silence displays* the behaviors described under the label "gestural adornments" in the examples above. These silent responses are, in fact, conventionalized acts which are choreographed predictably and perfunctorily in portraying alignments and attitudes. The reader can, no doubt, make an accurate guess as to which of the two students above would be designated as having a "bad attitude."

The student communicative silences that are most visible occur in teacher-student confrontations such as those shown in examples 1 and 2 above. Usually these encounters are ones in which the student is being reprimanded, and they often take place in front of other class members. In these cases I have observed two kinds of student silence displays, which can be called *submissive subordinate* and *nonsubmissive subordinate*. The first, submissive subordinate, is only observed in interactions with the teacher or another adult authority, never with peers. This display is marked with gestures such as a bowed head, quizzical expression around the eyes, a smile, a serious but relaxed facial expression, or, if the offense is not too serious, even a giggle.

By contrast, the nonsubmissive subordinate display of silence, which I have chosen to label *stylized sulking*, carries with it a very different bodily configuration (recall Example 2).

Stylized sulking differs for boys and girls. Girls will frequently pose with their chins up, closing their eyelids for long periods and casting downward side glances, and often turning their heads markedly sidewards as well as upwards. A girl also will rest her chin on her hand with her elbow supported by the desk. Striking or getting into the pose is usually performed with an abrupt movement that will sometimes be marked with a sound, either the elbow striking the desk or a verbal marker like "humpf." Since silence displays can easily go unnoticed, it is necessary to draw some attention to the silence and with the girls it seems to be primarily with a flourish of getting into the pose.

Boys usually display somewhat differently. Their stylized sulking is usually characterized by head downward, arms crossed at the chest, legs spread wide, and usually desk pushed away. Often they will mark the silence by knocking over a chair or pushing loudly on their desk, assuring that others hear and see the performance. Another noticeable characteristic of the boys' performance is that they sit down, deeply slumped in their chairs. This is a clear violation of the constant reminder in classrooms to "sit up" and "sit up tall."

The behavioral event of stylized sulking is a characteristic response in face-to-face clashes of will between student and teacher. Students who frequently used the displays were often students who were also identified as having "bad attitudes" and as a result were tracked out of academic programs.

Stylized sulking as a school problem seems age-related. Though these displays were not performed exclusively by students in the intermediate grades (4—6) they were significantly more prominent then. Sulking was primarily performed in a silent channel and an angry key. It seems, in fact, a last holding place to express defiance. For those students who do cross the line, the predictable verbal accompaniment transforms the crime from one of "bad attitude" to one of insolence and insubordination. These latter labels usually are associated with treatments more extreme than low-track classes (e.g., suspension, psychological guidance, and the like).

Stylized sulking was usually performed to an authority figure. The individual sulker is subordinate in status to the receiver of the display. Though the display, which is often used as a face-saving device, is certainly meant to be seen by onlooking peers, the primary audience is the adult in control. Sulking generally appeared in settings where an authority figure was in control and usually in direct conflict with the performer. Classrooms, hallways, lunchrooms, and the like are predictable settings for this kind of display. Further, the behavior appeared more in classes which have not "weeded out bad attitudes." In settings where propriety had been selected for, such as Academics Plus classes, few, if any sulking events were observed (even for the few students who had been observed sulking in the heterogeneous classes the year before). Certain agreed-upon expectations of attitude and behavior in the Academics Plus classes changed the classroom context in a way that made sulking no longer adaptive. The resistant demeanor was no longer appropriate for the teacher or the peer group in the setting. Though the act of sulking itself was rarely, if ever, mentioned, and was almost never consciously a part of the assessment of a student's attitude, students who repeatedly sulked had negative characteristics attributed to them as a result. Stylized sulking was selected out—not consciously, but nonetheless quite effectively—in the process of identifying "good attitudes."

Another concern focuses on how stylized sulking was treated in this community. The behavior seemed to be seen as a "cultural" variation of expression and communication. Sulking, in the highly stylized way it was performed by many of the students, was viewed by both black and white teachers as part of a stereotypic communicative style of blacks.

In addition to expressing emotion, displays provide evidence of an actor's alignment. Sulking displays therefore must also be considered in this latter regard. In general, sulking displays can function as face-saving devices which maintain dignity through individual autonomy when confronted by an authority in control. The display indicates the actor's refusal to align him- or herself with the authority figure. The stylized sulking characteristic of black communicative repertoire further seems to be interpreted as a statement of alignment with the student's own ethnicity and socio-economic class, and as a statement of resistance to the school ethos.

Steps

I noticed steps early in the spring of my first year of fieldwork. Girls would almost burst out of the hall at recess onto the playground, form lines and begin "doin' steps." These are chorally chanted rhymes similar to, yet distinct from, drills and cheers. The chanted talk is punctuated by a steady alternating rhythm of foot stepping and hand clapping. The steppers line up and perform in chorus as well as individually down the line. There are numerous rhymes, each with its own choreography and rhythm. Entire recess periods were spent "doin' steps," and it was often difficult for students to stop when they went back to their classrooms. Girls would chant or "step" in the room and be told to "stop" or "settle down." The "steps" were not unique to this school and in fact one could see the same performances in parks and driveways and on front steps all over the city, through the spring and summer months and until the cold weather came in the fall.

Within the community, challenges and competitions were held in which different neighborhood blocks would perform the rhymes for judging. Groups often had captains, who were in charge, and formal names, like "Stars" or "Bad Girls." In some cases groups had uniforms paid for by churches or community groups.

The staff and administration turned attention to the performance that spring also. The "dances" were labeled as "lewd," "fresh," "inappropriate for school," "disrespectful," and simply "too sexual." The principal banned the "dances" from the school in a formal announcement over the public address system one morning, saying "Nice girls don't do that." The genre was viewed as representing "deteriorating attitudes." It broke norms of propriety which were of central importance in the school ethos.

One of the stepping street rhymes, "Mississippi," seemed to be not only related to matters of propriety and attitude in general, but to literacy in particular. "Mississippi" is performed in a variety of ways, each version having its own choreography and rhythm to accompany and accent the verbal alternations. Each version has as its core the spelling of the word *Mississippi*. These variations include description of and metaphorical references to the letters and ongoing narratives which play with the letters as beginnings of utterances.

The performance of "Mississippi" is an intersection of visual and verbal codes. Steppers use the body dramatically as an iconic sign for the letters. The most prominent, noticeable, and controversial use of bodily representation of the letters is the formation of the letter *s*, or "crooked letter." The transformation of the body into the letter *s* is demonstrated in a limbo-like dancing movement with one arm forming a crook at the shoulder. It is not uncommon to find an elementary school teacher asking students to make their bodies shape a letter. Yet, in this case, although the steppers successfully perform such bodily letter representation, it was interpreted negatively. The iconic sign was viewed as being dressed with too sexual a body idiom for school, and, often family contexts.

It appears that few observers actually associated the dance movement with the words or letters. The performances were not studied but only casually observed, if observed at all, by most of the staff. The range of teacher responses to the dance movements in "Mississippi" ranged from "You have to be an adult to know it was suggestive," to "It's like an orgasm." Other examples were "It's like nothing I've ever seen before"; "It could be a nice kid, then all of the sudden it just comes over her"; "It's like an epileptic fit;" "It's bad"; and "Nasty."

"Mississippi": a display of literacy-related competencies

In informal interviews and discussions, teachers regularly commented that their students lacked necessary language and literacy skills. They were concerned that students had deficiencies in *word analysis skills* such as rhyming, syllabification, and identifying initial and medial blends. They said their students lacked *comprehension skills* such as being able to identify main ideas, develop narrative themes, recognize semantic differences in homonyms, and so on. Finally, they were concerned that their students lacked the *good citizenship skills* that were necessary for school instruction in language arts and literacy — listening to or cooperating with each other, getting organized, or working in groups. Bearing these teachers' concerns in mind, let us consider the following description of one of the most popular steps. Several versions are presented on the following page. These examples of oral group performances provide strong evidence that both the citizenship skills and the language skills identified by teachers as deficiencies for this population were demonstrated regularly in peer group contexts.

Each girl took a turn for an individual performance, stepping out of the line with an expression such as "Gimme room." Each was expected to have her own style within the conventions and boundaries of the performance, using embellishments and markers of individuality. The degree of oral composing varied, but performers who were creative were recognized for their virtuosity and often became captains, organizing and instructing the others.

While teachers and parents had heard and seen the steps performed enough to notice and ban them, most had never really listened enough to be aware of the general content. Instead, they were aware of isolated words (see, e.g., Example 4) or dance movements (e.g., the performance of the "crooked letter") that were considered too sexual or improper. Although stepping performances were public and prominent, the melodic prosody of the chants made the words and meaning almost unintelligible. Once the "sirens" lured a listener in, the taboo words could be heard with an assaulting clarity.

Stepping, like stylized sulking, seemed to be seen as a "cultural" variation of expression and communication. "Doin' steps" was something that black girls do. The musical chants and movements were referred to by several white and black teachers as "ethnic type dances," reminiscent of "African music" and "Caribbean music."

The particular community in which my observations were conducted might be characterized as being extremely responsive to the expressed norms of the school. Many parents who initially allowed the dances, once hearing that the school banned them, enforced the ban at home. One student who had been a stepping captain the year before told me the following fall that she no longer did steps because her mother wanted her to get into the Academics Plus program.

"Mississippi" conveys social messages

The performance of "Mississippi" can be examined as an "instructional routine." In many ways the routine sounds like what one might expect in a school classroom. Directions are called to an individual to spell a word: *Mississippi*, a

Oral Performance	Description
1. MISSISSIPPI	A straight spelling, reciting each letter in rhythmic, patterned clusters, the most concrete form of the rhyme.
2. M I crooked letter, crooked letter, I, crooked letter, crooked letter I, hump back, hump back, I	A spelling that includes a description or metaphorical reference to the physical features of some of the letters. In this version, "Crooked letter" refers to S and "hump back" to P. The children sometimes refer to the entire genre of steps as "Kookelater (crooked letter) Dances." The children perform the S in a limbo-like dance movement with one arm forming a crook at the shoulder.
3. for the money I if ya give it to me S sock it (to me) S sock it (to me) I if I buy it from ya S sock it S sock it I if I take it from ya P pump it P pump it I	This version is often followed by version 2 with a smooth transition. The spelling uses the letters of Mississippi to produce the first work of each line in an ongoing narrative.
4. Hey (name), yo You wanted on the phone. Who is it? Your nigger. I bet he wants my lips, my tits, my butt, my smut. My crooked letter, crooked letter, I.	A controversial narrative that is only punctuated with parts of the spelling. The play with the narrative rather than the orthography dominates the verbal content. The "crooked letter" by its position in a series of "wants" take on an ambiguous sexual meaning, especially as the letter is being adorned in dance.
5 Hey, Deede, yo Spell Mississippi Spell Mississippi right now You take my hands up high You take my feet down low I cross my legs with that gigolo If you don't like that Throw it in the thrash And then I'm bustin out With that Jordache Look in the sky With that Calvin Klein I'm gonna lay in the dirt With that Sergiert (Sergio Valente) I'm gonna bust a balloon With that Sassoon Gonna be ready With that Teddy I'm gonna be on the rail With that Venderbail With the is-M is-I Crooked letter crooked letter I	This version of Mississippi was performed by fewer individuals and was viewed as an accomplished recitation by peers. The jeans theme made it a favored version of the narrative performance.

difficult word to spell at that. Yet there are several aspects of the instruction that seem to break with expected norms of speech and politeness and with predictable co-occurrence rules of classrooms.

First, instead of a single teacher's voice, the entire group of steppers chant the request in loud chorus. This is the reverse of the stereotypic model of an individual teacher request followed by an entire class's choral response. The request itself has marked characteristics that countered expectations of what a classroom teacher would say.

> Hey, (Wendy). Spell Mississippi.
> Spell Mississippi, right now!

The request sounds more like a challenge or a dare. Consider some of the linguistic markers that run counter to expectations of co-occurrence rules. The use of the word "hey" is informal, is usually considered inappropriate for school, and has a slightly threatening quality—as if one is being "called out" rather than "called on." Further, there is an impatient tone to the demand as a result of the quick repetition "Spell Mississippi" and the conclusion "right now!" It has been pointed out that teachers tend to use politeness forms frequently in order to modify the power and control they have. These forms soften acts of instruction that might be interpreted as face-threatening to students (see Cazden 1979b). The teacher request in "Mississippi" seems to do exactly the opposite.

The stepper who is called on to perform the spelling task usually utters a quick phrase like "Gimme room" or "No sweat" as she jumps forward out of the line to begin her routine. These utterances indicate the stepper's willingness to take on the dare and the stepper's confidence that the performance is fully within the range of her competencies. Thus the instructional routine sets up an aggressive and suspicious teacher command and a student stepper who takes on the challenge with a sexual swagger and obvious confidence about her spelling prowess.

A spelling exercise, ordinarily practiced in the classroom, is transformed through linguistic play and dance with a market shift in ownership. By reframing the instructional exchange the literacy-related behaviors are recontextualized— taken from the school's mode of literacy instruction and made a part of the children's own world. Interpretive frames are created that signal to onlookers that this particular performance of literacy-related behaviors does not belong to or count for school.

The syncopation of this spelling lesson allows children, as subordinates, to mock school instruction. In much the same way skits and jokes present concrete formulations of an abstract cultural symbol, the images conveyed in the "Mississippi" performance can be seen as containing the children's symbolic social portraits of the dynamics of schooling.

Thus the message conveyed by these students through the performance of "Mississippi" can seem quite a poignant one. It is not merely defiant; it is not merely black. It can easily be seen as face-saving, a way of maintaining dignity through collective autonomy when confronted with the school's undermining doubt in their ability. At the end of "Mississippi" the entire group does the spelling performance in a striking flourish, declaring, for all to see, their excellence as literate spellers, as dancers, and as kids. When the steppers call out "Gimme room" they are asking for room to be seen, trusted and evaluated as skilled language users—as individuals who have the right to instructional circumstances where pride and ownership are the central features of learning.

Attitude, expectations, and instruction

In the case of assessing attitudes in the study site, in Bateson's (1972) terms, the "nip" becomes the "bite" rather than denoting it. The sign is read as the act rather than a suggestion of it. These narrow restrictions, born out of stereotyped fears and sensitivity, seriously limit teacher expectations and classroom instruction. Attitude and not literacy becomes the primary instructional focus. Though a good attitude was seen as a means to an end (i.e., literacy achievement), the focus was so intense and exclusive that instructional interaction simply got stuck there. Consider the effects of this ethos in the following example.

A teacher in one Academics Plus class was going over a list of homework vocabulary words with the class. The word they were doing next was *dismal*. She asked someone to use *dismal* in a sentence. One girl volunteered, "The clouds were *dismal*, dark and gloomy." The teacher answered, "No. Dismal *means* dark and gloomy. That's like saying "repeat again." Now a good sentence for *dismal* would be, "The clouds are dismal today."

Assuming the teacher is not stupid—which she is not—why would she reject the student's sentence of somewhat literary prose in favor of the rather bland and nonliterary one she herself offers. Consider first what the teacher is doing. She is testing her students to see if they know the meaning of the vocabulary words, which she likely assumes are new to their experience. The sentence will put the word in context so that the students can *prove* they understand the meaning. It might even be seen as cheating to use synonyms with the new word to disguise the fact that the word is not fully understood. Another sub-skill rule, to avoid redundancy, dominates the literary sense and poetic cadence. If the teacher believed the student could easily understand the word *dismal*, she might have been able to listen differently to the response. Only the suspicion that it hides ignorance registered. Seen in this light the teacher's sentence may have been offered more as an example of how to be honest (not hiding behind dictionary synonyms) than as an example of good prose and composition. This narrow pedagogy, driven by mistrust, will not provide the *room* for which the steppers have pleaded—the room which is required in order for them to demonstrate their competence.

Conclusion

Expressive forms such as stylized sulking or doing steps can essentially be viewed as metaphors for the human condition. The expressive forms used by the students can be seen as a message of individual (in the case of stylized sulking) or collective (in the case of "Mississippi") autonomy in the face of authority. The behaviors discussed here are both face-saving devices which allow for pride and ownership in circumstances where opportunities for such prizes are scarce.

Both sulking and stepping seem to be associated with a certain set of black communicative displays that have typically been a class marker for failure in our society. Like nonstandard vernacular, these "street" behaviors will tend to close rather than open doors for black children who are trying to be upwardly mobile in our society. No matter how legitimate a linguistic or behavioral analysis of such behavior is, the key factor of legitimacy is how these behaviors are interpreted in the social world in which they are performed. For the children in the study site, most of their parents and teachers agree that the cost is too high. Symbols of black "street" behavior such as stylized sulking and stepping are seen as ethnic and class markers which interfere with success and may, as the discussion has shown, even limit access to socially valued commodities such as literacy.

Since fear about and focus on good attitudes made community members especially sensitive to any markers associated with black vernacular "street" culture, little latitude was allowed for any displays concerning sex (particularly for girls) or aggression (particularly for boys). For example, sexual ambiguity in stepping dances was interpreted quickly as an indicator of the performer's sexual experience. The disgruntled looks and postures associated with stylized sulking were read as threats of violence and potential aggression.

One of the original concerns of this research was to identify problems that teachers saw as interfering with student achievement in literacy and language arts. "Attitude" was repeatedly offered as a major concern in the teaching of literacy skills. The research problem was to find out exactly what the label "attitude" meant in this community and how the term and concepts it en- compassed functioned in relation to literacy achievement. How was "attitude" communicated, interpreted, and understood? This was the question which guided the study. The focus of the investigation was on two specific social and linguistic behaviors that proved significant to the research. The ritual display of emotion which I have termed "stylized sulking" and the speech event of "doin' steps" were examined as metaphors for the everyday life of these children's social world. Through the use of these metaphors it became apparent that a "bad attitude" was closely associated with a conveyed message of alignment with black vernacular culture.

When I shared my findings with one of the mothers in the community, she commented on the fact that these two events appeared so prominent in the observations. Agreeing with the observations, she offered a dramatic parallel to sulking and stepping that struck her. She recalled that protrayals of black slaves in American history frequently depicted them as either *sullen* or *dancing*. The images of *sulking* and *stepping* youngsters suggests that we may not have come very far in our own brand of modern-day racism. Young students show their resistance to the authority in control through sulking facial gestures and body language, though they may go though the motions of their expected behaviors. Steps are reminiscent of some of the slave songs, sung almost in code, so that slave masters would not be able to comprehend the real content of their messages (e.g., songs such as "Follow the Drinking Gourd" and others associated with the Underground Railroad).

A study of attitude and literacy proved more to be a study of alignment and socio-economic status. The key factor for success in this school community seems to be demonstration of alignment with, if not allegiance to, the school's ethos—which in turn is compatible with, if not reflective of, the dominant ethos of the community.

Unfortunately there is a subtle confusion in the labeling process that has dramatic and lasting effects. Social alignment with the school is usually interpreted as literacy achievement while social resistance is often understood as literacy skill deficiency. The results are powerful and tragic. Stephen Jay Gould (1981) well describes them in the following way:

> We pass through this world but once. Few tragedies can be more extensive than the stunting of life, few injustices deeper than the denial of an opportunity to strive or even hope, by a limit imposed from without, but falsely identified as lying within.

As educators and researchers concerned with literacy our professional responsibility demands that we allow ourselves the room to see beyond the limiting and arbitrary boundaries of how we have traditionally defined the world of reading and writing. By examining literacy within its socio-cultural context we are in a much stronger position to understand the dynamics of its nature, acquisition, and development.

References

Anderson, E.S. (1977). Learning to Speak with Style: A Study of the Sociolinguistic Skills of Children. Doctoral Dissertation: Stanford University.

Bateson, G. (1972). In *Steps to an ecology of mind*. New York: Ballantine Books.

Bauman, R. (1982). Ethnography of children's folklore. In P. Gilmore & A. Glatthorn (Eds.), *Children in and out of school*. Washington, DC: Center for Applied Linguistics.

Cazden, C. (1979a). Language in education variation in the teacher talk register. In *Language in Public Life*. Washington, DC: 30th Annual Georgetown University Round Table, 1979.

Cazden, C. (1979b). Peekaboo as an instructional model: Discourse development at home and at school. Unpublished manuscript, Harvard University, 1979.

Cazden, C. (1982). Four comments. In Gilmore & A. Glatthorn (Eds.), *Children in and out of school*. Washington, DC: Center for Applied Linguistics, 1982.

Cazden, C., John, V. & Hymes, D. (Eds.). (1972). *Functions of language in the classroom*. New York: Teachers College Press.

Edwards, A., & Furlong, V. (1978). *The language of teaching*. London: Heinemann, 1978.

Gilmore, P. (1982). *Gimme room: A cultural approach to the study of attitudes and admission to literacy*. Unpublished doctoral dissertation, University of Pennsylvania.

Gilmore, P. (1983). Spelling Mississippi: Recontextualizing a literacy-related speech event. *Anthropology and Educational Quarterly*, 14(4), Winter, 235–255.

Gilmore, P. (1984). Silence and sulking: Emotional displays in the classroom. In D. Tannen & M. Saville-Troike (Eds.), *Perspectives on silence*. 139–162. Norwood, NJ: Ablex.

Gilmore, P. (1985-b). Sulking, stepping and tracking. The effects of attitude assessment on access to literacy. In D. Bloome (Ed.), *Literacy, language and schooling*, Norwood, NJ: Ablex.

Gilmore, P. (1985-a). Sub-rosa literacy: Peers, play and ownership in literacy acquisition. In B.B. Schieffelin & P. Gilmore (Eds.), *The acquisition of literacy: Ethnographic perspectives*. Norwood, NJ: Ablex.

Gilmore, P. & Glatthorn, A. (Eds.) (1982). *Children in and out of school*. Washington, DC: Center for Applied Linguistics.

Goffman, E. (1976). Gender advertisements. *Studies in the Anthropology of Visual Communication*, 3(2).

Gould, S.J. (1981). *The Mismeasure of Man*. New York: W.W. Norton & Co.

Hochschild, Arlie. (1979). Emotion Work, feeling rules and social structure. American journal of Sociology 85 (3): 551−575.

Hymes, D.H. (1962). The ethnography of speaking. In T. Gladwin & W.C. Sturtevant (Eds.), *Anthropology and Human Behavior*, Washington, DC: Anthropological Society of Washington, 1962.

McDermott, R.P. (1976). Kids make sense: An ethnographic account of the interactional management of success and failure in one first grade classroom. Unpublished doctoral dissertation, Stanford University.

Mehan, H. (1979). *Learning lessons: The social organization of classroom behavior*. Cambridge: Harvard University Press.

Mehan, H., Cazden, C., Coles, L., Fisher, S., & Maroules, N. (1976). *The social organization of classroom lessons*. San Diego: Center for Human Information Processing, University of California.

TWELVE

Reading Instruction and Social Class

Patrick Shannon

P ublic schools in the United States have traditionally served two functions: to instruct youth in academic subjects and to develop good citizens for the republic (Cremin 1977). These academic and socialization functions interact as educators believe that students cannot learn academic lessons unless they first learn the social rules of the classroom and that they will not prosper later in society unless they have a firm grounding in basic academics (Mehan 1979). However, some critics argue that the socialization function determines the academic function in classrooms because students from different social classes receive different academic and social lessons (Bourdieu and Passeron 1977; Bowles and Gintis 1976; Greer 1972; Jencks 1972). They contend that schools work primarily to reproduce the current economic and social conditions in society by providing middle- and upper-class children with preferential treatment — more freedom and higher levels of information — and by offering lower-class children highly controlled lessons concerning basic skills. As a basic academic subject, reading instruction should be a microcosm of the interactions between the socialization and academic functions within schools. This paper reviews recent research which suggests that reading instruction may unintentionally perpetuate social class stratification. Because much of the most recent research does not include social class as an explicit factor, it is first necessary to establish the connection between ability grouping for reading instruction and social class in order to understand how teachers' expectations for different social classes become the unequal treatment of social classes during reading instruction.

Social class and ability grouping

Perhaps the most well-known but controversial observational study of reading groups is Rist's (1970; 1973) investigation of the reading instruction received by

Source: Patrick Shannon, "Reading Instruction and Social Class," *Language Arts*, October 1985. Copyright 1985 by the National Council of Teachers of English. Reprinted with permission.

a group of black children during kindergarten, first, and second grades. Rist found that, in the absence of test information, a kindergarten teacher worked from her own implicit "ideal type" characterization of fast learners when she made decisions about reading groups; this ideal type was based on social rather than academic information. That is, children were assigned to the "fast learners" table (the high ability group) if they "appeared clean and interested, sought interactions, spoke with less dialect, were at ease with adults, displayed leadership within the class and came from homes which displayed various status criteria valued in the middle class" (1970, p. 444). Children who did not meet these implicit standards were placed at different tables (low ability groups) during instruction. All students remained in assigned groups throughout the first and second grades. Although Rist's appears to be an extreme case and parts of his study have been difficult to replicate (Haller and Davis 1980), several researchers have noted the permanence of ability groups within and across grade levels (Groff 1962; McDermott 1976; Pikulski and Kirsch 1979), and others have found a similar independent effect of family social class on ability group assignment across grade levels (Alexander and McDill 1976; Michaels 1981; Rosenbaum 1976).

When students' test results are available, teachers seem to rely heavily on this information when forming reading groups (Borko, Shavelson, and Stern 1981). In fact, teachers often overlook other relevant information and make their grouping decisions on test scores along (Russo 1978) — rank-ordering the achievement scores and then segmenting the ranks into high, middle, and low ability groups. However, achievement test scores have been found to be correlated with social class status (Fotheringham and Creal 1980; Harris and Amprey 1982; Rowan and Miracle 1983). For example, in a study of fourth grade boys of varying social class backgrounds, Low and Clement (1982) found that black and Hispanic students scored significantly lower than their white counterparts in lower, middle, and upper classes and that lower class children in general scored significantly below middle and upper class children on standardized reading tests. Although there is evidence that intellectual stimulation in the home can mediate the association between reading achievement scores and social class (Iverson and Walberg 1982), when students are assigned to homogeneous ability groups for reading instruction based primarily on reading achievement scores, to a degree, they are assigned according to social class (Hamilton 1983). Thus, whether teachers do or do not use achievement test scores as criteria, lower class children end up in lower ability groups. And frequently replicated research concerning the instruction offered ability groups can be interpreted as conclusions about the treatment of social classes during reading instruction, assuming that social class varies within schools (See Rist 1972 for an explanation of why this is a reasonable assumption).

Teacher expectations and social class

Several studies suggest that teachers have lower expectations of academic and social success for lower class children than they do for middle- and upper-class children (Cooper 1979; Hollingshead 1948; Ogbu 1978). Wilkins (1976) argued that these expectations are actually unconscious manifestations of a general societal philosophy which states that citizens are personally responsible for their position in society — that lower class people possess intellectual and character flaws which account for their lack of previous success and inhibit their prospects for the future and that middle- and upper-class people are successful because they are resourceful and industrious. Indeed, Feldman (1972) found that even college students during the "liberal 1960s" rated lower class people higher than other classes on the likelihood of being coarse and illiterate, but they rated middle and upper classes as more likely to be persistent, farsighted, striving, independent, complex, creative, and intelligent than lower classes. Teachers appear to ascribe similar stereotypical characteristics to lower class children and expect less from them during lessons (Braun 1976; Hamilton 1983; Rist 1973; Wilkins 1976).

In a review of research, Brophy (1979) concluded that "both naturalistic and experimental investigations have shown that teacher expectations can and often do affect how much students learn" (p. 738). For example, Seaver (1973) reported that teachers expected younger siblings of students they had previously taught to have similar aptitudes and deportment. Achievement test scores of these younger siblings after a year of instruction with these teachers "showed increments in pupil performance on all of the dependent variables resulting from favorable teacher expectations and decrements in performance from unfavorable teacher expectations" (p. 339). Good (1981) presented a model which describes how these expectations become real in their consequences: (a) teachers expect different specific behaviors and achievement from particular students; (b) because of these different expectations, they behave differently toward various students; (c) in turn, this different treatment sends different messages to students which affects their achievement, motivation, and self-concept; (d) over time, teacher actions shape students' behavior and teachers' initial expectations are met. Merton (1957) explained why these "self-fulfilling prophecies" are resistant to change.

> The self-fulfilling prophecy is, in the beginning, a "false" definition of a situation evoking a new behavior which makes the originally false conception come "true." This specious validity of the self-fulfilling prophecy perpetuates a reign of error. For the prophet will cite the actual course of events as proof that he was right from the very beginning. Such are the perversities of social logic (p. 423).

Consider Eder's (1981) study of first grade oral reading lessons as an example of Good's model. Eder found that first grade teachers expected greater general verbal competence from students who were considered to have longer attention spans (high ability group) than from students who were judged to have short attention spans (lower ability group) despite considerable evidence suggesting that language competence varies across social settings and that it is not a fixed general ability (Labov 1972; Mehan 1984). Because of these expectations for language competence, teachers allowed students in lower groups to interrupt one another during oral reading lessons in order to give them practice with oral language. On the other hand, these teachers discouraged high group students from any interruptions because they were considered verbally proficient. As a result, interruptions became more frequent in lower groups which required teachers to spend time on management rather than instruction; all of which contributed to lower levels of reading achievement for lower group students. Eder concludes:

> Because students are exposed to different learning contexts when they are assigned to ability groups, their behavior is likely to be differentially influenced in line with their group assignments. . . . If students tend to remain in the groups to which they are assigned initially, it is important that these assignments be accurate. However, since most students are assigned to ability groups within the first few weeks of first grade, it is highly unlikely that accurate assessment of students' aptitudes have been made. The lack of accurate measures of academic aptitude in early grades is particularly important since it increases the likelihood of ethnic and class bias in ability group assignment (p. 160).

Social class and teachers' unequal treatment of reading groups

As Good suggests and Eder demonstrates, teachers' expectations and their subsequent behavior toward students have pronounced effects on students' academic and social learning. Allington (1983) suggested that good and poor reading groups differ in reading competence as much from differences in instruction as they do from variation in individual aptitudes. These differences take many forms: teacher interruption behaviors, the amount of reading during reading lessons, the content of those lessons, and the difficulty of reading materials used.

Several researchers have found that teachers interrupt students in lower ability groups during oral reading between two and five times more frequently than they do students in higher ability groups, regardless of the type of mistake that was made (Allington 1980; Hoffman et al. 1984; Pflum, Pascarella, Boskwich and Auer 1980). Teachers give students in low groups less time to correct themselves, and are likely to pronounce any troublesome word immediately to keep the lesson moving. The frequent interruptions contribute to general hesitancy of low students during oral reading, to their frequent appeals for assistance from teachers, and to their reluctance or inability to monitor their own reading.

With both students and teachers interrupting, students in low reading groups have few opportunities for sustained reading (Allington 1977). In fact, students in high groups read about three times as many words per day in reading groups as poor groups do (Allington 1983). While seventy percent of the reading in high groups is done silently, only thirty percent of low group reading is silent. Allington (1983) argued that the greater amount of oral reading in low groups accounts for the discrepancy in the amount of overall reading time between groups because oral reading is slower paced and requires more management than silent reading. Moreover, the differences he reports may actually be greater for individual students because silent reading requires that all group members must read in order to accomplish the task, but oral reading requires but one reader. It seems that as students in high groups practice a more functional method of reading more often, those in low groups practice reading in a manner most suitable for reading lessons. This lead Allington (1977) to ask "If they don't read much, how they ever gonna get good?"

During oral reading, teachers are likely to direct the attention of students in low groups to the phonic characteristics of an isolated word, whereas their comments to students in high groups deal more often with the semantic and syntactic content which surround the troublesome word (Allington 1980). This phonic emphasis for students in lower groups was found in several other studies (Alpert 1975; Collins and Haviland 1979; Gambrell, Wilson and Gantt 1981). For example, Gambrell et al. (1981) found that fourth grade students in low groups: (a) worked on phonics in isolation twice as often as students in high groups, (b) spent half as much time on reading in context, and (c) engaged in nonreading activities during half of their reading lessons compared to only a third for high groups. These differences were even greater for students in low groups who found the assigned reading difficult. These students spent twice again as much time on isolated phonics instruction, half again as much time reading, and sixty-one percent of their instructional time on nonreading activities.

The relative difficulty of the assigned reading material is an additional difference between the treatment of students in low and high reading groups (Clay 1972; Gambrell et al. 1981; Hoffman et al. 1984). Students in high groups are often asked to read texts which are easy for them; however, students in low groups are often placed in difficult materials in which they misread at least one in every ten words. This difficulty inhibits low group students' use of context, forces them to read word by word, and makes them rely on the phonic characteristics of unknown words. Their frequent mistakes trigger student and teacher interruptions, and the unfortunate cycle begins anew.

This apparent unequal treatment also extends to the socialization lessons in classrooms. Hamilton (1983) suggests that "the most important finding of ecological research is that the socialization function of schools operates differently for students of different races and classes. Disadvantaged students tend to be socialized for subordination; advantaged students are socialized for responsibility" (p. 332). For instance, Leacock (1969) found that both black and white middle-class schools rewarded "nice" behavior and self control, and encouraged student interaction during social and academic activities. However, in lower class schools, proper behavior meant submission to authority; it was considered an end in itself; student interaction of any type was discouraged. Several researchers note that teachers use more language of control while working with low reading groups than they use with their high reading groups (Eder 1981; Brophy and Good in press; Rist 1970). Reading lessons for low groups are more teacher centered, more tightly monitored, and more likely to require literal interpretations of text (Brophy and Good in press). Allington (1983) speculated that postreading questions in low groups are more a behavior-monitoring device than an instructional tool because these questions are typically asked to see if silent readers can translate print into meaning. However, since most reading in low groups is done orally and most members have only listened to the passage, these questions simply check to see if the nonreaders are paying attention.

Of course, lower class children are not just pawns during reading instruction; their actions contribute to their fate. For instance, Ogbu (1974; 1978) has shown that minority lower class children do not expect schools to improve their social and economic lot in life and often do not invest much energy into school matters. Willis' (1977) study of working-class youths in England demonstrated how lower-class students can select themselves for lower-class status by rejecting all that the "earholes" (high ability group students) deem important. Labov (1972) has shown that lower-class black children appear mute and disinterested within traditional school settings.

This general lack of interest and persistence contributes to lower reading achievement (Butkowsky and Willows 1980; Dweck 1975), and Mosenthal and Na (1980) and Heath (1983) have demonstrated that a mismatch between culture and school or test setting can suppress reading acquisition and performance artificially. Anecdotal reports suggest that lower-class students are sometimes defiant within these situations — in reading groups, classrooms, and schools (e.g. Greenstein 1983). At times it appears that lower-class students and teachers engage in self-perpetuating miseducation during reading instruction along the lines of Allport's (1950) notion concerning how wars start through ignorance about other nations and mutual mistrust among nations. One side acts because it expects the other side will gain an advantage of some sort; then the other side reacts to prevent the first side from gaining the upper hand. In time, the cycle escalates until both sides lose and the cold war becomes war. In the case of reading instruction, teachers' and lower-class students' actions escalate until more time is spent on management and other nonreading activities than is spent on reading or reading instruction. Indeed, both sides lose.

Solutions to the apparent problem

What should be done about this unequal treatment of social classes during reading instruction depends on whom one listens to. Giroux (1983), Mosenthal (1984), and Walmsley (1981) suggested at least three alternative solutions — the academic, the affective, and the emancipatory solutions. These alternatives differ fundamentally concerning their postulates for the appropriate relationship between education and society and it is from these putative relationships that solutions arise.

The academic solution is founded on the notion that education should preserve the social culture and prepare students to fulfill the demanding roles in our technological economy. If schools produce students educated to the extent of their intellectual capabilities, these students will be able to compete actively for the best jobs that the economy has to offer. In this way, both society and the individual are served because students will reach a social class commensurate with their talents and the economy will have a highly trained workforce. From this perspective, the unequal treatment of social classes during reading instruction robs lower class individuals of their chance to succeed economically and society of a pool of potential talent.

Although there are many examples of the academic solution (See Brophy and Good in press), the most widely known expression is the University of Oregon Direct Instruction Model (Becker and Carnine 1980) and its Distar Programs (Becker 1977), which are based on three key assumptions: "1) all children can be taught; 2) to catch-up, low performing students must be taught more, not less; and 3) the task of teaching more requires a careful use of educational technology and of time" (Becker and Carnine 1980, p. 433). In this model, the knowledge and experience of teachers and students are bypassed—neither is free to escalate the behavior of miseducation—because a curriculum designer has developed scripted lessons which explain what teachers should say during lessons to insure maximum efficiency and how low students should respond. These lessons are based on tightly sequenced skills hierarchies which begin with phonics, are highly controlled by the scripted teacher who uses overt signals to elicit student response, and are highly effective in raising traditionally low-performing students' achievement scores. As this example shows, within the academic solution, the reading skills of the lower classes are improved while the social structure remains the same.

The affective solution concentrates on the individual's subjectivity and ignores society's objective constraints. That is, it is based on the idea that education should help each student develop as an individual to the limits of his or her intellectual and emotional potential in spite of social conditions. Through the socialization of students as individuals, education will improve society as each member will become psychologically secure. To effect this change, education must remake itself, losing its present authoritarian structure and replacing it with a spirit of cooperation and community. Students develop their own standards of performance and success and learn to express themselves emotionally. According to the affective solution, once students are socialized to "be themselves," their free and personal expression will give them the social and academic tools to become whatever they wish to become.

The open classroom (Kohl 1969) and the free school (Kozol 1972) movements of the late 1960s can be considered an attempt to implement the affective solution. One objective of these movements was to change the "oppressive" socialization of literacy programs which fostered competition for grades and stifled personal interpretation of literature. Reading programs in these schools were individualized by having students select their own materials, learn at their own pace, and evaluate their own progress, and in which adults acted as facilitators. From the very beginning of these programs, students were to understand that written language is a form of personal expression, and they were encouraged to develop unique understandings of the texts they read and to write as a means for self-development. Anecdotal reports state that these schools were helpful to lower class children's development of strong feelings of self-worth and to their achievement of academic success in terms of authenticity (Dennison 1972; Herndon 1971; Lopate 1974).

Advocates of the emancipatory solution postulate that American society is based on class exploitation and that discrimination against class and race serves the dominant classes by reserving privileged positions for its members (Apple 1982). However, through education, lower class students can develop a critical consciousness which should allow them to discover the historic reasons for their social position and provide them with possible methods with which they can end social domination. While the academic solution suggests that education should perpetuate the cultural structure, and the affective solution ignores society, the emancipatory solution calls for education to change the social order.

Paulo Freire's (1970; 1972; 1978) literacy pedagogy is considered an ideal vehicle for the emancipatory solution (Elasser and John-Steiner 1977; Giroux 1983; Kozol 1981). He maintains that the lower classes see themselves as objects of society rather than actors in society. That is, they have internalized the philosophy of social dominance to a point where they consider themselves beneath both knowledge and culture. In order to help the lower classes become literate, educators must engage groups in dialogue concerning mundane events in their lives which will allow them to recognize the problematic nature of knowledge and culture and the fact that they do indeed create both every day. Following the principles of language experience, these dialogues begin with the creation and interpretation of oral text stimulated by pictures and eventually work through written words and dictated sentences. According to the emancipatory solution, educators and lower class students work to eliminate the social and academic gaps within schools by understanding how and why they exist apart from schools.

Next steps

The research discussed and the theoretical solutions presented herein should give us pause for thought. It appears that social classes are treated differently during reading instruction which may contribute to the stratification of social classes in American society — at the very least, the evidence suggests that reading instruction does little to close the gap. Yet the rhetoric which surrounded reading instruction since the beginning of public schools proclaims that the ability to read and write will have liberating effects for anyone willing to learn. Regardless of the solution one considers as most appropriate, the status quo during reading instruction seems intolerable. Perhaps it is time for teachers to design lessons which will make this rhetoric a reality. Or shall reading instruction become one more instance where the rich get richer while the poor get poorer.

References

Alexander, K., & McDill, E. "Selections and Allocation Within Schools." *American Sociological Review 41* (1976): 969–980.

Allington, R. "If They Don't Read Much, How They Ever Gonna Get Good?" *Journal of Reading 21* (1977): 57–61.

Allington, R. "Teacher Interruption Behaviors During Primary Grade Oral Reading." *Journal of Education Psychology 72* (1980): 371–374.

Allington, R. "The Reading Instruction Provided Readers of Differing Reading Abilities." *Elementary School Journal 83* (1983): 548–559.

Allport, G. The role of expectancy. In *The Tensions that Cause Wars*, edited by H. Centril. Champaign: University of Illinois Press, 1950.

Alpert, J. "Teacher Behavior Across Ability Groups." *Journal of Educational Psychology 66* (1975): 348–353.

Apple, M. *Education and Power*. Boston: Routledge & Kegan Paul, 1982.

Becker, W. "Teaching Reading and Language to the Disadvantaged." *Harvard Educational Review 47* (1977): 518–543.

Becker, W., & Carnine, D. "Direct Instruction." In *Advances in Clinical Child Psychology*. Volume 3, edited by B. Lahey & A. Kazdin. New York: Plenum, 1980.

Borko, H., Shavelson, R., & Stern, P. "Teacher's Decisions in Planning of Reading Instruction." *Reading Research Quarterly 16* (1981): 449–466.

Bourdieu, P., & Passeron, J. *Reproduction in Education, Society, and Culture*. Beverly Hills: Sage, 1977.

Bowles, S., & Gintis, H. *Schooling in Capitalist America*. New York: Basic. 1976.

Braun, C. "Teacher Expectations." *Review of Educational Research 46* (1976): 185–213.

Brophy, J. "Teacher Behavior and Its Effects." *Journal of Educational Psychology 71* (1979): 733–750.

Brophy, J., & Good, T. "Teacher Behavior and Student Achievement." In *The Third Handbook of Research in Teaching*. Chicago: University of Chicago Press, in press.

Butkowsky, I., & Willows, D. "Cognitive-Motivational Characteristics of Children Varying in Reading Ability." *Journal of Educational Psychology 72* (1980): 408–422.

Clay, M. *Reading: The Patterning of Complex Behavior*. New York: International Publications, 1972.

Collins, A., & Haviland, S. *Children's Reading Problems*. Reading Education Report No. 8. Champaign: Center for the Study of Reading, 1979.

Cooper, H. "Pygmalian Grows Up." *Review of Educational Research 49* (1979): 389–410.

Cremin, L. *Traditions in American Education*. New York: Basic, 1977.

Dennison, G. *The Lives of Children*. New York: Vintage, 1972.

Dweck, C. "The Role of Expectancies and Attributions in the Alleviation of Learned Helplessness." *Journal of Personality and Social Psychology 31* (1975): 674–685.

Eder, D. "Ability Grouping as a Self-fulfilling Prophecy." *Sociology of Education 54* (1981): 151–162.

Elasser, N., & John-Steiner, V. "An Interactionist Approach to Advancing Literacy. *Harvard Educational Review 47* (1977): 355–369.

Feldman, J. "Stimulus Characteristics and Subject Prejudice as Determinants of Stereotype Attribution." *Journal of Personality and Social Psychology 21* (1972): 333–340.

Freire, P. *Pedagogy of the Oppressed*. New York: Seabury, 1970.

Freire, P. *Education for Critical Consciousness*. New York: Seabury, 1972.

Freire, P. *Pedagogy in Process*. New York: Seabury, 1978.

Fotheringham, J., & Creal, D. "Family Socioeconomic and Educational Emotional Characteristics as Predictors of School Achievement." *Journal of Educational Research 73* (1980): 311–317.

Gambrell, L., Wilson, R., & Gantt, W. "Classroom Observations of Task Attending Behaviors of Good and Poor Readers." *Journal of Educational Research 74* (1981): 400–404.

Giroux, H. *Theory and Resistance in Education*. South Hadley, MA: Bergin & Garvey, 1983.

Good, T. "Teacher Expectations and Student Perceptions." *Educational Leadership 38* (1981): 415–422.

Greenstein, J. *What the Children Taught Me*. Chicago: University of Chicago Press, 1983.

Greer, C. *The Great School Legend*. New York: Viking, 1972.

Groff, P. "A Survey of Basal Reading Group Practices." *Reading Teacher 15* (1962) 232–235.

Haller, E., & Davis, S. "Teacher Perceptions, Parental Social Status and Grouping for Reading Instruction." *Sociology of Education 54* (1980): 162–174.

Hamilton, S. "The Social Side of Schooling." *Elementary School Journal 83* (1983): 313–334.

Harris, D., & Amprey, J. "Race, Social Class, Expectations and Achievement." In *The Rise and Fall of National Test Scores*, edited by G. Austin and H. Garber. New York: Academic, 1982.

Heath, S. *Ways with Words*. Cambridge: Cambridge University Press, 1983.

Herndon, G. *How to Survive in Your Native Land*. New York: Bantam, 1971.

Hoffman, J., O'Neal, S., Kastler, L., Clements, R., Segel, K., & Nash, M. "Guided Oral Reading and Miscue Focused Verbal Feedback in Second-Grade Classrooms." *Reading Research Quarterly 19* (1984): 367–384.

Hollingshead, A. *Elmtown Youth*. New York: Wiley, 1949.

Iverson, B., & Walberg, H. "Home Environment and School Learning." *Journal of Experimental Education 50* (1982): 144–151.

Jencks, C. *Inequality*. New York: Basic, 1972.

Kohl, H. *Open Classrooms*. New York: New York Review, 1969.

Kozol, J. *Free Schools*. New York: Continuum, 1972.

Kozol, J. *Prisoners of Silence*. New York: Continuum, 1981.

Labov, W. *Language in the Inner City*. Philadelphia: University of Pennsylvania Press, 1972.

Leacock, E. *Teaching and Learning in City Schools*. New York: Basic, 1969.

Lopate, P. *Being with Children*. New York: Bantam, 1974.

Low, B., & Clement, P. "Relationships of Race and Socioeconomic Status to Classroom Behavior, Academic Achievement, and Referral for Special Education." *Journal of School Psychology 20* (1982): 103–112.

McDermott, R. *Kids Make Sense*. Unpublished Ph.D. dissertation, Stanford University, 1976.

Mehan, H. *Learning Lessons*. Cambridge: Harvard University Press, 1979.

Mehan, H. "Language and Schooling." *Sociology of Education 57* (1984): 174–183.

Merton, R. *Social Theory and Social Structure*. Glencoe, IL: The Free Press, 1957.

Michaels, S. "Sharing Time." *Language in Society 10* (1981): 423–42.

Mosenthal, P. "Defining Reading Program Effectiveness." *Poetics 13* (1984): 10–32.

Mosenthal, P., & Na, T. "Quality of Chidren's Recall under Two Classroom Testing Tasks." *Reading Research Quarterly 15* (1980): 504–528.

Ogbu, J. *The Next Generation*. New York: Academic, 1974.

Ogbu, J. *Minority Education and Caste*. New York: Academic, 1978.

Pflum, S., Pascarella, E., Boskwick, W., & Auer, C. "The Influence of Pupil Behaviors and Pupil Status Factors on Teacher Behaviors During Oral Reading Lessons." *Journal of Education Research 74* (1980): 99–105.

Pikulski, J., & Kirsch, I. "Organization for Instruction." In *Compensatory Reading Survey*, edited by R. Calfee & P. Drum. Newark: International Reading Association, 1979.

Rist, R. "Student Social Class and Teacher Expectations." *Harvard Educational Review 40* (1970): 411–451.

Rist, R. *Restructuring American Education*. New Brunswick, NJ: Transaction, 1972.

Rist, R. *The Urban School*. Cambridge: MIT Press, 1973.

Rosenbaum. *Making Inequality*. New York: Wiley, 1976.

Rowan, B., & Miracle, A. "Systems of Ability Grouping and the Stratification of Achievement in Elementary Schools." *Sociology of Education 56* (1983): 133–144.

Russo, N. *The Effects of Student Characteristics, Educational Beliefs, and Instructional Task on Teacher's Preinstructional Decisions in Reading and Math.* Unpublished doctoral dissertation, University of California, Los Angeles, 1978.

Seaver, W. "Effects of Naturally Induced Teacher Expectancies." *Journal of Personality and School Psychology 28* (1973): 333–342.

Walmsley, S. "On the Purpose and Content of Secondary Reading Programs." *Curriculum Inquiry 11* (1981): 73–93.

Wilkins, W. "The Concept of a Self-fulfilling Prophecy." *Sociology of Education 49* (1976): 175–183.

Willis, P. *Learning to Labor.* Lexington, MA: D.C. Heath, 1977.

THIRTEEN

Empowerment as a Pedagogy of Possibility
Roger I. Simon

I would like to start by thanking the organizers of this conference for inviting me to share my thoughts with you. A Canadian at a conference on American dreams! And so my problem begins — how should I participate in this debate? I share what I think is the assumption of this conference, that education is fundamentally about our hopes for the future given an understanding of current realities, that particular forms of educational practice offer both a particular version and vision of a future civic prospect and morality. So I want you to know — my dreams are Canadian dreams. My hopes for the future and my understanding of current realities reflect my location in a national culture that (while in many ways similar to yours) is fundamentally different in terms of its history, its economic realities, and its political traditions.

I'm not by any means suggesting that the ideas I offer you this afternoon have no relevance to education in the United States: but it is you that will have to decide if what I am about to say is helpful in formulating the direction in which it is desirable for you to dream.

Pedagogy as possibility

As I understand the purpose of this session it is to explore educational possibilities and open up the question of how classroom practice might be related to one's communal and national future. This means we must find a way of talking about practice that *simultaneously* references on the one hand what as educators we might actually do with students *and* on the other the political/cultural/economic visions such practices support.

This is why I was so pleased to see the word "pedagogy" used in the title of this session. I suspect that for many of us "pedagogy" is not a common term often heard in staff rooms or classrooms. For some it may sound slightly foreign and very much like academic jargon. Are we not just talking about teaching and if so why then do we have to use such a pretentious sounding word?

Well, I want to argue that there is an important distinction to be made between the words "teaching" and "pedagogy." Where I come from teaching usually refers to specific strategies and techniques to use in order to meet predefined, given objectives. It is talk exclusively carried out in the language of technique and usually its purpose is to provide do-able suggestions that can be tried out in the classroom the next day.

Such talk is, of course, important for sharing ideas and working out the details of what one actually does as a teacher. The problem is, however, that if we want to examine how our practice relates to future visions of community life such talk is insufficient. To debate what we should be doing in schools we need an alternative to the impoverishing construction imposed by an exclusive reliance on practical suggestions and the reduction of debate to questions of "what works."

I think talk about "pedagogy" is an alternative that points us in the right direction. To me "pedagogy" is a more complex and extensive term than "teaching," referring to the integration in practice of particular curriculum content and design, classroom strategies and techniques, a time and space for the practice of those strategies and techniques, and evaluation purposes and methods. All of these aspects of educational practice come together in the realities of what happens in classrooms. Together they organize a view of how a teacher's work within an institutional context specifies a particular version of what knowledge is of most worth, what it means to know something, and how we might construct representations of ourselves, others, and our physical and social environment. In other words, talk about pedagogy is simultaneously talk about the details of what students and others might do together *and* the cultural politics such practices support. To propose a pedagogy is to propose a political vision. In this perspective, we cannot talk about teaching practice without talking about politics.

Let me spell this out a bit. In his masterwork *The Principle of Hope* Ernst Bloch (1986) paid significant attention to the utopian impulse of daydreams. In a commentary on this text, he wrote:

> Dreams come in the day as well as at night. And both kinds of dreaming are motivated by the wishes they seek to fulfill. But daydreams differ from night dreams; for the daydreaming "I" persists throughout, consciously, privately, envisaging the circumstances and images of a desired, better life. The content of the daydream is not, like that of the night dream, a journey back into repressed experiences and their associations. It is concerned with, as far as possible, an unrestricted journey forward, so that instead of reconstituting that which is no longer conscious, the images of that which is not yet can be phantasied into life and into the world. (Bloch 1970)

Of what significance is Bloch's analysis of daydreams for us amid this national debate on the future of education. As I see it, education and daydreams share a common project: in Bloch's words the production of "images of that which is not yet." Without a perspective on the future, conceivable as a desired future, there can be no human venture. As an introduction to, preparation for, and legitimation of particular forms of social life, education always presupposes a vision of the future. In this respect a curriculum and its supporting pedagogy are a version of our own dreams for ourselves, our children, and our communities.

But such dreams are never neutral; they are always *someone's* dreams and to the degree that they are implicated in organizing the future for others they always have a moral and political dimension. It is in this respect that any discussion of pedagogy must begin with a discussion of educational practice as a form of cultural politics, as a particular way in which a sense of identity, place, worth, and above all value is in-formed by practices which organize knowledge and meaning. So this then is where I will start. My intent is to try to illustrate what a pedagogy of empowerment might mean when it is centered within a social project aimed at the enhancement of human possibility.

A project of possibility

When I speak about a pedagogy of empowerment I am speaking of an educational practice that is aimed at enabling a particular moral project, a particular "not yet" of how we might live our lives together. In other words, there is a particular cultural politics behind my view of a pedagogy of empowerment and, before I go any further, I want to introduce some of its dimensions.

The cultural politics from which I begin is one centrally committed to the task of creating specific social forms (such as schooling) that encourage and make possible the realization of a variety of differentiated human capacities; rather than denying, diluting or distorting those capacities. It is a cultural politics concerned with enabling ways of representing and understanding our social and material world that encourage, through the development of com-petencies and capabilities, the expansion of the range of possible social identities people may become (Corrigan 1987). In this respect I am proposing that as educators both our current problem and our future project should be an educational practice whose fundamental purpose is to expand what it is to be human and contribute to the establishment of a just and compassionate community within which a project of possibility becomes the guiding principle of social order.

What is this about? What is meant by a "project of possibility"?

I am using the term "project" here in the particular sense in which it was discussed by Sartre (1963), as an activity determined by both real and present conditions, *and* certain conditions still to come which it is trying to bring into being. In this sense a project of possibility begins with a critique of current realities. This critique suggests (and I think this applies to both Canada and the United States) that a contradiction exists between the openness of human capacities that we encourage in a free society and the social forms[1] that are provided and within which we must live our lives. It is this contradiction which is the starting point for a project of possibility and defines its broad aim: the transformation of the relation between human capacities and social forms. More particularly the project requires both the expansion of forms to accom-modate capacities and the expansion of capacities to make the realization of new forms possible. Such a project would reject the resolution of this contradiction between capacities and forms through narrowing of capacities to fit existing forms or through the narrowing of forms to fit preconceived, fixed, "naturalized" notions of capacities.

A clear example of the reduction of capacities by forms is the argument that "youth who embrace 'traditional values' make better high school students," putting the emphasis on school reforms that stress what is called "character development" (Ginsburg and Hanson 1985). What "character development" means here is a particular narrowing of human capacities to fit particular forms. Such a position calls for support on studies that examine the relation between student values and high school success seeking to identify those human capacities that best fit the existing forms of schooling. The results of such studies are then read as identifying the desired norm—the desired sense of identity, values, and sensibility—that students must "develop" to solve the school achievement problem. Those who fail to exhibit or "develop" such capacities are seen as deficient, lacking in appropriate character, simply of lesser worth. Taken to its logical conclusion, such deficient human character is seen as a national danger! And yet again we have a community which renders "natural" its existing historical social forms—celebrating them as the epiphany of morality—and rendering all versions of human possibility not in accord with the requirement of such forms as defective.

In the face of such approaches to education we surely should be asking who controls and defines what forms of education are available and who states what capacities are possible and acceptable. For a project of possibility rejects a moral neutrality in relation to regulation which normalizes, renders natural, takes for granted and as simply "obvious" what are in fact ontological and epistemological premises of a particular and historical form of social order. We need to hold those who seek to narrow human possibility morally accountable! We must be clear that the ways in which we are collectively represented to ourselves and in which permissible parameters and forms of individual liberty are defined and symbolized for us are simultaneously descriptive and evaluative. The narrowing of the range of possible relationships between capacities and forms is yet another practice which marginalizes those who express their difference differently—differences commonly organized within combinations of inequitable existing gender, race, ethnic, class, age, and regional relations (Corrigan and Sayer 1985).

A project of possibility would allow us to express our differences differently (Lewis and Simon 1986). It constitutes an agenda well beyond conventional notions of equal opportunity. Equal opportunity is defined in reference to an individual's position within given state or market-regulated social forms. Within a given form it means equal access to comparable opportunities provided within that form; be it a job, education, housing, protection, etc. A project of possibility on the other hand would require that we expand the range of both capacities and forms within our communities. The agenda is to create practices that encourage, make possible, and enable the realization of differentiated human capacities.

Such an agenda requires of course, not only our efforts in schools but as well our alliance with other transformative projects being undertaken in our homes, work places, and in our communities. The reality that schools are indeed only one site among many in which the practice of education takes place needs constant reemphasis, for the progressive renewal needed to advance our project of possibility will require new ways of defining and planning how and where education will take place.

A pedagogy of empowerment

The question, then, is what form of pedagogy is needed in order to support a project of possibility? What could a pedagogy of empowerment mean and would it be a means toward the realization of such a project?

Let's begin to try to answer these questions by considering what is meant by the term "empowerment." Empowerment literally means to give ability to, to permit or enable. When we hear the word empowerment used in education, it is usually being employed in the spirit of critique. Its referent is the identification of oppressive and unjust relations within which there is an unwarranted limitation placed on human action, feeling, and thought. Such limitation is seen as constraining a person from the opportunity to participate on equal terms with other members of a group or community to whom have accrued the socially defined status of "the privileged"/"the competent." To empower in this perspective is to counter the power of some people or groups to make others "mute." To empower is to enable those who have been silenced to speak. It is to enable the self-affirming expression of experiences mediated by one's history, language, and traditions. It is to enable those who have been marginalized economically and culturally to claim in both respects a status as full participating members of a community. Succinctly put by Bastian, Fruchter, Gittell, Greer, and Haskins (1985), empowerment is "the opportunity and means to effectively participate and share authority."

Now I will argue in a moment that such a conception of empowerment while important for formulating a pedagogy that supports the project of possibility is by itself woefully insufficient. But first let's see what orientation this concept of empowerment provides for pedagogy. A pedagogy that empowers (in the sense in which I just used the term) must do at least two things.

First, such a concept of empowerment has to provide a curricular and instructional agenda that enables students to draw upon their own cultural resources as a basis for engaging in the development of new skills and interrogating existing knowledge claims. This means finding ways of working with students that enable the full expression of multiple "voices" engaged in dialogic encounter. We cannot teach through forms that obliterate meaning. And we cannot teach through forms that silence. We must remember Roland Barthes' (1982) warning that "what is oppressive in our teaching is not finally the knowledge or culture it conveys—but the discursive forms through which we propose them." An education that creates silence is not an education.

Second, a pedagogy based on such a notion of empowerment must ask the question: empowerment for what? This, I want to emphasize, is the site of the insufficiency of the term empowerment. Without a vision for the future a pedagogy of empowerment is reduced to a method for participation which takes democracy as an end and not a means! There is no moral vision other than the insistence on people having a equal claim to a place in the public arena. Of course this is extremely important, but without something more empowerment becomes an empty and abstract moral project that is unable to call into question existing contradictions between human capacities and social forms. It provides us with no guidance as to what forms of knowing and learning might help enhance our chances of developing a just and compassionate society when justice and compassion are so urgently required.

Within the cultural politics of a project of possibility empowerment has got to be more than the individual enabling of the transformation of desire into reality and the opportunity to define what one desires. Too often education stops with the intent of ensuring that all students acquire the necessary knowledge, skills, and credentials to "make it" in the tough competitive world of existing social forms. Obviously we can never dismiss the importance of this. If we do not give youth a sense of how to "make it" within existing realities, all too often we doom them to social marginality: yet another high-minded way of perpetuating the structural inequalities in society.

But if we are to develop a pedagogy in support of a project of possibility this cannot be our sole nor primary orientation. An education that empowers for possibility must raise questions of how we can work for the reconstruction of social imagination in the service of human freedom. What notions of knowing and what forms of learning will support this? I think the project of possibility requires an education rooted in a view of human freedom as the *understanding of necessity and the transformation of necessity*. This is the pedagogy we require, one whose standards and achievement objectives are determined in relation to goals of critique and the enhancement of social imagination. Teaching and learning must be linked to the goal of educating students to take risks, to struggle with ongoing relations of power, to critically appropriate forms of knowledge that exist outside of their immediate experience, and to envisage versions of a world which is "not yet" — in order to be able to alter the grounds upon which life is lived.

Examples of a pedagogy of possibility

At the beginning of my talk I argued that talk about practice had to simultaneously reference the political, cultural, and economic visions which practices support and what we might actually do with students. And it is time that I begin to consider the latter. I want to share with you two examples which I hope will illustrate what a pedagogy for a project of possibility might mean.

A first example

My first example concerns a problem which is very much a reality for many elementary school teachers in my community. Simply stated they ask: when I encourage students to write and speak from their own experiences, what should my response be to my students' obsession with professional wrestling? This is, I want to assure you, a real and current issue. In Toronto (as elsewhere in North America) professional wrestling has become very popular with the support of cross-media marketing that has made use not only of broadcast TV but home videotapes, toys, and children's clothes.

To illustrate the extent to which this particular cultural commodity is having an impact on schools I want to read you the following excerpt taken from a principal's newsletter sent home to parents last spring.

> Spring brings a sense of relief to us at school as the grayness of winter is pushed into memory, when the sun shines and greenness begins to emerge. Children get involved with their marbles, skipping ropes, balls, kick ball, etc., and yard supervision is warm and fun, watching the children enjoy themselves.
>
> This year we are beginning to see another new game evolving that is influenced by television — Wrestlemania has taken us by force. The children talk of their heroes. Hulk Hogan, Big John Stud, Roddy Piper, Andre the Giant and many others. In their hero worship they also act the parts in friendly wrestling. Holds like the clothes line, the flying squirrel and others are sometimes demonstrated as the children model their heroes.
>
> I personally have difficulties with role model heroes like these. The children do not seem to understand that these characters are mostly actors who spend a lot of time learning to fall safely and how to act mean or hurt to get the crowd excited.
>
> We are stopping all such play because of the potential for accidental injuries. You may wish to take some home action too, if your family is an avid watcher of these wrestling shows, to make sure that they don't try the holds and throws they are watching.

Now the teachers I'm concerned with in this example are not like this principal. Rather than suppress the lived experiences of children they want to know how to deal with these experiences, how far to go with them. They do want to work out of a pedagogy of empowerment and so they ask: if I am to at least partly work from my students' interests, to acknowledge and make a place for what is meaningful and important to them, should I encourage the student voice that is constantly speaking about Hulk Hogan and Junkyard Dog and, if so, how should I engage that voice, how should I work with it?

In order to grasp the full importance of this question it is important to grasp what is meant by "the student voice." Giroux and McLaren (1986) argue that the category of voice refers to attempts through which students and teachers actively engage in dialogue. Voice then is related to the discursive means whereby teachers and students attempt to make themselves present and to define themselves as active authors of their own world. Frequently dominant school culture represents, legitimates, and privileges the voices of white, male, middle/upper classes (and, we may ask, the voice of principal in that newsletter to the parents?) to the exclusion of those economically and socially disadvantaged. As I argued earlier, a pedagogy of empowerment is important for it points to valuing legitimation of the expression of student voice. It recognizes that a student voice is a discourse that constitutes a necessary logic of identity — a cultural logic that anchors subjectivity.

Thus, from this point of view we can see that a teacher who has begun to ask such questions about her or his students' interest in wrestling has begun to consider their practice in a way consistent with the political vision of a project of possibility. What is recognized in this problem is that educational work is about helping students to make meaning and that part of this process must include making spaces for the expression of and engagement with student voices. Of course many of you will instantly recognize that a lot of "language arts" and "math" could be accomplished through giving students the opportunity to represent images and ideas and solve problems with narratives organized by the discourse of professional wrestling. But if we examine such ideas closely in the light of the desired cultural politics of a project of possibility, we are faced with a dilemma.

If education is not to be viewed as a process within which knowledge is transmitted or conveyed but rather as a process of production and regulation of our social and physical world, every time we help organize narratives in our classroom we are implicated in the organization of a particular way of under-standing the world and the concomitant vision of one's place in that world and in the future. And so the question remains, do we as teachers want to implicate ourselves in our classrooms in the production of narrative forms that celebrate violence and bigotry? This too is a question consistent with a pedagogy of possibility for it is a question which comprehends that knowledge is not neutral, that there is an indissoluble link between power and knowledge, that knowledge defines possibility, and that in this sense some ways of defining our world constitute taken-for-granted ways of thinking which justify war, racism, and indifference to human suffering.

So here then is a fundamental contradiction between a pedagogy that seeks (in the limited sense of the word) to empower students through developing language competencies and the expression of student "voice" and one that wishes to raise questions about the adequacy of existing social forms and what would have to be done for things to be otherwise. Within this contradiction is a fundamental dilemma of a pedagogy of possibility: how can we both legitimate the expression of a student voice and challenge at the same time those aspects of that voice which negate our educational/political vision? A pedagogy in support of a project of possibility would neither suppress the discourse of professional wrestling in classrooms nor simply employ such a discourse as a "neutral" vehicle in which supposedly neutral linguistic and mathematics skills could be developed.

So what's the solution? There is, of course, no "correct" answer, no multi-step model to follow. Besides, remember that we cannot reduce our talk about such problems to a list of "tips" or techniques. Rather we have to theorize our way to at least a provisional set of ideas.

To do this I think we could return again to the powerful notion of a student "voice" and reconsider some of its dimensions. A pedagogy of possibility proceeds from a view of language that views it as produced within discursive forms which organize and are organized by the everyday practices which constitute the social relations of our lives. What I think this means is that a "voice" does not constitute a person, a person can have and usually does have a multiplicity of voices that have been and can be constituted within a variety of social relations and material conditions (Emerson 1983).

The student voice that celebrates the displays of Hulk Hogan is a real one indeed, a voice that has been produced within a complex of practices that include not only the commodification of wrestling but, as well, the broad valorization of aggression, the reduction of people to black-and-white images of good and evil, and the reduction of empowerment to acquiring those characteristics and behaviors that "pay off" in rewards that can only be achieved at the expense of others. And furthermore, when one lives everyday in a world within which there is little opportunity to define the terms of one's participation and there is a rather restricted set of possibilities for making a better life for oneself, we should understand how a discourse such as professional wrestling becomes a "discourse of desire," one we should never suppress if we wish to avoid demeaning the lives of others.

But then again, professional wrestling is only one student voice among many possible voices that any individual might present. And further, since the classroom is a real material site of social relations, it is possible to organize new student voices there. Other voices can be introduced through such practices as storytelling, literature, and nonhierarchical classroom relationships which offer a variety of narratives demonstrating other possibilities for empowerment beyond the control and oppressive manipulation of others. The idea here is to introduce a counterdiscourse which provides the possibility for students to understand who they are in ways that are different from identities in-formed by the dominant culture. As a means for positive and meaningful resistance to taken-for-granted practices and beliefs such a counterdiscourse can provide the resources for a new voice within which students can define their experiences.

As Harold Rosen (1986) suggests, it does matter which stories we work with for to tell a story means to take a stance toward events and to create a world. Does this mean that we simply wish *our* stories to prevail? I suggest not. A teacher can set the stage for a pedagogy of possibility by ensuring that there are multiple voices in the classroom, but the crucial task is in finding ways in which these voices can interrogate each other.

Such an interrogation requires a serious dialogue (perhaps even a struggle) over assigned meaning, over the interpretation of experience, and possible versions of "self." It is this dialogue or struggle that forms the basis of a pedagogy that makes possible new knowledge that expands individual experience and hence redefines our identities and what we see as real possibilities in the daily conditions of our lives. It is a struggle that can never be won or pedagogy stops. The submission of all voices to one logic severs the process of education. This does not mean abandoning the authority of our knowledge and experience but only emphasizes that our authoritative voice is not oppressive by the weight of our own experience and knowledge but by its practice if it unwittingly subjugates other voices (Giroux).

Again Giroux and McLaren (1986) express well the intent here. They write:

> It is not just a matter of letting kids speak or write. Both student and teacher must develop an understanding of how both "local" and "official" knowledge gets produced, sustained, and legitimated. This further suggests that teachers need to develop pedagogical practices that link student experiences with those aspects of community life that inform and sustain such experiences. Teachers can better understand how students produce meaning by situating such a process within those wider aspects of community life that sustain, mediate, and legitimate it. In this way, the concept of voice can provide a basic organizing principle around which teachers can both develop a relationship to student

experiences, and also create a forum for examining broader school and community issues. Teachers must become aware of both the strengths and weaknesses of the community at large and develop this awareness into curriculum strategies designed to enable students to engage in the transformative work required to create a more just and humane society.

A second example

As many young people reach the point of leaving secondary school, questions about their future possibilities have a persistent way of being asked and reasked. Even if some young people do not raise these questions themselves, there are always parents, teachers, and friends to do so for them. My colleagues and I at the Ontario Institute for Studies in Education have recently been developing curriculum that has as its purpose helping youth confront questions about their future identities in such a way as to *empower them in defining an expanded range of possibilities for the future* (Simon 1983).

This curriculum is intended for use in high school cooperative education programs. These are programs of extended partial work entry in which students spend up to two-thirds of the time allocated for a course working in a work place within their community. The remaining one-third course time is spent in school in studies that are related to their work place experiences.

The teaching strategies and supporting material we have written are our attempt to further consider how a pedagogy of possibility might be undertaken. Our approach emphasizes the importance of a critical examination of a student's own work experience and the usually taken-for-granted aspects of a historically and socially organized Canadian work environment.

As a brief example, I have recently written a unit which provides a pedagogy for those teachers who include "self-assessment" activities in their course plans. This activity is often done with the use of psychometric tests or interest inventories. It is justified as helping students assess the appropriateness for themselves of different types of existing occupations. It is a way of helping young people entering the labor market to know how to structure their planning to fit the realities of that market. Indeed, an important task!

But we also think that our responsibilities as educators require us to help our students consider how they might act individually and collectively to alter the possibilities open to them. Thus we include in our pedagogy activities which are intended to facilitate a self-awareness that ties one's interests, abilities, temperament, and values to existing social arrangements within which people work, learn, play, and live. In other words, it is important that we help students to begin to consider how they are both created and limited by their particular life circumstances and to consider what alternative ways of working and living could be supported by other possible ways of defining one's work in the world. A pedagogy of work education consistent with the project of possibility must ask students to evaluate the desirability of existing ways work is made available to them and consider what it would take for the current world of work to be otherwise.

I will briefly give you a concrete sense of what this might mean. Self-assessment is commonly understood as a way of answering such questions as: "Am I right for this job?" "Does this career suit me?" "Can I do this type of work?" In determining whether a particular job or type of work is appropriate, the usual procedure is to compare some personal characteristics (e.g., interests, temperaments, aptitudes, etc.) against some set of job requirements. This means that jobs must be "objectively" described and defined and that such job descriptions become the standard against which people are counselled, hired, paid, and evaluated.

Those involved in work experience programs often take for granted that through working, students will learn enough about particular types of work to determine whether or not they want to pursue such occupations in the future. In the work place it is assumed that they can get the kind of firsthand knowledge of job requirements that will enable them to assess whether or not such work is "right for them." Teachers often comment that "work experience gives the kids a chance to find out if they are cut out for this or that kind of work."

There is, however, a problem in all this. When students use their experiences of particular jobs to find out whether they are interested or capable, they may be using their experiences to develop a false picture of themselves. I say false because students may assume that they have learned something about how they "fit" a particular job as it has come to be defined in the organization in which they have been placed.

What is often forgotten is that job requirements are not fixed but rather are dependent upon a range of decisions made by employers or managers or sometimes fellow employees as to how a set of tasks will be defined and related to each other. Organizations can and do differ in how the work they require is assigned and distributed among its members. Such decisions are based not only on the nature of the work itself but as well on the values held with regard to how work should be organized, the importance of hierarchy, the question of supervision, and the economic pressures the organization might face.

What is the importance of this situation for self-assessment? It means that teachers should attempt to help students understand that their reactions to particular work experiences are reactions to other people's plans and ideas for how a particular type of job should be done. Thus, self-assessment using work experience is not finding out about yourself (in terms of essential characteristics) but rather finding out about your interest in and ability to fit one version of the existing reality of work. This also means that students can be challenged to find out if there are alternative versions of what certain jobs entail within specific occupational areas. Further, they may assess what ways of organizing work and defining jobs would be most desirable for them. From this vantage point a range of questions can be posed. For example:

- How much variety in how work gets done exists between organizations?
- What accounts for this variety (or lack of it)?
- If you do not fit in with the way the work you want to do is most often defined, what are the consequences and why?
- *Are there any options?*

My point in providing you with these examples is to illustrate the enormous importance of the question of pedagogy. Our images of ourselves and our world provide us with a concrete sense of what might be possible and desirable. What we do in classrooms can matter; we can begin to enable students to enter the openness of the future as the place of human hope and worth.

Conclusion

I want to conclude here with an old Jewish story about a synagogue that had been without a rabbi for about twenty years, and was now on the verge of being torn apart by arguments about how to do some of the central prayer rituals. Finally, out of desperation they sent a delegation to the old rabbi, who had retired twenty years before, to inquire what the tradition was really supposed to be. Each side presented their case, denouncing the other side for distorting the true tradition. After they had concluded, the rabbi asked if it was true that each side was sure that their way was right. "Yes," said both sides. The rabbi continued, "And both sides seem to think that the other side is deeply mistaken and is about to ruin everything should their views prevail?" "Yes," both sides responded, "the other side distorts the truth and is ruining the community. So what *is* the tradition?" The rabbi had no problem responding: "The state of affairs you describe in our synagogue — *that is the tradition!*"

Our view in Canada of the best of American traditions has been your commitment to the ideas of possibility and diversity. This has always meant a lively, open debate about what such concepts really mean for everyday life. Any claim by one side to be the true faith while relegating all the others to the status of heretics has, in my view, stepped outside of the tradition. There is something to preserve and it is an openness to that which is "not yet."

We should not romanticize all dreams about the future. Not all phantasy is benign. The basis of what many people view as a "better tomorrow" sometimes includes the unjust and oppressive disparagement or control over others. Not all dreams are dreams of hope. There are those among us whose future dreams are structured by failure and hopelessness. But I will leave you with the thought that dreams can also be the lens through which we glimpse possibility; that which is not yet but could be if we engage in the simultaneous struggle to change both our circumstances and ourselves.

Notes

1. Corrigan, in a recent talk, suggests that social forms are the ways that social actions have to be done, the regulated pattern of the normal, expected and obvious, the precisely taken-for-granted dominant features of a given type of society. This includes categories of thought and emotion regarding social action, beliefs about means and ends and so on. We cannot discuss the effects of any given form without understanding its consequences for other contexts of regulation, e.g., what happens in families is linked to what happens in schools, work places, mass media, etc.

References

Barthes, Roland. "Inaugural lecture, College de France." In Susan Sontag (ed.) *A Barthes Reader* New York: Hill and Wang, 1982.

Bastian, Ann, Fruchter, Norm, Gittell, Marilyn, Greer, Colin, and Haskins, Kenneth. "Choosing Equality: The Case for Democratic Schooling." *Social Policy*, Spring 1985:34−51.

Bloch, Ernst. *A Philosophy of the Future*. New York: Herder and Herder, 1970.

Bloch, Ernst. *The Principle of Hope*. Cambridge, Mass: MIT Press, 1986.

Corrigan, Philip, and Sayer, Derek. *The Great Arch: English State Formation as Cultural Revolution*. New York: Blackwell, 1985.

Corrigan, Philip. "In/Forming Schooling." In David W. Livingstone and Contributors, *Critical Pedagogy and Cultural Power*. North Hadley, Mass: Bergin and Garvey, 1987.

Emerson, Caryl. "The Outer Word and Inner Speech: Bakhtin, Vygotsky, and the Internalization of Language." *Critical Inquiry*, *10* (1983).

Ginsburg, Alan, and Hanson, Sandra. *Gaining Ground: Values and High School Success*. Final Report to the U.S. Department of Education, Washington, D.C. 1985.

Giroux, Henry, and McLaren, Peter. "Teacher Education and the Politics of Engagement: The Case for Democratic Schooling." *Harvard Educational Review 56*, (1986): 213–238.

Lewis, Magda, and Simon, Roger I. "A Discourse Not Intended For Her: Learning and Teaching Within Patriarchy." *Harvard Educational Review, 56* (1986): 457–472.

Rosen, Harold. "The Importance of Story." *Language Arts*, *63* (1986): 226–237.

Sartre, Jean-Paul. *Search for a Method*. New York, Alfred Knopf, Inc.: 1963.

Simon, Roger I. "But Who Will Let You Do It: Counter-Hegemonic Approaches To Work Education." *Journal of Education*, *165* (1983): 235–256.

How

Is

Literacy

Taught?

FOURTEEN

Toward a Pedagogy of Possibility in the Teaching of English Internationally: People's English in South Africa

Bronwyn Norton Peirce

The project of possibility requires an education rooted in a view of human freedom as the understanding of necessity and the transformation of necessity.

(Simon, 1987, p. 375)

The phenomenal spread of the English language throughout the world is an uncontested fact: English is used by about 750 million people, only half of whom speak it as a mother tongue. More than half of the world's technical and scientific periodicals are in English, and English is the medium for 80% of the information stored in the world's computers. Three quarters of the world's mail, telexes, and cables are in English. As McCrum, Cran, and MacNeil (1986) state, "Whatever the total, English at the end of the twentieth century is more widely scattered, more widely spoken and written, than any other language has ever been. It has become the language of the planet, the first truly global language" (p. 19).

If English is indeed the first truly international language, it is also a subject of controversy. English has been recently described as both an "alchemy" (Kachru 1986) and a "Trojan horse" (Cooke 1988). For Kachru, "knowing

Source: From "Toward a Pedagogy of Possibility in the Teaching of English Internationally: People's English in South Africa" by Bronwyn Norton Peirce, 1989, *TESOL Quarterly* 23, pp. 401–420. Copyright © 1989.
Reprinted by permission.

English is like possessing the fabled Aladdin's lamp, which permits one to open, as it were, the linguistic gates of international business, technology, science, and travel. In short, English provides linguistic power" (p. 1). For Cooke, on the other hand, English is a language of "cultural intrusion...in a very real way, English is a property of elites, expressing the interests of the dominant classes" (p. 59).

This debate is important for teachers of English internationally: If we are implicated in producing and perpetuating inequalities in the communities in which we teach, we are accountable for our actions. Clearly, as Judd (1983, 1987) and Walters (1989) argue, teachers of English should be aware that teaching is a political act. Judd argues that the teaching of English as a second or foreign language can (and should) raise moral dilemmas for teachers. Are we contributing to the demise of certain languages or linguistic communities? Does the teaching of ESL or EFL serve to entrench the power of an elite, privileged group of people who may have little interest in the welfare of the majority of the people in the country? Do teachers of ESL sometimes participate in a process that "nurtures illusion" (Judd 1983, p. 271)? Cooke (1988) is less tentative than Judd in his conclusions:

> Faced with the doubts that seem to me to characterize English as a world language, I would argue that as teachers of EFL we need to be very aware of the potential dangers of English, and take them into account in preparation and teaching. (p. 60)

Although the issues raised by Kachru, Cooke, Walters, and Judd are important ones, I believe there is another approach to the teaching of English that can contribute, in a qualitatively different way, to the debate on the international role of English teaching. I argue, drawing on the work of Simon (Giroux and Simon 1984; Simon 1987, 1988), that the teaching of English can be reconceptualized as a pedagogy that opens up possibilities for students and teachers of English, not only in terms of material advancement, but in terms of the way they perceive themselves, their role in society, and the potential for change in their society. Such a conceptualization will necessitate a theoretical framework different from that presupposed by Kachru and Cooke, for an understanding of what language is and how it functions in society. It will also necessitate a reconsideration of the prevailing methodologies in the teaching of English internationally.

Proceeding from a reconceptualization of language as "discourse," in the sense in which it is used in poststructuralist theories of language, I argue against the prevailing emphasis on communicative competence as an adequate formulation of principles on which to base the teaching of English. This assessment leads to a proposal for a pedagogy of possibility to complement prevailing methodologies in ESL. Finally, the current movement in South Africa for "People's English" is examined to illustrate how the teaching of English can indeed be undertaken as a pedagogy of possibility, an approach that challenges inequality in society rather than perpetuating it. The attempts of organizations opposed to apartheid to appropriate both the form and functions of English in the interests of freedom and possibility are described. This discussion is thus an exploratory response to Judd's persistent question of what is to be done in the teaching of English internationally.

Theories of language

Despite differences in their interpretation of the function and role of English internationally, a common feature of the work of both Kachru (1986) and Cooke (1988) is their underlying view of the nature of language and its role in society. Kachru and Cooke both perceive language, in this case, English, as a *neutral* object that has political ramifications only insofar as it can lead to material advancement for those who are fortunate enough to acquire it. Thus, Kachru argues that "English is associated with a small but elite group, but it is in their role that the *neutrality* [italics added] of a language becomes vital" (p. 9). Similarly, Cooke argues that "it is not, of course, the nature of English itself that permits such high status, but the social foundation on which it is based" (p. 59).

To begin an exploration of the theory of language that dominates English language teaching, I would like to turn to Kachru's (1986) defense of the use of English in India on the grounds of its perceived neutrality.

> English does have one clear advantage, attitudinally and linguistically: it has acquired a neutrality in a linguistic context where native languages, dialects, and styles sometimes have acquired undesirable connotations. Whereas native codes are functionally marked in terms of caste, religion, region, and so forth, English has no such "markers", at least in the nonnative context. (p. 9)

I would argue, however, that this analysis is theoretically inadequate. The "nonmarked" nature of English (as Kachru perceives it) is not a reflection of the "neutrality" of English within a particular context, but a reflection of the very political nature of English within this context. Clearly, the way English is used in Indian society (whether this is considered marked or unmarked) has important implications for the way people perceive themselves and their relationship to others in their society. Surely this role is not a neutral one.

What theoretical framework would adequately reflect the powerful role of language, not only as Saussure's (1959) "system of signs that *express* [italics added] ideas" (p. 16), but also as a system that is implicated in constituting the way we perceive ourselves and our society? I would argue that the poststructuralist theory of language as *discourse* is sufficiently powerful to explain why English is far from neutral in the context described by Kachru above. Since the notion of discourse is already entrenched in the literature on English language teaching, I would like to draw a distinction between the way the term is currently used and the way I believe its meaning can be usefully extended.

In sociolinguistics, *discourse* refers to "a continuous stretch of (especially spoken) language larger than a sentence...at its most general, a discourse is a set of utterances which constitute any recognizable speech event e.g. a conversation, a joke, a sermon, an interview" (Crystal 1980, p. 114). Interest in discourse had led to a search for the sociolinguistic rules that determine the progress of discourse (Halliday 1973; Hymes 1979); investigation of the kind of discourse that takes place in classrooms (Sinclair and Coulthard 1975); research on how sentences are related in terms of cohesion and coherence (Widdowson 1978); and examination of how such a theory might influence the teaching of ESL (Brumfit and Johnson 1979; Widdowson 1978). It was within this set of theoretical positions that the field of ESL adopted a "communicative" approach to the teaching of English (Canale and Swain 1980).

This conception of discourse, although important and relevant to an understanding of language in use, should, I believe, extend beyond an exploration of units of language larger than the sentence if we are to understand why language in general, and English in particular, is not neutral. Discourses, in a poststructuralist theory of language, are the complexes of signs and practices that organize social existence and social reproduction. In this view, a discourse delimits the range of possible practices under its authority and organizes how these practices are realized in time and space: A discourse is thus a particular way of organizing meaning-making practices. The most powerful discourses in our society have established institutional bases in the law, in medicine, in social welfare, in education, and in the organization of the family and work. Different people can have different and unequal experiences of these discourses. The social meanings produced within these discourses are constituted in language and by language — hence the centrality of language to poststructuralist theory.

Although there are a range of positions that have been called poststructuralist, I am drawing specifically on the writings that reflect the relationship between language, power, and historical change (see Belsey 1980; Cherryholmes 1988; Foucault 1984; Terdiman 1985; Weedon 1987). In a poststructuralist theory of language, language is not only an abstract structure, but a practice that is socially constructed, produces change, and is changed in human life: "Language is the place where actual and possible forms of social organization and their likely social and political consequences are defined and contested. Yet it is also the place where our sense of ourselves, our subjectivity, is constructed" (Weedon 1987, p. 21).

Discourses thus have cultural and political corollaries and are implicated in the way we perceive ourselves and our role in society. The discourses of the classroom, the church, the family, and the corporation are implicated in relations of power within which participants take up different subject positions, positions that are constituted in and by language. Taking up a subject position implies that the subject — the person — is actively engaged in making meaning of his or her life, but is nevertheless constrained by the regulating norms of the discourse in question. When participants cannot find subject positions for themselves within a particular discourse, they may be silenced, or they may attempt to contest or challenge the dominant discourse. Thus, Terdiman (1985) argues that "no dominant discourse is ever fully protected from contestation...the counter-discourse always projects, just over its own horizon, the dream of victoriously replacing its antagonist" (p. 56).

English, like all other languages, is thus a site of struggle over meaning, access, and power. This struggle takes on different forms in different societies, communities, and organizations. Ndebele (1987), commenting on the future role of English in South Africa, states:

> I think we should not be critically complacent about the role and future of English in South Africa, for there are many reasons why it cannot be considered an innocent language. The problems of society will also be the problems of the predominant language of that society. It is the carrier of its perceptions, its attitudes, and its goals, for through it, the speakers absorb entrenched attitudes. The guilt of English must then be recognized and appreciated before its continued use can be advocated. (p. 11)

A poststructuralist theory of language helps to explain why English may be a tainted language for Ndebele and a neutral language for Kachru. Following Foucault (1984), I would argue that the discourse of which Ndebele is a part differs radically from that of Kachru, as a result of Ndebele's and Kachru's having taken up different subject positions vis-à-vis the discourse of English in their societies. In both cases, however, English is implicated in relations of power and dominance.

Pedagogical implications of a poststructuralist theory of language

How might the understanding of English as discourse affect the teaching of English internationally? I would argue that the teaching of English for communicative competence is in itself inadequate as a language-teaching goal if English teachers are interested in exploring how language shapes the subjectivities of their students and how it is implicated in power and dominance. What, then, are the limitations of a theory that has dominated English language teaching and research for the past 20 years? Hymes (1979), who first articulated this theory, argues (in response to Chomsky's distinction between competence and performance):

> We have to account for the fact that a normal child acquires knowledge of sentences, not only as grammatical, but also as appropriate. He or she acquires competence as to when to speak, when not, and as to what to talk about with whom, when, where, in what manner.... The engagement of language in social life has a positive, productive aspect. There are rules of use without which the rules of grammar would be useless. (p. 15)

Although it is important for the teacher and learner of English to know the "rules of use" of the language in a given society, I believe it is equally important for teachers and students to explore a second-order series of questions: Why do such rules exist? Whose interests do such rules serve? Have these rules been contested? Do these rules limit possibilities for our students? Are there other sets of rules that can expand possibilities?

If we teach students to use the English language in a way consistent with appropriate usage at a particular time and place, we may run the risk of limiting our students' perceptions of how English can be used in society. We may indeed be implicated in perpetuating inequalities in society. In South Africa, for example, it is still appropriate for black people within some communities to refer to white male supervisors as *master*. It might be appropriate in some societies for women to defer to men in social interaction.

Although students need to know how English is governed by certain rules of use within a society, they also need to explore how English can be used to challenge the very conditions on which these sociolinguistic rules are based. If we teach English in a way that promotes a student's uncritical integration into a society, students will lack the tools to question the predetermined roles established for them by that society. Conversely, if we teach our students that appropriate usage, although useful to acquire, is nevertheless historically and materially constructed to support the interests of a dominant group within a given society, we can open up possibilities for our students in terms of how they perceive themselves, their role in society, and the possibilities for change and growth in their society.

Thus, the teaching of English internationally is a discourse — a discourse in which teachers and students take up different subject positions. The nature of the subject positions we take up as teachers will be determined by our perception of the nature of the discourse and our role within it. If we adopt the view that the discourse of English language teaching is implicated in power relations within the classroom, the community, and society at large, we need to reexamine the methodology we adopt in our English language classrooms, the content from which we draw our lessons, and the learning goals that we set for our students.

The teaching of English, like any other pedagogical act, can reinforce existing inequalities in a society, but it can also help to expose these inequalities and, more important, help students explore alternative possibilities for themselves and their societies. It follows that if we wish to be part of a discourse that opens up possibilities for our students, we need a more powerful theory than that of communicative competence to inform our teaching.

Toward a pedagogy of possibility

The kind of methodology that can be adopted to explore the rules of English in use and to examine critically the conditions that give rise to these rules is what Simon (1987, 1988) calls a pedagogy of possibility. Because this pedagogy is central to an understanding of what teachers of English might do in their classrooms, let us explore these concepts in some detail.

It is significant that Simon (1988) draws a distinction between teaching and pedagogy:

> There is an important distinction to be made between the notions "teaching" and "pedagogy". Usually, talk about teaching refers to specific strategies and techniques to use in order to meet predefined, given objectives...however, it is an insufficient basis for constituting a practice whose aim is the enhancement of human possibility. What is required is a discourse about practice that references not only what we as educators might actually do; but as well, the social visions such practices would support....Pedagogy is simultaneously about the details of what students and others might do together *and* the cultural politics such practices support. Thus, to propose a pedagogy is to propose a political vision. (p. 2)

In essence, Simon is arguing that teaching, like language, is not a neutral practice. Teachers, whether consciously or not, help to organize the way students perceive themselves and the world. Thus, teachers of English are involved in a pedagogical practice of "cultural politics." The appeal of Simon's philosophy, however, is that such a situation, far from limiting the practice of what goes on in classrooms, offers many possibilities for growth among both teachers and students within a pedagogy of "empowerment":

> To empower is to enable those who have been silenced to speak. It is to enable the self-affirming expression of experiences mediated by one's history, language

and traditions. It is to enable those who have been marginalized economically and culturally to claim in both respects a status as full participating members of a community. (Simon 1987, p. 374)

Empowerment is a term that has little currency in the teaching of English. We are, however, familiar with the notions of "self-directed learning" (Dickinson 1987). Both approaches adopt the position that learners should take greater responsibility for their own learning: "Self-instruction is concerned with responsibility in learning. Individuals who are involved in self-instruction (as learners) have undertaken some additional responsibility for their own learning which in other circumstances would be held on their behalf by a teacher" (Dickinson 1987, p. 8).

What, then, is the distinction between empowerment and self-directed learning? It can be argued that whereas the self-directed learner is encouraged to take greater responsibility for success in learning, the empowered learner is encouraged to take greater responsibility for success in life. *Success* here is defined not only in terms of material advancement, but in terms of the learner's greater understanding and critical appreciation of his or her own subjectivity and relationship to the wider society. In particular, the empowered learner seeks to address the contradictions that might exist between the capacities that teachers encourage and the forms a society provides for these capacities to be realized.

As ESL teachers, we need to address the persistent question of whether our concern with communicative competence and self-directed learning limits the possibilities for growth in our students by emphasizing what is appropriate as opposed to empowering students by encouraging them to explore what might be desirable. Thus, a project of possibility empowers students "to critically appropriate forms of knowledge outside of their immediate experience, to envisage versions of a world which is 'not yet' in order to alter the grounds on which life is lived" (Simon 1988, p. 2).

Adopting a pedagogy of possibility is a bold venture. And it is not unreasonable to ask for examples of how such a pedagogy might operate in a particular place at a given time. For this I turn to South Africa, where teachers, parents, and students have indeed been sufficiently bold to attempt to develop a blueprint for what might constitute a pedagogy of possibility in the teaching of English in South Africa: People's English.

People's English in South Africa

The History of People's English

Language teaching is a site of struggle in South Africa (Janks in press). In a population of 30 million people, only 5 million people speak one of the two official languages of English and Afrikaans. The majority of the people, black South Africans, speak one, and frequently more than one, of a number of languages such as Sotho, Zulu, and Xhosa. The Soweto riots of 1976 were sparked off by the attempt to enforce Afrikaans as a medium of instruction in black schools (Peirce 1987). In a society in which inequality and the unequal sharing of resources are entrenched in the laws of the land, school unrest among the disenfranchised is marked only by differing degrees of intensity.

During the recent series of protests in South Africa, a National Education Crisis Committee (NECC) was established in an attempt to address the continuing crisis in black education. The theme of the first national conference, held in December 1985, was "People's Education for People's Power" (Muller 1987). Some of the resolutions passed at this conference include the following:

People's Education is education that:

- enables the oppressed to understand the evils of the Apartheid system and prepares them for participation in a non-racial, democratic system
- eliminates illiteracy, ignorance and exploitation of any person by another
- allows students, parents, teachers and workers to be mobilised into appropriate organizational structures which enable them to enhance the struggle for people's power and to participate actively in the initiation and management of people's education in all its forms (*SASPU* [South African Students Press Union] *National*, 1986/1987, p. 29)

At the second national conference, held in March 1986, a decision was made to establish two education commissions that would address the issue of what curricula and syllabuses would support the spirit of People's Education. It is significant that the first two commissions established were a People's History Commission and a People's English Commission. Clearly, the political nature of both these subjects was a focus of attention of members of the NECC. The struggle for People's English in South Africa must therefore be located within the struggle for People's Education because the proposals of the People's English Commission are informed by the resolutions of the National Education Crisis Committee.

A press statement issued by the NECC on November 27, 1986, contained the proposals of the People's English Commission and also called for a third national conference of the NECC to meet on November 29–30, 1986. Muller (1987) argues that it was at this stage—when People's Education began to take on a more explicit form within the guidelines proposed by the People's English and the People's History Commissions—that the NECC felt the full might of the state. Not only was the third national conference banned, but the state invoked the Public Safety Act of 1953, which provides for the prohibition of all nonapproved syllabuses, courses, books, and pamphlets. There was simultaneously a major crackdown on the leaders and activities of the NECC, which at the time of this writing (March 1989) was still in effect.

What was it that the state found so threatening in People's English? My argument is this: Because the People's English Commission made no claim to neutrality and paid little heed to linguistic rules of use in South Africa, People's English represents a pedagogy of possibility for the majority of South Africans and consequently a threat to minority rule.

People's English as a pedagogy of possibility

Gardiner (1987) captures the spirit of People's English in the following words:

People's English cannot construct itself upon the implementation of the English as a Second/Foreign Language principles generated so industriously and marketed so assiduously by British universities, publishers and agents of its Foreign

Office. That would be tantamount to changing the names of the actors but retaining the same old play. Not only should future syllabi be reconceptualised; they must proceed from different principles. (p. 60)

Gardiner's words explicitly challenge the principles on which the teaching of English internationally is based, principles that conform to rules of use within a given society and determine the communicative competence of second language speakers of English in that society. On what alternative principles, then, did the People's English Commission proceed?

1. *The recognition of the political nature of language.* Of crucial importance to an understanding of People's English is an understanding of the social vision embraced by members of the Commission. As a preamble, the Commission states that the proposals for People's English aim to assist all learners, among other things, to understand the evils of apartheid and to think and speak in nonracist, nonsexist, and nonelitist ways; to determine their own destinies and to free themselves from oppression; to use English effectively for their own purposes; to express and consider the issues and questions of their time (National Education Crisis Committee, 1986/1987).

   Implicit in these aims is the view that language, and English in particular, is not a neutral practice. It plays a constitutive role in determining how people think, speak, and act. In a society in which racism, sexism, and elitism are considered appropriate in many communities, the teaching of rules of use in these communities would simply perpetuate inequality. It takes a pedagogy of possibility rather than a communicative approach to enable these students of English to "free themselves from oppression."

2. A *reconceptualization of the meaning of* language competence. For the Commission, language competence extends *beyond* an understanding of the rules that govern the English language and the appropriate use of English within South African society. People's English redefines language competence to include the ability to say and write what one means; to hear what is said and what is hidden; to defend one's point of view; to argue, to persuade, to negotiate; to create, to reflect, to invent; to explore relationships, personal, structural, political; to speak, read, and write with confidence; to make one's voice heard; to read print and resist it where necessary (National Education Crisis Committee, 1986/1987). Language competence is thus redefined to include an understanding of language as socially and historically constructed, but at the same time open to dispute.

3. *An understanding of language education as process.* Process is understood to involve

   > exploration through language. It involves discussion and revision, and an understanding of how parts are eventually related to the whole. Process values the contributions of all the learners and makes every member of the group responsible for the learning experience. The teacher's role is to make this possible. (National Education Crisis Committee, 1986/1987, p. 38)

Although an emphasis on process in the learning of language is receiving a great deal of attention in the ESL literature, this emphasis in the South

African context is especially significant. In a society in which national school-leaving examinations play a large role in determining the future of most South Africans, product-oriented teaching and learning receive an inordinate amount of attention in schools. The state assumes the responsibility for determining what material is to be mastered, and the teacher has the responsibility for passing on this information to students. In such an environment, it is difficult for a teacher to engage in "pedagogy" as defined by Simon above. This is particularly true for black teachers, one of whom observed:

> The syllabuses are very full. They have so much in them we can never finish them. If we keep to the syllabus, we have no time at all to teach anything else. The Department makes sure of that! Packing the syllabus is one way of controlling what we can teach in schools. (cited in Christie, 1985, p. 149)

4. *The importance of consultation in the language learning and teaching process.* The People's English proposals were drafted as suggestions, not as a fixed set of objectives for a well-defined curriculum. The document (National Education Crisis Committee, 1986/1987) is punctuated throughout with questions such as the following:

> Do you support these aims? (p. 38)

> Do you agree with the specific proposals which follow? (p. 38)

> The committee needs your response to these specific suggestions about method, content and language competence. (p. 38)

Clearly, the proponents of People's English see themselves within the tradition of consultation that characterizes much of the literature and debate over People's Education (Alexander 1987) and that is consistent with the principles of a pedagogy of possibility. This approach stands in stark contrast to the authoritarian nature of schooling in South Africa, in which the state controls departments of education, departments control inspectors, inspectors control teachers, and teachers control students. As one black teacher said of the school inspectors:

> They're always visiting us and checking up on what we're doing! Every second week they're there. They make sure that we stick to the syllabus. They listen to our lessons. They look at the tests we set. They're there to control us, man, not to help us. With all this inspection, there's no time left for real education—only for drilling students. (cited in Christie 1985, p. 149)

Simon's (1987) views on what constitutes a "project of possibility" provide a theoretical framework for understanding the principles outlined above.

> A project of possibility...constitutes an agenda well beyond conventional notions of equal opportunity. Equal opportunity is defined in reference to an individual's position within given state or market-regulated social forms. Within a given form it means equal access to comparable opportunities provided within that form, be it a job, education, housing, protection, etc. A project of possibility on the other hand would require that we expand the range of both

capacities and forms within our communities. The agenda is to create practices that encourage, make possible, and enable the realization of differentiated human capacities. (p. 374)

It is clear that proponents of People's English do not view it as one of the "New Englishes" such as Indian English, Nigerian English, or Singaporean English (Kachru 1986, p. 121). People's English is not distinguished syntactically, semantically, or phonetically from the spectrum of English usage currently found in South Africa. Thus, it does not operate within a sociolinguistic frame of reference. If it did, it might have been referred to as South African English or Azanian English. The intention, however, is not to distinguish People's English from British English or American English, but People's English from Apartheid English.

The issues at stake here are *not* the linguistic features of English spoken in South Africa, but the central political issues of how English is to be taught in the schools; who has access to the language; how English is implicated in the power relations dominant in South Africa; and the effect of English on the way speakers of the language perceive themselves, their society, and the possibilities for change in that society. Thus, in South Africa, where language is an ongoing site of struggle, People's English is best understood as a counterdiscourse to the dominant discourse in which the English language is implicated in the current power relations in the country.

It follows that People's English is not conceived of as an English for nonnative speakers of English alone (M. Gardiner, personal communication, July 11, 1988). It is an English for all those people who support the principles and methods of People's English, whether black or white, rich or poor, male or female, native speaker of English or native speaker of Zulu, Xhosa, Sotho, or Afrikaans. What pedagogical tools, then, would proponents of People's English advocate? What content would best express the spirit of People's English?

The comic book as a pedagogical tool of People's English

An example of how an antiapartheid organization, the South African Council of Higher Education (SACHED), has given expression to a pedagogy of possibility in the teaching of English was the production and publication in June 1988 of *Down Second Avenue: The Comic*, which is based on the novel of the same name by esteemed South African writer Ezekial Mphahlele. It describes in pictorial form the experiences of the writer growing up under apartheid and his decision to go into exile in Nigeria. The first half of the comic book contains the pictorial story itself, and the second half of the book contains many interesting exercises that help readers to engage with the text as well as to develop their own writing and reading skills in imaginative and interactive ways. At the end of the comic book is a suggested bibliography of books for readers at different levels.

The organization that published the comic is unequivocal in its social vision. It describes itself on the inside cover of the comic as follows:

The SACHED Trust is an educational organization which aims to counter the imbalance created by the apartheid education system. The Trust is committed to establishing participatory, non-discriminatory and non-authoritarian learning processes. It seeks to transfer skills and resources in such a way that organisations, communities and individuals are empowered to take charge of their own projects.

The imaginative exercises and tasks set out in the second half of the comic provide many opportunities for exploration through language. Readers are encouraged to "work with a friend" in order to develop the skills of reading, writing, and critical thinking. The exercises draw on the visual representations in the comic, and multiple readings of the text are validated. Consider the following instructions:

> Look carefully at the following pictures. How much information can you get from them? Answer the questions about each one.…Compare your answer with a friend's. Pictures can be interpreted in different ways and so your ideas may differ. That is why we have not given you any answers to refer to. (South African Council of Higher Education, 1988, p. 15)

In addition, the text is punctuated with requests for readers to respond: "Did you find this comic interesting and enjoyable? Do you think we should produce more comics like this one? Please send us your comments. You may know of other stories which would make exciting comics. Write to…" (inside cover).

The kind of language competence encouraged in the comic, the methods used to enhance this competence, and the content covered in the comic are consistent with the spirit of People's English. The exercises in the comic enable students to "hear what is said and what is hidden; to create; to explore relationships; to read and write with confidence" (National Education Crisis Committee, 1986/1987, p. 39). In addition, they encourage the sharing and pooling of ideas, the collecting and recording of community-based experiences. It is significant that the comic draws attention to the young Mphahlele's developing consciousness: "At first political debates were just a jumble of words to me. Gradually as I listened I began to put in their proper place the scattered experiences of my life in Pretoria. Poverty, police raids, the curfew bell, humiliation…" (South African Council of Higher Education, 1988, p. 5).

The content covered in the comic differs markedly from the kind of content available in state-run English language classrooms. To quote the concerns of a Soweto English teacher:

> The reading books are all about white middle class children in England. This bears no relation to the culture of black children in Soweto—never mind the rural areas. It has nothing to do with the world they experience outside of school. These kinds of books do nothing to instil a love of reading in black children. (cited in Christie 1985, p. 149)

The form within which the content is presented is significant. It makes the writings of a respected black writer accessible to a wide audience, and it does so by utilizing the medium of the comic—an artifact of popular culture. Whereas a literary novel has a limited readership of highly literate people and is generally mediated by the interpretation given it within state-run institutions such as schools and universities, a comic book is far more easily accessible to the general public, is cheaper to buy, and needs no mediation by an external "expert." It becomes part of a popular cultural discourse in which many South Africans can take up subject positions that are outside the control of the state.

Significantly, Giroux and Simon (1988) posit a fundamental similarity between pedagogy and popular culture:

> Both exist as subordinate discourses. For both liberals and radicals, pedagogy is often theorized as what is left after curriculum content is determined. . . . popular culture is still largely defined in the dominant discourse as the cultural residue which remains when high culture is subtracted from the overall totality of cultural practices. (p. 11)

For SACHED, as for Giroux and Simon, the fundamental issue is how a pedagogy of possibility can incorporate aspects of students' lived culture into pedagogical work without depicting the students as exotic or marginal, as an "other" within the dominant hegemonic culture.

The comic book had only just been published when it was banned from distribution. As stated in *Upbeat* magazine (1988):

> If you want a copy of the comic Down Second Avenue you can't have it. The government banned it in July. . . . One reason given by the government for banning this comic was that: "with its bright cover and easily readable contents, this book will be read by thousands of scholars." (p. 3)

Why did the state choose to ban a comic based on a novel that had not only been available to the South African public since 1959 (*Down Second Avenue*, by Ezekial Mphahlele, Faber and Faber, London 1959), but had also appeared in the comic section of *Upbeat* magazine in 1981? It is likely that the state saw the comic book as a threat to its control over what is to be read, by whom, where, and for what purposes. If "thousands of scholars" had access to such a counter-discourse, the South African state's authority would certainly be challenged.

However, attempts by the state to stifle People's Education and People's English may be successful only insofar as they may drive the movement underground or curtail its activities. The state may be less successful in stifling a vision of a world that is "not yet." In the words of Alexander (1987):

> We have in the eighties in South Africa the great opportunity provided by the historic crisis into which the education particularly of the black people and their children has been catapulted to generate not only a new vision but also the means by which that vision can be realised. I have no doubt that our educators, our students and our parents will be willing and able to rise to the occasion. (p. 15)

In this section I have argued that People's English represents a pedagogy of possibility in the teaching of English in South Africa. The production of *Down Second Avenue: The Comic* provides an exciting example of how a text can be used to promote such a pedagogy of possibility in the South African context. Teachers of English in other parts of the world who are interested in opening up possibilities for their students could usefully draw on the South African experience: They could ask themselves the same kinds of questions that led the

People's English Commission to develop a blueprint for the pedagogical practice of English in South Africa. They could extend their students' focus on communicative competence and the prevailing linguistic rules of use to include the ability to "hear what is said and what is hidden," to deconstruct prevailing discourses in their societies and create new possibilities for themselves and their people.

In the South African context, a pedagogy of possibility in the teaching of English is predicated on the principles of process and consultation, with a view to the enrichment and expansion of human potential—albeit in the face of oppression and struggle. Its implementation is enhanced by a creative and critical use of language in a cooperative setting in which student and community experiences are validated. Teachers of English in other international settings would need to define the characteristics of the People's English that might prevail in their societies.

Conclusion

I would like to conclude on a note of reflection, one alluded to in Widdowson's (1980) research on discourse:

> All movements which attempt to set up a new scheme of values, whether these be political or pedagogic or whatever, are subject to distortion and excess. Practical action requires the consolidation of ideas into simple versions which can be widely understood and applied....The problem of application is: how can we consolidate without misrepresentation? How can we prevent our simple versions from being misleadingly simplistic? (p. 234)

In my attempt to locate People's English within the framework of a pedagogy of possibility, I hope I have not been guilty of misrepresentation. Equally, I hope that my attempt to give concrete expression to the principles of a pedagogy of possibility has not been misleadingly simplistic.

Clearly, a pedagogy of possibility will take on different forms at different times and in different places, and it must be understood with reference to the historical discourse within which it is located. But because a project of possibility addresses the relationship between language and the enhancement of human possibility, it has relevance to pedagogy in general and to the teaching of English in particular. A pedagogy of possibility allows for a reassessment and reconceptualization of the nature of language and of the role of communicative competence in the teaching of English internationally as well as providing a theoretical framework in which to analyze a dynamic counterdiscourse in South Africa—a counterdiscourse that may well extend beyond the borders of the country. It has indeed informed my practice as an ESL teacher, and in my view it opens up possibilities for the role of English internationally.

References

Alexander, N. (1987). Fundamentals of a pedagogy of liberation for South Africa/Azania in the eighties. *CEAPA* 2(1), 12–15. Johannesburg: Centre for Enrichment in African Political Affairs.

Belsey, C. (1980). *Critical practice*. London: Methuen.

Brumfit, C.J., & Johnson, K. (Eds). (1979). *The communicative approach to language teaching*. Oxford: Oxford University Press.

Canale, M., & Swain, M. (1980). Theoretical bases of communicative approaches to second language teaching and testing. *Applied Linguistics, 1*, 1–47.

Cherryholmes, C. (1988). *Power and criticism: Poststructural investigations in education*. New York: Teachers College Press.

Christie, P. (1985). *The right to learn: The struggle for education in South Africa*. Johannesburg: South African Council of Higher Education/Ravan.

Cooke, D. (1988). Ties that constrict: English as a Trojan horse. In A. Cumming, A. Gagné, & J. Dawson (Eds.), *Awareness: Proceedings of the 1987 TESL Ontario Conference* (pp. 56–62). Toronto: TESL Ontario.

Crystal, D. (Ed.). (1980). *A first dictionary of linguistics and phonetics*. London: Andre Deutsch.

Dickinson, L. (1987). *Self-instruction in language learning*. Cambridge: Cambridge University Press.

Foucault, M. (1984). *The Foucault reader* (P. Rabinow, Ed.). New York: Pantheon Books.

Gardiner, M. (1987). Liberating language: People's English for the future. In *People's Education: A collection of articles* (pp. 56–62). Bellville, South Africa: University of the Western Cape, Centre for Adult and Continuing Education.

Giroux, H.A., & Simon, R. (1984). Curriculum study and cultural politics. *Journal of Education, 166*, 226–238.

Giroux, H.A., & Simon, R. (1988). Schooling, popular culture, and a pedagogy of possibility. *Journal of Education, 170*, 9–26.

Halliday, M.A.K (1973). *Explorations in the functions of language*. London: Edward Arnold.

Hymes, D. (1979). On communicative competence. In C.J. Brumfit & K. Johnson (Eds.), *The communicative approach to language teaching* (pp. 5–26). Oxford: Oxford University Press.

Janks, H. (in press). Contested terrain: English education in South Africa, 1948–1987. In I. Goodson & P. Medway (Eds.), *Bringing English to order*. Basingstoke, England: Falmer.

Judd, E. (1983). TESOL as a political act: A moral question. In J. Handscombe, R.A. Orem, & B.P. Taylor (Eds.), *ON TESOL '83* (pp. 265–273). Washington, DC: TESOL.

Judd, E. (1987). Teaching English to speakers of other languages: A political act and a moral question. *TESOL Newsletter, 21*(1), 15–16.

Kachru, B.J. (1986). *The alchemy of English: The spread, functions and models of non-native Englishes*. Oxford: Pergamon Press.

McCrum, R., Cran, W., & MacNeil, R. (1986). *The story of English*. London: Faber & Faber/BBC.

Muller, J. (1987). People's Education for People's Power and the National Education Crisis Committee: The choreography of educational struggle. In *People's Education: A collection of articles* (pp. 106–113). Bellville, South Africa: University of the Western Cape, Centre for Adult and Continuing Education.

National Education Crisis Committee. (1987). NECC press release: 1986. In *People's Education for teachers* (pp. 38–39). Bellville, South Africa: University of the Western Cape, Faculty of Education.

Ndebele, N. (1987). The English language and social change in South Africa. *The English Academy Review, 4*, 1–16.

Peirce, B. (1987, April). *ESL under apartheid: Language in transition*. Paper presented at the 21st Annual TESOL Convention, Miami Beach, FL.

SASPU [South African Students Press Union] *National* staff. (1987). "People's Education for People's Power" loud and clear...In *People's Education: A collection of articles* (p. 29). Bellville, South Africa: University of the Western Cape, Centre for Adult and Continuing Education. (Original article published February 1986)

Saussure, F. de (1959). *Course in general linguistics*. New York: McGraw-Hill.

Simon, R. (1987). Empowerment as a pedagogy of possibility. *Language Arts, 64*, 370–383.

Simon, R. (1988). For a pedagogy of possibility. In J. Smyth (Ed.), *The Critical Pedagogy Networker, 1*(1), 1–4. Victoria, Australia: Deakin University, School of Education.

Sinclair, J., & Coulthard, R.M. (1975). *Towards an analysis of discourse*. London: Oxford University Press.

South African Council of Higher Education. (1988). *Down second avenue: The comic*. Johannesburg: Author/Ravan.

Terdiman, R. (1985). *Discourse/counter discourse*. New York: Cornell University Press.

Upbeat staff. (1988). Comic banned. *Upbeat, 7*, p. 3. Johannesburg: South African Council of Higher Education.

Walters, L. (1989). Language and politics: A new marriage? *TESOL Newsletter, 23*(1), 1, 5, 20.

Weedon, C. (1987). *Feminist practice and poststructuralist theory*. London: Basil Blackwell.

Widdowson, H.G. (1978). *Teaching language as communication*. London: Oxford University Press.

Widdowson, H.G. (1980). Conceptual and communicative functions in written discourse. *Applied Linguistics, 1*, 234–243.

FIFTEEN

Riverwest Neighbors Win New Fratney School

Sue Bietila   David Levine

This September, Fratney Street Elementary School will become the home of a bold initiative in innovative education. Responding to a groundswell of community support, and a carefully designed plan submitted by the "Neighbors for a New Fratney," the School Board has designated the school a "Two-way Bilingual, Whole Language, Site-based managed Neighborhood Specialty school."

On the night of January 19, seventy-five parents, teachers, and community activists braved freezing rain to show the School Board's Instruction and Human Relations Committee their support of the proposal. After listening to seventeen people testify in favor of the plan School Board president David Cullen said, "I appreciate everyone coming out here this evening. I was surprised—with the bad weather I thought we'd come out and see a near empty auditorium as we usually do. I think it's a tribute to that neighborhood and the people involved in this proposal."

The opportunity for a new program at Fratney emerged because the present staff and student body at Fratney will move in April to the newly re-built Gaenslen, a nearby school designed to integrate a combined population of disabled and able bodied students. Several parents and teachers who live in Riverwest began meeting to discuss how the soon to be vacated Fratney could become the home of a program which capitalized on the unique features of the neighborhood. As Marty Horning, a Riverwest parent and MPS [Milwaukee Public School] teacher put it, "We started to dream about a school that would provide the highest quality education for all of our children, black, white, and Hispanic."

Source: Sue Bietila and David Levine, "Riverfront Neighbors Win New Fratney School," *Rethinking Schools* 2, 3 (1988): 1, 7. Reprinted with permission.

A different kind of school

The new Fratney will be built on four essential features: relying on the cultural strengths of the neighborhood, teaching all students Spanish and English, involving parents and teachers in decision-making, and basing instruction on the child-centered "whole language" approach.

Local cultural resources will be easy to find. The Riverwest community is composed of blacks, whites, and Hispanics. Over the past several years its residents have initiated cultural, political, and artistic activities notable for their diversity and vitality. Food, housing, kindergarten, and childcare co-operatives have been set up to meet basic needs and enhance the cohesiveness of the neighborhood.

Churches, block clubs, and political groups generate a lively community life. Many craftspeople and artists have made Riverwest their home.

The New Fratney proposal anticipates that the school will make heavy use of these resources: "The community can provide tutors, interesting visitors, artists in residence (paid and volunteer), financial support in fundraising campaigns, and places where students and teachers can visit and study (such as local businesses, community organizations, art galleries, and workshops.)" Denise Crumble, director of the Inner City Arts Council and a Riverwest parent for the past eight years, explained the importance of a strong school–community link this way: "I'm real concerned about stabilizing the neighborhood and helping to create a program that's going to make parents more active in the school. I think this kind of a program goes a long way toward doing that. It builds upon the strength that already exists in the community."

For many parents, a key drawing card of the school will be the chance to provide their children with an integrated education without busing. As the plan explains, "The multiracial character of our neighborhood offers the opportunity to create a naturally integrated school with little busing, drawing on the diversity of the populace to enhance the educational program. The actual content of the curriculum will reflect and be strengthened by the multiracial character of the surrounding neighborhood. The development of such a specialty would be an incentive for families to remain in this neighborhood, thus stabilizing an integrated housing pattern."

This integrated school in an integrated neighborhood will be an excellent context in which to use two-way bilingual instruction. The plan proposes that half the student body be children who speak Spanish as their first language and half be students whose first language is English. Children will learn to read initially in their mother tongue, and then be well on their way to becoming bilingual and biliterate by the end of fifth grade. Bilingual education, besides its increasing practical value, will give all students more tolerance of and appreciation for other cultures. And as Rita Tenorio, a bilingual kindergarten teacher, pointed out at the hearing, integrated bilingual education encourages a healthy interdependence. "Each child who comes into the program would have something to offer another student in that same classroom. No matter who you were, or where you came from, the child would have something, their language, that is needed by another child in the same class.

The self-esteem of all children would be enhanced in such a situation, and especially in the context of a whole-language approach which utilizes and builds on the language and experience of each child."

"Whole-language" instruction will also be a pedagogical cornerstone of the program. According to the proposal, this means an emphasis will be placed "on using language skills — reading, writing, speaking and listening — as the means to learn and acquire language as well as a way to learn about the real world. This 'real use' will be valued over drills and practice exercises, not only because such use provides integrated practice in phonics, spelling, semantics, etc., but also because it shows children that language is for making meaning, for accomplishing something."

The final key element of the new Fratney will be an approach to site-based management which gives teachers and parents substantive involvement in major decisions concerning the school. To make this possible, the New Fratney group hopes to secure funds to hire three "parent literacy organizers." Besides helping parents and community members become active in all aspects of the life of the school, these organizers will "work to develop a full range of literacy activities in the school and community." Such activities would include training classroom parent volunteers, planning cultural events that include both parents and students, and helping parents establish positive homework environments and habits at home.

Overcoming obstacles

From the outset, most school board members were warmly supportive of the efforts of the New Fratney group. Nevertheless, the group had to contend with substantial obstacles in order to win MPS approval of the plan.

One serious objection to the proposal came from parents and community members associated with the new Gaenslen school. Strongly committed to a Gaenslen which would integrate disabled and able bodied students, they were worried that a new attendance area specialty at Fratney would entice many neighborhood students and thereby turn Gaenslen into an inadvertently segregated facility containing mostly disabled students. New Fratney advocates were able to reassure this group by pointing to the demographic realities of the school age population in the area. Because of inadequate space in existing neighborhood schools, over 2,600 students in the Fratney Street district and the six adjacent districts are bused out to other schools. Thus there should be plenty of students to fill up both the new Fratney and the new Gaenslen.

Another problem arose because MPS had originally planned to turn Fratney into an "Exemplary Teaching Center." The staff at this center was to be comprised of "master teachers" with master degrees and at least ten years teaching experience. Their job would have been to work with MPS teachers who were having classroom difficulties and were brought in for 2 and 1/2 week long training sessions. The administration was interested in combining this plan with the New Fratney proposal, but the New Fratney group saw the two proposals as fundamentally incompatible. The school board may in part have been swayed in favor of the community proposal by the fact that a teacher training center could be implemented at any building in the school system while the New Fratney proposal can only unfold as envisioned at its present site.

The future

Exhilarated by the their hard fought victory, members of "Neighbors for a New Fratney" are beginning to grapple with the difficult challenge of organizing an entirely new school from the ground up. Their desire to see the school open in September of 1988 can only be realized if they establish a strong working relationship with Dr. Faison and the MPS administrators directly responsible for implementation of the program. A mountain of work lies between the School Board's approval of the initial plan and the actual opening of the school. A principal, an entire staff, and a student body must be recruited. A curriculum and a system of school governance must both be created. Substantial building improvements are also needed.

The members of Neighbors for a New Fratney face this mountain of work with some trepidation, but also with a sustaining vision of a very different kind of school. In a letter of support to the School Board, Dan Grego, director of Shalom High School, eloquently summed up the potential value of the New Fratney: "Here in one package you have everything that studies have shown to be necessary for the creation of a truly effective school, dedicated and empowered educators, concerned and involved parents, site-based management in an integrated neighborhood. If the parents and teachers of every school would be so organized and enthusiastic, Milwaukee Public Schools would become the best in the country."

SIXTEEN

A Vision in Two Languages: Reflections on a Two-way Bilingual Program
Rita Tenorio

I n June of 1989 when the last students said goodbye to their teachers and friends for the summer, La Escuela Fratney had reached a milestone — we had completed our first year. More accurately, we had survived our first year and all the difficulties it presented. It was a time for congratulations and celebration, but more importantly it was a time for reflection and planning for year two. I felt the greatest successes came in the building of our "identity," in the way we became a school community of students, staff, and parents. My greatest concerns were in how we would strengthen our program to ensure the quality of instruction for this new community.

Our program is designed to focus on several important components: multi-cultural education, a whole language approach to literacy, cooperative learning, and school based management. Other schools in Milwaukee are also dealing with one or more of these areas, but what makes our school unique is the addition of a dual language program, a "two-way" bilingual component that is the only one of its kind in Wisconsin.

La Escuela Fratney is one of fifteen Milwaukee Public Schools with a bilingual program. In our city, the struggles of the Hispanic community to ensure quality education for their children took the form of parents, teachers, students, and community members demanding bilingual programs that would meet the academic needs of the students. The school board and the state legislature made the commitment to bilingual education in the early 1970s. Because the Hispanic community continues to advocate for quality, Milwaukee has gained a reputation as having one of the best bilingual programs in the country. MPS has a "developmental" program, a Spanish maintenance program in which both the first and second languages of the students are valued and

Source: Rita Tenorio, "A Vision in Two Languages: Reflections on a Two-Way Bilingual Program," *Rethinking Schools* 4, 4 (1990): 11–12. Reprinted with permission.

nurtured from kindergarten through 12th grade. Becoming bilingual and bi-literate is the primary focus. Students learn English during classroom instruction and with English as a Second Language (ESL) teachers. Yet, one of the greatest strengths of the program is that the students' native language is developed too. Cultural pride is an important goal of the program. The bilingual schools serve approximately 2000 students in Milwaukee, and are located in several parts of the city. While all of them are under the "bilingual department" umbrella, each has its own individual character and strengths based on the school population, curriculum focus and local emphasis.

Two-way bilingual education

La Escuela Fratney was opened in 1988 as the result of an unusual effort by the community that surrounds the school. Faced with the opportunity to build curriculum from scratch, the parents, teachers and community members who made up "Neighbors for a New Fratney" decided they wanted to design a bilingual program that would build on the strengths of the local multicultural community. We wanted all the classrooms and students to be involved in the bilingual program in order to avoid separating the language groups and to give meaning and purpose to the acquisition of two languages.

Recent research on second language acquisition confirms that children can excel in two languages and that they benefit from early exposure to the second language. Over time, cognitive abilities are strengthened as a result of learning another language. It is no wonder that parents in middle and upper class communities value second language acquisition for their children. Foreign language has held high prestige in these communities for a very long time and "immersion" programs for English-speaking students are very popular. The research also points to the importance of developing a child's native language first. It has been shown that a student's abilities in the second language can actually surpass those of the native speaker if they have a rich understanding of their first language. Concepts and skills that are acquired in the child's first language are easily transferred to the child's second language.

The "two-way" model dispels the notion of bilingual education as a remedial or compensatory program. It builds on the research and promotes the desirability of bilingualism for all students, both English and Spanish speaking.

The two-way model does this by striving for a 50/50 balance of native English and Spanish speakers in each classroom. All students are learning a second language. Both languages are valued equally and all students receive instruction for significant amounts of time in each language. The focus of instruction is primarily academic; students are gaining knowledge in many subjects in two languages. Language is a vehicle for instruction, not simply an end in itself. I am not "teaching Spanish," but rather teaching kindergarten "in Spanish."

At Fratney, we use the "Natural Approach" to second language learning as described by Steven Krashen and Tracy Terrell in their book, *The Natural Approach* (*Alemany Press 1983*). It promotes second language acquisition through the "real use" of the language for communicative purposes. The authors state: "Language is best taught when it is used to transmit messages, not when it is explicitly taught for conscious learning." This approach works nicely alongside a "whole language" program for literacy where the focus is giving students many experiences with reading and writing and involving them in activities with true meaning and purpose.

When students of both language groups come together in a two-way program they see first-hand the value of the second language. The program fosters interaction of children from a variety of races, cultures and two language groups from early on. On one day, the English-speakers may have "an advantage," but when the target language becomes Spanish on the next day, the students will see a whole different group of their peers excel. The students become the language models for each other and they are motivated to learn the second language both out of the need to learn the content being taught and the desire to communicate with their peers.

First year struggles

This plan, this ideal, seemed so clear and feasible to us as we began in September of 1988. The reality was somewhat different. At the kindergarten level, we did not have the 50/50 balance of language. Only one third of my students spoke Spanish. While we strove to put a whole language literacy program into place, we quickly realized the difficulty of finding quality materials in Spanish for the emergent reader. As strict as I tried to be in implementing an "alternate day approach," one day in English, one day in Spanish, the tendency for students to use English was an ever present dilemma. Even the Spanish dominant children were quickly "pulled" into English by their desire to acquire this very important tool.

As we reflected on our first year, both five-year-old kindergarten teachers, Betsy May and I, felt that the children learned a great deal in two languages, but we also knew that it wasn't enough. We knew that the Spanish-speakers were not receiving an equal amount of instruction time in their native language. This was significant in light of the research that stressed the importance of developing fully the students' first language. We knew that deep down, English was perceived as more valuable than Spanish, that we were still lacking an adequate supply of Spanish materials, and that the class coming in September would still be short of the 50/50 balance.

The new model

Over the summer we contemplated a change in our model — a pilot of sorts to try to improve the instruction in both languages and really focus on the objective of promoting bilingualism in all of the students. In August at a "Welcome to Kindergarten" picnic, Betsy and I presented the plan for the year to the parents of the incoming kindergartners:

- Betsy and I would team-teach and together be responsible for the 50 students.
- The students would be divided into two balanced groups, the Rainbow and the Stars with speakers of English and Spanish in both groups.

- Betsy would teach the English component of the program; I would teach the Spanish component.
- An alternate day model would be used where the students would spend one day in the English environment in Betsy's classroom and the next day in Spanish in mine.

We hoped this model would insure the balance of the two languages and offer consistent, in-depth development of each. All the Spanish resources would be in one location rather than two. Most importantly, we felt that this model would greatly encourage the use of the second language. We hoped that these separate environments would "create a boundary" for each language, making its use an absolute necessity for both teacher and students. We felt that this model would give stronger meaning and purpose to the use of the second language.

The parents had many questions. Some had serious concerns about the ability of the children to adjust to such a model with two environments and two teachers. Betsy and I answered the parents' questions as best we could, asking their support and trust as we began the implementation. It would be a learning experience for us all.

As one might expect, the children adjusted quickly to the logistical aspects of the program, while we as teachers struggled over how to deal with attendance, journal folders, resting mats, and assessment. We gradually increased the amount of time in the target language over the first weeks until the children were comfortable spending an entire day in Spanish or English. Since we each taught all the students, we had the luxury or rearranging the groups to better balance them in terms of language dominance and verbal abilities. I used the reading funds available to order Spanish language materials, buying multiple copies of books, as well as acquiring resources for science and social studies.

While Betsy and I saw growth in both languages from early on in the year, there were many complications and concerns too. Finding enough time each week to collaborate and plan was difficult. We were able to schedule music and art with our specialists back-to-back, and we have used our before-, after-school and recess times to the best advantage. It is still not enough. We struggled with the issue that initially some students "preferred" one class or the other. It was hard when the English speakers would cheer, knowing they would be in Betsy's class the next day. We both spent time reassuring English-speaking parents that their children were learning even though they were not yet "producing" a lot of Spanish. Being consistent and supportive on discipline matters was another challenge.

Gradually the students felt comfortable enough to begin speaking in their second language. By January, many of the English speakers were experimenting with language, "babbling" in Spanish, trying to use as many words as they could. I went through another phase of trying to convince the Spanish-speakers to "stay" in Spanish when they were in the Spanish classroom. They too, were experimenting in their second language and were anxious to try it out.

As the second semester concludes I see huge gains in the language abilities of the students. Children who were fearful and hesitant to take risks in Spanish are now comfortable and outspoken in the group. While at one point it was hard to stay in Spanish all day, we now find that there isn't enough time to "get everything in each day." At the beginning of the year I had to focus parts of each day on building vocabulary and learning words and phrases in Spanish. Now for the most part all the students participate in the content area instruction that takes place each day. They all add to the discussion of Earth Day, the parts of plants or the translated version of Leo Leonni's "Swimmy."

In the native Spanish speakers I see better growth this year in their literacy skills. Their self-esteem is enhanced as they become the language resources for the English speakers. The Spanish-speakers can "read" a Big Book to the whole group. They beam with pride as they stand up to tell a story, or share a book they've written in the writing center. Because Spanish is "equal" to English in school, there is more emphasis on developing the language, and the native speakers have benefited.

As we watch them interact with each other, I feel that they are gaining a sensitivity to the process of learning a second language. They have learned to be patient with each other's mistakes and take great pleasure in coming to their teacher with the exciting news that "Reinaldo said good morning. He spoke English!" Once children are familiar with the words for common classroom objects, and phrases used in daily routines, they know that I will expect them to use those words and phrases. While they know that I really do understand their comment or question in English, they also know that I will only accept words in Spanish at certain times. If they forget or "get stuck," there is always someone else, one of their peers, who is ready to be their resource. We try to stress that they can help each other, rely on each other, and that each student, Black, white and Hispanic has something important to give to the group in his or her language.

Parents respond

Now that we've reached the end of our second year, it's time again to celebrate and reflect. As teachers, Betsy and I have seen the successes. The growth of the students in both their first and second languages has shown us that implementing this model was a good idea. Beyond ourselves, though, we needed to hear the responses of the parents, and so an after school meeting was scheduled to listen to their feedback and concerns. Almost 30 people attended, and the positive response to this year's instruction was overwhelming. The same parents who in August were concerned that their child would be receiving only "half as much" instruction were now testifying that their child had gained a great deal of knowledge in two languages. The children were not "losing" their academics while learning a second language. As one parent stated, "He's picking up things in English that I thought would take a lot longer. It's carrying over into his reading. I think he's learned a whole lot this year!"

Many parents felt that it was "good that they hear things in both English and Spanish." The children were developing interest in other languages too. Parents were happy that their children had the opportunity to learn from two teachers and experience two styles of teaching. They saw their children learning to be flexible and comfortable in different situations.

Both English and Spanish speaking parents commented that they now saw the advantages of separating and putting equal emphasis on both languages. One Spanish-speaking mother spoke of how her son now sees Spanish as being "validated" and not just something that she and his grandmother feel is important. School becomes more connected to home. One parent said that "Children see the advantage of being bilingual at an early age."

Parents also raised concerns. What about the different personalities of the students — those who are not so anxious to use the second language? How long will it take for the children to be really bilingual? How can I help my child in the second language when I don't know it? They raised concerns about reading, being "immersed" in the second language, and planning time for teachers. The biggest concern that afternoon, though, was "Will the program model continue for them next year?" The strong consensus was that it should.

Challenges ahead

Next year, the staff at La Escuela Fratney will take on the challenge of expanding the "two environment" model to the other grade levels. We must strive to provide the best environment — one that fosters growth in two languages, that builds the self-esteem of all children and stretches them academically as well. Some issues will be ever present: how to provide planning time and inservice for teachers, how to best teach reading and writing in two languages, how to recruit and maintain a school population that reflects the 50/50 language balance.

There are other issues though that will challenge us even more — questions we must raise if we are to really provide a program that reflects the vision we hold. Will the "reliance" that this year's kindergartners of many cultures have on each other carry over into the next grade and beyond? How can we help them to continue to see each others' strengths, here at school and in their own communities as well? What structures, what vehicles can we as educators put in place to promote a multicultural experience that goes beyond the end of the school day?

While we may have a balance of language at school, the reality in our society is that in the minds of many people Spanish is certainly not equal to English. Can we help our students to understand why that is and challenge them to reconsider that perception? We must also challenge our own perceptions that reflect a bias toward English. For example, parents and teachers will express their concern about the length of time English speakers are immersed in Spanish. Parents raised concerns about how much Spanish the children would be comfortable with in the program. Teachers feel unsure about "keeping" the children in Spanish all day. Yet our sensitivity doesn't always extend to what the Spanish-speakers are experiencing in the English environment. Maybe because English is the dominant language, we somehow feel that the Spanish-speaking students will cope more easily and adjust more quickly. Yet, anyone who has been immersed in a foreign language knows the difficulty that both language groups face. As teachers, we must strive to lessen the anxiety for all students.

The true test of our vision will come as these children grow. Success will be evident when the learning that takes place at school begins to connect with what goes on at home. We'll see it when students are eager to carry their projects home to share and when parents feel welcome and eager to be at school to share in their child's experience here. La Escuela Fratney is breaking new ground. Children, parents and educators of many cultures and two language groups are offering an exciting vision of bilingual, multicultural education. In this vision bilingualism is an advantage, a strength, and all students can benefit from learning in two languages.

SEVENTEEN

Commercial Reading Materials, a Technological Ideology, and the Deskilling of Teachers

Patrick Shannon

One way to think about commercial reading materials in elementary classrooms is to consider the array of offerings they present to teachers. For example, these materials include (*a*) anthologies of stories and essays considered appropriate for students of various reading levels, (*b*) a scope and sequence of objectives reflecting areas that are often considered necessary for children in order to learn to read, (*c*) directions for instruction and practice activities to meet the stated objectives, (*d*) tests to determine whether objectives have been met, and (*e*) recording systems to keep track of student progress. Perhaps all of these features could be subsumed under the rubric of time saving devices because through the use of one or all of them teachers save production and collection time — the time it would take to produce the materials themselves. Since time seems to be a precious commodity in elementary classrooms, in this one vein alone commercial reading materials do seem to be a boon for elementary teachers.

As with most aspects of life, one must give up something in order to get something in return. Another way to look at commercial reading materials, then, is in terms of what teachers must risk to reap these time-gain benefits and whether or not it is a good exchange. This second perspective is the one I intend to take in this paper (Mills 1959). In this article, I want to explore what teachers give up by using commercial materials by first determining the role of commercial reading materials in American reading instruction and discussing an empirical explanation for that role. Second, I attempt to place this explanation

Source: Patrick Shannon, "Commercial Reading Materials, a Technological Ideology, and the Deskilling of Teachers," *The Elementary School Journal* 87 (1987): 307–329. © 1987 by The University of Chicago. Reprinted with permission.

in the larger social context of twentieth-century Western society and then to return to reading programs via the notion that commercial reading materials are considered the technological solutions to the problems of reading instruction. Third, I compare the ascent of commercial reading materials' importance with the decline of teachers' responsibilities during reading instruction and comment on teachers' reactions to this inversion of the subject and object of teaching. Finally, I evaluate the exchange and describe the constructive core of this seemingly negative perspective (Marcuse 1960) on commercial reading materials in elementary reading programs.

I use the term commercial materials rather than basal materials for two reasons. First, I find it more descriptive of the materials readily available within most elementary classrooms. Basal reading series usually connote the readers, teacher's manuals, workbooks, worksheets, management component, and skill kits developed and produced by one commercial publishing company. For example, Aukerman (1981) lists 15 basal reading series, all labeled by commercial publishing companies. Yet, no mention is made of the plethora of other workbooks, worksheets, or kits that students are asked to complete daily. Commercial reading materials is a more inclusive term. Second, I believe and argue in this paper that it is partly the commercial production of these materials that gives school personnel the mistaken notion that the materials can teach students to read. The distance of the production process from classrooms, the glitter of advertising, and the number available make the materials mysterious to a degree. The term "commercial reading materials," then, also signals this mystification in the way that the label "basal" cannot.

The role of commercial reading materials

As Nila Banton Smith (1965) demonstrated in her historical treatment of American reading instruction, it is often difficult to tell where commercial reading materials end and where teachers' reading instruction begins. Smith devoted half of her 426 pages to detailed descriptions of reading materials and another third to an explanation of how those materials were used from colonial times until 1965, when the updated edition of her book was published by the International Reading Association. Smith's emphasis suggests that American teachers of reading have routinely used commercial materials. Moreover, Smith implies that progress in reading instruction in this century can be related directly to the improvements made in commercial materials based on scientific study of reading and instruction.

In this paper, science is defined as the attempt to discover lawlike generalizations about physical, natural, and social phenomena. The principal assumptions of this science are that these generalizations are universal, not dependent on situational constraints or values, and that any phenomena can be divided into discrete causal variables that can be measured quantitatively. Popkewitz (1984) labels this definition "empirical-analytical science" and states that it is the definition most often used by both "hard" and "soft" scientists. Mosenthal suggests that most educational scientists use this definition and seek literal definitions of progress by "a conscious attempt to apply definitions of progress in the physical and natural sciences to descriptions of progress in the social sciences" (1985, p. 5). Perhaps the best objective evidence of the association of science and reading instruction is the development in the early 1920s of the teacher's manual, which was to direct teachers and students in using the materials during reading instruction.

Others were more explicit concerning this putative relationship between science and commercial reading materials. Donovan says, "In these places we find teachers instructing children as they themselves were taught, absolutely ignorant and oblivious that science had discovered for us truths and that little children are entitled to the benefit of these discoveries" (1928, p. 107) and "One of the most potent factors in the spreading of the results of research is through a well prepared set of readers and their manuals" (1928, p. 106). "Furthermore," Gray states, "prepared materials are, as a rule, more skillfully organized and are technically superior to those developed daily in classrooms. Because they follow a sequential plan, the chance for so called 'gaps in learning' is greatly reduced" (1936, pp. 90–91). Finally, "In general, it appears that systematic reading instruction on the differentiated basis can be achieved, for the time being, through carefully prepared teacher's manuals for basal materials" (Betts 1943, p. 59).

Early professional books on reading and methods textbooks for training teachers also carried the message that scientific instruction depended on the use of commercial reading material according to the directions in teacher's manuals. In *Silent and Oral Reading: A Practical Handbook of Methods Based on the Most Recent Scientific Investigation*, Stone suggested that "the best practice will involve the use of all three types of primers during the first few months of instruction" (1922, p. 45). Dolch (1950) and Durrell (1940) were more forthright in their support of the primacy of commercial materials. Durrell writes, "The advantage of orderly procedures in reading instruction is such that few, if any, teachers can serve all pupils well by incidental or improvised reading methods. . . . The well planned basal-reading systems presented by experienced textbook publishers have many advantages. . . . A detailed study of the manuals of basal-reading systems is the first step to learning how to teach reading" (1940, p. 22). Furthermore, Dolch states, "A basic reader is really one part of a 'system for teaching reading.' This system includes the basic books themselves, the workbooks that go with them, and the teacher's manual, which tells what to do with the textbooks, what to do with the workbook, and also tells all the other activities a teacher should go through in order to do a complete job teaching reading" (1950, p. 319).

Authors of recent reading methods textbooks seem equally convinced of the advantages of teachers relying on commercial reading materials during reading instruction (Shannon 1983a). In a systematic analysis of a random sample of six (of 30) methods textbooks in which we analyzed physical characteristics, scope and emphasis, suggestions for use, and language of description, seven reader reviewers concluded that five of the six textbooks presented three reasons for a relatively unqualified endorsement of the use of commercial reading materials: (*a*) the reading selections are of high quality, (*b*) the teacher's manuals offer suggestions for comprehensive and systematic instruction, and (*c*) the materials are based on scientific investigation of the reading process. If space devoted to commercial materials can be taken as one indication of an author's commitment to teachers' use of commercial materials, five authors devote between 11 and 36 pages to these materials, accompanied by six to 19 reproductions from the materials themselves. In comparison, they devoted between zero and 1.5 pages to a discussion of perhaps the most important comprehension skill, main idea. In addition, the language these authors used suggested their endorsement. Terms like "best routines," "developed by teams of reading experts," "bring children to a higher degree of reading proficiency," "objective, tightly structured, and logically ordered," and "with sufficient repetition to insure mastery" appeared frequently in five of the six methods textbooks examined. The author who qualified her endorsement suggested that commercial reading materials were more a product of logic than science and that teachers should be selective in their use of the suggestions in teacher's manuals. Although she set aside 36 pages for discussion of commercial materials and provided 40 reproductions, she qualified her endorsement with the following: "more a product of convention than research," "claims and guarantees... await...verification" and "the perfect materials do not exist."

In fact, other experts believe that commercial materials recently have become an impediment rather than an impetus to scientific reading instruction (see Anderson, Osborn, and Tierney 1984): "Currently, there would appear to be a lag as long as 15–20 years in getting research findings into practice" (Anderson et al., 1984, p. x). That is, current reliance on commercial materials precludes teachers' implementing the findings of the most recent research. Since research on reading has more than doubled in the past decade (Weintraub et al. 1982), this gap between commercial reading materials and what is currently considered scientific reading instruction may indeed be wide. To remedy this situation, the contributors to *Learning to Read in American Schools: Basal Readers and Content Texts* (Anderson et al., 1984) suggest that a concerted effort be made to bring about appropriate alterations of those materials. "It stands to reason therefore that researchers who wish to have scholarship influence practice ought to give high priority to interacting with publishers" (Anderson et al. 1984, p. ix). Apparently, commercial reading materials are still considered to be the appropriate vehicle for "scientific" reading instruction.

To be sure, not all those concerned with reading instruction in the twentieth century have agreed that commercial reading materials are appropriate. Huey commented that "after all we have thus far been content with trial and error; too often allowing the publishers to be our jury, and a real rationalization of the process of inducing the child into the practice of reading has not been made" (1908/1968, p. 9). Germane and Germane found that "unfortunately too many teachers use only one book—the regular school reader" (1922, p. 92), which precluded teachers from encouraging the "more effective and efficient" practice of silent reading. Boney (1938, 1939) offered three criticisms of the *Thirty-sixth Yearbook of the National Society for the Study of Education's* wholehearted support for teachers' use of commercial reading materials: (1) trade books had better content, (2) commercial materials were expensive, and (3) their use did not ensure thoughtful instruction.

More recently, others have found that teachers' adherence to the suggestions in teacher's manuals precludes attention to students' individual needs (Austin and Morrison 1963; Durkin 1974; Goodlad 1970), that it stymies attempts at instructional innovation (Chall 1967; Rosecky 1978; Singer 1977), and that it defines schooling, literacy, and childhood in less than optimal ways (Freebody and Baker 1985). One researcher went so far as to suggest, in a description of management components of commercial materials, that "literacy in this competency-based, highly structured, empty technology is reduced to a tight sequence of arbitrary skills. The teacher becomes a technician, part of a delivery system" (Goodman 1979, p. 663).

Despite these frequent objections, teachers' use of commercial reading materials was virtually universal by the 1960s. In the Columbia-Carnegie Study of Reading Research and Its Communication, Barton and Wilder found that over 90% of the teachers in 300 schools they surveyed used commercial reading materials on "all or most days in the year" (1964, p. 162). By 1977, the percentage was over 94% of a sample of 10,000 elementary teachers (Education Product Information Exchange 1977). Moreover, the teachers in Barton and Wilder's survey suggested that their beliefs concerning reading instruction were formed primarily by the teacher's manual and their practice teaching, and 70% agreed that suggestions in teacher's manuals were based on definite scientific proof. In a series of studies, Durkin (1978–1979, 1981, 1983) found that teachers use commercial materials consistently but that they skip certain parts of suggested lessons to keep their classes running smoothly. Duffy and McIntyre (1980) concluded that teachers typically monitored students' progress through commercial materials, checking the accuracy of their work, and that teachers believe that this monitoring constitutes reading instruction. In their study's conclusion, Barton and Wilder point out an apparent contradiction in teacher thinking: "Teachers think they are professionals — but want to rely on basal readers, graded workbooks, teacher's manuals, and other materials prefabricated by the experts" (1964, p. 382).

Barton and Wilder's (1964) comment suggests that, although teachers may think of themselves as professionals, their heavy reliance on commercial reading materials makes observers of their work skeptical of their professionalism. Professionals control their work and make critical judgments about what procedures and materials are most suitable for specific situations (Lortie 1975). However, advocates of the use of commercial reading materials, and even the authors of the materials (Chall 1967), question teachers' judgment concerning their devoted use of the materials "as if they were divinely inspired" (Durkin 1978, p. 45).

An empirical study of teachers' reliance on commercial reading materials

In an attempt to determine why elementary teachers rely so heavily on commercial reading materials during reading instruction, I sought to identify subjective (Shannon 1982a) and objective (Shannon 1982b) factors that might contribute to this dependence in one large school system. To investigate teachers' beliefs (subjective factors), I developed a 20-item forced-choice questionnaire and a follow-up interview schedule. These survey instruments were based on four hypotheses gleaned from previous studies of elementary reading instruction: (1) teachers are not involved with their instruction (Durkin 1978–1979), (2) teachers believe that commercial reading materials can teach students to read (Austin and Morrison 1963), (3) teachers believe that the materials embody scientific truth (Barton & Wilder 1964), and (4) teachers think that they are fulfilling administrative expectations when they use these materials (Chall 1967). Three openended questions that probed why, how, and when teachers used commercial reading materials were the final component of both the questionnaire and the interviews.

Because teachers do not participate in reading instruction uninfluenced by others, I sought to identify contributing factors beyond teachers' control (objective factors). The investigation of these factors was an attempt to determine the organization and policies of the reading program within the school district. Toward that end, a comparison of classroom teachers', reading teachers', and administrators' perceptions concerning the four hypotheses was made using questionnaire and interview data. I informally observed interactions among these personnel over a 1-year period and made an examination of the school district's printed explanations of the reading program. By placing teachers' subjective opinions among the objective factors, I assumed that I would get a clearer picture of why teachers in this district used commercial reading materials (Shannon 1983b).

The results of the investigation to identify subjective factors suggested that 445 teachers believed foremost that they were fulfilling administrative expectations when they used commercial reading materials (Hypothesis 4). This opinion held across the three types of data collection techniques: forced-choice items, open-ended "why" questions, and interviews. In fact, some teachers ridiculed me for even considering any other hypotheses. This strong belief seemed based primarily on teachers' negative reactions to the district's textbook selection process and its method of monitoring student progress. Twenty-three of the 26 teachers who were interviewed stated that the textbook selection process was controlled too much by administrators. The teachers thought that teachers were underrepresented on the selection committee in comparison with the number of administrators and that the decision to adopt the new edition from the same publisher was made before the committee was even convened. The monitoring system required teachers to record students' criterion-referenced test scores on cards, which reading teachers and principals reviewed biweekly. Most teachers considered this to be pressure to push students through the materials regardless of their reading ability and progress.

However, teachers agreed that basal reading materials can teach reading (Hypothesis 2) and that they are based on science (Hypothesis 3). With the exception of one item, teachers considered themselves involved with their instruction (Hypothesis 1). The exception was that teachers agreed that others could teach reading in the same way as they did, a finding that suggests that teachers devalue the contribution of their individual personalities and intellects to instruction.

The first analysis compared classroom teachers' opinions with those of reading teachers' (N = 23) and administrators (N = 18). There was little disagreement concerning Hypotheses 1 and 2. However, administrators were more likely than either teachers or reading teachers to agree strongly that commercial reading materials were based on science (Hypothesis 3). In addition, neither reading teachers nor administrators agreed as strongly as classroom teachers that teachers use the materials in order to meet administrative expectations (Hypothesis 4), although they did agree that administrators expected teachers to use the materials. In response to the open-ended "why" questions on the questionnaire, one-third of the reading teachers and over half of the administrators (10) suggested that commercial reading materials can teach students to read.

The second analysis was an attempt to understand the organization and procedures of the reading program. During interviews, teachers, reading teachers, and administrators related that the reading program was organized hierarchically according to authority, with the board of education and the superintendent at the top, teachers at the bottom, and four levels in between. Both the description of the district program and the results of interviews confirmed that the curriculum for reading instruction was supplied by a set of commercial reading materials and that teachers were not to alter either the scope or the sequence of skills listed in the teacher's manuals. Instruction was to be based on the principles of mastery learning and paced according to students' abilities to reach critical scores on criterion-referenced tests that accompanied the commercial materials. However, 69% of the teachers suggested that the requirements for administering these tests, recording the results on students' records, and submitting the records to reading teachers and administrators on a biweekly basis applied pressure on teachers "to push students through the materials." Because the curriculum and administrators sought instruction consistent among classrooms within schools and across schools within the district, teachers were "limited" to one set of commercial materials, which was selected by an administratively appointed committee.

At first glance, it seems that Hypothesis 4 explains teachers' reliance on commercial reading materials in the district under study. The analyses of subjective and objective factors point toward administrative expectations as the appropriate conclusion. Administrators offered Hypotheses 2 and 3 as justification for their expectations, implying that the materials can teach reading because they are based on scientific investigations of the reading process. Administrators reasoned that, if teachers stick closely to the suggestions in the teacher's manuals, all students will master the basic skills of reading. And, in fact, when I asked teachers to describe what they would do if administrators did not expect them to use the materials, 84% of the teachers offered the same rationales as administrators for their instruction. These teachers said that they would continue their present practice of relying on commercial materials, with one slight deviation — they would include more sets of commercial materials in order to meet students' needs while remaining within the parameters of the original curriculum.

My initial attempt to understand why teachers rely so heavily on commercial reading materials during their reading instruction, then, ended with a question instead of an answer: Why do administrators and teachers believe that commercial reading materials can teach students to read?

Technological ideology

In an attempt to answer this question, I sought an explanation that would relate school personnel's thoughts about their reading instruction to the way in which others view their work. After all, as a group, teachers are not that different from other workers in our society. Basing my work loosely on Georg Lukács's theory of reification (1970), I developed a model of reading programs that suggests that school personnel's beliefs can be best interpreted as a natural development of the "rationalization" of everyday life in Western society. Lukács argued that, in order for countries to prosper materially, all parts of their society, both public and private, had to be made or considered predictable in order to reduce the risk of capital investment. Accordingly, along with standard laws, social norms, and other institutions, school became organized and measured by business and scientific principles. For Lukács, the process of rationalization could be explained by the relationship of reification, formal rationality, and alienation, and, in this section, I attempt to show how a dialectic among these three factors explains school personnel's beliefs and actions concerning the relationship between commercial reading materials and reading instruction. My point in this discussion is to demonstrate that school personnel's belief that commercial reading materials can teach is really deeply ingrained in the fabric of American culture.

Reification

Reification is the treatment of an abstraction as a concrete object or an immutable procedure. In my study, it seems that school personnel reified reading instruction as commercial reading materials because, rather than engaging in many of the possible ways of teaching reading, school personnel relied on only one method—the application of commercial materials. An explanation of why this happened is not so straightforward as we would perhaps like. It seems that school personnel have confused the materials' contribution to students' reading development in a way similar to the way in which others confuse the contribution of capital to the commercial production of any commodity. In both cases, what are really transactions among people (past and present labor) are understood as transactions among things. In a factory, the machines appear to do the work, rather than the craftsmen who designed the routine and the toolmakers who developed the machine. In my study, rather than a collaboration among author, teacher, and student, reading instruction is understood as an exchange between commercial materials that have the power to teach and students who can absorb that instruction.

   This general confusion about commodities, I believe, underlies school personnel's conceptions of reading instruction. The psychological, intellectual, and physical distance from the production of these materials, coupled with the everyday confusion over the properties of commodities and the dazzle of advertising, leaves school personnel with the illusion that the materials—not the labor of authors, artists, typesetters, and so on—can teach students to read. Of course, no participants in my study used these terms to describe their work, but their actions, the examples they offered from their classroom practice, and their comments on the materials pointed in this direction.

   When forced to justify their beliefs on the questionnaire, most respondents offered the scientific nature of the materials as the basis for the materials' instructional powers. In fact, teachers' and administrators' responses were significantly correlated concerning items dealing with the instructional capabilities of the materials (Hypothesis 2) and the scientific nature of the materials (Hypothesis 3); their prose explanations concerning why they used the materials were replete with such associations. This deference to science also fits Lukács's (1970) explanation of rationalization of Western society because it seems based on two generally accepted ideas: an understanding of science as technology and a use of science as the major form of evaluation of social institutions and customs.

Huxley (1963) and Snow (1959) commented on the gulf between the scientific community and everyday life. They suggested that people who are not directly engaged in scientific investigations do not understand the human process of scientific inquiry. Rather, most people see only the material results of scientific endeavors—increased quantity, standard means, and efficiency (Habermas, 1970). Science does not appear to them as a human activity, but as an object or unalterable procedure. In other words, most people reify science as technology. For my study, this meant that school personnel treated the directions in teacher's manuals as the science of reading instruction. The reification of reading instruction and of the scientific study of reading instruction as the format and directions of commercial materials has important consequences for school personnel: they become uninformed spectators of the scientific, instructive activity of the commercial materials, and they see no need or way to alter the course or content of their reading instruction except to change the commercial materials used in their classrooms.

A second consequence of the misunderstanding of science is the increased role that measurement and efficiency have come to play in our daily lives. In earlier times, most social institutions were judged primarily in ethical and moral terms; that is, people wondered if an institution was just or good. However, with the rise of industrialization, with its requirement that all aspects of life become rationalized, more and more public and private matters have come under the scrutiny of scientific principles (Heilbronner, 1985). Currently, it seems that everything is judged in terms of quantity and efficiency. In fact, science is considered the sole method with which to define and solve the problems we face. For example, the problem of equal opportunity for employment is defined as the numbers of various groups in the workplace, and scientific studies are conducted to isolate factors that impede or encourage achievement of a balance. In a similar manner, the administrators in my study attempted to solve the problem of teaching large numbers of students to read by defining reading as verified competence in the basic skills of reading (i.e., certain achievement and criterion-referenced test scores) and by requiring all teachers to use the technology of reading instruction—one set of commercial reading materials.

Reification, then, explains that three social forces are working when school personnel believe that commercial reading materials can teach. First, when they reify reading instruction, teachers and administrators lose sight of the fact that reading instruction is a human process. Second, their reification of the scientific study of the reading process as the commercial materials means that their knowledge of reading and instruction is frozen in a single technological form. Third, school personnel's reification of science requires that they define their work in terms of efficiency of delivery and students' gains in test scores.

Formal rationality

This use of science to reorganize reading programs explains in part administrators' interest in teachers following the commercial reading materials and the recognition by teachers in my study that they were expected to use them. These school personnel were simply describing their respective roles in a scientifically arranged organization in the same way that any worker who is employed in a large modern corporation would. In other words, they have internalized a system of thought that Max Weber (1964) called formal rationality in his attempts to describe the impact of capitalism on everyday life. Formal rationality is distinguished from traditional uses of reason because the former, like science, excludes all consideration of values and moral questions. Thus, reorganization of production processes according to the principles of formal rationality emphasizes the development of the most efficient means with which to maximize the productivity of each worker in a coordinated unit rather than the "qualitative human and individual attributes of the worker" (Weber 1964, p. 99).

For Lukács (1970), such reorganization meant the segmentation of the production process into standard, easily defined sets of actions in which the worker becomes a specialized part rather than the producer of whole goods, as he was under previous economic systems. The development and coordination of this reorganized system require the separation of planning of production from its execution in order to maximize efficiency and productivity. According to Lukács, few workers would choose such a reduction and organization of their work, and, therefore, a hierarchical arrangement is necessary, with planning becoming purely an administrative function and acting according to that plan becoming the workers' role. Lukács considered the Taylor System the culmination of this trend. Taylor used time as the hone to develop scientific management procedures by first dismantling the specific process of production as performed by a very able worker to its elemental parts, timing each part to remove nonessential movements and then reassembling the streamlined procedures into subgoals to be performed repeatedly by groups of workers. In this way, the practices of the best worker could be introduced to all workers, thereby making production and productivity calculable.

Although the reorganization in schools is not a direct parallel of industrial production processes, according to Callahan (1962) and Franklin (1976), the Taylor Scientific Management System had a considerable impact on education. Instead of using time, however, curriculum theorists such as Frank Spaulding and Franklin Bobbitt argued for a three-step approach to the design of instruction: (*a*) analyze the learning environment during instruction to identify instructional methods, (*b*) measure the effects of various methods with specifically designed tests, and (*c*) adopt the means that yield the highest results. To oversee the transition from unscientific to scientific instruction, a hierarchical administration was required to plan, coordinate, and maintain the new organization.

Reading programs in elementary schools were also subject to the principles of formal rationality. At one time, elementary teachers taught students of various ages to read simultaneously from books on many subjects according to the teachers' own directions (Smith 1965). Over time their role became to teach reading to a certain age group using commercial reading materials according to a teacher's manual under the watchful eyes of administrators. We are currently told that "America will become a nation of readers when verified practices of the best teachers in the best schools can be introduced throughout the country" (Anderson et al. 1985, p. 120). Reading, itself, is also segmented in elementary schools: "Reading, as a complex skill, is comprised of subordinate

units that must be mastered and integrated to form higher-order skills. Consequently, to accomplish this developmental task, a variety of subskills thought
to be essential are taught to students. The order of progression in these skills is
from prerequisite small units to larger units" (Samuels & Schachter 1978,
p. 48).

According to the second analysis of objective factors, the school district
that I studied was organized according to the principles of formal rationality: it
had a hierarchical administration, a separation of planning of goals from
instruction, separate roles for administrators and teachers, a standard technology
in the form of the commercial materials, and a monitoring system of production
(students' achievement) and productivity (teachers' instruction) through the
criterion-referenced tests that directly paralleled the materials. Because it was
organized in the name of science and high student achievement, few within the
district questioned the organization of the reading program in which teaching
became following the lead of those who do not teach because most work seems
to be organized this way. Rather, school personnel responded according to
their roles—teachers pointed toward administrative plans and administrators
toward science.

Alienation

Alienation is the process of separation between people and some quality
assumed to be related to them in natural circumstances. This process can be
consciously recognized (subjective alienation) or be beyond the control of the
individual (objective alienation). The organization of the reading program
according to the principles of formal rationality and school personnel's responses
to questionnaires and during interviews suggested that both forms of alienation
were apparent in the school district I studied. First, the fact that school
personnel's roles, by their own accounts, did not include goal setting or directions
for instruction (both were set by the authors of the commercial materials)
means that administrators and teachers were objectively alienated from reading
instruction. Of course, I am assuming here that reading instruction is the work
of all school personnel, or that it once was, and that work and people are
related in natural circumstances. The separation of teachers from the totality of
reading instruction seemed to prevent school personnel from recognizing that
the organization of their reading program was but one of many possible
arrangements that would accomplish the task of teaching children to read. Like
the workers in industry (Noble 1983) and in offices (Howard 1985), these
school personnel assumed that their present circumstances were "just the way
it is."

This sense of fatalism was apparent in many teachers' answers to the open-
ended questions on the questionnaires and during interviews. Although teachers
complained loudly about the textbook adoption process and the recording
system for students' test scores, very few teachers and literally no administrators
challenged the separation of the planning of goals from the process of teaching,
the definition of reading as the summation of basic isolated skills, or the
directions for lessons from teacher's manuals. By accepting their roles with
only minor complaint, school personnel acknowledged that they were subjec-
tively alienated from reading instruction.

In summary, my model of reading programs is based on the notion that school personnel understand and describe reading instruction in a manner similar to how workers in other occupations discuss their work because they all are subject to the same societal influence, that is, the process of rationalization. The model suggests that school personnel believe that commercial materials can teach because they have reified reading instruction as commercial materials. This illusion of instructional power is supported by school personnel's reification of the scientific inquiry concerning reading instruction as the directions for lessons in teacher's manuals and by the use of formal rationality in the organiz-ation of reading programs. According to the model, this combination of re-ification and formal rationality alienates school personnel from a central feature of their work in elementary schools — the development of students' literacy. Thus, administrators expect the use and teachers use commercial reading materials because they have internalized the process of rationalization, and, like other workers, they apply its business and scientific principles to the task of teaching reading. From this point of view, it would be more startling if teachers and administrators thought reading instruction was a human transaction rather than an interaction between objects — commercial materials and students.

Tests of the model

I have tested this model in three separate studies in school districts in different states. In each case, reification, formal rationality, and alienation were apparent, although they combined in different ways in each district, giving each a unique character. However, in these districts, school personnel's views of commercial reading materials remained substantially the same as they were in my original study.

In the first test (Shannon, 1984b), I compared quotes from Chicago admin-istrators and teachers concerning the philosophy and organization of the Chicago Mastery Learning Reading Program (CMLR) with those of administrators and teachers from my original study in order to demonstrate how the organization of a reading program according to the principles of formal rationality contra-dicted each district's underlying philosophy of reading instruction based on mastery learning. Basically, I argued that mastery learning was adopted as a philosophy as much to assuage managerial concerns as it was for pedagogical reasons. Mastery learning, with its assumption that everyone can learn to read, was acknowledged as a method, perhaps the method, by which these school districts could regain the confidence of their skeptical publics by insuring that all students learned to read at appropriate and verifiable levels of competence before leaving elementary school, junior high, or high school. However, in order to meet these quotas, instructional time was segmented, which violates a mastery learning assumption of adequate (unlimited) time to learn to read. Furthermore, reading goals were reduced to elemental levels to insure that all students would be considered competent, thereby subverting Bloom's (1976) notion that mastery learning would enable "higher levels" of learning. Finally, instructional methods were reified as commercial reading materials, counteract-ing the theoretical concern of mastery learning that teachers prepare their own materials and tests to insure that they are clearly aware of the instructional goals and the formats in which those goals will be tested. According to Schmidt

(1982), a teacher in the Chicago system, teachers' alienation from their reading instruction using the CMLR program was similar to what I found in my original study.

In the second test of the model (Shannon 1986), I sought to explain how a merit pay program based on increased test scores (a form of formal rationality) would affect school personnel's thoughts concerning reading and reading instruction. Using questionnaires, interviews, observation, and district printed materials, I found a reading program in which central administrators set specific achievement test scores as goals for average pupil performance for each school in the district, offered merit pay incentives to teachers and administrators of schools that reached those goals, and developed standard methods for the use of the teacher's manuals for commercial reading materials. Although several teachers resented certain aspects of this formal rationality and some rejected the reification of reading as achievement test scores, most teachers and all administrators demonstrated that they accepted their respective roles to apply the materials according to plan and to monitor teachers' instruction closely. However, even when accepting their role, many teachers considered reading instruction less fulfilling within the merit pay program than they had under other circumstances. This alienation is captured best in one teacher's statement.

> At my previous school [in another district], I felt no pressure about reading instruction. I felt good at my job and gave 100 percent. At this school, the principal stresses that it is important to teach tested skills. "Adapt your instructional time to raise those scores with your top group," she says. "Worry about your low group, but you need those high scores to bring them up." I do feel pressure from the principal and the other teachers. When the scores came in, we had a faculty meeting and the scores were distributed to all faculty listed by room number....It's quite evident who has done the best. For example, the third-grade teachers felt that the second-grade teachers must have cheated to get scores that high because there was such small growth from second to third grade. All of this is unprofessional....On my Christmas card that my principal sent me she did write. "I know that your [standardized achievement test] scores will be better this year." I swear to God.

In the third investigation (Shannon, in press), I used questionnaires and interviews to investigate school personnel's commitment to the goals and means of their reading program, which was organized according to the principles of formal rationality. Administrators were overwhelming in their support for the rationalized program, with its emphasis on centralized decision making, test scores, and uniform use of commercial reading materials. However, teachers were much less enthusiastic about the goals of the rationalized program, although they were equally convinced that commercial reading materials were the appropriate means for reading instruction. That is, although administrators saw formal rationality and reification of reading instruction as integrally related, teachers saw them as separate issues. In fact, teachers spoke of their resentment of administrative intervention into their classroom instruction, which they considered "their territory." To avoid this confrontation, administrators developed a monitoring system based on the criterion-referenced tests that accompany commercial reading materials. Since these tests are based closely on the format and vocabulary of their parent materials (Johnson & Pearson 1975), this monitoring system accomplished administrators' goals indirectly. Teachers, who reified reading instruction as the materials themselves, wholeheartedly backed this system, although they complained about "the pressures of teaching reading."

These three studies, along with the original investigation, suggest that the model of reading programs based on the dialectic among reification, formal rationality, and alienation will account generally for school personnel's actions and beliefs in a variety of situations. The central feature of each reading program was the notion that commercial reading materials were the technology of the scientific study of reading and instruction and that they possessed instructional powers to teach students to read. Reified reading instruction was the foundation on which each program was organized. Standard use of these materials was considered essential for skill mastery, merit pay, and continuity across classrooms, grade levels, and schools. However, in each study, many teachers recognized, at least tacitly, that they had to give up something in order to get the full benefits of the rationalized program and the use of commercial reading materials. Although they were not always certain what they were giving up or to whom or what to affix the blame, these teachers were uneasy about the circumstances of their reading instruction.

The deskilling of teachers

Marcuse (1964) argued that teacher uneasiness should be considered a typical reaction to the control required in the rationalization of an institution or process. In reading programs, as in most institutional work, this control comes in three forms: simple, bureaucratic, and technical (Apple 1982). Simple control is one person persuading others by whatever means to follow directions concerning their behaviors. The institutionalization of this simple persuasion is called bureaucratic control, wherein the right of control, authority to direct the activities of others, is given to someone or some group. Clearly, both simple and bureaucratic control were apparent in the reading programs I studied, if they are not in most reading programs. Usually, teachers' complaints about "the pressures of teaching reading" were attributed to either of these types of control. However, technical control is more subtle; that is, it seems natural to the definitions and physical realities of the job to be performed. In reading programs, commercial materials supplied the means for the technical control of reading instruction in order to render it more predictable and more productive.

Since both administrators and teachers reified reading instruction as commercial reading materials, few questioned the legitimacy of this form of technical control. In these materials, administrators found an economical and less confrontational means for instructional accountability, and teachers found both the source and the tools of reading instruction. Teachers willingly accepted this technical control as simply "the way to teach reading." Commercial reading materials, then, controlled the program goals, methods of instruction, main source of texts for reading, and evaluation procedures without noticeable objection on the part of teachers. However, teachers were not mere puppets; they did object to what they considered arbitrary exercise of administrative bureaucratic authority (e.g., limitation to one set of commercial materials, restriction of promotion based on skill mastery alone, setting quotas for average pupil performance, or requirements of standard pace for instruction).

Yet, it is the technical, not the simple or bureaucratic, control that has the greatest repercussions for teachers. In a very real sense, as commercial reading materials became more pervasive, teachers became less important in the process of reading instruction in America. To understand this inverse relationship — the deskilling of teachers — it is necessary to look once again at the history of reading instruction and of commercial reading materials.

Just before the turn of the twentieth century, the work of Johann Herbart was translated into English and had a wide impact on American teacher education and reading instruction. In fact, John Dewey, in *How We Think*, stated, "Few attempts have been made to formulate a method, resting on general principles of conducting recitation. One of these is of great importance and has probably had more influence upon the hearing of lessons than all others put together; namely the analysis by Herbart of a recitation into five successive steps" (1910, p. 202). In these five steps teachers (1) prepared students for new information by referring to relevant known information, (2) presented the new information, (3) associated the new information directly with materials and ideas learned in the past, (4) systematically used examples to illustrate these points of connection, and (5) tested students' ability to apply the new information.

Smith (1965) suggested that "Herbartianism" affected early twentieth-century reading instruction in two ways: first, the recitation steps became commonplace in reading instruction, and, second, Herbart's notion of the effects of literature and history on moral development influenced the reading selections in commercial reading materials. At the time, these materials consisted of a graded set of textbooks, and, although teachers used them frequently, they had to devise their own procedures for using them. To be sure, professional books concerning how to teach reading began to appear in the early 1900s, but commercial reading materials did not include teacher's manuals, workbooks, or tests until the 1920s. Thus, teachers were responsible for the goals of reading, the methods of instruction, designation of practice activities, and procedures for evaluation.

Compare those expectations and responsibilities with the teachers' role in present-day rationalized reading programs. Just as happened to the craftsman in manufacturing, teachers lost much of their responsibility and, over time, their skills to the technology. With the advent of teacher's manuals, teachers began to lose control of the goals and methods of instruction. Today, some experts on teacher effectiveness recommend teacher's manuals in the form of scripts for teachers to perform (Carnine and Becker 1980; Rosenshine 1981). The development of workbooks relieved teachers of the responsibility and soon the skill for developing practice activities. Today, Durkin (1978–1979) suggests that workbook and other practice activities (worksheets, skill boxes, etc.) account for most of the time designated for reading instruction, to the detriment of children learning to read. Criterion-referenced tests that accompany virtually all sets of commercial reading materials have become substitutes for teachers' judgment concerning students' reading ability (Johnson and Pearson 1975). In each case, skills that Dewey (1910) and Smith (1965) described as being in the repertoires of classroom teachers are now considered to be in the domain of commercial reading materials.

The rise of commercial reading materials as technical control was and is fueled by at least two sources. First, each of the parts of commercial reading materials was originally introduced as an improvement over the reliance on teachers' subjectivity because the teacher's manuals, workbooks, and tests would standardize reading instruction, improve teachers' productivity, and extend scientific reading instruction to all students. Second, this standardization of teacher's instructions and their subsequent loss of instructional skills rendered teachers dependent on the materials and thus created a market for this technological solution. Teachers and administrators expect commercial reading materials to provide complete programs that specify goals, means, and evaluation for reading instruction. Recognizing this expansion of their market, publishers supply the commodities to fulfill these expectations. This commercialization of reading instruction has produced a highly lucrative, highly competitive, and highly conservative market. In fact, when Scott, Foresman and Company published reading materials that required more teacher judgment in the early 1970s, they lost 65% of their school market (Tierney 1984). Thus, technical control and the deskilling of teachers find support in science and the economy. And, of late, some teacher education experts have begun to acknowledge teachers' fate in this process: "Teacher education programs are often designed as if teachers were responsible for establishing appropriate educational objectives for their students, preparing appropriate curriculum materials, conducting and evaluating the outcomes of instruction, and making whatever adjustments should prove necessary in these activities. Teachers may have done all of these things in the distant past, but at present, most of these functions are performed by school boards, school administrators, and commercial publishers" (Brophy 1982, p. 11).

The reskilling of teachers

If the technical control of reading programs (the commercial reading materials) deskills teachers by supplying the goals, means, and evaluation of their reading instruction and the bureaucratic control (state education departments, school boards, and centralized administration) limits teachers' access to choices among these materials, what then are the new skills of teaching reading? For a "state of the art" perspective, I turn to the *Handbook of Reading Research* (Pearson 1984).

In chapter 23, "Classroom Instruction in Reading," and chapter 24, "Managing Instruction," the authors explain the new skills of reading instruction. Identified in a manner reminiscent of Spaulding and Bobbitt's three-step adaptation of scientific management, these new skills "seek a universal system of managing instruction...evaluated in terms of standardized achievement tests" (Otto, Wolf, and Eldridge 1984, p. 320). In chapter 23, Rosenshine and Stevens (1984) divide these new skills into three categories: (1) general instructional procedures, (2) specific instructional procedures, and (3) indexes of effective instruction. Generally, teachers are encouraged to lead instruction, to teach to small groups, and to project an academic focus. Specifically, teachers should follow a variation of Herbart's five steps while maintaining a swift pace, students' attention, and high student success. These last three variables are considered indexes of effective instruction. Conspicuous by its absence is a discussion of teachers' knowledge of the content of reading instruction, the reading process, their students, and the source of instructional goals and means in elementary classrooms.

Ironically, Otto et al. (1984) highlight Rosenshine and Stevens's omission in the first sentence of chapter 24—"Reading instruction involves not only selecting and presenting a curriculum to students, but also structuring a context in which teaching and learning can occur" (1984, p. 799). However, Otto et al. then proceed only to elaborate on specifics from Rosenshine and Stevens's argument (e.g., grouping, delivery systems, and feedback cycles). Apparently, in the reskilling of teachers of reading according to the *Handbook on Reading Research*, it is not who is teaching, what is taught, or to whom it is taught that is important; rather, effective instruction is a matter of how students are guided through commercial reading materials.

The technical control of reading instruction through the required use of commercial reading materials, with its deskilling and reskilling of teachers, should not be overemphasized—teachers are not factory workers and students' reading is not easily understood as a commodity—but the technical control's effect on elementary teachers and students should not be underestimated either. Depending on the type of materials and administrative perspective, teachers and students relinquish some or most of the control over their actions during lessons (Cuban 1984; Shannon 1984a): they are asked to routinize their lessons, eliminating nonacademic comments and content, asking primarily low-level questions to monitor student success, and maintaining a "businesslike" but not cold atmosphere (Rosenshine and Stevens 1984, p. 752). Because the materials supply the goals, directions, practices, and evaluation and because instruction is defined as managing students through the materials, teachers may see little incentive to improve their knowledge of reading, instruction, their students, or appropriate literature. Additionally, in the reification of reading instruction, with all but management predetermined, teachers have little need to reconsider goals of instruction, to reflect on the meaning of their work, or to interact with one another concerning curricular or instructional matters, all of which exacerbate the isolation of elementary school teaching. Moreover, the reskilling of teachers according to which behaviors raise achievement test scores elevates the role of testing to a point at which students' reading becomes reified as test scores and the primary focus of teachers' attention becomes narrowed to this one part of students' literacy development—in other words, test scores become the bottom line of the reading instruction tally sheet.

Although students' test scores usually rise under prescribed conditions of reskilling and sometimes their self-esteem scores rise also (Rosenshine and Stevens 1984), students are expected to forfeit much of their control over their learning to read in typical school lessons (Shannon 1984a). Just as with teachers, commercial reading materials as technical control means that students lose any control over the content to be learned. Still, they are expected to attend to task religiously, to participate in every lesson, and to be successful (Otto et al. 1984, p. 814). Yet several writers have recently challenged the putative social, emotional, and intellectual benefits for students attending, participating in, and being successful in lessons based on commercial reading materials. For instance,

Freebody and Baker (1985) suggest that socialization into the culture of literacy through the language of primary-grade reading textbooks promotes sexism and subservience: Bettelheim and Zelan (1981) argue that the content of stories in these textbooks stifles children's imaginations and stunts their emotional attachment to reading; and Anderson (1984) reports that seatwork directed by commercial workbooks and worksheets usually emphasizes completion over understanding.

It is in this individual, segmented practice that the effects of teachers' reliance on commercial reading materials for students may be most readily apparent: students are separated from reading and writing on topics that they consider important, they are kept from reflecting on the potential meaning of literacy in their lives because they are busy completing assignments, and, finally, they are denied the social aspects of literacy because they work alone. In fact, all of the acts typically included in definitions of mature reading (Purves 1984) seem absent from reading instruction in American elementary schools.

I began this article with two questions. First, I asked what teachers must give up in order to enjoy the benefits of commercial reading materials. At least under present rationalized conditions, teachers give up control over the means and ends of their work, subjectivity in their teaching, ability concerning construction of reading lessons and tests and knowledge about scientific investigations of reading and instruction, the respect due professionals that comes from outside observers, authority over their classroom activities, working relationships with other teachers and students concerning student literacy development, and, in fact, the history of teaching reading. Second, I asked whether or not this is a good exchange. For teachers and students, I think not.

Constructive change

Max Weber (1964) called the rationalization of everyday life and social institutions an "iron cage" from which there was no escape except to return to preindustrial society and to give up its considerable material benefits. Recently, several educational critics have reiterated Weber's conclusion, suggesting that schooling in America cannot be just or equitable for students or teachers because schools are designed and function in order to reproduce contemporary social structure (Bourdieu and Passeron 1977; Bowles and Gintis 1976; Jencks 1972). Although my analysis of elementary school reading instruction may appear equally bleak (if all of society is fragmented and appears unchangeable, how can reading instruction be any different?), I do not accept this pessimistic conclusion that leaves teachers and teacher-educators impotent. In other words, I do not think that reading instruction must be rationalized, and I believe there are teachers and teacher-educators who have reached the same conclusion.

Simply because students and teachers are controlled in rationalized reading programs does not mean that they totally acquiesce to the directives of commercial reading materials. Anyone familiar with classroom reading instruction recognizes that students find both positive (reading a book behind an elevated desk top) and negative (refusal to participate) ways to subvert the classroom routine of reading group and seatwork. Furthermore, teachers also resist the simple translation of the directives into practice. For example, Durkin (1983) and Shake and Allington (1985) have found that, although teacher's manuals direct activities during reading instruction, teacher quasi decisions about which parts of packaged lessons to emphasize are not always improvements on the information included in the manuals. However, many teachers do find some time outside the reading lesson proper for so-called enrichment activities — sustained silent reading, oral reading to children, library time — that take students beyond the skills emphasized in commercial reading materials.

Moreover, my third test of the proposed model of reading programs found that the majority of teachers in a rationalized reading program rejected the assumptions of rationalized instruction — the separation of planning from instruction, the centralization of decision making, and the primacy of test scores — even if they did accept commercial reading materials as the appropriate means of instruction. These teachers sought to reemphasize their subjectivity during reading instruction: to know their students and to form cordial relationships in order to share the joys, not just the skills, of reading; to decide which reading goals were worth pursuing for their students; and to judge students' reading competence for themselves. Most of these teachers were unaware that other teachers, even ones in their building, felt the same way, and they closed their classroom doors and "made do." Few were satisfied with the status quo; many expressed frustration. How, then, can these incidents of resistance to the rationalization of reading instruction be coordinated in order to affect reading programs? How can teachers' subjectivity (their knowledge, understanding, and emotions) regain its status in American reading instruction?

Although I do not have any quick and ready-made answers for these questions, I think there are three places where we can start to redirect reading instruction from its current course: (1) reconsider the foundations of reading instruction, (2) separate business principles from reading programs, and (3) develop a notion of science that appreciates teachers' contributions to children's literacy development.

Currently, most people interested in reading instruction consider it in psychological and technical terms. That is, they think primarily about the cognitive effects of teachers' actions and material's content on students and how modification of these factors based on experimental research can increase or decrease those effects. Because they do not question the basic assumptions and organization of school reading programs, they subscribe to the illusion that reading programs have always been and will always remain as they are right now. However, a view of reading instruction early in this century and Mosenthal's (1984) and Giroux's (1984) work on evaluation of reading programs and their ideological bases suggest that reading programs are not immutable givens, but rather that they are historically constructed entities that people brought into existence and maintain for various reasons. If we begin to reconsider the foundations of reading instruction in historical and philosophical terms rather than psychological and technical ones, we can begin to see through the curious and conservative reasoning of the following passage on nonformally rationalized reading instruction (whole language approaches, in this example): "It is noteworthy that these approaches are used to teach children to read in New Zealand, the most literate country in the world, a country that experiences very low rates of reading failure. However, studies of whole language approaches in the United States have produced results that are best characterized as inconsistent. In the hands of very skillful teachers, the results can be excellent. But the average result is indifferent when compared to approaches typical in American classrooms, at least as gauged by performance on first- and second-grade standardized reading achievement tests" (Anderson et al., 1985, p. 45). To think historically and philosophically about this quote, consider what is left unsaid. First, an industrialized, albeit smaller and somewhat socialist, nation has a nonrationalized basis for reading instruction in its schools. Why then must U.S. reading instruction be rationalized? Second, skillful New Zealand teachers do not have the proposed reskills of rationalized "effective" instruction, yet they contribute to the development of the most literate population and prevent most reading failures. Why do the authors of this quote imply that the average New Zealand teacher "is very skillful" but the average American teacher is not? Finally, why is New Zealand society willing to trust its teachers' subjectivity and the United States apparently is not?

These questions cannot be answered in psychological and technical terms, yet they are fundamental to reading instruction in the United States. As an initial concrete step toward the redirection of the foundations of reading instruction, those interested in change might write letters to editors of journals and authors of statements like the one just quoted, asking them to explain the historical and philosophical consequences of their work. Such questions might also be asked of administrators, teacher-educators, and conference speakers. Unfortunately, little help can be expected from colleges of education because historical and philosophical considerations are often relegated to one course and usually isolated from subject matter altogether in that environment. However, it does not really take formal training to wonder about and to ask questions concerning why things are the way they are.

Second, perhaps one of the reasons reading instruction is different in New Zealand than in the United States is that New Zealanders seem to have been able to separate reading instruction from the rationalization pervasive in most social institutions in Western society. That is, they have not used business or scientific principles to measure the effectiveness of reading instruction. In the United States, the process/product metaphor from business has led to a separation of planning from instruction, a perseverance on standardization, and the primacy of the educational bottom line — achievement test scores (Cuban 1984). Although each of these changes in reading instruction was originally made to save teachers time and to increase their productivity, in fact, each change now confronts teachers, often placing external expectations on them and giving them little time to reflect on the meaning or the potential of their work.

Some progress can be made on each of these fronts. In Michigan, for example, a group of teacher-educators has been successful in changing the official state definition of reading and student competence (Wixson and Peters 1984). Because of this change, teachers' groups have been able to obtain state funding to reeducate themselves and other teachers concerning this new definition (e.g., Plymouth, Michigan's Strategic Ongoing Application of Reading Research [SOARR] program). Although this is certainly not a grass-roots movement, and it seems likely at this point to end with the substitution of one test for another, it is a modest example of individuals from outside and lower levels of the educational bureaucracy attempting to reunite planning and instruction.

An example of resistance to the standardization of reading instruction comes from Substitutes United for Better Schools (SUBS) in Chicago. From 1980 to 1985, this teachers' group carried on a running battle with the Chicago School Board over the Chicago Mastery Learning Reading Program (CMLR), which I studied in the first test of my model of reading programs. By attending each school board meeting, scrutinizing each written communiqué from the district office, and carefully analyzing the social, political, and psychological principles on which the program was designed, SUBS (along with other teacher and parent groups) was instrumental in prompting a reduction in the number of skills required in the program, the redesign of the materials, and, finally, a total abandonment of the program. In the words of one teacher, "[CMLR] has made robots out of imaginative teachers. I have been teaching the same stuff for years, but in my own way" (Johnson 1981, p. 7).

The problem of achievement test scores was recently highlighted in a report sponsored by the National Academy of Education and the National Institute of Education, *Becoming a Nation of Readers* (Anderson et al. 1985). After advocating one instructional method over others based solely on its superior effects on students' achievement test scores (e.g., the statement dismissing whole language instruction for American classrooms cited earlier), the authors state, "The strength of a standardized test is not that it can provide a deep assessment of reading proficiency, but rather that it can provide a fairly reliable, partial assessment cheaply and quickly" (p. 98). Here we have the catch-22 that confronts teachers—they are told to adopt reskilling practices because they boost test scores, but then the same experts denigrate improving test scores as a goal for instruction. However, the authors of *Becoming a Nation of Readers* unconsciously suggest a way out of this paradox: "A more valid assessment of basic reading proficiency than that provided by standardized tests could be obtained by ascertaining whether students can and will do the following: Read aloud unfamiliar but grade-appropriate materials with acceptable fluency; write satisfactory summaries of unfamiliar selections from grade-appropriate social studies and science textbooks; explain the plots and motivations of the characters in unfamiliar grade-appropriate fiction; read extensively from books, magazines, and newspapers during leisure time" (Anderson et al. 1985, p. 99). Underlying this more valid assessment of basic reading proficiency are teachers' subjective views concerning appropriate materials, acceptable fluency, satisfactory summaries, and extensive leisure-time reading. Yet, the reskilling of teachers of reading ignores teachers' knowledge and understanding. Indeed, the rationalization of reading instruction is founded on the principle that teachers' subjectivity is to be neutralized by standardized, more efficient practices. Clearly, there is contradiction at the heart of the rationalization of reading instruction in the United States, and, therefore, there is opportunity for change.

Third, this movement away from the unambiguous ends of cheap and fairly reliable achievement test scores toward the ambiguous, messy conceptualization of more valid assessment of reading calls for a different type of science than the currently popular formal rationality. Within formal rationality, general theoretical principles are considered the highest level of knowledge and concrete problem solving is considered the lowest. From this view, the real knowledge of reading instruction lies in the theories and techniques of basic and applied sciences that university-based scientists and scholars create and then translate for teachers into the technology of commercial reading materials. These theoretically correct routines *may* work well in the pursuit of unambiguous goals like test scores within controlled experiments of limited duration, but for the problematic goals mentioned as more valid means of assessing reading in the uncertainty of real world classrooms, teachers cannot rely on formal rationality or university experts for solutions.

Rather, what is needed is a new type of science — what Schon (1983) calls "reflection in action" — in which practice is recognized for its theory generation rather than its theory reception. Schon argues that "with the emphasis on problem solving (in formal rationality), we ignore problem setting, the process by which we define the decisions to be made, the ends to be achieved, the means which may be chosen. In real world practice, problems do not present themselves to practitioners as givens. They must be constructed from the materials of problematic situations which are puzzling, troubling, and uncertain" (1983, p. 40). And although problem setting is probably necessary for problem solving, it is not a formally rational problem. To describe this ability for problem setting, Schon contrasts knowledge of practice — the application of set routines in attempts to solve problems — with reflection in action with a statement about how Leo Tolstoy taught children to read in Russia during the nineteenth century: "Tolstoy thinks of each of his pupils as an individual with ways of learning and imperfections peculiar to himself. The teachers are astonished by the sense behind a student's mistake. In each instance, the practitioner allows himself to experience surprise, puzzlement, or confusion in a situation which he finds uncertain and unique. He reflects on the phenomena before him, and on the prior understandings which have been implicit in his behavior. He carries out an experiment which serves to generate both a new understanding of the phenomena and a change in the situation" (Schon 1983, p. 68).

Perhaps the clearest illustration of attempts to change American reading instruction through the development of reflective practitioners is the teacher development projects that Jane Hansen and Donald Graves conduct in New Hampshire. There, teacher-educators act as facilitators for the development and maintenance of small teacher cadres who reflect on instruction through group discussions and close analysis of their own writing. Similar reliance on teachers to reflect on their work and to find their own way toward more valid instructional practices has also been documented in Meeks's (1983) *Achieving Literacy* and in the second half of Heath's (1983) *Ways with Words*. In each case, teachers' practice, their subjectivity, and their careful analysis of their subjective practice were the basis on which reading programs could be developed.

Some may argue that many teachers are not prepared for the freedom to use their subjectivity during reading instruction — that, at least, we must set alternatives between which teachers may choose. This strikes me as logic akin to Mary McCarthy's observation that Americans find the poverty of others romantic. Would reading researchers, policymakers, or administrators sit still while others choose the objectives, methods, materials, and intended outcomes of their work? I think not. Why, then, do the majority of these groups condone the rationalization of reading programs? What should be done, it seems to me, is to provide teachers with information and *allow them* (not require, prescribe, or legislate) the opportunity to formulate the available choices, to argue over them, and then to choose for themselves. Perhaps it is unwise to underestimate teachers' capabilities outside their alienated circumstances of rationalized present practice, even if it elevates the importance of the positions of reading researchers, policymakers, or administrators to do so.

I close with a quote from Bertolt Brecht's "A Worker Questions History" because I believe it shows that we can learn as much about reading, reading instruction, and ourselves from the subjectivity of literature as we can from the "objectivity" of science.

> Who built Thebes, with its seven gates?
> In books we find the names of Kings.
> Did the kings drag along the lumps of rock?
> And Babylon, many times destroyed—
> Who rebuilt it so many times?
> Where did the builders of glittering Lima live?
> On the evening, when the Chinese Wall was finished,
> Where did the masons go?

References

Anderson, L. (1984). The environment of instruction: The function of seatwork in a commercially developed curriculum. In G. Duffy, L. Roehler, & J. Mason (Eds.), *Comprehension instruction: Perspectives and suggestions* (pp. 93–103). New York: Longman.

Anderson, R., Hiebert, E., Scott, J., & Wilkinson, I. (1985). *Becoming a nation of readers: The report of the Commission on Reading*. Washington, DC: National Institute of Education.

Anderson, R., Osborn, J., & Tierney, R. (1984). *Learning to read in American schools*. Hillsdale, NJ: Erlbaum.

Apple, M. (1982). *Education and power*. Boston: Routledge & Kegan Paul.

Aukerman, R. (1981). *The basal reader approach to reading*. New York: Wiley.

Austin, M., & Morrison, C. (1963). *The first R*. New York: Wiley.

Barton, A., & Wilder, D. (1964). Research and practice in the teaching of reading. In M. Miles (Ed.), *Innovations in education* (pp. 361–398). New York: Teachers College Press.

Bettelheim, B., & Zelan, K. (1981). *On learning to read: The child's fascination with reading*. New York: Knopf.

Betts, E. (1943). Systematic sequences in reading. *Elementary English Review*, 20, 54–59.

Bloom, B. (1976). *Human characteristics and school learning*. New York: McGraw-Hill.

Boney, C. (1938). Basal readers. *Elementary English Review*, 15, 133–137.

Boney, C. (1939). Teaching children to read as they learn to talk. *Elementary English Review*, 16, 139–141, 156.

Bourdieu, P., & Passeron, J.C. (1977). *Reproduction in education, society and culture*. Beverly Hills, CA: Sage.

Bowles, S., & Gintis, H. (1976). *Schooling in capitalist America*. New York: Basic.

Brecht, B. (1977). A worker questions history. In M. Hoyles (Ed.), *The politics of literacy* (p. 62). London: Writers and Readers Publishing Cooperative.

Brophy, J. (1982). How teachers influence what is taught and learned in classrooms. *Elementary School Journal*, 83, 1−13.

Callahan, R. (1962). *Education and the cult of efficiency*. Chicago: University of Chicago Press.

Carnine, D., & Becker, W. (1980). Direct instruction. In B. Lahey & A. Kazdin (Eds.), *Advances in clinical child psychology* (pp. 121−157). New York: Plenum.

Chall, J. (1967). *Learning to read: The great debate*. New York: McGraw-Hill.

Cuban, L. (1984). Transforming the frog into a prince: Effective school research, policy, and practice at the district level. *Harvard Educational Review*, 54, 129−151.

Dewey, J. (1910). *How we think*. Boston: Heath.

Dolch, E.L. (1950). *Teaching primary reading*. Champaign, IL: Garrard.

Donovan, H. (1928). Use of research in teaching reading. *Elementary English Review*, 5, 104−107.

Duffy, G., & McIntyre, L. (1980). *A quantitative analysis of how various primary grade teachers employ the structural learning component of the direct instruction model when teaching reading* (Research Series No. 80). East Lansing: Michigan State University, Institute for Research on Teaching.

Durkin, D. (1974). Some questions about questionable instructional materials, *Reading Teacher*, 28, 13−18.

Durkin, D. (1978). *Teaching them to read* (3rd ed.). Boston: Allyn & Bacon.

Durkin, D. (1978−1979). What classroom observation reveals about reading comprehension. *Reading Research Quarterly*, 14, 481−533.

Durkin, D. (1981). Reading comprehension instruction in five basal reading series. *Reading Research Quarterly*, 16, 515−544.

Durkin, D. (1983). Is there a match between what elementary teachers do and what basal readers manuals recommend? *Reading Teachers*, 37, 734−744.

Durrell, D. (1940). *Improving reading instruction*. Yonkers, NY: World.

Education Product Information Exchange. (1977). *Report on a national survey of the nature and the quality of instructional materials most used by teachers and learners* (Technical Rep. No. 76). New York: EPIE Institute.

Franklin, B. (1976). Curriculum thought and social meaning: Edward I. Thorndyke and the curriculum field. *Educational Theory*, 26, 298−309.

Freebody, P., & Baker, C. (1985). Children's first schoolbooks: Introductions to the culture of literacy. *Harvard Educational Review*, 55, 381−398.

Germane, C., & Germane, E. (1922). *Silent reading: A handbook for teachers*. Chicago: Row, Peterson.

Giroux, H. (1984). *Theory and resistance in education*. South Hadley, MA: Bergin & Garvey.

Goodlad, J. (1970). *Behind the classroom door*. Worthington, OH: Jones.

Goodman, K. (1979). The know-more and the know-nothing movements in reading: A personal response. *Language Arts*, 56, 657−663.

Gray, W. (Ed.). (1936). *The teaching of reading. Thirty-sixth yearbook of the National Society for the Study of Education, part I*. Chicago: University of Chicago Press.

Habermas, J. (1970). *Toward a rational society: Student protest, science, and politics*. Boston: Bacon.

Heath, S.B. (1983). *Ways with words*. New York: Cambridge University Press.

Heilbronner, R. (1985). *The nature and logic of capitalism*. New York: Norton.

Howard, R. (1985). *Brave new workplace*. New York: Viking.

Huey, E.B. (1968). *The psychology and pedagogy of reading*. Boston: MIT Press. (Original work published 1908).

Huxley, A. (1963). *Literature and science*. New York: Harper & Row.

Jencks, C. (1972). *Inequality*. New York: Basic.

Johnson, C. (1981). Teachers critical of new reading plan. *Substance*, 7, 7.

Johnson, D., & Pearson, P.D. (1975). Skills management systems: A critique. *Reading Teacher*, 28, 757−764.

Lortie, D. (1975). *Schoolteacher*. Chicago: University of Chicago Press.

Lukács, G. (1970). *History and class consciousness*. Boston: MIT Press.

Marcuse, H. (1960). *Reason and revolution*. Boston: Beacon.

Marcuse, H. (1964). *One dimensional man*. Boston: Beacon.

Meeks, M. (1983). *Achieving literacy: Longitudinal studies of adolescents learning to read*. London: Routledge & Kegan Paul.

Mills, C.W. (1959). *The sociological imagination*. New York: Oxford University Press.

Mosenthal, P. (1984). Defining program effectiveness: An ideological approach. *Poetics*, 13, 1−22.

Mosenthal, P. (1985). Defining progress in educational research. *Educational Researcher*, 14, 3−9.

Noble, D. (1983). *Forces of production: A social history of industrial automation*. New York: Knopf.

Otto, W., Wolf, A., & Eldridge, R. (1984). Managing instruction. In P.D. Pearson (Ed.), *Handbook of reading research* (pp. 799−828). New York: Longman.

Pearson, P.D. (Ed.). (1984). *Handbook of reading research*. New York: Longman.

Popkewitz, T. (1984). *Paradigm and ideology in educational research*. Philadelphia: Falmer.

Purves, A. (1984). The challenge to education to produce literate citizens. In A. Purves & O. Niles (Eds.), *Becoming readers in a complex society: Eighty-third yearbook of the National Society for the Study of Education, Part I* (pp. 1−15). Chicago: University of Chicago Press.

Rosecky, M. (1978). Are teachers selective when using basal guidebooks? *Reading Teacher*, 31, 381−385.

Rosenshine, B. (1981, April). *Meta-analyses of process-product research*. Paper presented at the Invisible College of Researchers on Teaching, University of California at Los Angeles.

Rosenshine, B., & Stevens, R. (1984). Classroom instruction in reading. In P.D. Pearson (Ed.), *Handbook of reading research* (pp. 745−798). New York: Longman.

Samuels, S.J., & Schachter, S. (1978). Controversial issues in beginning reading instruction: Meaning versus subskill emphasis. In S. Pflaun-Connor (Ed.), *Aspects of reading education* (pp. 44−62). Berkeley: McCutchan.

Schmidt, G. (1982). Chicago mastery reading: A case against skills-based reading curriculum. *Learning*, 11, 36−40.

Schon, D. (1983). *The reflective practitioner: How professionals think in action*. New York: Basic.

Shake, M., & Allington, R. (1985). Where do teachers' questions come from? *Reading Teacher*, 38, 432−439.

Shannon, P. (1982a). Some objective reasons for teachers' reliance on commercial reading materials. *Reading Teacher*, 35, 884−889.

Shannon, P. (1982b). Some objective reasons for teachers' use of commercial reading materials. *Reading Improvement*, 19, 296−302.

Shannon, P. (1983a). The treatment of commercial reading materials in college reading methods textbooks. *Reading World*, 23, 147–157,

Shannon, P. (1983b). The use of commercial reading materials in American elementary schools. *Reading Research Quarterly*, 19, 68–85.

Shannon, P. (1984a, December). *Control over learning events: A classification system for direct instruction*. Paper presented at the Thirty-fourth National Reading Conference, St. Petersburg, FL.

Shannon, P. (1984b). Mastery learning in reading and the control of teachers and students. *Language Arts*, 61, 484–493.

Shannon, P. (1986). Teachers' and administrators' thoughts on changes in reading instruction with a merit pay program based on test scores. *Reading Research Quarterly*, 21, 20–35.

Shannon, P. (in press). Consensus on conflict: Views of reading curriculum and instructional practice. *Reading Research and Instruction*.

Singer, H. (1977). Resolving curricular conflict in the 1970's. *Language Arts*, 54, 158–163.

Smith, N.B. (1965). *American reading instruction*. Newark, DE: International Reading Association.

Snow, C.P. (1959). *The two cultures*. London: Oxford University Press.

Stone, C. (1922). *Silent and oral reading. A practical handbook of methods based on the most recent scientific investigations*. Boston: Houghton Mifflin.

Tierney, R. (1984, April). *Research on reading comprehension instruction in basal reading programs*. Paper presented at the annual meeting of the American Educational Research Association, New Orleans.

Weber, M. (1964). *The theory of social and economic organization*. New York: Free Press.

Weintraub, S., Smith, H., Plessas, G., Roser, N., Hill, W., & Kibby, M. (1982). *Summary of investigations relating to reading July 1, 1980 to June 30, 1981*. Newark, DE: International Reading Association.

Wixson, K. & Peters, C. (1984). Reading redefined: A Michigan Reading Association position paper. *Michigan Reading Journal*, 17, 4–7.

EIGHTEEN

Consensus and Difference in Collaborative Learning
John Trimbur

Kenneth A. Bruffee, Harvey S. Wiener, and others have argued that collaborative learning may be distinguished from other forms of group work on the grounds that it organizes students not just to work together on common projects but more important to engage in a process of intellectual negotiation and collective decision-making. The aim of collaborative learning, its advocates hold, is to reach consensus through an expanding conversation. This conversation takes place at a number of levels—first in small discussion groups, next among the groups in a class, then between the class and the teacher, and finally among the class, the teacher, and the wider community of knowledge. In Bruffee's social constructionist pedagogy, the language used to reach consensus acquires greater authority as it acquires greater social weight: the knowledge students put into words counts for more as they test it out, revising and relocating it by taking into account what their peers, the teacher, and voices outside the classroom have to say.

The purpose of this essay is to examine two important criticisms of the politics of collaborative learning in order to explore one of the key terms in collaborative learning, consensus. This seems worth doing because the notion of consensus is one of the most controversial and misunderstood aspects of collaborative learning.

One line of criticism argues that the use of consensus in collaborative learning is an inherently dangerous and potentially totalitarian practice that stifles individual voice and creativity, suppresses differences, and enforces conformity. Thomas S. Johnson, for example, believes that consensus is just another name for "group think" and conjures images of 1984. Pedro Beade

Source: John Trimbur, "Consensus and Difference in Collaborative Learning," *College English*, October 1989. Copyright 1989 by the National Council of Teachers of English. Reprinted with permission.

worries that consensus might be used to justify the practices of "a crazy, totalitarian state" (708). These critics of collaborative learning want to rescue the sovereignty and autonomy of the individual from what Johnson calls collaborative learning's "peer indoctrination classes." Underlying these political objections is the sense, as David Foster puts it, that the human mind is "far too mysterious and fascinating" to take the social constructionist route and "ground its utterances" in a "normative social community." According to Foster, collaborative learning is based on an epistemological mistake: Bruffee's "overeager application of the social constructionist label" causes him to overvalue social practices and thus to deny the primacy of individual consciousness in creating knowledge.

A second line of criticism, on the other hand, agrees with Bruffee that things like selves, knowledge, discourse, readers, and writers are indeed socially constructed. What left-wing critics such as Greg Myers do worry about, however, is that Bruffee's social constructionist pedagogy runs the risk of limiting its focus to the internal workings of discourse communities and of overlooking the wider social forces that structure the production of knowledge. To understand the production and validation of knowledge, Myers argues, we need to know not just how knowledge communities operate consensually but how knowledge and its means of production are distributed in an unequal, exclusionary social order and embedded in hierarchical relations of power. Without a critique of the dominant power relations that organize the production of knowledge, left-wing critics hold, the social constructionist rationale for collaborative learning may, unwittingly or not, accommodate its practices to the authority of knowledge it believes it is demystifying.

In this essay I propose to extend the left critique, not to abandon the notion of consensus but to revise it, as a step toward developing a critical practice of collaborative learning. I want to concede that consensus in some of its pedagogical uses may indeed be an accommodation to the workings of normal discourse and function thereby as a component to promote conformity and improve the performance of the system. My point will be, however, that consensus need not inevitably result in accommodation. The politics of consensus depends on the teacher's practice. Consensus, I will argue, can be a powerful instrument for students to generate differences, to identify the systems of authority that organize these differences, and to transform the relations of power that determine who may speak and what counts as a meaningful statement.

Before I outline the critical and transformative projects I believe are implied in collaborative learning, I want to address the fear of conformity in the first line of criticism — the fear that collaborative learning denies differences and threatens individuality. It is important to acknowledge that this fear points to some real problems that arise when students work together in groups — problems such as parochialism, demagoguery, narrow appeals to common sense, an urge to reach noncontroversial consensus without considering alternatives. After all, we cannot realistically expect that collaborative learning will lead students spontaneously to transcend the limits of American culture, its homogenizing force, its engrained suspicion of social and cultural differences, its tendency to reify the other and blame the victim. But if the fear of conformity is a legitimate one, it is not for the reasons the first group of

Bruffee's critics gives. Their effort to save the individual from the group is based on an unhelpful and unnecessary polarization of the individual and society.

The limits of these critics' fear of conformity can best be seen, I think, by emphasizing the influence of John Dewey's educational pragmatism on collaborative learning. What Bruffee takes from Dewey is a strong appreciation of the generativity of group life and its promise for classroom teaching. Consensus represents the potentiality of social agency inherent in group life — the capacity for self-organization, cooperation, shared decision-making, and common action. From a pragmatist perspective, the goal of reaching consensus gives the members of a group a stake in collective projects. It does not inhibit individuality, as it does for those who fear consensus will lead to conformity. Rather it enables individuals to participate actively and meaningfully in group life. If anything, it is through the social interaction of shared activity that individuals realize their own power to take control of their situation by collaborating with others.

For Deweyans, the effort to save the individual from the group is at best misguided and at worst reactionary. On one hand, pragmatists see no reason to rescue the individual from "normative communities" because in effect there is nowhere else the individual can be: consciousness is the extension of social experience inward. On the other hand, the desire to escape from "normative communities" and break out of the "prison house of language" by grounding utterances in the generative force of individual consciousness springs from an ideological complex of belief and practice.

Dewey's educational pragmatism recasts the fear that consensus will inevitably lead to conformity as a fear of group life itself. Pedagogies that take the individual as the irreducible, inviolate starting point of education — whether through individualized instruction, cultivation of personal voice, or an emphasis on creativity and self-actualization — inscribe a deeply contradictory ideology of individualism in classroom practice. If these pedagogies seek to liberate the individual, they also simultaneously constitute the student as a social atom, an accounting unit under the teacher's gaze, a record kept by the teacher. The fear of consensus often betrays a fear of peer group influence — a fear that students will keep their own records, work out collective norms, and take action. Rather than the liberation of the individual it claims to be, the fear of "group-think" is implicitly teacher-centered and authoritarian. It prevents a class of students from transforming themselves from an aggregate of individuals into a participatory learning community. The mode of teaching and learning remains what Bruffee calls "authoritarian-individualist": the atomization of students locks them into a one-to-one relation to the teacher, the repository of effective authority in the classroom, and cuts them off from the possibilities of jointly empowering activities carried out in the society of peers. In short, the critique of consensus in the name of individualism is baseless. Consensus does not necessarily violate the individual but instead can enable individuals to empower each other through social activity.

We may now take up the left-wing critique. Here the issue is not the status of the individual but the status of exchange among individuals. We should note, first of all, that Bruffee and his left-wing critics occupy a good deal of common ground concerning the social relationships of intellectual exchange as they are played out in the classroom. For teachers and theorists looking for a critical pedagogy, Bruffee's work has been important because it teaches us to read the classroom and the culture of teaching and learning as a social text.

How we teach, Bruffee suggests, is what we teach. For Bruffee, pedagogy is not a neutral practice of transmitting knowledge from one place to another, from the teacher's head to the students'. The pedagogical project that Bruffee initiated in the early seventies calls into question the dynamics of cultural reproduction in the classroom, a process that normally operates, as it were, behind our backs. What before had seemed commonsensical became in Bruffee's reading of the classroom as a social text a set of historically derived practices — an atomized and authoritarian culture that mystifies the production of knowledge and reproduces hierarchical relations of power and domination. Bruffee's formulation of collaborative learning in the early seventies offers an implicit critique of the culture of the classroom, the sovereignty of the teacher, the reification of knowledge, the atomized authority — dependence of students, and the competitiveness and intellectual hoarding encouraged by the traditional reward system and the wider meritocratic order in higher education.

In his early work, Bruffee sees collaborative learning as part of a wider movement for participatory democracy, shared decision-making, and non-authoritarian styles of leadership and group life. "In the world which surrounds the classroom," Bruffee says in 1973, "people today are challenging and revising many social and political traditions which have heretofore gone unquestioned"; if education has been resistant to collaboration, "[e]lsewhere, everywhere, collaborative action increasingly pervades our society" ("Collaborative Learning" 634). In Bruffee's account, collaborative learning occurs — along with free universities, grass-roots organizing, the consciousness-raising groups of women's liberation, the anti-war movement, and so on — as a moment in the cultural history of the sixties, the name we now give to signify delegitimation of power and the search for alternative forms of social and political life. I think it is not accidental that collaborative learning emerged initially within open admissions programs, as part of a wider response to political pressures from below to extend literacy and access to higher education to black, Hispanic, and working-class people who had formerly been excluded.

From the late seventies to the present, Bruffee has asked what it means to reorganize the social relations in the classroom and how the decentering of authority that takes place in collaborative learning might change the way we talk about the nature of liberal education and the authority of knowledge and its institutions. Bruffee's ongoing efforts to find a language adequate to this task — to theorize collaborative learning as a social constructionist pedagogy — have turned, in the ensuing discussion, into the source of recent left-wing challenges to his work. One of the central issues of contention concerns Bruffee's appropriation of Richard Rorty's notion of conversation.

The term conversation has become a social constructionist code word to talk about knowledge and teaching and learning as social — not cognitive — acts. Knowledge, in this account, is not the result of the confrontation of the individual mind with reality but of the conversation that organizes the available means we have at any given time to talk about reality. Learning, therefore, cannot be understood strictly on cognitive grounds; it means rather joining new communities and taking part in new conversations. Learning, as Rorty puts it, "is a shift in a person's relations with others, not a shift inside the person that now *suits* him to enter new relationships" (*Philosophy* 187). By organizing students to participate in conversation, Bruffee argues, collaborative learning forms transitional communities to help students undergo the stressful and anxiety-inducing process of moving out of their indigenous communities and acquiring fluency in the conversation of liberally educated men and women. For Bruffee, Rorty's notion of conversation provides a rationale for collaborative learning as a process of re-acculturation, of learning to participate in the ongoing discussions of new communities.

This is a powerful rationale because it translates a wider reinterpretation of knowledge taking place in contemporary critical theory to the classroom — and gives us a way to incorporate what Bruffee calls the "social turn" in twentieth-century thought into the theory and practice of teaching. Still, for left-wing teachers and theorists, there is something troubling about Rorty's notion of conversation, something in the metaphor worth unpacking.

For Rorty, the term conversation offers a useful way to talk about the production of knowledge as a social process without reference to metaphysical foundations. Rorty's notion of conversation describes a discourse that has no beginning or end, but no crisis or contradiction, either. Cut loose from meta-physical moorings and transcendental backups, the conversation keeps rolling of its own accord, reproducing itself effortlessly, responsible only to itself, sanctioned by what Rorty sees as the only sanction credible: our loyalty to the conversation and our solidarity with its practices. All we can do is to continue the conversation initiated before we appeared on the scene. "We do not know," Rorty says, "what 'success' would mean except simply 'continuance'" (*Consequences* 172).

In political terms, what Rorty calls "postmodernist bourgeois liberalism" hangs onto the "ideals of the Enlightenment" but gives up the belief in Enlightenment reason. In Rorty's hands, the metaphor of conversation invokes an eighteenth-century vision of freely constituted, discoursing subjects taking part in polite speech, in Enlightenment salons and coffee houses, in the "republic of letters" emerging in the interstices of the absolutist state. To historicize Rorty's metaphor is to disclose what Terry Eagleton calls the "bourgeoisie's dream of freedom": "a society of petty producers whose endlessly available, utterly inexhaustible commodity is discourse itself" (16–17). As Eagleton argues, the "bourgeoisie...discovers in discourse an idealized image of its own social relations" (16). Conversation becomes the only truly free market, an ideal discursive space where exchange without domination is possible, where social differences are converted into abstract equalities at the level of speech acts.

Only now, Rorty says, the discourse must operate without the consensus of universal reason that eighteenth-century speakers took to be the normative grounding of their utterances. Given the postmodernist's disbelief in metanar-ratives of reason and freedom, Rebecca Comay argues, the conversation loses its emancipatory edge and "adapts to the episodic rhythms of commercial culture" (122). If we've traded in the old metaphysical comforts for a cheerful, if ungrounded, affirmation of conversation, we do so, Rorty says, so we can "read more, talk more, write more" (*Philosophy* 375). The logic of planned obsolescence drives the conversation as we look for the "new, better, more interesting, more fruitful ways of speaking" (*Philosophy* 360). In a world without foundations, "nobody is so passe as the intellectual czar of the previous generation...the man who redescribed all those old descriptions, which, thanks in part to his redescriptions of them, nobody now wants to know anything about" (*Consequences* xl–xli). According to the idealized exchange of a free and open market, conversation keeps circulating in a spectacle of production and consumption. The new becomes old, the fashionable out-of-date, but the conversation itself is inexhaustible. "Evanescent moments in a continuing conversation...we keep the conversation going" (*Philosophy* 378).

Stripped of its universalist principles, the conversation turns into an act of assimilation. Unpacked, Rorty's metaphor of conversation offers a version of non-foundationalism without tears. The consensus that keeps things rolling is no longer based on higher purposes but instead on the recognition that if we cannot discover the truth in any final sense, what we can do is to keep on talking to each other: we can tell stories, give accounts, state reasons, negotiate differences, and so on. The conversation, that is, gives up teleological ends to reaffirm the sociability of intellectual exchange. And if, as Rorty says, the conversation is simply the way we justify our beliefs socially, then we might as well relax, get good at it, and enjoy it.

Of course there are considerable attractions to this view. But there are some problems too. Rorty acknowledges, for example, the tendency of discourse to normalize itself and to block the flow of conversation by posing as a "canonical vocabulary." The conversation, as Rorty starts to acknowledge here, is perpetually materializing itself in institutional forms, alloting the opportunity to speak and arbitrating the terms of discussion. But Rorty, finally, backs away from the full consequences of conversation's normative force. At just the point where we could name the conversation and its underlying consensus as a technology of power and ask how its practices enable and constrain the production of knowledge, privilege and exclude forms of discourse, set its agenda by ignoring or suppressing others, Rorty builds a self-correcting mechanism into the conversation, an invisible hand to keep the discourse circulating and things from going stale. This is abnormal discourse or, as Rorty says, "what happens when someone joins in the discourse who is ignorant of...conventions or who sets them aside" (*Philosophy* 320).

Rorty's view of abnormal discourse is, I think, a problematical one. On one hand, it identifies abnormal discourse with a romantic realm of thinking the unthinkable, of solitary voices calling out, of the imagination cutting against the grain. In keeping with this romantic figure of thought, Rorty makes abnormal discourse the activity par excellence not of the group but of the individual—the genius, the rebel, the fool, "some*one*...who is ignorant of...conventions or sets them aside." This side of abnormal discourse, moreover, resists formulation. There is, Rorty says, "no discipline which describes it, any more than there is a discipline devoted to a study of the unpredictable, or of 'creativity'" (*Philosophy* 320). It is simply "generated by free and leisured conversation...as the sparks fly up" (321).

At the same time, though we can't know abnormal discourse on its own terms, we can identify how it functions, but now from a pragmatist perspective, to keep the conversation going. In other words, at just the moment Rorty seems to introduce difference and destabilize the conversation, he turns crisis, conflict, and contradiction into homeostatic gestures whose very expression restabilizes the conversation. What remains, once we've removed universal reason, narratives of emancipation, or "permanent neutral frameworks" as the grounds for adjudicating knowledge claims, is civility, the agreement to keep on talking. The "power of strangeness" in abnormal discourse "to take us out of our old selves" and "to make us into new beings" (*Philosophy* 360) simply reaffirms our solidarity with the conversation.

Left-wing critics are uncomfortable with this position. They want to interrupt the conversation, to denaturalize its workings, and to talk about the way conversation legitimizes itself by its very performance. Left-wing critics worry that Rortyian conversation downplays its own social force and the conflict it generates, the discourses silenced or unheard in the conversation and its representation of itself. They suspect there are other voices to take into account — voices constituted as otherness outside the conversation. For this reason, left-wing critics want to redefine consensus by locating it in the prevailing balance of power, as a marker that sets the boundaries between discourses. As Myers suggests, we need to see consensus in terms of differences and not just of agreements, "as the result of conflicts, not as a monolith" (166). Redefining consensus as a matter of conflict suggests, moreover, that consensus does not so much reconcile differences through rational negotiation. Instead, such a redefinition represents consensus as a strategy that structures differences by organizing them in relation to each other. In this sense, consensus cannot be known without its opposite — without the other voices at the periphery of the conversation.

By looking at consensus in terms of conflict rather than agreement, we get a somewhat different picture of the relationship between normal and abnormal discourse than the one Rorty and Bruffee have offered. Redefining consensus leads us, I think, to abandon the view that abnormal discourse functions as a complement to normal discourse, something which, as Bruffee says, students can turn to from time to time to question business as usual and to keep the conversation going. Instead, abnormal discourse represents the result at any given time of the set of power relations that organizes normal discourse: the acts of permission and prohibition, of incorporation and exclusion that institute the structure and practices of discourse communities. Abnormal discourse is not so much a homeostatic mechanism that keeps the conversation and thereby the community renewed and refreshed. Instead, it refers to dissensus, to marginalized voices, the resistance and contestation both within and outside the conversation, what Roland Barthes calls acratic discourse — the discourses out of power. Abnormal discourse, that is, refers not only to surprises and accidents that emerge when normal discourse reaches a dead end, when, as Wittgenstein puts it, "language goes on holiday." In the account I'm suggesting, it also refers to the relations of power that determine what falls within the current consensus and what is assigned the status of dissent. Abnormal discourse, from this perspective, is neither as romantic nor as pragmatic as Rorty makes it out to be. Rather it offers a way to analyze the strategic moves by which discourse communities legitimize their own conversation by marginalizing others. It becomes a critical term to describe the conflict among discourses and collective wills in the heterogeneous conversation in contemporary public life.

Bruffee argues that such an emphasis on conflict has led his left-wing critics to want to "turn to 'struggle' to force change in 'people's interests'" (Response 714). I would reply that struggle is not something people, left-wing or otherwise, can "turn to" or choose to do. "Struggle," at least the way I understand it, is something we're born into: it's a standard feature of contemporary social existence. We experience "struggle" all the time in everyday life precisely because, as Bruffee points out, we "all belong to many overlapping, mutually inclusive communities." We "experience belonging to each of these communities as both limiting and liberating" (715) in part because we experience the discourses, or what Bruffee calls the "vernacular languages of the communities one belongs to," as a polyphony of voices, an internal conversation traversed by social, cultural, and linguistic differences.

Bruffee uses the term vernacular to call attention to the plurality of voices that constitute our verbal thought. The intersecting vernaculars that we experience contending for our attention and social allegiance, however, are not just plural. They are also organized in hierarchical relations of power. The term vernacular, after all, as Houston Baker reminds us, "signals" on etymological and ideological grounds "'a slave born on his master's estate'" (2). The term vernacular, that is, cannot be understood apart from the relations of domination and subordination it implies. The conversation, in Bakhtin's word, is "heteroglot," a mosaic of vernaculars, the multi-accented idiomatic expression of race, class, and gender differences. The conversation gives voice to the conflicts inherent in an unequal social order and in the asymmetrical relations of power in everyday life.

Bruffee worries that "struggle" means interrupting the conversation to "force change in people's interests." Bruffee's worries here betray what seems to me a persistent anxiety in non-foundationalist versions of social constructionist thought about its own radical disclosure: that once we give up extra-historical and universal criteria and reduce the authority of knowledge to a self-legitimizing account of its own practices, we won't have a way to separate persuasion from force, validity claims from plays of power. As Rorty puts it, to "suggest that there is *no* . . . common ground seems to endanger rationality. . . . To question the need for commensuration seems the first step toward a return to a war of 'all against all'" (*Philosophy* 317). In the account I'm suggesting, "struggle" is not a matter of interrupting the conversation to replace consensual validation with force. It refers rather to the relations between the two terms — intellectual negotiation and power — in what we think of as rational argument and public discourse. The term "struggle" is simply a way of shifting rhetorical analysis, as Victor Vitanza has suggested, from Aristotelean persuasion or Burkean identification to an agonistic framework of conflict and difference — to a rhetoric of dissensus.

The choice, as I see it, does not consist of solidarity with a self-explaining conversation or violence. I want to preserve, along with Bruffee and Rorty, the value of civility and consensus. But to do this we will need to rehabilitate the notion of consensus by redefining it in relation to a rhetoric of dissensus. We will need, that is, to look at collaborative learning not merely as a process of consensus-making but more important as a process of identifying differences and locating these differences in relation to each other. The consensus that we ask students to reach in the collaborative classroom will be based not so much on collective agreements as on collective explanations of how people differ, where their differences come from, and whether they can live and work together with these differences.

To think of consensus in terms of dissensus is to challenge a central rationale Bruffee has offered for collaborative learning. Bruffee currently holds that one of the benefits of collaborative learning is that its consensual practices model the normal workings of discourse communities in business, government, the professions, and academia. Myers argues, correctly I think, that Bruffee's use of consensus risks accepting the current production and distribution of knowledge and discourse as unproblematical and given. The limit of Myers' critique, however, is that it concedes Bruffee's claim that consensus is in fact the norm in business, industry, and the professions. In this regard, both Bruffee and Myers seriously underestimate the extent to which the conversations of these discourse communities are regulated not so much by consensual negotiation and shared decision-making as by what Jurgen Habermas calls a "success orientation" of instrumental control and rational efficiency.

It can be misleading, therefore, to tell students, as social constructionists do, that learning to write means learning to participate in the conversation and consensual practices of various discourse communities. Instead, we need to ask students to explore the rhetoric of dissensus that pervades writing situations. As Susan Wells argues, even such apparently prosaic and "unheroic" tasks as writing manuals for the computer-assisted redesign of an auto body section take place within a complicated network of competing and contradictory interests. In the case of the design manual that Wells cites, the technical writer faces three different audiences. Concerned with the overall operation of a computer system, the first audience of systems programmers may be just as likely to guard their professional knowledge of the system as to collaborate with others. They may, in fact, see the second audience, application programmers responsible for writing programs for specific design tasks, as "enemies" looking for ways to "tweak" or "jiggle" the system to get their work done — and who thereby threaten the overall performance of the system. The third audience of users, on the other hand, needs to know how to operate the system on narrow job-related grounds. But from both the programmers' perspective, this group is an unknown variable, men and women who may be "demonically curious" and want to play with the system, to see how it really works.

By exploring the differential access to knowledge and the relations of power and status that structure this writing situation, Wells says, students can learn not only how technical writers "write for success" by adjusting to multiple audiences. (As it turned out, the technical writer produced a separate manual containing quite different information for each of the audiences.) Students can also learn to articulate a rhetoric of dissensus that will lead them to see that the goal of discourse in this case, as Wells puts it, "is systematic misunderstanding and concealment...the total fragmentation and dispersal of knowledge" (256). They can learn, that is, not how consensus is achieved through collaborative negotiation but rather how differences in interest produce conflicts that may in fact block communication and prohibit the development of consensus.

Of course, it is true, as Wells notes, that not all organizations rely upon such a rigid division of labor. Collaboration and consensual decision-making, after all, have become buzz words for "new age" managers and technocrats.

Part of the current conventional wisdom about the new information society is that cooperation and collaboration will replace the competitive and individualistic ethos of the entrepreneurial age of industrial capitalism. But finally what collaboration and consensus amount to are not so much new paradigms for a high-tech post-industrial order as new versions of an older industrial psychology adopted to late capitalism—human relations techniques to bolster morale, promote identification with the corporation, legitimize differential access to knowledge and status, and increase productivity. Even in the ostensibly disinterested realm of academics, the production of knowledge is motivated as much by career moves as by consensus, by the efforts of individuals to enhance their credentials and relative position in a field, to build up their fund of cultural capital.

At issue here is not whether collaborative learning reflects more accurately than traditional pedagogies the actual social relations that produce knowledge and make organizations run. Surely it does. But by modeling collaborative learning on the normal workings of discourse communities, Bruffee identifies the authority of knowledge with the prevailing productive apparatus. For social constructionists, this is an uncontroversial point. In one sense, it is the point— that the present configuration of knowledge and its institutions is a social artifact. But in another sense, this line of thought also concedes the authority of knowledge to the professional judgment of experts, to academic specialties and professional training, to the wider meritocratic order of a credentialed society.

If one of the goals of collaborative learning is to replace the traditional hierarchical relations of teaching and learning with the practices of participatory democracy, we must acknowledge that one of the functions of the professions and the modern university has been to specialize and to remove knowledge from public discourse and decision-making, to reduce it to a matter of expertise and technique. By the same token, we must acknowledge that it devalues the notion of consensus to identify it with the current professional monopolies of knowledge. If anything, the prevailing configuration of knowledge and its institutions *prevents* the formation of consensus by shrinking the public sphere and excluding the majority of the population from the conversation.

The effect of Bruffee's use of consensus is to invest a kind of "real world" authority in the discursive practices and tacit understandings that bind the discourse communities of specialists and experts together. It makes the conversation a self-explaining mechanism that legitimizes itself through its performances. "This," we tell students, "is the way we [English teachers, biologists, lawyers, chemical engineers, social workers, whatever] do things around here. There's nothing magical about it. It's just the way we talk to each other." The problem is that invoking the "real world" authority of such consensual practices neutralizes the critical and transformative project of collaborative learning, depoliticizes it, and reduces it to an acculturative technique.

To develop a critical version of collaborative learning, we will need to distinguish between consensus as an acculturative practice that reproduces business as usual and consensus as an oppositional one that challenges the prevailing conditions of production. The point of collaborative learning is not simply to demystify the authority of knowledge by revealing its social character but to transform the productive apparatus, to change the social character of production. In this regard, it will help to cast consensus not as a "real world" practice but as a utopian one.

To draw out the utopian possibilities I believe are implied in collaborative learning, we will need to distinguish between "spurious" and "genuine" consensus, as grounded and problematical as these terms may appear to be. In his theory of "communicative action," Habermas defines "genuine" consensus not as something that actually happens but instead as the counterfactual anticipation that agreement can be reached without coercion or systematic distortion. Consensus, for Habermas, is not, as it is for social constructionists like Bruffee, an empirical account of how discourse communities operate but a critical and normative representation of the conditions necessary for fully realized communication to occur. In Habermas' view, we should represent consensus not as the result at any given time of the prevailing conversation but rather as an aspiration to organize the conversation according to relations to non-domination. The anticipation of consensus, that is, projects what Habermas calls an "ideal speech situation," a utopian discursive space that distributes symmetrically the opportunity to speak, to initiate discourse, to question, to give reasons, to do all those other things necessary to justify knowledge socially. From this perspective, consensus becomes a necessary fiction of reciprocity and mutual recognition, the dream of conversation as perfect dialogue. Understood as a utopian desire, assembled from the partial and fragmentary forms of the current conversation, consensus does not appear as the end or the explanation of the conversation but instead as a means of transforming it.

To cast consensus as a utopian instead of a "real world" practice has a number of implications for the collaborative classroom. For one thing, a utopian representation of consensus offers students a powerful critical instrument to interrogate the conversation — to interrupt it in order to investigate the forces which determine who may speak and what may be said, what inhibits communication and what makes it possible. The normal workings of collaborative learning, as Bruffee describes them, ask students to generate an interpretive response to a literary work or a rhetorical analysis of a piece of writing and then to compare the results to the responses or analyses of their teacher and the community of scholars the teacher represents. The pedagogical goal is to negotiate a common language in the classroom, to draw students into a wider consensus, and to initiate them into the conversation as it is currently organized in the academy. The utopian view of consensus, on the other hand, would abandon this expert-novice model of teaching and learning. Instead consensus would provide students with a critical measure to identify the relations of power in the formation of expert judgment.

Let me give an example here. Collaborative learning in literature classes is often based on the idea that students need to avoid, on the one hand, the objectivism that assumes the meaning is in the text and, on the other, the radical pluralism that assumes we cannot distinguish the merits of one reading from another. Collaborative learning, that is, seeks to locate authority in neither the text nor the reader but in what Stanley Fish calls interpretive communities. From the perspective I am suggesting, however, the identification of collaborative learning with interpretive communities takes for granted the enterprise of interpretation as an end in itself.

In contrast, I think we need to begin collaborative classes by asking why interpretation has become the unquestioned goal of literary studies and what other kinds of readings thereby have been excluded and devalued. We would be interested in the forces which have produced dissensus about how to go about reading a literary text and about what constitutes a literary text in the first place. Students, of course, already know a good deal about all this: they are used to naming Shakespeare and Dickens and Hemingway as literature and disqualifying Stephen King, thrillers, and science fiction. What students have had less opportunity to do is to investigate collectively these implicit hierarchies in terms of the relations of power that organize them. Their literature classes have taught them to segregate kinds of reading but without asking them where these differences come from.

For this reason, we might begin the conversation in literature classes by talking not about how to read a literary text but rather about how the students in the course have been trained to read literature and how their schooled reading differs from the way they read outside of school. By examining these differences, freshmen and sophomores in introductory literature courses, I have found, can begin to examine critically the prevailing representation of literature and the institutional base on which it rests. Students rather quickly will distinguish between literature — which is assigned by teachers and is "good for you" — and the other reading they do — which is "for fun." They explain to each other and to me that literature is filled with "hidden meanings" and that the point of schooled reading is to dig them out, while the reading they do for "fun" produces strong identification with characters and teaches them about "life" or gives them the opportunity to escape from it.

The point of such discussion is not to reach agreement about what properly belongs in the realm of literature and what lies outside of it. Nor is it to abandon the usefulness of schooled reading. Rather what students begin to see is that literature exists as a social category that depends on its relation to non-literature. Students, that is, can begin to sketch the rhetoric of dissensus that structures the dominant representation of what literature is and is not and that produces marked differences in the way they read and experience texts.

Such discussions, moreover, give students permission to elaborate what they already know — namely, that schooled reading for "hidden meanings" reinforces the authority of expert readers and creates professional monopolies of knowledge. By drawing on their own experience as readers in and out of school, students regularly and spontaneously make the same telling point William E. Cain makes in *The Crisis in Criticism* that the institution of literature depends upon the "close reading" of specialist critics. In this regard, one of the most valuable things students bring to a literature class is what we as professional readers have largely forgotten — the imprecise, unanalytical act of non-close reading, the experience of ordinary readers at home, on the subway, or at the beach in the summer, the kind of reading that schooled reading marks as different.

One of the benefits of emphasizing the dissensus that surrounds the act of reading is that it poses consensus not as the goal of the conversation but rather as a critical measure to help students identify the structures of power that inhibit communication among readers (and between teachers and students) by authorizing certain styles of reading while excluding others. What students in introductory literature classes learn, I think, is to overcome the feeling that they don't get the point of literature or that they just like to read "trash." Instead, they learn why readers disagree about what counts as a reading, where the differences they experience as readers come from, and how we might usefully bring these differences into relation to each other. They learn to probe not only the ideology of the institution of literature but also the ideologies of popular reading. Just as they learn how schooled reading constitutes them as students in a complicated relationship to the authority of teachers and the institution of literature, students also learn that the reading they do outside of school is not simply a pastime but more important represents an act of self-formation that organizes their experience and desire in imaginary relations to the popular culture of late capitalism and its construction of race, class, and gender differences.

The revised notion of consensus I am proposing here depends paradoxically on its deferral, not its realization. I am less interested in students achieving consensus (although of course this happens at times) as in their using consensus as a critical instrument to open gaps in the conversation through which differences may emerge. In this regard, the Habermasian representation of consensus as a counterfactual anticipation of fully realized communication offers students a critical tool to identify the structures of power which determine who may speak and what may be said. But more important, this notion of consensus also offers students utopian aspirations to transform the conversation by freeing it from the prevailing constraints on its participants, the manipulations, deceptions, and plays of power. Through a collective investigation of differences, students can begin to imagine ways to change the relations of production and to base the conversation not on consensus but on reciprocity and the mutual recognition of the participants and their differences.

Unlike Habermas, however, I do not believe removing relations of domination and systematic distortion, whether ideological or neurotic, from the conversation is likely to establish the conditions in which consensus will express a "rational will" and "permit what *all* can want" (108). Instead, I want to displace consensus to a horizon which may never be reached. We need to see consensus, I think, not as an agreement that reconciles differences through an ideal conversation but rather as the desire of humans to live and work together with differences. The goal of consensus, it seems to me, ought to be not the unity of generalizable interests but rather what Iris Marion Young calls "an openness to unassimilated otherness." (22). Under the utopian aegis of consensus, students can learn to agree to disagree, not because "everyone has their own opinion," but because justice demands that we recognize the inexhaustibility of difference and that we organize the conditions in which we live and work accordingly.

By organizing students non-hierarchically so that all discursive roles are available to all the participants in a group, collaborative learning can do more than model or represent the normal workings of discourse communities. Students' experience of non-domination in the collaborative classroom can offer them a critical measure to understand the distortions of communication and the plays of power in normal discourse. Replacing the "real world" authority of consensus with a rhetoric of dissensus can lead students to demystify the normal workings of discourse communities. But just as important, a rhetoric of dissensus can lead them to redefine consensus as a utopian project, a dream of difference without domination. The participatory and democratic practices of collaborative learning offer an important instance of what Walter Benjamin, in "The Author as Producer," calls the "exemplary character of production" — the collective effort to "induce other producers to produce" and to "put an improved apparatus at their disposal" (233). In this regard, the exemplary character of production in collaborative learning can release collective energies to turn the means of criticism into a means of transformation, to tap fundamental impulses toward emancipation and justice in the utopian practices of Habermas' "ideal speech situation."

It would be fatuous, of course, to presume that collaborative learning can constitute more than momentarily an alternative to the present asymmetrical relations of power and distribution of knowledge and its means of production. But it can incite desire through common work to resolve, if only symbolically, the contradictions students face because of the prevailing conditions of production — the monopoly of expertise and the impulse to know, the separation of work and play, allegiance to peers and dependence on faculty esteem, the experience of cooperation and the competitiveness of a ranking reward system, the empowering sense of collectivity and the isolating personalization of an individual's fate. A rehabilitated notion of consensus in collaborative learning can provide students with exemplary motives to imagine alternative worlds and transformations of social life and labor. In its deferred and utopian form, consensus offers a way to orchestrate dissensus and to turn the conversation in the collaborative classroom into a heterotopia of voices — a heterogeneity without hierarchy.

Works cited

Baker, Houston A., Jr. *Blues, Ideology, and Afro-American Literature*. Chicago: U of Chicago P, 1984.

Beade, Pedro. Comment. *College English 49* (1987): 708.

Benjamin, Walter. "The Author as Producer." *Reflections*. Ed. Peter Demetz. New York: Schocken, 1986, 220–38.

Bruffee, Kenneth A. "Collaborative Learning: Some Practical Models." *College English 34* (1973): 634–43.

———. Response. *College English 49* (1987): 711–16.

Cain, William E. *The Crisis in Criticism: Theory, Literature, and Reform in English Studies*. Baltimore: John Hopkins UP, 1984.

Comay, Rebecca. "Interrupting the Conversation: Notes on Rorty." *Telos 69* (1986): 119–30.

Eagleton, Terry. *The Function of Criticism*. London: Verso, 1984.

Foster, David. Comment. *College English 49* (1987): 709–11.

Habermas, Jurgen. *Legitimation Crisis*. Trans. Thomas McCarthy. Boston: Beacon, 1975.

Johnson, Thomas S. Comment. *College English 48* (1986): 76.

Myers, Greg. "Reality, Consensus, and Reform in the Rhetoric of Composition Teaching." *College English 48* (1986): 154–74.

Rorty, Richard. *The Consequences of Pragmatism*. Minneapolis: U of Minnesota P, 1982.

———. *Philosophy and the Mirror of Nature*. Princeton: Princeton UP, 1979.

Vitanza, Victor. "Critical Sub/Versions of the History of Philosophical Rhetoric." *Rhetoric Review 6.1* (1987): 41–66.

Wells, Susan. "Habermas, Communicative Competence, and the Teaching of Technical Discourse." *Theory in the Classroom*. Ed. Cary Nelson. Urbana: U of Illinois P. 1986, 245–69.

Young, Iris Marion. "The Ideal of Community and the Politics of Difference." *Social Theory and Practice 12.1* (1986): 1–26.

What Is Possible In Literacy Education?

NINETEEN

Conversations with Parents: Talking about Literacy and Living
Lynn Moody

I greet Maria, a Winnipeg woman, at the principal's office door. We have never met before. I am immediately struck by her dark, stylishly coiffured hair and gold business suit. She looks like an executive in a major corporation. I am puzzled about why the principal has chosen her to represent the inner city. As I listen to Maria's story, I understand. Choosing her words slowly and apologizing along the way, Maria begins:

I went last year and two years ago [to the school's Parent–Child Center to learn English]. I never have time before. When I came to Canada about eleven years ago, the Portuguese community is that way. You want to come, you have to work. You want a house, you have to work damn hard. When I come here, this is the way that my people teach me. Go work—if you want the good life. I work day and night. I had no time to go to school.

In the factory, I work hard, about eight hours...with cold chicken and ice....Hard work...same as a man's. I have good money, okay? But after, I lose my health. I am sick. Sick all the time. Paralyzed two times—my legs. From the cold. And I quit. But when I felt sick, I went to the hospital. I am there about one month and a half. I realize you need English. I realize I was stupid I never went to school. My daughter comes all the time to tell my feelings. I feel low. After that, I think about to go to school. I came here. I found out about the program.

Salena sits across from me at a table in a Toronto public school library. We have just met. She, like Maria, has agreed to talk to me, a visiting teacher, about kids, parents, and schools. As the tape-recorder hums in the background, I am conscious that her deep, black eyes lead the telling of her story. When they dance, I know this chapter is full of happy memories and hope. When they

---

The names of parents have been changed to maintain confidentiality.

glaze over, her lashes flicking away the pools of moisture collecting in the corners of her eyes, I know what I'm hearing is painful. Speaking of her oldest daughter and her attitude towards school, Salena says:

> She's so excited by it. She loves to talk about it. She wants me to listen. She wants to go right up to university. She wants to be a principal of a school. So it means education right through in her life. She likes designing. So she designs the clothes for them [both daughters]. I'm a dressmaker by trade.... Sometimes I see a fashion in the store. I cannot draw, so she does the drawing. I come home and I cut and I sew and it's even better than what I saw at the store.
>
> My own school life...it was a struggle. Learning was very hard for me. My mom was always busy in the grocery. My dad was not there. He passed away when I was four. [My mother] couldn't read. Why did I leave [school in grade nine]? Most of the girls had boyfriends and got into trouble. I stayed at home and learned dressmaking. I was not a career-minded woman. I would like to go back to school now.

The hour goes by too quickly. Another parent is waiting in the hall to talk to me. I stand up, thanking Salena for her time. Our eyes meet again. Salena reaches her arms around my shoulders, drawing me to her chest. "Thank you!" she whispers, her words breaking with emotion. "You made me feel so important...so special...thank you."

Back home in Halifax, I meet Vanessa, a parent in an inner-city school where I will be teaching when my sabbatical ends. Vanessa shares her experiences as a former student in this school her children now attend.

> In some ways it's just the same. In other ways it's different.... It feels strange.... I liked it and I hated it. The only thing I liked about school was Math and English. I did good in those. If I was late in the morning, I hated having to stay an hour after school. It never did no good. I still came late.... Then I moved to Cole Harbour. I got pregnant, so I quit. I knew I couldn't keep my baby if I went back to school.

Joan, a parent who lives in the community and who works with students from the same inner-city school, shares her story of struggle and success,

> I was an outspoken child. I lived in Mulgrave Park [a public housing complex built by Halifax City when Africville was demolished]. I was the oldest. I had a tough side in that "You're not going to walk over me or my family." I had to fight a lot.... One teacher had a prejudice problem. My mother knew. She let me stay home so I had a tutor the rest of that year in grade seven. Without the support from home, I don't know...God knows where I'd be. It wasn't anything she [mother] ever really said verbally. It was just from seeing her. She was a single parent. Seeing what she did. Seeing her sisters, even in the same boat as her, and them not accomplishing.... I was lucky because my mom had connections.
>
> I worry about my kids. They're more intimidated by other people. He's [one child in same school] more quiet than me. I know he's bullied. He doesn't fight back. Kids are always trying to bring him down. I was always bright. I had no problems in school. He does. He has learning problems. I worry about him

getting back and forth because of my knowledge of people in the neighborhood. People putting him up to things.

I think the expectations of the school are too low. I don't know why. The parents' attitudes, too. They could be "upped." Give the kids more credit.

These stories are excerpts from four (of forty) conversations that took place during the 1989−90 school year in inner-city schools in Winnipeg, Toronto, and Halifax. Having spent most of my teaching years in inner-city schools, I was disturbed by the messages of failure that pervaded these schools. No matter how hard educators, parents, and the children themselves appeared to try, the majority of these inner-city kids weren't making the grade in school. Yet the out-of-school experiences of these same students seemed to suggest that they were very competent in other ways. Stories of individual and group success in community sports, youth groups, local film roles, poetry and rap contests as well as the children's shared experiences of daily family responsibilities, perseverance, and street smarts indicated that many of these students were successful in environments other than school.

Were the kids failing the school system, or was the school system failing the kids? I wanted to find out what people in the inner city thought about the problem. How did they define it? What ideas for solving the problem or at least beginning to address it could they offer?

My concerns led me to design an independent course of study with my advisor. Along with reading a considerable amount of the research related to inner-city education, I planned visits to inner-city schools to talk with staff and parents. I was new to the interview process and spent much time reading about and designing open-ended questions to guide my inquiry. I knew that I needed enough structure in each interview to allow me to compare answers among individuals, but I was also concerned that too much structure could create superficial and stilted talk. What I hoped for was real conversation that allowed people the opportunity to share personal interpretation and individual life stories. At the beginning of each interview, I explained that there were no right or wrong answers to my questions. I was only interested in honest interpretations. People trusted and shared. As a result of their candor, my thinking about literacy, success, and failure was challenged and changed.

Prior to these conversations, I viewed literacy rather traditionally as the ability to use language to speak, read, and write. Because I was teaching in an English-speaking community, I interpreted my teaching role as assisting students in becoming literate using standard English. As a result of my conversations and reading, I now think that literacy and literacy teaching cannot be so simply defined. Gee (1987) and Heath (1983) suggest that each of us is privy to a variety of literacies. Some literacies we are born into, or acquire, and other literacies we consciously learn. If school literacies are similar to students' acquired literacies (in actions, values, and ways of using language), then success in learning them is both possible and even probable. However, as in the case of many inner-city families, if the acquired literacies do not match or prepare the student for learning school literacies, students can find such new learning confusing and contradictory.

Until I talked with inner-city parents, I had little appreciation of the possibility that school failure might be linked to the contradictions between acquired and learned literacies. As I listened to parents' stories, I began to realize the importance of knowing about student success in acquiring other literacies. That knowledge could help me recognize and value acquired literacies as well as guide my teaching as I helped students learn new literacies.

While my conversations with teachers and administrators were meaningful and revealing, it was the voices of parents that most affected my rethinking of the inner city, failure, and success. As parents shared their stories, I began to understand how ways of thinking about family, culture, race, gender, education, and work intersected to shape people's choices and experiences. I began to appreciate success and competence in terms of out-of-school living. I was forced to look beyond the traditional school definitions. I began to have a better understanding of factors other than school success or failure that contributed to people's educational decision making.

Through the voices of Salena, Joan, and Maria, I learned about growing up in single-parent, mother-led homes. I began to see how this experience limited one woman's educational choices and how it provided a strong, successful role model for another woman's success. I heard how gender affected the way their families, their cultures, and their society viewed them and how these views influenced their personal decision making (girls were getting "into trouble. I stayed at home and learned dressmaking"; "I got pregnant so I quit"; "My brother wanted to send me to secretarial school"). I came to know about the work these women did. ("I couldn't keep my baby if I went back"; "I worked in the factory...day and night....I have good money,...but I lose my health"; "I am a dressmaker by trade"; "Hard work....same as a man's").

As each woman talked about education, I first heard about their personal experiences. Stories of success were sometimes punctuated with periods of frustration, pain, and prejudice. Themes of abandoned dreams and still-unfulfilled wishes became evident ("I liked...English and Math....I knew I couldn't keep my baby if I went back to school"; "I would like to go back"). Like all parents, these women talked hopefully to me of better things for their own children. Success in the future was often linked to better education ("She's so excited by it....She wants to be a principal"; "I think the expectations of the school are too low").

I learned about cultures different from my own. Salena shared how her protective East Indian family practices (ones that allow children outside the home only if accompanied by a parent) helped her control her children's out-of-school experiences. These beliefs made it difficult for her to understand why so many other inner-city children were permitted to be in malls and streets unsupervised. She also explained her husband's "very strict" role as father and her own "more flexible" role as mother. When I listened to Maria's story of accepting, then questioning and abandoning her Portuguese culture's emphasis on work, I began to appreciate the cultural alienation she risked. I admired her willingness to learn a new language and how she transformed that new language ability into community action as a translator and as a teacher of others. Joan's story of racial prejudice sensitized me to the issue of racism in education in my own city.

These conversations with parents were individually, then collectively, critical incidents for me. Newman (1990) describes critical incidents as "those occurrences which let us see with new eyes some aspect of what we do. They make us aware of the beliefs and assumptions that underlie our instructional practices" (p. 17). By listening to these parents' stories, I came to appreciate how my new knowledge of these out-of-school literacies and competencies could affect and inform my teaching practice. Had I been a teacher of any of their children, I now understood how talking to these parents would help me understand the students and their families in ways I had never known before. I would know about the child at home and in the community. I would not be limited by my narrow understanding of their success or failure in the school environment only. I recognized that I would have a much better appreciation of the whole child.

As parents shared their life stories, I also faced the fact that our views and interpretations of the world did not always agree. I began to see that honest collaboration with parents realistically involves not only consensus but also dissensus, "agreeing to disagree" (Trimbur 1989). The background knowledge of other contributing literacies helped me appreciate the importance of valuing and living with differences of view.

Having an enriched view of the whole child would help me shape curriculum to validate the child's out-of-school experiences. It would force me to examine how these other definitions of literacy are supported or hindered by the school's definitions and expectations. I was beginning to see ways of teaching that could bring into the classroom differing cultures, literacies, and ways of examining school literacies critically (Heath 1983; Bigelow 1989). By understanding success and competence in my students' out-of-school life, I might begin to examine the problem of academic failure endemic to inner-city schools. But I needed parents and students to inform me.

Challenging and changing

Why had I never experienced the intensity of this kind of conversation with any of my own students' parents? Why, after only forty-five minutes, did I feel closer to these strangers than to the parents of children I taught all year long? I tried to recapture images of past parent–teacher conversations:

> I'm sitting at my desk, chair positioned to watch the clock. A friend of mine has taught me this trick to avoid "running into" the next time slot. My appointment schedule is pinned to the bulletin board, and a second copy is posted on the classroom door for parents. Children's folders are organized outside the classroom on a table for parents to view before their appointment. Inside, I am enthusiastically explaining a child's progress to a parent. I occasionally stop the running commentary to suggest ways the parent could support classroom efforts at home.
>
> At the end of the time period, with thirty seconds left on the clock, while walking the parent to the door, I politely ask if the parent has any questions. The parent, as usual, says "No" — my assurance that I have done my job well. I turn to greet the next parent and "Beat the Clock" starts again. Twenty-one parents later, head pounding, voice hoarse, I gather my belongings and drive home, thankful that I have several months before the procedure is repeated. I am dog-tired, but I've done a good job, right?

Is the above description an exaggerated scenario? Perhaps a bit. But it reflects enough elements of truth for me to question what I have done in these ritualistic encounters (Lightfoot 1978). Sure, I've allowed a few questions. Yes, I've listened to a few bold or angry parents. Certainly, I've tried encouraging children to accompany their parents and I've shared taped sessions of individual children's reading. But in each meeting, I was so busy telling that I didn't allow for listening.

I realized that most of my parent−teacher encounters to date had not been conversations at all. They had been one-way transmissions. I also knew that for many inner-city parents the information I was transmitting was negative. Often their already stressed lives were burdened with my pleas to assist my job by engaging in educational endeavors at home. No wonder attendance at these parent−teacher interviews declined with each succeeding grade. No wonder parents of "problems" learned to avoid coming.

I also saw that my past experiences with parents did not create opportunities for me to learn about and from parents. The interviews I had conducted — my "critical incidents" — had demonstrated how important that kind of information could be for learning about my students and improving my teaching. How could I change my one-way talk *to* parents to become conversation *with* them? Parents expected and had a right to information about their child at school. But I needed to make time for parents to inform me. Then I could respond to students and their learning in more meaningful ways, valuing their perspectives and planning curriculum with them — curriculum that supports students critically "reading the word and the world" (Shor and Freire 1987). Rather than seeing teaching as limited to exploring what is and what was, I was beginning to see it as creating a learning environment in which students could question what was and what is and explore what is possible in terms of a more just and democratic world.

As I thought about what this new kind of parent−teacher relationship might be like, I began to examine some of the current buzzwords in the research literature: "parent−teacher−child partnerships"; "collaboration with parents"; "parent participation." At first, these terms conjured up wonderful egalitarian relationships. I read many accounts of successful parent participation in the school. But then, nudged by Dillon (1989), I became more suspicious of the lopsided nature of some of these relationships. Yes, the parents might be visibly helping the school, but how was the school supporting the parents? Parents might have a greater appreciation for the work of the school, but did the school have a better appreciation for the work and the world of individual parents? Were there ways to bridge the home−school worlds (Lightfoot 1978) in meaningfully reciprocal ways?

What's possible? What's realistic?

My conversations with parents have confirmed for me the need and the value of hearing about each other's worlds. Now that I am committed to authentic partnerships with parents in my school, what can I do this coming year to develop such relationships?

First, I plan to welcome parents into the classroom on a regular basis so we can begin to get to know each other. I also plan to make home visits in the fall. Rather than just arriving with a cute bag of educational tricks, I intend to listen and learn from the family. When parent—teacher interview sessions are scheduled, I will try to arrange longer appointments, limit my talk, address parents' concerns, and value their perceptions of the child at home and in the community. I will use this parent knowledge to inform my own developing knowledge of the child and to help me negotiate meaningful curriculum.

I also plan to suggest other, very different ways of getting together to learn about each other — perhaps biweekly or monthly "Family Nights" (such as one Toronto school was attempting) or "Family Afternoons" during school hours. I hope that these informal get-togethers will provide opportunities for school staff and families to meet and explore a variety of projects. My hope is that we would become a community of learners. Our joint time could be open to a wide number of enterprises limited only by our collaboratively defined needs and goals. These endeavors might range from publishing a community newspaper to addressing community issues of a social or environmental nature to writing community and cultural histories for our student library.

We could begin to learn about each other and each other's literacies on a schoolwide level. If parents feel welcome to examine the world of school in real ways, they may begin to see possibilities for change, too. As my new principal observed, "No parent here ever questions curriculum. They should be. They should be looking to see what we're not doing and demand that we do it." In the kind of community climate I am suggesting, the demand may more likely be expressed as a shared commitment among parents and staff to work toward common goals.

I see many possibilities for small and large group projects. Discussions might include topics of community culture, social, environmental, and educational issues. Reading and writing projects might result in articles for local community newspapers or publications of personal narratives, poetry, or community histories. We might explore oral storytelling, visual or performing art experiences together to communicate our ideas. The key feature of such a learning community seems to be, however, the inclusion of family voices, not just teachers', in defining what shape the Family Night or Family Afternoons will take. Rather than becoming just another school effort done to people, the concept of a community of learners has the possibility to create something worthwhile for all of us. Through the spirit of such a community, we should be able to find many creative and meaningful projects to engage in — projects aimed at making the school and the community better places in which to work and live; better places in which to learn about and from each other.

As I think about the possibility of such conversations and projects, my enthusiasm is countered with realistic concerns and fears. Will parents trust my sincerity? Will my new principal support such projects? Will my teaching colleagues value these projects? Will they want to become personally involved, or will they be threatened by my attempts to change my relationship with my students' parents? If our get-togethers uncover discomforting problems and issues, will we be able to talk honestly and frankly about them, and will we be willing to explore avenues of change?

I realize that the kinds of changes in parent—teacher—student relationships I am exploring confront and challenge a long history of tradition and ritual. For some people, past and present home—school relationships are accepted as necessarily confrontational roles. For these people, there is no perceived need to change. For others, myself included, the idealism of better things is a dream that is tempered with realistic constraints of time and resources.

I am not so romantic to believe that opening up conversation among people in the school and the community will (or even should) produce only happy encounters. There is much about life in the inner city that is frustrating, painful, and unjust. Attempting to change traditional home—school relationships will no doubt be a slow process met with much resistance. Many parents will have to go against their own histories and trust schools. Teachers may be uncomfortable with their new sense of vulnerability. As parents become more aware of current educational philosophies and teaching practices, there may be extremes of false hope and reactionary fear that these trends represent access or denial to the better life they so desperately want for their children. The opportunity to voice these concerns, explore the underlying assumptions, and make some attempt at reasonable interpretations would be important.

Exploring issues openly carries not only the potential for liberating experiences but also the risk of alienating ones (Harmon and Edelsky 1989). Social, cultural, and religious views from acquired and learned literacies may compete with one another. Exploring beliefs and values among them may uncover differences in views among family members and cultural group members. Working together to identify change that is possible might reveal considerable differences in opinion. These will be the times when we will most benefit from listening to and recognizing each other's perspectives. Agreeing to disagree is more important to productive and collaborative talk than trying to achieve false consensus that risks silencing or marginalizing some voices (Trimbur 1989). But unless the invitation for collaborative learning together is extended, we will be limited in our understanding of home and school worlds by the stereotypes of our own perspectives.

The conversations I experienced with parents this sabbatical year tell me that there are parents who are willing to begin to bridge the home—school worlds if teachers will only extend the invitation. Thanks to those wonderful parents, I now see reasons why I must extend those invitations to the parents in my own school. I now realize why, in my own small way, I need to begin to change the way I talk with and relate to parents of my students. I can learn so much about them, from them, and with them, if I am willing to make the effort to begin.

Taking stock—months later

Several months have passed since I first explored my ideas for a "project of possibility." Like most meaningful change, the process of implementation has been slow and challenging. Much of this first year has been spent building relationships with staff in the school and with children and parents in the community.

In September, a number of parents often met casually in the classroom as they brought their children to school. From that group, several accepted the invitation to work in the classroom on a regular basis. Other parents, in particular working parents, have been writing to me about home literacy events through a weekly journal that the children carry from school to home in their Reading Tote Bags.

My determination to talk with rather than at parents has affected my relationships with them. I really am learning to listen, and in the process I am learning more about the children I teach. Although much that I hear confirms and supports my own interpretations, some anecdotes challenge or change my thinking. Even during the time constraints of more traditional parent–teacher interviews, I am experimenting with ways to open conversation. This past term I began by asking parents if they found any surprises in their children's work or in their anecdotal progress report. By focusing on parents' interpretations (rather than merely restating my own), we were each able to come away with new understandings of the children.

Recent chats with several Vietnamese parents, for example, have helped me appreciate their culture, their language, and their recent refugee experiences. I also have learned how certain Canadian customs, gestures, and clothing practices conflict with Vietnamese ones. A recently arrived Iranian family has been teaching me some language as well as helping me understand a culture I knew nothing about. Single-parent mothers have shared their struggles and successes in education, day care, and employment.

This valuing of other literacies has spilled over into the classroom, too. By encouraging the Vietnamese and Iranian students to teach the rest of us how to speak their languages, these children have felt an importance and valuing of their acquired literacies as they take risks to learn new ones. Black and white Canadian students, in turn, have learned to value the native language competence of these new students rather than waiting for them to prove themselves in English. They actively seek out the ESL children to exchange words and phrases in both languages. Our school's year-round multicultural theme, "My World, Your World, Our World," has provided a focus for understanding each other's similarities and differences.

The home visits I planned to make in September have taken place with a few families over the course of the year. The children have been the natural conversationalists, tripping over their words and feet trying to share their whole home world in a precious half-hour. I need to find more time in future years to make these visits with all the families who feel comfortable having me spend some time in their home. I need to think about working families and how to keep in contact with them, too. The weekly journal has been a good beginning for communicating with English-speaking families.

My idea to get together with parents, children, and teachers at school is still in the planning stages. As I talk with parents, I am even more convinced that it could be a meaningful enterprise. There are stories to tell, issues to be tackled, and challenges to be met. But I realize that this year needed to be a "listen and learn" year for me. Perhaps with my newly formed friendships among staff and parents, there will be enough of us ready to begin the larger "project of possibility" next year. But whether the school project is launched or not, I am convinced that my willingness to value and understand literacies from a more open-minded, less ethnocentric perspective will continue to influence how I talk and learn with parents and children.

References

Bigelow, W. 1989. "Discovering Columbus: Rereading the past." *Language Arts* 66 (6): 635–43.

Dillon, D. 1989. "Dear Readers." *Language Arts* 66 (1): 7–9.

Gee, J. 1987. "What Is Literacy?" *Teaching and Learning* 2 (1): 3–11.

Harmon, S., and C. Edelsky. 1989. "The Risks of Whole Language Literacy: Alienation and Connection." *Language Arts* 66 (4): 392–406.

Heath, S. 1983. *Ways with Words*. New York: Cambridge University Press.

Lightfoot, S. 1978. *Worlds Apart*. New York: Basic Books.

Newman, J., ed. 1990. *Finding Our Own Way: Teachers Exploring Their Assumptions*. Portsmouth, NH: Heinemann.

Shor, I., and P. Freire. 1987. *A Pedagogy for Liberation*. Granby, MA: Bergin & Garvey.

Trimbur, J. 1989. "Consensus and Difference in Collaborative Learning. *College English* 51 (6): 602–16.

TWENTY

How It All Starts

Cathy Townsend-Fuller
Jill Hartling-Clark

Even in Nova Scotia, students take standardized tests. We say "even" because Nova Scotia's Ministry of Education has published language arts curricula that gives the impression that standardized testing is not an adequate, or even useful, measure of students' capability or achievement. But standardized testing is still very much a part of many students' lives, particularly those whom teachers identify as having problems at school. Children from non-middle-class discourse communities and linguistically, culturally, and racially diverse students take standardized tests in disproportionate numbers. Questions of the validity and reliability of these tests are legion. However, rarely are these concerns shared with students, their parents, or the general public.

We sought a way to share our concern for testing and the consequences that it brings, a way that would inform and empower consumers of tests and testing without bias. The result of our efforts is a pamphlet, "Standardized Testing and Your Child." We consider a pamphlet to be the appropriate genre because many parents, our selected audience, are used to getting pamphlets for information. Moreover, the brevity of a pamphlet makes it more likely to be read and used.

We began our pamphlet with a short definition and rationale and encouraged parents to ask questions and expect that the testing make sense. Our aim was to prepare parents to discuss the issue of testing and become more actively involved in their children's schooling.

We entitled our pamphlet "Standardized Testing and Your Child."

Standardized testing and your child

You have just been notified by the school that your child is going to be given a **standardized test**.

What does this really mean?

What are standardized tests?

A standardized test is an instrument designed to measure an individual's performance on a specific set of tasks. These tasks are administered the same way by each examiner. The test results generally compare an individual to a group who were given the test when it was first developed. Such tests are called *standardized, norm-referenced tests*.

Examples of standardized tests:

- Wechsler Intelligence Scale For Children-Revised (WISC-R^{TM})
- Wide Range Achievement Test (WRAT^{TM})
- Stanford-Binet^{TM}
- Standardized Achievement Test (SAT^{TM})

Why do educators give these tests?

Standardized tests are generally used to assist in the educational planning for your child—for example:

- Your child may be experiencing difficulty with his/her schoolwork. Through testing it is hoped that a specific cause for this problem will be found.
- Students of the same age are often compared to the normative group on their progress to master certain skills.
- Sometimes tests are used to measure a student's intelligence quotient or I.Q. in order to estimate his/her ability to handle academic challenges.

What are some important points to consider once you've received your child's results?

- Researchers have suggested that intelligence is difficult to measure because there are many components of intelligence which are believed to be untestable.
- They have also discovered that test scores are not 100% accurate, nor are they always used in the way their authors intended.
- Your child's results on the test are usually represented by a number. Be sure to ask the school to translate this number into a percentile ranking, which can held you understand how your child compares with the norm group.
- Teachers must translate the test number into specific instructional goals because the tests do not provide specific information on your child's academic abilities.

Why might some children not score well on a standardized test?

- There is controversy over the fact that standardized norm-referenced tests are culturally biased because they are often developed by white, middle-class males, and they are normed on white, middle-class groups of children. Children of different backgrounds are considered to be at a disadvantage.
- Think about this:
  Your child has an allotted amount of time to complete the test. During this time, many factors may affect his/her performance. Some of these factors may include:
  - fatigue
  - anxiety
  - stress
  - illness
  - emotional upset

- setting
- rapport with the examiner
- cooperation
- motivation

OR, your child may simply have had a bad day!

How might the results of the test affect your child?

Students are often classified as fast, average, or slow learners and placed into advanced, regular, or resource classes on the basis of their scores on standardized tests. As a result, the following may occur:

- The educational programming that your child will receive will differ according to their placement.
- A student's self-esteem will be affected by the program he/she is placed in.
- Teachers' expectations of your child's potential will be altered.
- A student's expectations for himself/herself will be altered.

The following are examples of questions you may want to ask the school concerning standardized testing. Ask for specific information in words you can understand.

- Why is the standardized test being administered?
- Who will administer the test, and what are their qualifications?
- Who will interpret the results for the instructional goals and programs? Do they know my child?
- What is the percentile ranking of my child's results, and how will this be used? (Be sure to question until you fully understand.)
- Who will have access to my child's results? How can he/she change programs?
- How does my child's educational program compare to other programs offered in the school?

As a parent, you have the right to be well informed of any educational decision affecting your child. Be sure to exercise that right!

For more information:

- Stephen Jay Gould. *The Mismeasure of Man*. New York: W.W. Norton & Co., 1981.

- Hugh Mehan et al. *Handicapping the Handicapped*. Stanford, CA: Stanford University Press, 1986.
- Jeannie Oakes. *Keeping Track*. New Haven: Yale University Press, 1985.
- Frank Smith. *Insult to Intelligence*. Portsmouth, NH: Heinemann, 1986.

During the past six months we have tried to distribute our pamphlet to as varied an audience as possible, including parents, fellow teachers, administrators, educational consultants (test administrators), family, and friends.

The reactions to the pamphlet have been diverse. Some readers found it quite informative, saying that it helped to raise specific questions and concerns they had not considered before, it helped to clarify their understanding of testing, and it provided some background knowledge about testing and the procedures used in testing. Others, however, had some difficulty with the pamphlet. Some parents and teachers felt that the pamphlet was unnecessary, as they had no qualms or questions regarding testing or its validity. One point that was brought to our attention was our mention of percentile ranking; it was felt that the use of standard scores would provide a more realistic indication of the student's ability.

The reactions to our pamphlet have been helpful and greatly appreciated. We felt the pamphlet was a worthwhile endeavour. Information provided through the pamphlet gave parents an opportunity to be exposed to facts that schools often neglect to pass on to them, thus "empowering" them in the situation. Test administrators became uncomfortable with this "empowerment" of parents, thus making them more accountable. Both the creation and distribution of the pamphlet proved to be learning experiences. The end result provided a much needed resource for parents and educators.

TWENTY-ONE

Rethinking Whole Language: The Politics of Educational Change

Susan M. Church

am basically an optimist. I suppose that is why I became a teacher. I believed I could make a difference in children's lives.

But in recent months I have found my usual positive feelings about my work increasingly overshadowed by a sense of frustration and even anger. I've wondered whether all the energy I'm expending is really helping children and teachers. I've looked back over the several years of curriculum changes associated with whole language philosophy, which have been occurring in the province and in my own district, and asked myself how substantive the changes have really been.

I have a large stake in what's been happening, having been involved in whole language since the early 1980s, first as a teacher and then as a curriculum supervisor. I helped write the provincial guide *Language Arts in the Elementary School* (1986), which mandated programming consistent with "an integrated approach and a holistic perspective" (p. 1). I've led many inservices, both within my own district and around the province. I've written about my own classroom experiences and those of others (Church 1985a, 1985b, 1987, 1988). In fact, because I have played such an active role, someone once jokingly dubbed me "Ms. Whole Language."

In my district we've been using "student-centered learning" as an umbrella term to try to dispel the notion that whole language philosophy applies only to language arts programming. The district has made the implementation of student-centered learning from primary (the first year in school) to grade twelve a system priority and thus the focus of professional development.

So why am I so frustrated and angry? Let me share some experiences that have contributed to these feelings. Most of these have not been monumental events; rather, they have been snatches of conversation, brief encounters in everyday situations, or comments overheard.

Not too long ago at an inservice on student-centered learning, an elementary teacher asked me: "Are there any teachers you know who are doing it all the time? I just can't seem to manage it." We talked a bit more about what she meant by "doing it." She wasn't quite sure, but it was evident she felt she was not measuring up.

A junior high teacher told me about a staff meeting in her school at which the teachers were complaining about the new grade seven students. The teachers found the group an irresponsible lot, not picking up after themselves and failing to complete assignments. Someone suggested asking the elementary school about the children to find out if the problem had occurred before. One teacher commented: "Yes, maybe they have had so much of this student-centered learning that they are used to leaving their garbage around."

At a meeting of senior high teachers, an experienced English teacher expressed her confusion: "I think a lot of what I've been doing seems to fit. I keep wondering what else there is to this. My kids work in groups a lot, and I've been working on writing process, too." I could not offer an easy or quick answer. She wanted to know if she is doing it right, and I'm supposed to be the expert.

I attended a gathering of supervisors called to discuss the implications of student-centered learning for the secondary school. They developed a long list of changes that need to be made. They talked about inservicing teachers — doing something to them — to get them ready. Most of the participants rarely get into a school and have been away from the classroom for years.

These situations are typical of what has occurred throughout this change process, whether we called it whole language or student-centered learning. It began as a grass-roots movement, led by teachers who were exploring theory and practice through reading, course work, study groups, and other forms of personal professional development. In the early to mid 1980s, however, an intensive, top-down implementation began. Elementary teachers attended inservices on using real literature, on process writing, on moving away from fixed ability groups, on using Big Books, on reading and writing conferences, and sometimes on theory. The focus of these sessions was primarily on the "what" of the change. Even the theory, which was and is continually evolving, became a set of principles developed by experts and handed to teachers.

Most teachers tried to incorporate new methodologies, many without much understanding about why they were making changes. "Am I doing it right?" was a primary concern: What kinds of questions should I ask when I conference? When should I stop accepting invented spelling? How can I manage all these different groups?

Many misconceptions also arose: whole language means doing themes; never tell a child how to spell a word; teaching phonics is not part of whole language; children must always work in groups; teachers must always facilitate and never intervene; and on and on (Newman and Church 1990).

With these misconceptions came frustrations. Teachers who had seen themselves as successful in a skills-based model abandoned phonics against their better judgment or did phonics exercises behind closed doors. Others moved children's desks together or sat them at tables and then struggled with the management problems of dealing with small groups. Many said, "If you'll just tell me what to do, I'll do it." (Perhaps not willingly or with much knowledge, but I will try to do it.) Fortunately, many teachers knew they didn't understand what was being asked of them, and assumed responsibility for their own professional development through formal and informal study.

A number of us involved in leadership roles recognized the difficulties. We ourselves were exploring whole language philosophy, seeking ways we could apply our beliefs about teaching and learning in our work with teachers. I wrote articles about how inservice could change (1985c) and about how teachers in some schools were collaborating (1987; 1988). I also tried to create situations more supportive to teacher growth.

One project involved the development of a district guideline dealing with language for learning in grades four through nine. A committee of teachers and administrators spent eighteen months meeting regularly — talking, writing, thinking, arguing, and learning together. As chair, I tried to structure a whole language environment in which we all could participate actively in an enterprise with a real purpose and audience. We struggled with ideas and with structure, taking several months to hammer out underlying learning principles and to discover voice and form.

Throughout our many months together, the teachers commented over and over again about how privileged they felt to have time, with paid substitutes, to reflect on their work. One told me, "I truly feel like a professional, like someone values what I know and can do."

The teachers wrote about their own classrooms, sharing their struggles and insights. We began to see that these personal reflections conveyed a powerful message. Committee members encouraged other teachers in their schools to write in a similar way. We asked teachers of subjects other than language arts to explore the role of language for learning in their subject areas. We decided that students' voices also needed to be heard, so we asked the teacher-authors to include student writing, talk, and artwork.

What evolved was a collection of classroom narratives, framed with and connected by a common underlying philosophy. We decided to publish it not as a coil-bound directive, but as a book, *From Teacher to Teacher: Opening Our Doors*. We hoped this title would convey our intention: to extend an invitation to teachers to speak directly with one another about their work. As further support for this intention, we held a reception to launch the book, and invited the authors, school and district administrators, and school board members to celebrate with us.

We all had very high expectations for our book. I thought the process held much promise as a model for professional development. Why couldn't other teachers have similar sorts of opportunities to learn together? The authors hoped their writing would encourage colleagues to reflect on their own teaching and to open the doors of their classrooms. Committee members talked of starting small support or study groups within their own and neighboring schools and of finding ways to tell decision makers about their concerns regarding class size, teaching loads, schedules, and evaluation policies.

Our initial excitement soon turned to dismay. Although some administrators and teachers welcomed the publication as a valuable resource that could support them in their ongoing growth, the majority treated it just like any other system directive. Many administrators distributed it to teachers with little or no discussion. In a number of schools the books were piled on staff room tables for teachers to take if they wanted them.

It soon became obvious that the book, instead of being an invitation to engage, was becoming yet another barrier to learning. And many teachers saw the authors not as colleagues reflecting on their own teaching, but experts who somehow had figured out how to "do it right." Polarization seemed to be increasing rather than diminishing, and I felt responsible for putting the authors at risk—for alienating them from other teachers.

The authors felt the alienation strongly. In one author's school a group of junior high language arts teachers met to discuss ways they could bring the January exams more in line with student-centered learning. As the teachers shared examples of exam questions, one teacher said, "I'm putting all my grammar questions in under 'revision.' That'll keep them [the administration] happy. We need to teach these kids grammar. I see their writing as having a disease which I have to cure." Five of the other teachers applauded and then looked to see how the *Opening Our Doors* author would react.

Another author described her feelings about moving to a new school: "There seems to be some expectation from the administration that I'll be a leader, but most of the other teachers are reluctant to include me in their discussions. I've tried to play a low key role but my classroom is so different from most of theirs that I stand out even if I don't say anything. And the students know the difference and make comments about it."

This negativity toward the teacher-authors was a particularly intense form of a general problem. Teachers who had nothing to do with the book, but who seemed to their colleagues to have some kind of special knowledge of the curriculum change told me of similar incidents. Like the authors, these teachers were working hard to revise beliefs and practice and certainly did not feel they had arrived. I was distressed to hear the feelings of alienation expressed in their comments:

> I just can't find anyone in the staff room who is interested in talking about what I'm learning from my students.

> I see what some teachers are doing in the name of whole language and I get really concerned. So much of what happens is still so teacher-centered. But I don't dare make suggestions or question what others are doing.

> I feel so alone in my classroom sometimes. I don't have anyone to help me grow.

My frustration and anger grew as this evidence of misunderstanding, alienation, and lack of communication accumulated. What more could I do? Why had my attempts to help teachers explore whole language—a philosophy with so much promise for freeing people to learn—seemed to create barriers to learning for so many? Why hadn't we been able to sustain the powerful learning context provided by the *Opening Our Doors* project? Why had empowering some teachers been so threatening to others?

I wanted to understand what had happened, so I began to look for answers to these questions. David Dillon, editor of *Language Arts* from 1983 to 1990, helped me rethink the situation and raised a number of interesting questions of his own. His editorials explored a theme he returned to again and again in different contexts over his seven years as editor. In reflecting upon the articles submitted for the November 1984 issue on "Teacher as Researcher," Dillon commented:

I was saddened by the greatly differentiated and often adversary, camps, teams, and roles embedded throughout so much of the discussion....Each appears to be ideologically pure, out to confront and change—not to dialogue with—other groups with different ideologies....While it is natural for like-minded learners to draw together and support each other in the best sense of "community," the pureness and close-endedness of the ideologies left me wondering about the role of critical questioning in any inquiry. At what point do we ask, as Margaret Spencer often does, "What if it's otherwise?" What role and value do we provide for dissenters? (p. 680)

In subsequent issues of the journal Dillon asked readers to consider "What if it's otherwise?" in many different ways. He wrote about "seeing with new eyes" (October 1985); about differences not needing to be divisive (April 1987); about what it means for teachers to take control of their own learning (November 1987); about what it means to be critically literate (October 1988); about what it means to be reflective in our practice (November 1988); and in his final editorial (April 1990), about liberation education as "a way of finding and raising critical questions" not just for students but for teachers.

As I thought about my experiences with change and Dillon's persistent challenges to the status quo, some critical questions began to emerge: What are the implications for my own work with teachers if I act upon what I believe about teaching and learning? How can we create communities of learners that are open rather than closed? What does empowerment really mean? What does it mean for teachers to have voice? What could it mean for me to see my own role as leader with "new eyes?"

If I believe that learning occurs as learners actively construct meaning in a social environment in which language is used for a range of real purposes, what does that mean for teachers' learning? If I agree with Harman and Edelsky (1989) that in whole language philosophy "the most powerful of these beliefs and practices—and therefore both the most liberating and potentially alienating—is the whole language commitment to a democratic relationship both between the student and the teacher, and between the student and the material" (p. 397), how might that affect how I view curriculum change?

What about empowering teachers? Simon (1987) maintains that our concept of empowerment must be expanded. In education, whether referring to students or teachers, we have thought of empowerment as simply enabling all to "participate on equal terms with other members of a group or community to whom have accrued the socially defined status of 'the privileged'/'the competent'" (p. 374). Given that definition, I could say I had been working to empower teachers by giving all of them a variety of opportunities to join our community of learners in exploring whole language theory and practice.

But Simon believes this concept of empowerment is "woefully insufficient." In his view, to empower means to adopt a political agenda: first, to enable multiple perspectives to be expressed—to hear all voices; and second, to ask "empowerment for what?" For Simon,

Teaching and learning must be linked to the goal of educating students to take risks, to struggle with ongoing relations of power, to critically appropriate forms of knowledge that exist outside their immediate experience, and to envisage versions of a world which is "not yet"—in order to be able to alter the ground upon which life is lived. (p. 375)

In our efforts to bring about curriculum change, we have not allowed all voices to be heard. Giroux and McLaren (1986) define voice as "the means at our disposal—the discourses available to us—to make ourselves understood and listened to, and to define ourselves as active participants in the world" (p. 235). Only those people who agree with whole language can voice their views in socially sanctioned ways. There has been no way for dialogue to occur—for those with differing views to interrogate each other. Instead, those who don't agree with or understand the mandated curriculum have used passive resistance (I'll keep quiet, close my door and do what I believe is right) or have distanced those who seem to have bought in by baiting them with barbed comments or by isolating them from their peers.

Ironically, the majority of those who have embraced whole language philosophy have changed, not because they "bought in" to system philosophy, but because they have been on a personal journey of discovery through self-directed professional development. Most have continued to learn and grow, questioning what they believe and what they practice. I doubt very much if even one teacher changed through our laid-on inservices, unless they were already engaged in a process of inquiry. For we did not allow the beliefs or practices to become the focus of critique.

It's not surprising the questions became "what" and "how" rather than "why" and "what if." We did not invite open dialogue or encourage multiple perspectives. We failed to create for teachers a democratic learning environment in which we, as their teachers, valued critical literacy and thinking. In contradiction of our own philosophy, we tried to enforce the kind of consensus Trimbur (1989) critiques: "To develop a critical version of collaborative learning, we will need to distinguish between consensus as an acculturative practice that reproduces business as usual and consensus as a oppositional one that challenges the prevailing conditions of production" (p. 612).

The teachers who believe in and practice whole language have largely been silenced, too, except among themselves. They cannot engage in productive dialogue with colleagues who feel threatened by their expertise and apparently privileged knowledge or question those who may have taken on some of the practices of whole language but not the philosophy. They also cannot easily give voice to their own concerns. Through their exploration of whole language philosophy and practice, many of these teachers have empowered their learners. As they have worked to create democratic environments in their classrooms, they have begun to recognize that they, like their students, need greater control over their work—what and how they teach.

But the teacher–authors of *Opening Our Doors* who began asking hard questions about schedules, teaching loads, and evaluation policies felt that their voices fell on deaf ears. They became angry and frustrated at trying to deal with a hierarchical system that vests the decision making about these issues outside the classroom and often outside the school. Many of them, too, said, "Well, maybe I'll just close my classroom door and do what I can for my students."

These teachers are beginning to define empowerment, for both their students and for themselves, through Simon's expanded sense of the concept. They recognize the contradictions between what the system is telling them to do in their classrooms (whole language) and how they themselves live and work in the system. For many of them, however, the difficulty of challenging existing power relationships seems almost insurmountable. They see no way of having their voices count. Some of them have told me they feel burnt out, angry, and discouraged.

They, and I at times, feel much like the teacher who wrote an angry reply to Pat Shannon (1990) when he asked her to describe an ideal literacy education. Her response was a diatribe against the authoritarian system that prevents her from doing what she knows is right for her students. And his analysis of her reaction ("...she exhibits a rage that only comes from the frustration of inaction when you know you must act," p. 182) might also be said of me and of the teachers who have fallen silent. His further description of her situation is equally apt:

> Even with a radical ethic, a democratic view of authority, a sense of a better literacy program, a developing critical voice, and an understanding that things must change drastically if her concept of a good and just literacy program is to help her students, this teacher feels totally powerless to bring about the needed changes. (p. 182)

So here is an alternative to anger: Shannon telling me I need a sense of history—a connection with dissenting movements of the past—and a sense of hope. His book shows how others have struggled with the same kinds of issues that engage me and ends with a challenge and an invitation to continue their work.

Where does that lead me? I understand my anger better. I can see that a whole language agenda needs to be a political agenda—that the philosophy challenges not only the ways we view teaching and learning in the classroom but the ways in which children and adults live and work in schools. I see that our well-intentioned attempt to open classroom doors and teachers minds through *Opening Our Doors* foundered because of the teachers' subjectivities: system publications are directives to be ignored if possible; talking with other teachers about our work is a threat, not an opportunity; teaching is competitive — if a colleague does well it reflects badly on me—rather than collaborative; whole language or student-centered curriculum is a set of "correct" practices.

These subjectivities, and others, have developed through the teachers' experiences in working within a hierarchical system that sets up certain expectations about the way schooling works both for children and teachers. The challenge for someone in my position is to find ways of making the subjectivities the focus of inquiry. I know I can't personally revolutionize the hierarchy, but I might begin to raise questions about the contradictions between our espoused beliefs and our practices of curriculum change. If we truly believe in whole language philosophy, how can we create democratic learning environments— ones in which multiple perspectives are heard and valued—for administrators and teachers? How can we open the conversation so that differing views become the subject of critical inquiry? How can we shift attention from "Am I doing it right?" to "What am I learning about my students, and what does that mean for my teaching?" How can we help administrators and teachers examine what stops them from changing?

For me, Schon's (1983) ideas about reflective practice suggest a new way of thinking about schooling. He argues that professional practice is not the application of specialized technical knowledge (doing it right) but a process of reflection in action involving uncertainty, surprise, and experimentation. The professional is a researcher in the context of practice, constantly recreating theory through reflection while doing.

Schon believes reflective practice has significant implications for bureaucracies:

> When a member of a bureaucracy embarks on a course of reflective practice, allowing himself to experience confusion and uncertainty, subjecting his frames and theories to conscious criticism and change, he may increase his capacity to contribute to significant organizational learning, but he also becomes, by the same token, a danger to the stable system of rules and procedures within which he is expected to deliver his technical expertise. (p. 328)

To take reflective practice seriously suggests a political agenda in which a thinking, inquiring, professional teaching staff would begin to question the status quo — to demand the right to make decisions about their work. As Schon points out, a bureaucracy, such as the education system, depends upon its members complying with the written and unwritten institutional expectations — the subjectivities of schooling.

Schon envisions a different sort of institution, one sustained through reflection and critique at all levels:

> In a school supportive of reflective teaching, a supervisor would advocate his own standards of educational quality while at the same time inquiring into teachers' understandings, confronting what he sees as poor teaching while at the same time inviting teachers to confront his own behaviour.... In a school supportive of reflective teaching, teachers would challenge the prevailing knowledge structure. Their on-the-spot experiments would affect not only the routines of teaching practice but the central values and principles of the institution.... An institution congenial to reflective practice would require a learning system within which individuals could surface conflicts and dilemmas and subject them to productive public inquiry, a learning system conducive to the continual criticism and restructuring of organizational principles and values. (pp. 335−336)

This is the language of possibility — a vision of how things might be. Like Giroux's (1987) teachers as intellectuals who "engage in a critical dialogue among themselves and others in order to fight for the conditions they need" (p. 180), Schon's reflective practitioners actively critique themselves and the institution. Schon himself here is clearly using the language of critique to question the traditional role of teacher as technician.

Reflective practice could be a means for teachers to find their voices — to become empowered in Simon's sense. For if teachers behave in the way Schon described they will empower themselves "to raise questions about the existing social forms and what would have to be done for things to be otherwise" (Simon 1987, p. 377). They will develop very different subjectivities about what it means to be a teacher.

I saw this happen with the authors of *Opening Our Doors*. When they had the opportunity to ask themselves and each other hard questions about the institutional implications of whole language philosophy, they began to challenge the authoritarian school system. Why is the democratic learning environment limited to my classroom? Why do I have to struggle with constraints — schedules, marking schemes, evaluation practices — imposed from outside? Why am I such a threat to other teachers and to administrators? I'm struggling to create communities of inquiry for my students; where are mine?

I've come to see that *Opening Our Doors* was not a failure. It was an example of empowerment in action. We were successful in writing about learning and teaching from the perspective of teachers and students, but we underestimated the power of the institution and the teachers' subjectivities to subvert our intentions. What we perceived as professionalism on the part of the teacher-authors many in the system saw as a challenge to authority — teachers taking control of the curriculum. What we perceived as an open invitation to explore ideas and ask questions many teachers saw as a challenge to their beliefs and practices — definitive whole language answers being imposed on them.

I now recognize the wisdom of the environmental movement: "Think globally, act locally." I know I can't affect the lives of huge numbers of teachers. What I can do is engage the fifteen principals with whom I work in more open dialogue regarding program, inviting and valuing their dissenting views. I can ask, and encourage them to ask, "What if it's otherwise?" I can support them in fostering similar opportunities for the teachers in their schools. I can encourage teachers to write about their teaching — to explore questions that interest them. Just as happened with the *Opening Our Doors* authors, new communities of inquiry might emerge through the process of struggling for voice and form.

I can try to play a different role in schools, not the "snoopervisor" coming around to see if people are "doing it right," but a teacher and a learner, grappling with the same issues that concern the teachers. I can lend my energies and expertise to long-term projects within individual schools, establishing a social environment in which we give voice to multiple perspectives.

I haven't abandoned my whole language agenda. I still believe the philosophy has endless potential for leading us toward the creation of truly democratic learning environments for adults and children. I am encouraged as I visit classrooms in which teachers and students are grappling with important issues (Church 1990). I can envision projects similar to *Opening Our Doors* giving many teachers and administrators opportunities to be professionals. I might even see a day when supervisors would meet not to discuss how best to direct the work of principals and teachers, but to engage in critical inquiry about our beliefs and practices.

Through these kinds of efforts we might move toward Trimbur's (1989) notion of consensus "not as an agreement that reconciles differences through an ideal conversation but rather as the desire of humans to live and work together with differences." We might begin to "imagine alternative worlds and transformations of social life and labor" (p. 615).

Considering these possibilities helps to restore my natural optimism. I've learned some valuable lessons about the politics of change, not the least of which is the necessity to find ways, however small, to act on my beliefs — to redirect the energy wasted by venting anger and frustration in order to make a difference where I can. I now understand that sustaining my sense of hope, and helping others to do the same, is the most powerful way that I, as a leader, can promote lasting educational change.

Postscript, February, 1991

A number of months have passed and I am back in the world of multitudinous memos and seemingly neverending meetings, facing the problems of too little money and too little time to do what I would like. How have I changed? How am I doing with my project of possibility?

Although my work world is much the same as previous years, I am aware that I am seeing it with different eyes and hearing it with different ears. I've become more sensitive to the language we habitually use—language which reflects our subjectivities about the organization.

Rarely a day goes by that I don't hear someone refer to movement up or down in the system: teachers or administrators move up from positions in elementary to positions in secondary; teachers move up to being vice-principals and then principals; and principals move up to supervisory jobs. Decisions, on the other hand, almost without exception, come down.

I am less likely than I was in the past to let this kind of language go by without comment. And, I am encouraged to find myself engaging in an ongoing conversation with a number of colleagues, not only about the pervasiveness of the hierarchy but about how we might change it.

Support for our inquiry is coming from an unexpected source. Our CEO has returned from a year's sabbatical during which he studied organizational change and looked at different administrative models. In his conversations with staff he's been using language which reflects his changing views of the organizational structure. He's been asking us to consider what it would mean to have a flat organization. He's been talking about teacher and student empowerment. I can see him struggling to overcome his subjectivities about his own role within the organization in order to act in ways that are more consistent with his evolving beliefs. It is clear he also is seeking ways to modify the expectations of others who neither understand nor accept his need to change.

Fortunately, within my own administrative unit of three supervisors and fifteen principals, there is great interest in these issues. Like me, many of them have become increasingly aware of the many contradictions between our beliefs and our practice and increasingly sensitive to the political implications of our beliefs. In our principals' meetings, the dissemination of administrivia has yielded to discussion—and as people develop more trust, argumentation—about topics of substance: What does flat organization mean? What would we have to give up? Do all teachers really want the responsibility of shared decision-making? Can we change at the school level if the larger organization is still strongly hierarchical?

Although these discussions are healthy and useful, the structure of the principals' meeting seems to impose some constraints. It may take some time before people feel comfortable enough to be honest about what they are doing in their own schools. At a recent meeting this issue was raised when I found myself continuing discussion with three female principals who landed in the women's washroom during a break. Although we had been in different small groups, we had felt the same frustration. One said, "If what they say is happening in their schools is really happening, I want to be the first one there to see it. I am struggling with sharing leadership, and some of them talk as if it is easy."

As a group, we decided we needed more time to talk, outside the context of the meetings. So, we have formed our own small study group. We hope, as we develop trust, to be able to be honest with each other—to create a community of inquiry through which we can think together. We have lots of questions: What do we believe about empowerment and about collaboration? How does our gender influence how we view our roles? We have a sense our view of leadership is different—more compatible with flat organization than most of our male colleagues—but is that valid? And, does the system really value that kind of leadership? We have lots of evidence that the ability to impose authority from on high is still what counts. How do we raise these issues without forming camps along gender lines?

For now, four people seems to be the right size as we tentatively explore our commonalities and differences. We all have lots we want to get on the table and are able to do so in our small group. We can vent the frustrations we hold back in other situations and deal honestly with our doubts and questions.

Just as political issues have gained precedence in my talk, they are increasingly the focus of my writing, both for self and for publication. My writer's notebook is filling with examples of language use which catch my attention. In my most recently published writing, I have highlighted the work of teachers who are pursuing projects of possibility in their classrooms.

In the big picture, a small study group and a few pieces of writing might not seem like much. But, for me, they are powerful ways of sustaining my energy and enthusiasm. They are also ways for me to continue to rethink both what I believe and how I can act on those beliefs—to keep the sense of possibility alive.

References

Church, Susan. 1985a. "Blossoming in the Writing Community." *Language Arts* 62(2): 175–79.

———. 1985b. "The War of the Words." In J.M. Newman (ed.), *Whole Language: Theory in Use*. Portsmouth, NH: Heinemann.

———. 1985c. "Inservice Education: Becoming Our own Experts." *Reading Canada Lecture* 3: 182–86.

———. 1987. "Fostering Change from Within." *Reading Canada Lecture* 5: 158–60.

———. 1988. "It's Almost Like There Aren't Any Walls." *Language Arts* 65(5): 448–54.

———, ed. 1989. *From Teacher to Teacher: Opening Our Doors*. Halifax County, NS: Halifax County–Bedford District School Board.

———. 1990. "Helping Children Learn to 'Read the World.'" *Reading Today* 8(3): 25.

Dillon, David. 1984. "Dear Readers." *Language Arts* 61(7): 679–80.

———. 1985. "Dear Readers." *Language Arts 62*(6): 585–86.

———. 1987a. "Dear Readers." *Language Arts 64*(4): 359–60.

———. 1987b. "Dear Readers." *Language Arts 64*(7): 707–9.

———. 1988a. "Dear Readers." *Language Arts 65*(6): 535–36.

———. 1988b. "Dear Readers." *Language Arts 65*(7): 631–32.

———. 1990. "Dear Readers." *Language Arts 67*(4): 333–35.

Giroux, Henry. 1987. "Critical Literacy and Student Experience: Donald Graves' Approach to Literacy." *Language Arts 64*(2): 175–81.

Giroux, Henry, and Peter McLaren. 1986. "Teacher Education and the Politics of Engagement: The Case for Democratic Schooling." *Harvard Educational Review 56*(3): 213–38.

Harman, Susan, and Carol Edelsky. 1989. "The Risks of Whole Language Literacy: Alienation and Connection." *Language Arts 66*(4): 392–406.

Language Arts in the Elementary School. 1986. Halifax, NS: Nova Scotia Department of Education.

Newman, Judith, and Susan Church. 1990. "The Myths of Whole Language." *The Reading Teacher 44*(1): 20–26.

Schon, Donald. 1983. *The Reflective Practitioner*. New York: Basic Books.

Shannon, Patrick. 1990. *The Struggle to Continue: Progressive Reading Instruction in the United States*. Portsmouth, NH: Heinemann.

Simon, Roger I. 1987. "Empowerment as a Pedagogy of Possibility." *Language Arts 64*(4): 370–82.

Trimbur, John. 1989. "Consensus and Difference in Collaborative Learning." *College English 51*(6): 602–16.

TWENTY-TWO

A Rationale and Unit Plan for Introducing Gay and Lesbian Literature into the Grade Twelve Curriculum

Roberta F. Hammett

In response to the AIDS crisis, my school board decided that all senior high school students should receive some AIDS education every year. Senior high students do not have an option to take health or physical education courses, so central office personnel decided that regular subject teachers would, if they agreed voluntarily, deliver the AIDS education that supervisors, with input from various sources, had prepared. In preparation for our task, the volunteers were given one and a half days of inservice by the secondary curriculum supervisor, aided by a public health nurse. We reviewed such aspects as the biology of the disease and discussed what messages and education we would give regarding prevention. We were told to emphasize abstinence and not to give condom demonstrations. In class, particularly after the first year, I discovered that most students understood the basic scientific or medical explanations of the virus and had heard, though perhaps not heeded, the messages of abstinence, condom use, and non-sharing of needles. Added the second year, at the teachers' request, were condom demonstrations (on a model wooden penis) by a public health nurse. I found I had time left over in the five days set aside for the lessons.

As an English teacher, I had limited interest in the science of AIDS. But I was/am interested in the human aspects: How does society treat people living with AIDS? How do we deal with AIDS-related moral questions? How does literature and the media portray AIDS victims? How do individuals, families, and friends deal with certain death? In exploring these questions with my students, I discovered that their homophobia (fear and hatred of homosexuals) stems, I believe, from their ignorance or lack of knowledge and understanding of homosexuality and from institutionalized heterosexism. I believe that literature (as well as human rights legislation and other changes in the laws) can help to overcome homophobia. I have pondered adding gay and lesbian literature to my grade twelve English course and purchasing such to create a special shelf in the library. The school principal and librarian tentatively agreed, giving me the responsibility for selecting, establishing, and using such a collection.

I found a good deal of material to support the importance of such a unit in a variety of sources. Stafford (1988) quotes the London Borough of Ealing Education Committee Policy Statement on Sexual Equality (approved on January 20, 1987):

> There are pupils who will themselves grow up to be lesbian or gay. It is vital that they be reassured that homosexuality is not a disease or "perversion" but simply another variation of human sexuality. Many pupils will also be unsure as to their sexuality, and it is important that they be able to decide for themselves without being subjected to pressure at school. Education also involves encouraging respect for and acceptance of others. (pp. 11–12)

Stafford goes on to cite statistics that showed that one-sixth of gay male respondents in the survey had been beaten. Our newspapers carry stories of gay murders as well as "gay bashings." Television talk shows bring us discussions of Ku Klux Klan and neo-Nazi railings against homosexuals. As Stafford says, "I regard it as scandalous that Tingle [a writer very critical of the policy] should condone the intolerance which gives rise to these evils" (p. 14). Stafford's article is also helpful in that it explores the question of positive image, rightly pointing out that positiveness is relative to one's perspective. Stafford concludes:

> This policy requires that young people be exposed to images of caring and humane homosexuals who are, or become, secure and confident in their own sexuality and responsible in the relationships they form. (p. 16)

Many sources cite the Kinsey statistics on adult sexual behavior. Margaret S. Schneider (1988) translates these into a school-related profile:

> The relevance of these figures lies in what they reveal about the world in which we work and live.... Teachers can estimate that about five to ten per cent of the young people in their school will grow up to be gay or lesbian. That means that 25 to 50 students in a school of 500 will define themselves as gay or lesbian when adult. (p. 19)

Talking About School (Warren 1984) argues that schools are failing to support the young homosexuals in their charge and that this results directly in these students' feelings of isolation and alienation, teasing, physical abuse, and pressure to conform; and indirectly in low grades, feelings of insecurity and paranoia, anxiety and stress, dropping out, and attempted suicides.

That gays and lesbians are invisible is proven by the fact that we teach literature by gays and lesbians and never mention their homosexuality. I have taught the play *A Raisin in the Sun* for fifteen years without knowing to mention that Lorraine Hansberry was a lesbian. A good deal more gay and lesbian literature has been similarly mainstreamed, without the literature courses considering that fact. Heterosexism, like racism and sexism, censors by omission. Demands for investigations of the education system for racism and awareness of sexism may change attitudes and practices over the next few years. It is time to similarly address heterosexism. True, Hansberry's sexual orientation has no direct relation to the subject of her play, *A Raisin in the Sun*, but as long as homosexuality is left invisible, homophobia and heterosexism are likely to continue.

Talking About School lists "Katherine Mansfield, E.M. Forster, W.H. Auden, Virginia Woolf, Walt Whitman, Emily Dickenson, [Christopher] Isherwood, [Joe] Orton, [Oscar] Wilde, [Christopher] Marlowe, Tennessee Williams, and Denton Welsh [as] writers whose own homosexuality and experience of oppression greatly influenced their work" (p. 27). The homosexuality of these writers is largely ignored in schools. The issue should be addressed in geography, history, politics, music, art, theatre, home economics, and sociology as well as the more obvious courses like sex education and health, though I am told that even in those courses teachers have been instructed to deal with homosexuality only if the issue is raised by students. *Talking About School* suggests the issue could be raised indirectly even in math, in problems as well as statistics.

Grayson (1987) argues that "homophobia...is a primary barrier to our society's ever achieving gender equity. Most people agreed that this fear is a primary factor in maintaining the traditional male role stereotype and that much of it is rooted in sexism" (p. 133). She explains how schools maintain control of students through "rigid sex role definition" (p. 135). She also asserts that we must examine "all aspects of the curriculum for bias in content and materials," as well as other "factors which influence academic achievement" (p. 137). Grayson's four-step approach for action (p. 142) calls for the following:

1. Increase awareness. This includes expanding one's own knowledge base through reading literature, attending workshops, and obtaining concrete information on the topic.
2. Examine attitudes. Starting with ourselves and then working with others, look at language, beliefs, stereotypes, and the sources of information in our own environment and background. Identify how homophobia has influenced our lives, clothing, behavior, activities, and choices.
3. Look at alternatives. What guidelines for name-calling, labeling, harassment, and teasing might be applied from prior experience? What positive role models and/or experiences might be shared?
4. Take supportive action. Include homophobia when discussing discrimination and gender issues.

Grayson's article (which, in addition, defines terms such as gay, dyke, etc.) might be useful as a resource for class or group discussion.

Rofes (1989) discusses the silence, despair, and victimization of gay youth and describes two schools, in Los Angeles (Project 10) and New York (Harvey Milk School) that support gay and lesbian students with counselling services, special programs, and student-centered curricula.

The subject of homosexuality is a natural outgrowth of a number of themes and texts already part of the English curriculum. McCarthyism, an implicit theme of Arthur Miller's *The Crucible*, was a witch-hunt against homosexuals as well as communists. The mass hysteria described in the play is similar to attitudes toward and treatment of gays and lesbians throughout history. The censorship of gay and lesbian literature and issues, both covert and overt, is like the censorship of the theory of evolution, as described in *Inherit the Wind* by Laurence and Lee. Robert Bolt's *A Man for All Seasons* leads easily into discussions of moral courage, a theme very appropriate to much gay and lesbian literature. These connections to the regular curriculum, as well as the study of AIDS and related issues, serve to justify a unit on gay and lesbian literature.

In accordance with my school board's policy, I will not make the study of any one book or article mandatory. I extend to my students the option of individual study programs in lieu of almost all my units of study. In addition, this unit will be set up to include mainstream literature by gay and lesbians, some of which is already in the curriculum, and books about homophobia. The sensibilities of no students or their parents will be forcefully challenged.

I still feel I need to be prepared for possible censorship challenges. The controversial Clause 28 of the local Government Bill in London forbids "the deliberate promotion of homosexuality" (*The Times Education Supplement*, April 1, 1988, p. 17). My lessons might be seen as promoting homosexuality. I believe it would be beneficial for students to anticipate and prepare for such censorship battles. They would thus learn how to argue a case, find evidence to support a point of view, interview people who are opposed or supportive, examine their own values and motives, and make judgments from an informed point of view.

Kings County District School Board, for which I teach, adopted a policy for dealing with textbook challenges in 1983. The policy establishes a Materials Evaluation Committee made up of school board members, parents, and a school librarian or teacher. It states, in part, "When a formal objection to a text or material is made, the burden of proof shall rest with the complainant. . . ." There is a set procedure for the teacher and the complainant parents to follow.

The Nova Scotia Department of Education (1983) leaves the selection of supplementary materials to the teacher's discretion, expecting her to "exercise discretion" (p. 13). Additional Department of Education evaluation guidelines detail procedures for examining proposed materials for content, organization, bias, style and format. A question to detect bias asks, "What indications are there of bias (racial, ethnic, religious, sex, occupational, class, other)?" Neither heterosexism nor homosexuality is addressed specifically in any of the evaluation guidelines for selecting school texts supplied by the Department of Education. Sexism and racism are addressed directly in *Guidelines to Eradicate Prejudice, Bias and Stereotyping in Textbooks*, and certain statements in that pamphlet might be taken as admonitions to pursue such a study as I am proposing:

Avoid derogatory slants and slurs on minority groups. (Social no. 4)

A variety of life styles and living environments should be shown. (Ethnic Concerns no. 5)

Materials should endeavour to lead students to a self-awareness in such a way that they examine their own attitudes and behavior and acquire an understanding of their responsibilities in our society. Prejudice and discrimination should be examined objectively with reference to the date and place and people concerned. (Ethnic Concerns no. 13)

An attempt should be made to seek freedom and justice and equal opportunity for every individual. (Ethnic Concerns no. 14).

Material should stress the uniqueness of each individual within the framework of basic similarities among all members of the human family. (Ethnic Concerns no. 15)

Reading *A Pedagogy for Liberation* (Shor and Friere 1987) renewed my interest in introducing this literature into my course. The subject is ideal for a liberatory pedagogy and might well liberate students from boredom, apathy, routine, passivity, alienation, disruptiveness, and rebellion. Believing, to some extent, as Shor suggests, that "mass culture socializes people to police themselves against their own freedom" (p. 25), I see a unit on gay and lesbian literature as an opportunity for students to experience the liberating nature of fringe culture as well as understand the oppression of the majority. I am not so naive as to think that all students will be or will want to be so liberated. I anticipate the kind of student resistance Shor and Freire describe (pp. 26, 54). I also anticipate attempts to censor. I will need to encourage in my students an open mind, not instantaneous condemnation. And I will need to recognize signs of their confusion and reluctance.

Also as Shor and Freire suggest, my students and I would all be learners, for this topic and material would all be new to me. I have no experience with gay and lesbian literature. Indeed, there would be a great deal of possibility for student input — a challenge for them to find articles and books and to remember film and television or songs with which they are already familiar. (Care would need to be exercised in opening up the classroom to student-selected materials, however, as all my careful precautions to avoid parental censorship might be undermined.) I would gather together a getting-started resource file, but additions would be needed and encouraged.

I also intend to borrow some ideas for unit and lesson plans from *A Pedagogy for Liberation*. Critical dialogue, as well as reading and writing, would be an important element of the course. Freire says, "Through critical dialogue about a text or a moment of society, we try to reveal it, unveil it, see its reasons for being like it is, the political and historical context of the material" (p. 13). That is exactly what I want to do with gay and lesbian literature and homophobia. I believe close textual analysis, or deconstruction, and candid discussion would facilitate understanding of the controversial elements of this subject. I am well aware that guidance, structure, and strong teaching will be essential. For example, I think it will be important at first for students not to name or discuss individuals they know or who are part of the community. This might cause upset and misunderstandings. I also think it will be important to encourage students to look for underlying moral codes and motives to behavior, emphasizing a kind of moral nature to the whole study as is common in studies of the politics of equality, for example.

In addition to critical dialogue, this unit offers excellent opportunity for intensive language study of the type Shor suggests for sexism and racism (p. 166). Among other topics and assignments, I can foresee making dictionaries and examining the definitions, connotations, and etymology of words they use and encounter. For example, as Jay Friedman (1989) says, "Homophobia begins in elementary school when 'girl', 'sissy,' 'queer,' 'virgin,' and 'fag' are the worst put-downs boys can hear" (p. 8). This language is sexist as well as heterosexist.

Shor's description of his Literature and Environment class provides a model for the opening classes in my unit.

> I asked the students to write down questions that came to them when they thought about the [subject. In my case it would be homophobia]. Next, in groups of three the students read their questions to each other and developed composite lists which each group then read to the class. As a recorder, I copied down the verbal reports and then read back the questions the students raised. We had some discussion on the issues that stood out in the lists. Then, I asked each student to choose one...theme or question and write on it for 20−30 minutes in class. Once again, students read their essays to each other in groups of three, chose one to read to the whole class, and let us hear what that person wrote. (1987, pp. 41−42)

Although I like this plan very much, I would have to determine (as much as possible) when students were ready for such public exposure on so controversial and sensitive an issue as homophobia. Additional topics students might explore in their talk, writing, and reading are such issues as myths about homosexuals, problems gays and lesbians face, negative stereotypes, and mainstream literature by homosexuals.

A better starting place for my students than exploratory writing might be articles, such as three from *Rolling Stone* magazine (White and Black 1985−86; Van Gelder and Brandt 1986; Tierney 1988). All describe the hysteria and homophobia resulting from fear of AIDS. The *Rolling Stone* articles are very readable and would be viewed favorably by students as the magazine is part of their culture. A number of controversial issues and varying attitudes are discussed in the articles. John Tierney's article (1988) argues that AIDS is not much risk for heterosexuals; I would be sure to provide a strong article arguing otherwise. Van Gelder's and Brandt's article (1986) does in fact present a contrasting point of view on heterosexual vulnerability. I might add that these articles are fairly explicit in their references to heterosexual and homosexual sex, and have what will be considered by some to be rather offensive language.

I would try to keep the discussions of all readings on intellectual and theoretical grounds; I would not feel comfortable with class members discussing their own sexual orientation, although I realize personal explorations of attitudes and their source are the aim of the unit. It might be helpful to give AIDS and, coincidentally, homosexuality a "face" by inviting a gay male living with AIDS to the class, as we did last year. This might well be the least threatening plan as far as parents are concerned, for a warning against promiscuity might be implicit in the disease.

Another possible and appropriate teaching strategy would be a panel discussion, for it could present a variety of points of view at one time. Students, in preparing the questions, would both reveal and anticipate various ideas and attitudes.

Role playing and skit writing and performing also provide opportunities for students to examine their own points of view and experience another person's point of view.

Journals and other forms of personal communication, with the promise of confidentiality, would "free students to examine their thoughts and feelings in safety and encourage them to assume responsibility for their intellectual and emotional growth" (Gardner et al. 1989, pp. 72–73).

Another approach could be to study essays, like Coral Ann Howell's, which on Marie-Claire Blais's writing and thus not specifically on her lesbianism. Howell (1987) discusses Blais's images, language, themes, and similarities to heterosexual literature. Blais's novel *La Belle Bete* is on the curriculum translated as *Mad Shadows*. This essay would help link the topic of gay and lesbian literature to mainstream literature and provide a basis for understanding lesbian literature.

There are a number of other books and articles I have now in my possession for possible use in this class. While I need a unit plan to get started, I think it is important that I be flexible and encourage students to develop their own projects of possibility. My agenda is to expose homophobia, to raise consciousness. As long as that idea is being developed, I will ensure whatever freedom I can to students' collaborative learning projects. John Milton wrote in *Areopagitica*: "Where there is much desire to learn, there of necessity will be much arguing, many opinions; for opinion in good [people] is but knowledge in the making." And as Jonathan Kozol (1980) wrote:

> To awaken people to intelligent and articulate dissent, to give voice to their longings, to give both lease and license to their rage, to empower the powerless, to give voice to those who are enslaved by their own silence—certainly this represents a certain kind of danger. It is, indeed, the type of danger which a just society, or one that aspires to justice, ought to be eager to foster, search out and encourage.

I feel what I am proposing to do is worthwhile, even important. I fear I may face criticism and censorship. But where much is ventured, much is gained. It's worth the risks.

Epilog

I prepared my unit plan in the summer of 1990. That September, I showed it to my school principal. He said that he continued to support the inclusion of gay and lesbian materials in the school library. He suggested that before making the unit part of the curriculum I would have to discuss it with supervisory personnel, students, fellow teachers, and parents. I felt encouraged by my discussions with him despite his words of caution.

I sent the unit plan to the supervisor of secondary curriculum, whose reaction was very negative and who sent copies without permission to senior central office personnel. The principal was called in to defend such a potentially controversial plan to three supervisors, all apparently very opposed to the proposal. I met later with the supervisor of secondary curriculum to discuss the unit and his action. I indicated I had been seeking his reaction and was upset that he had photocopied the essay without permission and had discussed it with the principal instead of with me. We discussed the unit and later exchanged written comments on the essay and our meeting. He, like the other supervisors who read the unit plan, warned me that my own sexual orientation would be questioned. He also wanted the unit rewritten in traditional lesson-plan style. He set out several other requirements to road block my proceeding with the unit.

In the meantime, I decided to seek funding for books and materials from my the Professional Development Assistance Fund of my teachers' union. I had embarked on a unit of study with my grade twelve English classes, The Portrayal of Native People in Literature and the Media, that required the purchase of additional resources. I was planning several other units that would similarly require resources not in the current curriculum offerings. I wrote the application for funding for a variety of units under the title Projects of Possibility. In the application I explained my beliefs regarding literacy as a political issue, student-centered learning, and critical thinking. I also suggested probable topics, though I explained the students would be selecting the issues they would address. I attached a copy of my unit plan for the native study and for introducing gay and lesbian literature.

A copy of the gay and lesbian literature unit plan had been sent by the curriculum supervisor to the superintendent of schools, who had been away when the principal was called in to answer for my actions. The superintendent and I met when he returned to discuss the unit and the PDAF grant application, which had to be accompanied with a letter of approval by the superintendent of the school district. He said that he was seldom required to read materials that challenged him to reconsider his assumptions, as my essay had done. He agreed to support the application, but felt that he should consult a few people, including selected school board members and the central office personnel of my teachers union, before we went any further with either the application or the gay and lesbian literature unit. Time passed. Whenever the superintendent and I met, he claimed to be busy but still planning to help with my application. It was his last year before retiring, and he did have a lot of additional responsibilities and commitments. He was very often absent from the district. In the end both he and I let the whole matter drop.

It is now the beginning of the new school year 1991−92. There is a different principal in my school and a new superintendent in the school district. I don't know either of them personally, as I did their predecessors. The year began for me with an attack on my supposed feminist politics by two sets of parents who see my requiring my students to use inclusionary, non-sexist language as imposing my personal political beliefs on my students. In addition, our school's schedule is changed to accommodate the semester system. Right now I have too much to contend with to enter into a new conflict over the teaching of gay and lesbian literature.

I am continuing to address political issues in literature study, and to purchase additional needed resources with my own money. The grade ten unit I am doing now is about culture. The students will present an assembly in the school during Cultural Awareness Week, October 21 to 27. The grade eleven unit is called Reflecting on the Environment Through Reading, Writing, and Viewing. They are studying poetry, films, and other curriculum materials and their own selected resources that relate to the topic. They will carry out group action projects that require them to read, write, and speak to adults and others outside the school and to do something that in some way relates to the environment. The grade twelve class has not decided on an issue yet, but are looking at agism as they begin a study of *The Stone Angel* by Margaret Laurence.

Last year the schools did not do the AIDS education because all concerned felt there is need to address it only two out of three years. I should be teaching that subject later this year. I may request permission to introduce gay and lesbian literature then.

Although I did not use my proposed unit last year, I did take opportunities to mention gay and lesbian literature, homophobia, and heterosexism in class. During a grade eleven unit on Afro-Canadian literature, we had several discussions on discrimination against homosexuals. One student made her required formal speech on the subject of homophobia, and several students spoke on prejudice and discrimination, referring to gays and lesbians in their examples.

I believe my students are becoming ever more politically aware, and are seeing the hidden curriculum in the literatue they study. I hope that awareness is applied in other classes. I will continue to make the teaching of literature as holistic as I can, integrating reading, writing, speaking, viewing, and literary analysis around issues of concern to my students.

I have certainly learned a great deal about the politics of education. I know first hand that literacy education is political. Although I have in many ways empowered myself within the closed doors of my classroom, I have learned I have no real power in the education system. Although I can encourage my students to empower themselves as learners, I cannot provide them with the instruction and resources that will allow them to consider political issues that are not part of the mainstream curriculum. I guess I'll continue to have "School Teacher Blues."

Library list/course bibliography

The following lists resources I would like to have available in the library and classroom.

Adam, Barry D. *The Rise of a Gay and Lesbian Movement*. Boston: Twayne Publishers G.K. Hall, 1987.

Alda, Alan, "What Every Woman Should Know About Men.", *Ms*. magazine, October 1975.

Baldwin, James. 1985. *Giovanni's Room*. New York: Dell, 1985.

Bargar, Gary. *What Happened to Mr. Forster*? Boston: Houghton Mifflin/Clarion Books, 1981.

Bell, Alan P., Martin S. Weinberg and Sue Kiefer. *Sexual Preference, It's Development in Men and Women*. Bloomington: Indiana University Press, 1981.

Blais, Marie-Claire. *Les Nuits de l'Underground/Nights in the Underground*. Toronto: New Press Canadian Classics, 1982.

Borhek, Mary V. *Coming Out to Parents: A Two-Way Survival Guide for Lesbians and Gay Men and Their Parents*. New York: Pilgrim Press, 1983.

Brown, Rita Mae. *Ruby Fruit Jungle*. New York: Bantam, 1983.

Callwood, June. *Jim: A Life with AIDS*. Toronto: University of Toronto Press, 1988.

Chabon, Michael. *The Mysteries of Pittsburgh*. New York: Harper and Row, 1989.

Cline, Victor B., ed. *Where Do You Draw the Line?: An Exploration into Media Violence, Pornography, and Censorship*. Provo, Utah: Brigham Young University Press, 1974.

Cruikshank, Margaret. *Lesbian Studies: Present and Future*. Old Westbury, NY: The Feminist Press, 1982.

Curtin, Kaier. *"We Can Always Call Them Bulgarians": The Emergence of Lesbians and Gay Men on the American Stage*. Boston: Alyson Publications, 1987. (The introduction is a good historical overview, with comments on Shakespeare and several plays.)

Davis, Christopher. *Joseph and the Old Man*. New York: St. Martin, 1987.

———, *Valley of the Shadow*. New York: St. Martin, 1988.

De Cecco, John P. *Bashers, Baiters & Bigots: Homophobia in American Society*. New York: Harrington Park Press, 1985.

Duplechan, Larry. *Blackbird*. New York: St. Martin, 1987.

Dworkin, Andrea. *Ice and Fire*. Toronto: Stoddart, 1986.

Farrell, Warren. *Why Men Are the Way They Are: The Male-Female Dynamic*. New York: McGraw-Hill, 1986.

Forster, E.M. *Maurice*. New York: W.W. Norton, 1987.

Foster, Jeannette H. *Sex Variant Women in Literature*. Tallahassee: The Naiad Press, 1985.

Fricke, Aaron. *Reflections of a Rock Lobster—A Story About Growing Up Gay*. Boston: Alyson Publications, 1981.

Garden, Nancy. *Annie on My Mind*. New York: Farrar, Straus and Giroux, 1982.

Gay Fathers: Some of Their Stories, Experience and Advice. Toronto: Gay Fathers of Toronto, 1981.

Gersoni-Edelman, Diane. *Sexism and Youth—Addresses, Essays, and Lectures*. New York: Bowker, 1974.

Hall Carpenter Archives staff. *Inventing Ourselves: Lesbian Life Stories*. New York: Routledge, Chapman, and Hall, 1989.

———. *Walking After Midnight—Gay Men's Life Stories*. New York: Routledge, Chapman, and Hall, 1989.

Hall, Radclyffe. *The Well of Loneliness*. New York: Doubleday, 1990.

Hankel, Frances, and John Cunningham. *A Way of Love, a Way of Life: A Young Person's Introduction to What it Means to Be Gay*. New York: Lothrop, Lee and Shepard, 1979.

Heron, Ann, ed. *One Teenager in Ten: Writings By Gay and Lesbian Youth*. Boston: Alyson Publications, 1983.

Holmes, Sarah, ed. *Testimonies: a Collection of Lesbian Coming out Stories*. Boston: Alyson Publications, 1988.

Howells, Coral Ann, "Marie-Claire Blais…" *Private and Fictional Words: Canadian Women Novelists of the 1970's and 1980's*, London: Methuen, 1987.

Hunt, Morton M. *What Teenagers Should Know About Homosexuality and the AIDS Crisis*. New York: Farrar, Straus and Giroux, 1987.

Ireland, Timothy. *Who Is Inside?*

Jones, Clinton R. *Understanding Gay Relatives and Friends*. New York: Seabury Press, 1978.

Kahn, Coppelia. *Man's Estate: Masculine Identity in Shakespeare*. Berkley: University of California Press, 1981.

Kantrowitz, Arnie. *Under the Rainbow: Growing up Gay*. New York: Morrow, 1977.

Katz, Jonathan. *Gay American History*. New York: Thomas Y. Crowell, 1976.

Kirk, Marshall and Hunter Madsen. *After the Ball: How America Will Conquer Its Fear and Hatred of Gays in the 90's*, New York: Doubleday, 1989.

Kirkwood, James. *Good Times, Bad Times*. Mississauga, ON: Fawcett, 1983.

Klein, Norma. *Now That I Know*. New York: Bantam, 1988.

Kramer, Larry. *Reports from the Holocaust: The Making of an AIDS Activist*. New York: St. Martin's Press, 1989.

Leavitt, David. *Family Dancing*. New York: Alfred A. Knopf, 1984.

————. *The Lost Language of Cranes*. New York: Alfred A. Knopf, 1986.

Lenskyj, Helen. *Out of Bounds — Women, Sport and Sexuality*. Toronto: The Women's Educational Press, 1986.

The Lesbian Writing and Publishing Collective. *Dykeversions — Lesbian Short Fiction*. Toronto: The Women's Educational Press, 1986. (I find this collection quite explicitly erotic and may well decide not to shelve it in the library. I have selected two stories I would like to use in class: Michele Paulse's "Keynotes" and Carol Allen's "The Report Card".)

Levy, Elizabeth. *Come Out Smiling*, New York: Delacorte Press, 1981.

Loovis, David. *Straight Answers about Homosexuality for Straight Readers*. New York: Prentice-Hall, 1977.

McCauley, Stephen. *The Object of my Affection*. Markham, ON: Distican, 1990.

McEwen, Christian and Sue O'Sullivan, eds. *Out the Other Side: Contemporary Lesbian Writing*, London: Virago, 1988.

Miller, Isabel. *Patience and Sarah*. New York: Fawcett Crest, 1973.

Milligan, Don "Fighting the Epidemic." *Rouge* 2: 12−14 (Spring 1990).

Mohin, Lilian, ed. *Beautiful Barbarians: Lesbian Feminist Poetry*. London: Onlywomen, 1986.

Navratilova, Martina, and George Vecsey. *Martina*. New York: Alfred A. Knopf, 1985.

Naylor, Gloria. *The Women of Brewster Place*. New York: Penguin, 1988.

New Internationalist 201:4−25. (A series of articles in this issue relate to homosexuality and homophobia from a global perspective.)

Pearson, Carol Lynn. *Good-bye, I Love You*. New York: Randon House, 1986.

Pilon, Debra. "Double Discrimination: Racism and Heterosexism". *Breaking the Silence*, December 1987, 10−12.

Pogrebin, Letty Cotten, "The Secret Fear That Keeps Us From Raising Free Children", *Ms*. magazine. 9:4 (October 1980).

Puig, Manuel. *Kiss of the Spider Woman*. Trans. Thomas Colchie. New York: Random House, 1985.

Rafkin, Louise, ed. *Different Daughters: A Book by Mothers of Lesbians*. Pittsburgh: Cleis Press, 1987.

Reading, J.P. *Bouquets for Brimbal*. New York: Harper and Row, 1980.

Reid, John. *The Best Little Boy in the World*. New York: Ballantine Books, 1986.

Renault, Mary. *The Last of the Wine*. New York: Random House, 1975.

————. *The Persian Boy*. New York: Random House, 1988.

Roberts, J.R. *Black Lesbians — An Annotated Bibliography*. Tallahassee: The Naiad Press, 1981.

Rogers, Donald J. *Banned!—Book Censorship in the Schools*. New York: Simon and Schuster, 1988.

Rule, Jane. *After the Fire*. Tallahassee: The Naiad Press, 1989.

———. *Desert of the Heart*. Tallahassee: The Naiad Press, 1985.

———. *A Hot-Eyed Moderate*. Tallahassee: The Naiad Press, 1985.

———. *Memory Board*. Tallahassee: The Naiad Press, 1987.

Schneider, Margaret S. *Often Invisible—Counselling Gay and Lesbian Youth*. Toronto: Central Toronto Youth Services, 1988.

Snyder, Anne. *The Truth About Alex*. New York: New American Library, 1987.

Stevenson, Richard. *Ice Blues*. New York: Penguin, 1987.

Thurston, Carol. *The Romance Revolution: Erotic Novels for Women and the Quest for New Sexual Identity*. Champaign: University of Illinois Press, 1987. (The book makes a brief reference to lesbians in Harlequin-style novels, but the discussions of images, etc., of women in this book are quite relevant to the overall topic.)

Walker, Alice. *The Colour Purple*. Orlando, FL: Harcourt Brace Jovanovich, 1982.

———. *In Search of Our Mothers' Gardens*. Orlando, FL: Harcourt, Brace, Jovanovich, 1984. (The book is a series of essays on writers, experiences, etc. "Gifts of Power" and "Breaking Chains and Encouraging Life" deal with lesbianism.)

Waugh, Evelyn. *Brideshead Revisited*. Boston: Little, Brown, 1982.

Weinberg, George "Homophobia." *Forum*. 1982.

White, Edmund. *The Beautiful Room is Empty*. New York: Alfred A. Knopf, 1988.

———. *A Boy's Own Story*. New York: New American Library, 1983.

Winterson, Jeanette. *Oranges are not the Only Fruit*. New York: Atlantic Monthly Press, 1987.

Zaremba, Eve. *A Reason to Kill*. Toronto: University of Toronto Press, 1990.

———. *Work for a Million*. Toronto: University of Toronto Press, 1990.

References

British Columbia Ministry of Education. 1990. *Learning Resources Evaluation Guide*. Victoria: British Columbia Ministry of Education.

Crumpacker, Laurie, and Eleanor M. Vander Haegen. 1987. "Pedagogy and Prejudice: Strategies for Confronting Homophobia in the Classroom." *Women's Studies Quarterly* 15 (Fall—Winter): 65—73.

Friedman, Jay. 1989. "The Impact of Homophobia on Male Sexual Development." *SIECUS Report* (May—July): 8—9.

Gardner, Saundra; Cynthia Dean; and Deo McKaig. 1989. "Responding to Differences in the Classroom: The Politics of Knowledge, Class, and Sexuality." *Sociology of Education* 62 (January): 64—74.

Grayson, Delores A. 1987. "Emerging Equity Issues Related to Homosexuality in Education." *Peabody Journal of Education* 64 (Summer): 132—144.

Howells, Coral Ann. 1987. *Private and Fictional Words Canadian Women Novelists of the 1970's and 1980's*. London: Methuen.

Hyde, Janet Shibley. 1986. *Understanding Human Sexuality*. 3rd ed. New York: McGraw-Hill.

Kings County District School Board. 1983. *Policy Manual*. Kentville: Kings County District School Board.

Kozol, Jonathan. 1980. *Prisoners of Silence: Breaking the Bonds of Adult Illiteracy in the United States*. New York: Continuum.

Lee, Helen. 1988. "Precautions Principals Can Take To Avert Censorship Protests", *NASSP Bulletin* 72 (May): 70−76.

Nova Scotia Department of Education. 1977. *Criteria for Evaluation of Learning Materials*. Halifax: Nova Scotia Department of Education.

Nova Scotia Department of Education. 1983. *English Language Arts Grades 7−12*. Halifax: Nova Scotia Department of Education.

Nova Scotia Department of Education. 1977. *Guidelines to Eradicate Prejudice, Bias and Stereotyping in Textbooks*. Halifax: Nova Scotia Department of Education.

Rofes, Eric. 1989. "Opening up the Classroom Closet: Responding to the Educational Needs of Gay and Lesbian Youth." *Harvard Educational Review* 59 (November): 444−53.

Schneider, Margaret S. 1988. *Often Invisible − Counselling Gay and Lesbian Youth*. Toronto: Central Toronto Youth Services.

Shor, Ira and Paulo Freire. 1987. *A Pedagogy for Liberation − Dialogues on Transforming Education*. Granby, MA: Bergin and Garvey.

Squirrell, Gillian. 1988. "Clause Without a Rebel." *The [London] Times Education Supplement*. (April 1) 17.

Stafford, J. Martin. 1988. "In Defence of Gay Lessons." *Journal of Moral Education*. 17 (January): 11−19.

Stanek, Lou Willett. 1976. *Censorship: A Guide for Teachers, Librarians, and Others Concerned with Intellectual Freedom*. New York: Dell.

Tierney, John. 1988. "Straight Talk" *Rolling Stone* 539 (November 17): 122−37.

Van Gelder, Lindsy, and Pam Brandt. 1986. "AIDS on Campus." *Rolling Stone*. 483 (September 25): 89−94.

Warren, Hugh. 1984. *Talking About School*. London: London Gay Teenage Group.

White, Edmund, and David Black. 1985−86. "AIDS: The Story of the Year." *Rolling Stone*. 463−464 (December 19−January 2): 121−24.

TWENTY-THREE

Developing a Community of Learners Inside and Outside the Classroom
Audrey Sturk

When grade twelve students come to my class for the first time in their graduating year, each brings a "discourse as an identity kit which comes complete with the appropriate costume and instructions" (Gee 1987, p. 3). These discourses vary according to student backgrounds. For example, the primary discourse of a farmer's son, who has had to finish his chores before six in the morning and who has not traveled far beyond Nova Scotia, differs greatly from that of the Base Commander's son, who spent a year in French immersion in France and was schooled in Germany, British Columbia, and California; and both, in turn, differ from the primary discourse of the mountain boy who lives by himself because of a family breakdown. And all differ from the primary discourse of young women in similar circumstances. Each in his or her way, has a "socially accepted association among ways of using language, of thinking, and of acting that can be used to identify oneself as a member of a socially meaningful group or social network" (Gee 1987, p. 3).

Despite these different primary discourses, grade twelve students bring to the classroom a remarkably similar secondary discourse. They have some very traditional expectations of teachers and how English should be taught. They expect me to give them a text, to put notes on the board (although they prefer handouts), to test them on my notes, to tell them what and when to learn, and to transmit knowledge through lecturing. Finally, they expect to write an essay on what the text is about. They acquired these expectations during their eleven previous years of schooling. They believe that I am the English expert and that I should feed them information, interpretations, and language, which they, in turn, will religiously memorize so that they can pass my course and get on to university. They expect to remain disinterested and to absorb externally determined knowledge; that is, students expect me to continue to "thwart (their) natural curiosity and treat them as passive recepticles rather than as active, sensitive human beings" (Shannon 1990, p. 164). Clearly, they are members of the discourse called student.

I must confess that prior to working with Patrick Shannon in 1990, I never consciously focused on the relationship between discourse and schooling. Before, I had been process oriented and student centered, providing students with choices and opportunities to gain control of standard English so that they might gain access to the elite discourse community called "university student." I did not see how the very structure of schooling and traditions of teaching favored the discourse of military personnel over farmers and people from the mountains. In my efforts to help individuals, I did not see why some groups of individuals found it nearly impossible to break into the discourse of school and why even fewer could gain acceptance as university students, even when they have control over standard dialect. Although I have not backed away from my responsibility to prepare these students for university, I now understand and practice this responsibility differently. I agree with Shor and Freire (1987) that "education is politics and that language is political" (p. 61) and with Giroux (1987) that "schools need to be seen as vital sites for the development of democracy" (p. 180). After all, as Shannon told me "education is the backbone of democracy." I ask myself: What kind of politics am I doing in the classroom? and "How many or how few do I want to have this education?" (Rose 1988, p. 194).

My answers to these questions have added a political edge to my process approach, and I now attempt to align my work according to two goals. One of my goals must be to create an environment in the classroom to ensure that all students can work together in harmony and to promote learning opportunities that will be beneficial to all social groups equally. A second goal is to provide opportunities for students to question authority, to think for themselves, and to act democratically, responsibly, and compassionately among themselves in the classroom and within our community. To realize these goals, as Giroux (1987) suggests, "Schools need to provide the opportunity for literate occasions for students to share their experiences, work in social relations that emphasize care and concern for others, to take risks, and to fight for a quality of life in which all human beings benefit" (p. 181). I want to "stand back and observe from a critical distance" (Shannon 1989, p. 163) as we produce "images of that which is not yet" (Bloch 1970 in Simon 1987, p. 371).

In theory, this sounds glorious; however, I am not God, and I search for some practice that will enable and allow me to act on my pedagogical *and* political goals. For me, it takes up to six weeks of each school year for students to trust that we are here to learn and progress together and that each student's focus or contribution is important even though it may differ from others in the class. Too, it takes six weeks to eliminate the questions: How much does this count? How long does it have to be? I confront our different expectations directly. I tell them I want them to write, research, read, discuss, collaborate, make judgments; to examine the label placed on their backgrounds; to perform on cable television or video; to share; and to get out into, and contribute to, the community. I want to develop a community of voices and "a community of learners" (Shannon 1990, p. 169) who can make a difference inside and outside the classroom. After our first meeting, some students leave the classroom excited; some are skeptical because they don't trust my thinking; some are flabergasted and reluctant because the have no idea how their grades will be determined. To gain their trust, I work on two fronts.

The first plan to close the gap between student and teacher expectations begins with controversial articles from newspapers or magazines. The goal here is to make students conscious of the explicit social and political issues that surround them every day. Moreover, I want to make students aware of the politics of writing; in particular, the political, moral, and social assumptions that authors typically leave unstated. We look at articles on illiteracy and attacks on teachers so that we can learn to question what is not said. We look at articles on vandalism in the local newspapers; and we read reports on controversies over the Meech Lake Accord, the wage freeze, and the GST. Our job is to probe deeply into the assumptions behind what is written and to ask who is served by them and how issues can be distorted in the pursuit of personal or class interests. I want students to make connections within the text and with the political, social, and moral issues outside the text. This type of activity sets the background for reading critically. So, we work at "how to look" and we talk about why most readers do not question the articles. Like Bigelow (1989), I find this a new experience for most of the grade twelve students.

Dealing with controversial articles is now important for me. I need to feel that students realize that I want them to take a questioning stance as they head into any text. All students may not learn to question and challenge the written word, but I need to know that I have provided an opportunity for them to do so. I do not want students to continue to equate print with authority and truth. Through our reading and discussion, the students and I learn to deal with diversity of legitimate opinion in the classroom and community. Trimbur's article, "Consensus and Difference in Collaborative Learning," (1989) has strongly influenced my thinking as I work with students toward developing a critical practice of collaborative learning. Trimbur writes that the "use of consensus is inherently dangerous and politically a totalitarian practice that stifles individual voice and creativity and suppresses differences and enforces conformity" (p. 602); however, it is how consensus is used that is important here. "Consensus can be a powerful instrument for students to generate differences, to identify the systems of authority that organize these differences, and to transform the relations of power that determine who may speak and what counts as a meaningful statement" (Trimbur 1989, p. 603). I think this is the crux of education and what I have tried to do by beginning with controversial articles and working them through in order to get students to ask: What can we do? What should we do? What will we attempt to do, and for whom?

The second front on which I attempt to build trust is through student writing. My students are not different from the freshmen at UCLA that Rose (1988) describes. They write fragments, use repetition (usually to gain length), deny that they are less than a 70 percent language student (70 represents the university requirement average in Nova Scotia), feel lonely (especially the transient students), have memorizing and summarizing down pat, have experienced "their culture denied and the brazenness of power" (Rose 1988, p. 169), have been labeled cheaters because they collaborated, and have had their primary discourse ridiculed. So, as I work with their first piece of writing, I find that some students copied from Coles' Notes; some summarized rather than analyzed; and some did not understand the difference between quotations that support their opinion and those that simply repeat or hang in mid-air.

My job, as a teacher, must be "to address their weaknesses (and) nurture their strengths" (Rose 1988, p. 187) and to overcome the myth that "test scores and tallies of errors" (Rose 1988, p. 187) determine a student's privilege to learn and become literate in all environments in which the students may find themselves. "Error marks the place where education begins" (Rose 1988, p. 189) is a beautiful line, one that I discuss with my students. The level of language skills that I expect from my students is my personal judgment call; this is based upon the belief that because I have remained a part time student at university for twenty five of my thirty four years of teaching, I am capable of judging what kind of writing is expected at the university level. The practical here and now in preparation for making a student's life a little easier as he or she heads out to the first year of university far outweighs any criticisms of sometimes teaching grammar in a traditional way. Moreover, "stressing the 'deficits,' 'deficiencies,' and 'handicaps' of the students" (Rose 1988, p. 202) and shifting the blame for their lack of success from the teacher, the school, and the upper sectors of society to the students, the victims, must be turned around. The subsequent pieces of writing they compose do improve. Students begin to trust that I am not here to bury their writing, their sensitivity, or their ability with ridicule, and they soon begin to take pride in working with language to make their writing more powerful.

Five to six weeks into the term, I feel confident that I have students headed in a certain direction—a democratic direction—one that works for me and my personality. I have a "flexibly rigid" control that makes me feel good about myself, the program, and the students. So much in school and in life, depends upon having a direction. When students and I are in limbo about where an essay, a novel study, a class, or our lives may be going, there is chaos. The direction may change its course or focus as we build upon what we already know from our reading, writing, discussions or whatever, but we all have to have a direction. My direction as we head into a novel study is to develop communities of learners within and outside the classroom who will collaboratively direct their learning. I see each class as thirty-plus "projects of possibility" (Simon 1987, p. 372): each can make a difference as we share the role in what our community learns.

A logical progression from, and extension of, the first six weeks of school for one class of thirty-seven students was to move to Sheila Watson's novel, *The Double Hook* (1969), a challenging novel for any level. I wanted to look at our community of learners in an attempt to understand how we make meaning from a text and how we make social, political, moral, and educational connections within and outside the text. Additionally, I wanted to look at how students responded to my bowing out of the direction for the study.

Watson's novel is filled with symbolism, a language device to which the students had little previous exposure, but that capitalizes on students' recent experience in critical reading. Moreover, the book's style and characters' discourse is other than mainstream middle-class Canadian. We discussed this as a class and we examined an introduction to the novel done by Grube (1969). Right away, one student challenged the fact that Grube's introduction may influence what a student was to think. She was right, of course, and I had to sort out whether I was promoting what I was trying to defeat: that students must learn to not accept print as authority.

The students chose to begin with the whole class reading the first chapter aloud together, followed by small group discussion. The symbolism and the apparently bizarre social relationships within *The Double Hook* afforded almost continuous discussion and debates concerning the prospects for remediation of the physical and social pollution within the fictional community. During small group discussion, students struggled with the characters' often unsavory and, at times, illegal efforts to overcome the stigma of labels and social pressure to conform. Efforts to reach consensus in our class often resulted in disagreement because students' primary discourse led them to different conclusions.

All groups had many questions as they dealt with this novel. It was delightful, as a teacher who had pretty well bowed out, to watch the students sharing opinions and to listen to the buzz of talk that was being used to make meaning. This, I believe, is the basis of language and literacy and what readers should be doing with a text as they put Trimbur's idea of "dissensus" into action.

That the students dealing with this novel became a community of learners and a community of people who care about others showed up specifically on three occasions. One class began with a student's questioning why Greta, a central character in the novel, had said nothing about her brother, James, killing their mother. The class reaction was that when we don't know what others are thinking or we don't know the cause of something in life, we fear: we fear the silence; we fear the unknown. This led immediately to a student's saying, "It's like Richard (a boy in our class); he doesn't know what killed his father yesterday and he's scared. He knows his parents had a quarrel, but that's all he knows." The rest of the class was spent on what the classmates could do to ease Richard's pain. Some decided to go see him; some would send cards; two wanted to write a poem for him; some would go to the funeral home; two would gather notes and work from school for him while he was out; and one volunteered to work his night shifts at a nursing home if needed.

A few classes later, students were dealing with the passage in the novel on leaving as no escape. The discussion was centered on James's running from his self-created ills in the community. The main passage being discussed was the following:

> Beasts aren't much different from men....I've seen them knock down fences and kick themselves out of corrals. But I've seen them come wandering back to the barn and the hay. Some...are pure outlaw. But there's the torment of loneliness and the will of snow and heat they can't escape. (Watson 1969, p. 76)

One girl broke in here with: "My mother's like a beast. She's just left again and said the kids could fend for themselves until after the new year. But she'll come wandering back when the novelty and money wear off." The group fell silent and let her talk out the frustrations she must have been feeling. It was interesting here to see that the novel passage prompted this student to reveal her home problems. Another student referred to his mother as a "beast" too.

He confessed that he dreaded Christmas by saying: "I haven't had a wrapped Christmas present since Mother left when I was thirteen." The original "beast" passage being dealt with by some students not only meant understanding a text; for them, it also meant understanding real life and its complexities.

On some occasions, I intentionally came into the classroom up to fifteen minutes late, just to test whether the students had taken control of their learning and if they had a direction. The first come-in-late session was rewarding, to say the least. I found Elizabeth reading aloud to Robert. She knew that he had difficulty with print and organizing his thoughts. He had told her he was having trouble sorting out "this gibberish" in the text. Melanie was arguing with a group of boys that Angel should be the leader of the small community in which the novel is set. She concluded her argument with, "That's what I'm writing my paper on." This, of course, was an assumption that there would be a paper expected. (She read me right, again.) Rachel's group was discussing Kip's saying, "People go shutting their doors. Tying things up. Fencing them in. Shutting out what they don't rightly know" (Watson 1969, p. 58). Another group was trying to decide whether it was language or lack of it that separated households in this novel, whether it was that they didn't have the social skills to deal with their problems, or whether it was the social skills that caused the problems. Two students were discussing the use of Coyote in the novel and trying to make sense out of the following passage:

> Fear making mischief. . . . Fear skulking round. Fear walking round in the living shape of the dead. No stone was big enough, no pile of stones, to weigh down fear. (Watson 1969, p. 61)

All groups were making meaning out of the text in their own way. They were making connections and interconnections; they were talking of language; and they were using their varied discourses and sensitivities to learn. It was rewarding to see how they shared interpretations, figured out meaning, and related the novel to their own lives. My bowing out was, for the most part, accomplished by the seventh week of the school year and I felt the struggle to do so was well worthwhile as I watched the students from so many backgrounds become a community of learners within the classroom.

With the collaborative skills of group activity in place, the writing phase of the novel study went very smoothly. In my journal I recorded a sampling of what students were doing with the text. As I came into the classroom, three boys were arguing over who had the best thesis statement or direction for their piece of writing. Stephen called out to me, "Come check this, quick, Mrs. Sturk, it'll blow your mind." Michael broke in with, "I can beat that." As I read Michael's opening, he said, "Now, doesn't that just say it all?" Marcus said, "Bet you fellows don't have an opening line with *cosmos* in it." From across the room, Elizabeth's comment baffled Stephen: "Stephen, I bet you didn't make the connection between Greta's burning herself and James's escape from his fears." The students worked with words and made words work for them. For a week, the argued; they discussed; they changed their direction; they shared sections of their writing; they laughed; they talked about symbols in the text; and they asked each other for a word. Language became an enjoyable challenge.

Of the thirty seven essays I received on Sheila Watson's novel, there were thirty two different focuses of interest; for example, one student explored the woman's position in society in the late 1940s; another explored the laws of the time; others looked at who should become the leader of the community and so on. Through making their own decisions about events in the novel and how these related to their own lives, all the students were "introduced to a language of morality that allowed them to think about how a community should be constructed; to recognize constraints; to make choices; and, to believe that they can make a difference in the world" (Giroux 1987, p. 179).

Margaret Laurence's *The Stone Angel* (1964) helped a different class of thirty-six students to discover education outside the classroom. One of the concerns of Laurence's novel is aging. I began this novel study by asking students to write a description or to perform an image of a senior citizen. Words and images of having wrinkles, slobbering, and being old, senile, feeble, thin, toothless, and a burden were used in most of the descriptions in some way. The consensus was that senior citizens, for the most part, are a burden to their families. I then asked them to write a description of Hitler. My next step was to have students read a poem entitled "Think About It" (which I had received from a history professor many years ago) and to write a description of what kind of person would write such a compassionate poem about a dying mother. While they had the adjectives that described the poet and the Hitler descriptions in front of them, I told them that my history professor told me that Hitler, in fact, had written the poem. Exercise completed: we reached a conclusion that things are not always as they seem, which implied that maybe their assumptions about senior citizens may not be accurate. I am not sure whether this lead-in to the novel study was devious, good teaching, or nonsense. It did, however, provide a two-pronged approach to the study of aging: the literary investigations through *The Stone Angel* and an empirical investigation of senior citizens in our community. My objectives were to move beyond the language of possibility in order to attempt projects to expand student discourse through community work and to establish new relationships between young and old. Clearly, these objectives could not be met in the traditional or even process classroom. Students were allowed to leave the school grounds and move out into the communities of senior citizens because of the unusual degree of flexibility teachers are given in my school.

Students working with *The Stone Angel* began their study in small groups. The number of ideas skyrocketed in this setting as students negotiated their curriculum, made decisions on what they wanted to know about seniors, and thought about who would benefit from their knowing. They set up clearcut guidelines for their field trips: to give me their leaving time, destination and phone number, purpose, method of travel, and expected arrival time back at the school; to work out time slots for the trip so as to avoid missing other classes; to introduce themselves to whomever they were visiting and to explain the purpose of their visit; to take a copy of *The Stone Angel* with them and offer it to the senior or others who were being interviewed; to come to some agreement on how to interview, what questions to ask, how to ask them, and how to dress; and to determine what we want to know and why we want to know it prior to going out into the community.

In this class of thirty-six students, thirteen groups emerged with very different interests. The thirteen groups had very different projects of possibility to put into action, in very different ways, and in many different places, but the underlying consensus was: What can we do to make the lives of senior citizens in our communities happier and more worthwhile? The projects included:

1. Interviewing lawyers, law enforcement officers, and social workers concerning the laws governing the operation of nursing homes in Nova Scotia.
2. Interviewing seniors living in nursing homes to determine what changes would make their living there happier.
   With permission from the home's administrator and the interviewee, some students audio- or videotaped the interview; some took notes.
3. Interviewing seniors who still lived in their own homes to determine what students could do for these people to make their lives easier and, thus, happier.
4. Writing stories and poems about seniors. (This quickly changed to writing *for* seniors).
5. Bringing seniors together for entertainment at the local hall in the community in which they lived. Students and seniors alike would provide the entertainment. Students learned through the reports of interviews the kinds of entertainment that seniors liked.
6. Helping in senior citizens' homes by cleaning, mowing lawns, taking them for groceries, and so on.
7. Helping in nursing homes with meals, taking residents out for walks or in wheelchairs, and other tasks requested by the nursing home staff.
8. Determining what the expulsion of the Acadians meant to seniors who were French compared to those who were English. (Similar to what Bigelow (1989) did with his history class on Columbus).
9. Investigating seniors' pensions and supplementary payments in an attempt to find out from where the money comes, how the amount is determined, and whether the amounts received met financial needs.
10. Typing stories and poems written by students for seniors. (One student had reported the lack of reading materials in the homes he had visited.) Once typed, the materials were distributed to any seniors with whom the students had made contact.
11. Producing twenty-minute television programs on the local station for seniors in the viewing area. (This was suggested by one of the seniors interviewed who was active in the Senior Citizens' Association.) By the end of the novel study, every member in this particular class had performed on television, the purpose being to entertain and inform senior citizens in the viewing audience. This was wonderful public relations for the student-designed curriculum.
12. Inviting senior citizens to the classroom, where they could become a student and then explain how this experience differed from their own school days.
13. Summarizing points of view on political issues. Students interviewed members of the various political parties at all levels of government, attempting to include all sides and versions of the issues. They then made

notes on their findings, using language that was easy to understand. The final judgement about the issues was left totally to the individual senior.

The results of the groups' efforts on the senior-citizen theme were exciting to all of us. We had no idea when the theme was created that it would prove so fruitful and take so many directions, or that the grade twelve students could make such a difference in the lives of the senior citizens in our area. Every group fulfilled its expectations, and, in fact, went far beyond what it had initially set out to do.

The in-class study of *The Stone Angel* was "situated amid the historical forces that shaped it" (Rose 1988, p. 191). Some students wrote about nursing homes of the 1940s and the stigma attached to them compared to the 1990s; some looked at Nova Scotia's present demographics and concluded that given the facilities available in the 1990s, there will be a major crisis for seniors who need placement in homes by the year 2000; some looked at all the experience-notes gathered and related them to the novel. Newspaper articles flooded the classroom; some students challenged the publishers on "covert censorship (which) contains the same elements of negation and affirmation as overt censorship" (Shannon 1989a, p. 103).

The essays I received showed that each of the thirty-six students felt a different emphasis on what was important in this novel study as a whole. Many barriers were removed for students who feared interviewing authorities and seniors outside the school setting; many were appalled as they gathered and shared information and dealt with Section 21 of Canada's Criminal Code. One nursing home was closed and the owner convicted for violation of the laws governing nursing homes, as a result of two students confiding in a law enforcement officer who had read the novel. After being interviewed, this officer joined our class in its attempt to make life better for senior citizens. Some students worked with this officer putting locks on houses of seniors who lived in remote areas and convincing them to put their money in the bank, rather than under a mattress. One student wrote, "The functions of the RCMP cannot be successfully carried out if police are alienated from the rest of society. To consider that police work is 'their' responsibility is dead wrong." Here again was an unexpected change of attitude. Each project resulted in tipping the "balance between individual and social needs in favor of social and community needs" (Shannon 1990, p. 165).

How to do a fair assessment on so many different projects was the only difficult part of this novel study. I respect the school's requirement to have a numerical mark for all students to send home to parents, but to determine that mark fairly for this study created problems for me because I agree with Shannon (1990) that assessment should focus on what students can and do practice when using literacy for real purposes. I included the students in the various groups in negotiating how the mark was to be determined and what questions would be asked on the upcoming examination. (Although my school does not require that students write an English examination at the grade twelve level, I require this to prepare them for the university examination experience that they will face.)

At the social gatherings that the students and the senior citizens had, each group confessed its opinions about the other. Much laughter ensued when some students read their initial descriptions of senior citizens and the seniors told their tales of thinking that most young people today were into drugs! Both sides changed their attitudes as students made connections from the novel and the school to the community and as seniors came into the school and attended gatherings planned by students. Both seniors and students clearly demonstrated why and how it is possible for literacy to be more than reading and writing.

One of the most touching times for one group of students came after graduation. One couple, in their late seventies, had no flush toilet or hot water in their home. The students had raised money, hired a carpenter and plumber, and supplied this couple with a luxury the students could not imagine being without. The outhouse was torn down and the debris buried; then the couple was presented with a receipt for the work, marked "Paid in full."

The critical reading and writing about controversial articles of the first few weeks of school and the novel studies of Sheila Watson's *The Double Hook* and Margaret Laurence's *The Stone Angel* demonstrate that the politics of literacy education has a wonderful and positive future if students are provided the opportunity to exercise the direction and control of their learning. With teacher and community support, students can learn to appreciate different primary discourses in order to work and live in harmony; they can expand student discourse to allow themselves the freedom to question the authority of text, to think for themselves, and to act democratically, responsibly, and compassionately; and they can use literacy to make sense of their lives. I believe that these novel studies are good examples of negotiations between and among students and teacher and a sharing of control, authority, and responsibility over learning, and that we developed a community of learners inside the classroom with the study of *The Double Hook* and outside the classroom with *The Stone Angel*.

References

Bigelow, William. 1989. "Discovering Columbus: Rereading the Past." *Language Arts* 66(#6): 635–643.

Gee, James Paul. 1987. "What is Literacy?" Prepared for the Mailman Foundation Conference on Families and Literacy, Harvard Graduate School of Education.

Giroux, Henry A. 1987. "Critical Literacy and Student Experience: Donald Graves' Approach to Literacy." *Language Arts* 64(#2): 175–181.

Grube, John. 1969. "Introduction." In Sheila Watson, *The Double Hook*. Toronto: McClelland and Stewart. 5–14.

Laurence, Margaret. 1964. *The Stone Angel*. Toronto: McClelland and Stewart.

Rose, Mike. 1988. *Lives on the Boundary*. New York: Free Press. 167–204.

Shannon, Patrick. 1985. "Reading Instruction and Social Class." *Language Arts* 62(#6): 604–613.

———. 1989a. "Overt and Covert Censorship of Children's Books." *The New Advocate*. 2(#2) 97–104.

———. 1989b. "The Struggle for Control of Literacy Lessons." *Language Arts* 66(#6): 625–634.

———. 1990. *The Struggle to Continue: Progressive Reading Instruction in the United States*. Portsmouth, NH: Heinemann. 163–183.

Shor, Ira and Paulo Freire. 1987. *A Pedagogy for Liberation*. Granby Ma.: Bergin and Garvey.

Simon, Roger I. 1987. "Empowerment as a Pedagogy of Possibility." *Language Arts* *64*(#4): 370−382.

Trimbur, John. 1989. "Consensus and Difference in Collaborative Learning." *College English 51*(#4): 602−616.

Watson, Sheila. 1969. *The Double Hook*. Toronto: McClelland and Stewart.

TWENTY-FOUR

Opportunity Through Politics: The Game of Schooling

Jeanette L. Bishop
Susan M. Cameron

Schools consist of humans interacting both cognitively and socially. Historically the nature of the educational system has been a teacher–learner paradigm, the teacher being in control of knowledge that is required by the learner. More recently, the educational system has been undergoing progressive change in an attempt to incorporate alternate philosophies of education that create a more natural and just learning environment. Whether in a traditional or progressive setting, however, surrounding these seemingly simple relationships is a complicated hierarchy of players with various degrees of control and power.

The Canadian educational structure is composed of provincial departments (as well as two territorial departments) under the umbrella of the Federal government. Each province governs its municipal school boards through its Department of Education headed by a Minister of Education. In turn, each municipal school board is comprised of several elected members and several government-appointed members. Within each municipality exists a central office supervisory staff (the Chief Education Officer/Superintendent and various assistants and subsystem supervisors). Completing this hierarchy is the core of the system, the schools, which contain principals, teachers, and students. The other crucial players in the system are parents, whose role is somewhat ambiguous but certainly prominent.

Opportunity Through Politics is a game that presents political issues that affect the more visible people within the system—students, parents, teachers, and principals. Because relationships exist on various levels, some players are affected more than others. For example, policies mandated by supervisory staff regarding discipline procedures have effects on principals, teachers, and students.

However, each player is affected in a different way. The effects may be positive or negative depending on the issue, the player, and the context. One specific issue may positively affect a principal but negatively affect a student. Conversely, an issue that positively affects a student may have a negative effect on a teacher.

The issues that comprise the Opportunity, Politics, and Issue cards in the game were compiled after a survey of the nearly one hundred teachers and administrators who attended the Summer Institute. These informants were asked to list examples of the politics of their jobs. The issues that we used fit our Nova Scotia circumstances to varying degrees. Appendix A includes the statements collected at this time — some are written as problems; others are just phrases or topics. Although these issues may be universal to some degree, the game will be improved if a similar survey is conducted for potential players from different parts of the globe. Use our issues or make your own, but play the game.

By playing Opportunity Through Politics, teachers, parents, and others interested in schooling can discuss the politics of everyday events in schools. During these discussions, players can identify the opportunities and constraints that events present for participants in school. As players learn to name the politics, their talk may lead them to discussions of how to change the politics of schooling to ensure that the benefits of education will be shared equally by all.

General notes on play

Opportunity Through Politics can best be described as the ups and downs of a year at school. Players land on squares that describe events or situations that occur within a school system. For example, as students, parents, teachers, or principals, we all remember the inservice day and the much-anticipated spring break. When players land on a politics or an opportunity square, the issue they choose from the deck will be an event or situation that has actually occurred in at least one school or board office somewhere at some time.

As four players respond to a particular issue chosen, they experience a wide range of reactions, from satisfaction and confidence to frustration and anger. The issue of the tracking of students in secondary school programs is a good example. While a student in a lower track may feel frustrated and deflated because he or she had wanted to go to university eventually, the parent may be satisfied that the child was placed in a mediocre track rather than the lowest one of all. In this case, the player who is the parent moves ahead two squares, while the child — the student — moves back two squares. The emotions symbolized by these moves become very real, so that by the end of the game, players may feel cynical and unhappy about their trip through school — as is the case, we are sure, in real life.

The advanced version of Opportunity Through Politics enables players to discuss the issue before them in order to reach a consensus. Upon playing this version, we found that by having to discuss an issue from the point of view of a particular player, one becomes much more sensitive to the needs of that player. We could move closer to feeling how a downtrodden principal or an elated parent feels.

As the game nears the finish line, each player knows that any issue arising from the deck can have either devastating or positive effects on their fate. Students and parents hold their breath as they approach graduation. Will they arrive first, or will the school personnel beat them and win the game? Will June bring positive changes for the teacher, but damaging ones for the student? It's anyone's guess!

Rules for playing opportunity through politics—version 1

Players

- For two, three, or four players.
- Players are designated as:
  - Student.
  - Parent.
  - Teacher.
  - Principal.
- Highest roll of the die chooses which role a participant will play, next highest has second choice, etc.
- Since there is no advantage to being the first player, players decide among themselves who will start the game.

Objective

Each player must attempt to be the first to complete the education course and reach the finish line.

Setup and rules of play

1. Place the board on a flat surface. Place the Opportunity and Politics cards on the designated places.
2. Following the rules of player selection, each player places his or her token on the start position for his or her player. Each token is marked: S for student, Pa for parent, T for teacher, Pr for principal.
3. The first player rolls the dice and proceeds forward. Play moves to the left.
4. As a player moves forward he or she will land on squares that may or may not contain additional directions and moves.

   - A player landing on a Politics square must select a Politics card from the top of the deck of cards and follow the directions given on the card. Each card contains directions for each of the four players. Some cards instruct "all players" to follow the directions given. When this is found on the card, *all* players must follow the directions. Replace cards at the bottom of the deck.
   - If a player lands on an Opportunity square he or she must pick a card and follow the directions. (See the rules above for landing on a Politics square.)

- If the directions on a card state that the player loses a turn, he or she must wait until each player has completed a turn, skip, and wait until his or her turn comes around again.
- If a player lands on a square that directs him or her to move (or a card directs him or her to move), that player must move and then wait until his or her turn comes around again before attempting to go ahead or following the directions on a square landed on. When the turn comes, the player must follow the directions contained on the square first and then roll the die for your turn.
- Some issues will have no effect on specific players. A "no effect" indicates you are to stay on your present square.
- Some directions for students or parents include combined moves. For example, a student may be instructed to move ahead two with the parent. In such a case, student and parent each move ahead two squares.

5. If, after a card has been read, a player contests a directive, all players must discuss the issue and come to a consensus on the move contested. If consensus cannot be reached, the player must follow the directive given. If it is agreed to change the directive, players must decide what that move will be.
6. When approaching the finish line, a player must roll the exact number to land on Finish. If the exact number is not rolled, the player must wait until his or her turn comes around again before attempting another roll.
7. The player to reach Finish first ends the game.

Rules for playing opportunity through politics – version 2 (advanced)

Players

- For two, three, or four players.
- Players are designated as:
  - Student.
  - Parent.
  - Teacher.
  - Principal.
- Highest roll of the dice chooses which role a participant will play, next highest has second choice, etc.
- Since there is no advantage to being the first player, players decide among themselves who will start the game.

Objective

Each player must participate in discussion of randomly chosen educational issues in an attempt to negotiate their movement toward the finish line.

Setup and rules of play

1. Place the board on a flat surface. Place the deck of Issue cards in the center of the board.
2. Following the rules of player selection, each player places his or her token on the start, position as described in Version 1.
3. The first player selects an Issue card from the top of the deck and reads the issue aloud.
4. *All* players must then discuss the issue and its implications for their particular role (student, parent, etc.) in the game. Players are encouraged to draw upon past educational experiences, whether as a student, a parent, or an educator in an attempt to discern the effects of the particular issue being discussed.
5. Players must come to a consensus as they decide who moves in what direction (backward or forward) and by how many spaces on the game board.
6. The first player to reach the finish line 'ends' the game.

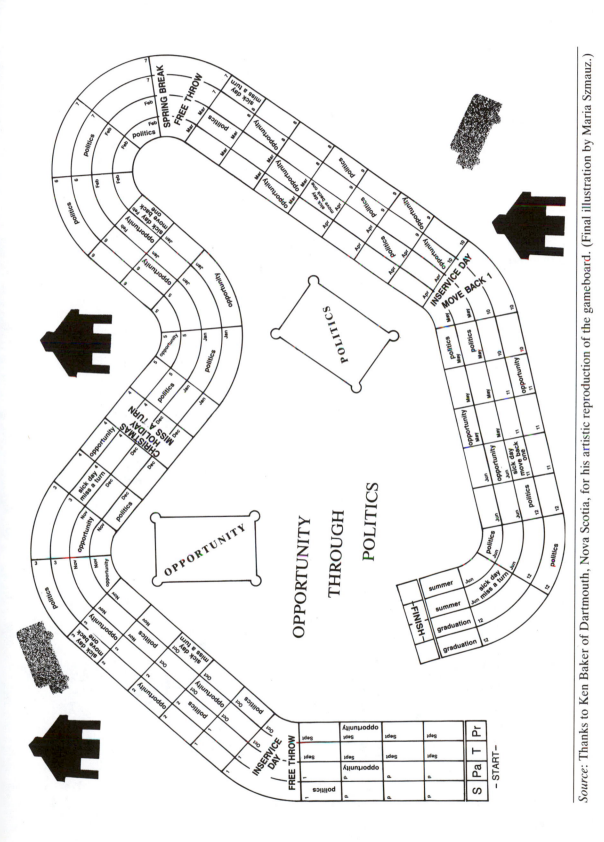

Source: Thanks to Ken Baker of Dartmouth, Nova Scotia, for his artistic reproduction of the gameboard. (Final illustration by Maria Szmauz.)

Opportunity cards (for version 1)

Issue: Novels by native authors are introduced into L.A. curriculum.
S: Access to good literature from another cultural perspective. Move ahead 3.
Pa: Native parent invited to class to talk about self-government. Move ahead 2.
T: Students appreciate cultural differences. Take another turn.
Pr: Sat on censorship committee. Voted for access to previously banned novels. Move ahead 2.

Issue: All standardized tests that are judged to be culturally biased are banned.
S: Black student scored well on achievement test. Move ahead 3.
Pa: Child is not labeled. Pleased with progress. Move ahead 1.
T: Achieve valid evaluation results from all students. Move ahead 2.
Pr: Struck a committee to develop additional culture-free evaluation materials. Take another turn.

ALL PLAYERS
Issue: Freedom of action is given to students during budget restraints.
S: Cutbacks threaten to close school. Your campaign sways school board vote. Take another turn.
Pa: Your child develops a sense of control and responsibility. Move ahead 1.
T: Freedom given to students is abused. Move back 2.
Pr: Student power prevents school from closing. Move ahead 1.

Issue: Budget allows for expansion of school programs.
S: New Music program implemented, which gives you access to music careers. Move ahead 3.
Pa: New Fine Arts program recognizes child's talent. Move ahead 3 with student.
T: Sense of fulfillment to see students motivated. Move ahead 2.
Pr: Students, parents, and staff content with new programs. Move ahead 2.

Issue: New Teacher gives students more curriculum control.
S: New materials in English—collaborative choice. Move ahead 2.
Pa: Feels a lack of structure in curriculum. Not pleased. Move back 1.
T: Positive feedback from students, but not parents. Lose a turn.
Pr: New teacher acts as guide to other programs. Move ahead 2.

ALL PLAYERS
Issue: Request made for additional funding is granted.
S: Individual access to new computer lab. Move ahead 1.
Pa: Attended workshop on L.A. curriculum. Move ahead 2.
T: Bought books for classroom library. Move ahead 1.
Pr: Hired another classroom assistant. Move ahead 2.

Issue: Curriculum is to meet student's needs.
S: L.A. program uses personal experiences. Move ahead 2.
Pa: Child is highly motivated in school. Move ahead 1 with student.
T: Enjoyable class environment. Pleased with progress. Move ahead 3.
Pr: Receives positive feedback from parents and staff. Move ahead 2.

ALL PLAYERS
Issue: Evaluation is individualized for all students.
S: Allowed to take oral exam due to learning disability. Take another turn.
Pa: Positive evaluation of child. Highly motivated. Move ahead 1.
T: Not enough time for individual evaluation. Miss a turn.
Pr: School shows high success rate. Move ahead 1.

ALL PLAYERS
Issue: Staff shows cultural variety.
S: Exposed to multiculturalism. Move ahead 2.
Pa: Child questions values. Do not move.
T: Curriculum includes censored materials that limit cultural exposure. Move back 2.
Pr: Cooperative community effort to address racial issues. Move ahead 2.

Politics cards (for version 1)

Issue: Teacher is not suitable for Primary grade; is used to teaching grade 5; remains in primary. S: Teacher not used to primary. Bad year. Move back 3. Pa: Teacher in wrong grade. Bad year. Move back 2. T: Hate primary. Want out. You and S lose a turn. Pr: Placed teacher in wrong grade. Bad move. Move back 4.	ALL PLAYERS **Issue: Curriculum is set without student and teacher input.** S: Social Studies content has no relevance for you. Move back 1. Pa: Must push child to attend in boring class. Move back 1. T: Subject you teach has no relevance for students. Move back 1. Pr: Must handle discipline problem that stems from boredom. Move back 1.	ALL PLAYERS **Issue: Students are tracked into secondary programs—little opportunity for change. Expectations adjust accordingly.** S: In general program, would like to go to university. Need different courses. Move back 2. Pa: Insisted that son be put in general, not adjusted class, succeeded. Move ahead 2. Pr: Expect those in occup. classes not to do well. They don't. Move back 3.
ALL PLAYERS **Issue: Format of report cards** S: New report cards implemented that credit individual traits. Move ahead 2. Pa: New report cards made easier to understand. Move ahead 2. T: Old report cards do not allow room for individual comments (restricted). Move back 1. Pr: New proposal for report card format is rejected. Move back 1.	ALL PLAYERS **Issue: Cutbacks in Special Ed program** S: Resource help is canceled. Move back 2. Pa: Special Ed service for your child is limited. Move back 2. T: Recommendations given are not accepted. Lose a turn. Pr: Fight to maintain Special Ed is lost. Move back 3.	ALL PLAYERS **Issue: Few administrative positions are held by women.** S: I need to talk to guidance counselor. Since I am female, he may not understand my problems. Move back 2. Pa: Single mom with many problems. Would relate better to female principal. Move back 1, with student. T: Want to become a principal. Seems more difficult since I am a woman. Lose turn. Pr: Female Vice-Principal-feel subordinate to male V.P. Lose turn.
Issue: Specialists used to relieve classroom teachers—limited consultative/collaborative time. S: No resource help today; resource teacher substituting. Move back 2, with parent. Pa: Child had no extra help today. Upset at system. Lose a turn. T: Didn't meet with specialist. Unsure of program plans. Lose a turn. Pr: Got class covered by specialist. No need for a substitute. Move ahead 2.	**Issue: Integration is mandated, yet funds for Special Ed personnel are reduced** S: Reading help I need is not available. Move back 2, with parent. Pa: Reading more at home with child. Not enough time. Move back 1. T: No support in class for difficult child. Stressed. Lose turn. Pr: More parents upset about lack of support. Lose turn.	**Issue: Parental involvement in curriculum and methods used in schools.** S: Your parents insist on diversified reading material. Move ahead 2. Pa: You are a member of PTA and help establish new evaluation system. Move ahead 2. T: Parental assistance with curriculum helps establish relationship with students. Move ahead 2. Pr: Parental feedback on curriculum helps decision-making process. Move ahead 1.

Appendix A

Gender, race, religion

- There are no women besides the regular classroom teacher in positions of authority (guidance counselors, vice-principal, etc.). Therefore, there is no one for girls to go to when they need advice, counseling, etc. The administration cannot work with females in such close proximity.
- Women in administration—men have traditionally held administrative positions—few women as v.p./principals—principals in Elementary only—v.p.—token positions
- Why do schools or school boards seemingly classify teacher areas in terms of gender? For example: Primary Education teachers—predominantly female Elementary—mixed Jr. High—predominantly male
- Administrative positions predominantly held by males
- There are only three female principals in Lun. Co.—27 schools. Are they not hired because they are female? Are the three token females? Maybe females don't apply.
- Women as second class citizens.
- In a certain school system, a principal can refuse enrollment of a child on a religious basis—for example, a Roman Catholic child may not be enrolled in an integrated school if there is a Catholic school in the community. This is often used to the advantage of the school if enrollment is down. (This may not be a written rule or agreement, but it is common practice.)

Curriculum control

- Parental involvement in curriculum and methods used in the schools
- You teach English Language Arts in a large high school (1750 students). There are five or six teachers per grade. The board policy is that all students in the school taking a given course must write a common exam. The exam is worth 50 percent of the final grade. Effectively this means that all six hundred students in grade ten must read the same books and cover the same material. The decision about which books to assign is made several removes from the student.
- Every year the school holds Christmas concerts and such. Teachers and students are never consulted as to whether or not they want a concert. It is assumed that they want it and will attend.

Evaluation

- the format of report cards
- a confrontation with university president over the issuing of a grade before the course and then assisting them to achieve it.
- You are involved in a controversy over the number of reporting sessions. Some schools want three reporting periods instead of four but this has been met with resistance by the administration.

Control of knowledge

- You are asked to participate in a project, but you find that some people are withholding information others deem significant.

- hidden agendas (when we are told differently) — whose involved — students, teachers, professors.
- who is "we" — the teacher is the authority in the classroom

Staffing/hierarchy

- Why can't a teacher who is not suited for a primary classroom be asked to move back to a grade-five classroom from which he initially came?
- A school principal was not promoted to the Superintendent of Schools position, mainly because he is the kind of person with the knowledge, confidence, and courage to question the board on many issues. How can educators foster thinking when the school board rejects it?
- A principal of a college department is told not to continue to talk to the press about budget cuts and the effect they had on a high-profile program.
- Specialists are used as a means to provide free time for the classroom teacher and are therefore not encouraging collaborative situations.
- You notice that some teachers within the school system are going over the principal's head to talk to the supervisor or superintendent.
- A teacher has been employed by her board for nine years as a term teacher — and fired each year.
- Specialists (in such areas as physical education and French) are used for administrative duties. principal — specialists and classroom teachers
- Confrontation with university president over the issuing of a mark before the course and assisting the students to achieve it.
- In your school, teachers are responsible for child supervision both in the lunch room and outside. Should teachers be responsible for this? Should parents? Should lunchtime be a free hour for teachers to do things they cannot do while in class?
- duty — some boards hire outside supervisors
- prep time — some Canadian boards give teachers back their owed preps if missed for any reason. The number of preps per teacher — teachers in high school — some may teach 4 different subjects and need more prep time than a teacher who teaches the same subject for 5 classes.

Labeling for funding

- You need a certain number of special ed students in the school in order to maintain a teaching unit (teacher). The principal goes from door to door making a list of special ed students. If there aren't enough students considered special ed, others who may have minor learning difficulties are added to the list.

Student placement

- Your school is divided into academic, general, academic support, work experience, adjusted, remedial, and secondary occupational classes. In the 1989–90 school year a parent demands that his child be moved from the general to the academic classes; a teacher demands that one student be moved from work experience to general classes. The school has 925 students. Once a label is pinned on a student, he or she rarely if ever gets rid of the label.

- The teachers' collective agreement states a limit to the number of students per class. If the enrollment goes beyond that number, you may be asked to sign a paper agreeing to accept one more student. But once you sign, you find that there is no limit to the number of extra students you are asked to accept.
- The Education Department for the province is pushing for mainstreaming. The classroom teacher and the students need more and more help from resource teachers. However, the province is now cutting back on support for these resource teachers.

Patronage

- It is well known within your school system that if you belong to a certain club, frequent that club, and socialize with its members, who are in high administrative positions, your chances for advancement are much greater.
- You work in a system that hires people as junior high reading specialists whose backgrounds are primarily as primary teachers over other qualified people.
- Your board advertises an administrative position and goes through the process of setting up interviews when it is obvious that higher management has already picked a person for the job. This person is not necessarily the best candidate, but is one who conforms to certain views, values, and politics valued by management.
- Your board advertises for a position when they already have one particular candidate in mind. They word the advertisement to fit that candidate.
- A full-time teacher for several years leaves the school for several years, then returns as a substitute for several more years. She then applies for a full-time position without success. She continues to substitute. Meanwhile, another candidate is hired into a position. She has no teaching experience, but belongs to the right political party and is a high-profile member of the community. The first teacher complains to the superintendent, who says, "Come on, don't be naive. We both know what's going on and why. These things happen. Keep trying; your turn will come."
- Principals are placed in elementary schools with little or no understanding or educational background in this area.
- In a job interview, you are asked what your father's name is to establish the political ties you may have.

Parental pressure

- Your principal tried to suspend a child for misbehavior on the bus. The child's parents went to the school trustees and appealed. The trustees backed the parents and said the school had no right to suspend the child, as it did so seven days after the incident. The child returned to school laughing and telling everyone his side. He could do no wrong, it seemed — everyone was afraid of his parents.

Cutbacks

- Certain special ed and alternate classes are closed. You are unable to determine who made the decision. Was dictated by the supervisors? the board? There was no input from parents and a disregard of the teachers' feelings, suggestions, and reservations.
- The Education Department in your province is pushing for mainstreaming. The classroom teacher and the students need more and more help from resource teachers. However, the province is now cutting back on support for those resource teachers.

Financial control

- Where you teach, four buildings are considered one school. A single item must be shared.
- Your school and its classrooms have to hold fundraisers to buy the materials they need.

Imposing dominant discourse

- Students are not allowed to wear hats in school.
- Students must call their teachers "Ms.," "Miss," "Mrs.," or "Mr." while the teachers call the students by their first names.

Censorship

- In your school district, members of a local committee conducted a study of discipline in schools. When the results of the study were presented to the school board, they became public and were discussed by members of the media. The director of education for the district stated publicly that he found the report "interesting" but would be conducting his own study of discipline in district schools. There was no further official comment on the matter. Teachers and local committee members felt as if their concerns were unimportant and as if the director took it upon himself to publicly reprimand the committee for conducting this study on their own.

TWENTY-FIVE

Out of the Straightjacket
Linda Cook

"**M**rs. Cook, I have to talk to you. I *have* to. It's important." I turned to face the pale, freckle-faced girl who stood anxiously in front of me and knew she needed my attention. Asking my other students to go about their group work, I took her aside.

Heather spoke in a low voice as she explained to me that her father had forbidden her to undertake her planned research on Israel. Just that week I had asked each student to choose a topic from their novel reading about which they wished to learn more. Heather had finished reading *From Anna* by Jean Little, and the story about a German girl who made reference to the war had sparked her interest. She wanted to find out what exactly had happened to the Jews during that time and why Anna's family had felt it imperative to emigrate to a safer country like Canada. She had also heard about *The Diary of Anne Frank*, which had made her wonder what it meant to be Jewish and how it was that Anne's family came to be persecuted. A few of the students had done some searching for information on World War II, but Heather was nagged by larger moral issues that augmented her desire to research Israel.

On questioning Heather why her father disapproved of her study, she replied that he had said he "just didn't like those people." I told her I was sorry her father thought that way, that unfortunately we often have to face opposition to what we want to do whether or not it is justified. She would have to reconsider her plans. I suggested she go back to one of the other books she had read and perhaps join another group to research a different topic. She said she would think about it, but that she really had wanted to do Israel.

The next morning Heather arrived at school, bright with the news that she had decided to stick with Israel. She told me she had thought it through and knew this was what she wanted to do most. Somewhat concerned, I asked Heather if she had considered the consequences of her father's feelings regarding her choice, and that it wasn't pleasant to go against a parent, even if you didn't agree with his or her wishes. Yes, she assured me, she had. What I suspected is that Dad would be left out of this enterprise. I said no more.

Heather worked every minute of her project time and more, at recesses and at lunchtime, to find out all she could about Israel. She drew pictures of whatever interested her and asked to photocopy those that were too difficult to draw. Frequently she could be heard off in a corner or seen sitting on a mat somewhere in the classroom, explaining some little tidbit to a classmate who wanted to listen. Finally, when her research was finished, she proudly displayed it on bristol board. She then signed up for a time to present her information, extending an invitation to the principal. If it were possible, I think she would have presented her information to the entire world!

Heather's presentation was a strong indication of the benefits of self-motivated research. She had delved deeply enough into Israel's history to know that it had been a country torn by conflicts. She talked about the land, touching on several of its political divisions, referring to Jerusalem's Old City and Israel's three main religions. In the follow-up discussion Heather was able to answer many of the questions her classmates asked of her. She explained why Anna's family had emigrated from Germany during the events leading up to World War II, and why Anne Frank and her family had had to take drastic measures to hide from their oppressors. Heather's learning, generated by incidents in her reading of novels, had come out of a need to know, not from some perfunctory assignment I had given as part of the social studies curriculum guide.

Thinking back to when Heather had first entered grade four, few could have imagined this turnabout. I remembered how shy and insecure she had been when first asked about her reading. Brimming with tears, her eyes mirrored her pain of failure as she explained her inability to read. All she focused on was that she had failed grade three and that she had been on resource for the past year. During the initial parent–teacher interviews, her mother had mentioned that Heather didn't feel good about herself, calling herself "stupid" when her younger sister had caught up to her in school. She cried a lot. She also fought with her brothers and sisters, which made life around home difficult. Her mother had been concerned that Heather might not "snap out of her moods."

Heather reached my class at a propitious time. I was returning to teaching after a year's sabbatical at Mount Saint Vincent University, where I had joined other teachers who were also taking their masters of education degree. I had been stimulated by reading the current work of educational scholars and exchanging ideas with my peers. I internalized the whole language ideology. For the first time I was aware of how collaborative and social learning was. I was relearning how to learn. One of the ideas that particularly struck me was the literature-based program, and I read various theorists' views on the values of implementing such a program. I was determined to make it work in my grade-four classroom.

That summer I scrounged for books, enlisting the services of the subsystem's curriculum consultant, who helped me put together a starting library. I structured the program with a reading/writing workshop approach, an eclectic mix of ideas from educators who had written of their experiences: Calkins, Graves, and Atwell from the United States; Newman and various local teachers in

Halifax County. Although I faced the opening day of school with paradoxical feelings of euphoria and terror, there was no going back to basal readers. I knew I was going to make my program work.

As the months passed, I watched Heather become a reader in the true sense of the word. She always had a book in her hand and constantly shared her ideas with others. Frequently she organized her classmates into presenting some aspect of their novel reading and extended invitations to students, parents, and teachers who might like to attend. At the end of that year she had read a varied list of twenty-three novels, ranging from E. B. White's *Stuart Little* to Peggy Parish's mysteries. Heather got together with one of her friends who was also interested in Parish's mysteries to write a mystery of their own in Parish's style. As the presenters read it (complete with sound effects), the class was thoroughly entertained. Given all this, it was no surprise to me when Heather announced she had decided to go against her father's wishes and research Israel. I had watched her take charge of her learning and grow in her knowledge of what it meant to be a learner.

It wasn't until much later, when I was challenged in conversation with a colleague, that I became aware of the full implications of Heather's choice. I was accused of irresponsibility in allowing a ten-year-old child to make a decision that, in effect, would pit her against her father. In my colleague's eyes there was no worse sin, and she felt that whole language teachers, in their rigorous attempts to render the acquisition of literacy skills more attractive, were alienating students from their homes and their cultures. Harman and Edelsky (1989) have addressed this issue:

> As students become literate and begin to feel the liberating effects of their ability to use their language, they paradoxically begin to feel the constraints of estrangement from their roots.
>
> Because the explicit purpose of education is to assimilate subordinate groups into the dominant culture, much has been written about the pressure on these groups to reject their home communities. Labov (1969) and Ogbu (1987) have described black teenagers refusing to succeed in school in order to avoid being "white." (p. 395)

As women embark upon the road to literacy, it is often with a bittersweet duplicity. "This is especially true for women engaged in heterosexual relationships when their men feel threatened by the images of power [independence and success] attached to education" (Rockhill p. 315). I am one of these women. Since my return to university to upgrade my education, my husband has felt, and continues to feel, excluded from the world of the university that nurtures me. I know the paradoxes that lie in furthering my education.

I considered my colleague's accusation. In my mind the alternative was to deny Heather a right to intellectual freedom, to shackle her to her father's bigotry; this was the same father who would not allow her to take books home from the school library for the sole reason that they cluttered up the house. It seemed to me that, in not deferring to her father's command, Heather was on some level formulating her own response to society's ideological construction of the male voice as the voice of authority.

Men are invested with authority as individuals not because they have individual special competencies or expertise but because as men they appear as representative of the power and authority of the institutionalized structures that govern society." (Smith 1989, 253)

Had Heather's father found out that she had defied his command, he might have made the issue a legal challenge. Had he gone to the school board with a complaint against me, I am not sure how much support I would have received. The Department of Education lists under its The Goals of Public Education to "develop the habits and methods of critical thinking and reasoning to foster the natural desire to learn and understand." [p. 11, 4] The Education Act (Province of Nova Scotia, Department of Education 1986) has listed amongst the duties of the teacher "to encourage in the pupils by precept and example a respect for religion and the principles of Christian morality, for truth, justice, love of country, humanity, industry, temperance and all other virtues" [Section 74(f), p. 36].

But words are cheap, and the jargon of programs and acts are deliberately ambiguous and obscure. What it boils down to is that if Heather's father had become enraged with my supporting Heather in her research enterprise and had wanted to lodge a formal complaint with the school board, I would have been out on a limb. Just as Heather's growth in literacy may get her in trouble at home, I was just as much at risk by providing her with opportunities to make choices regarding what she wanted to learn, and in supporting her in those choices.

Ira Shor talks to Paulo Freire about this problem in their conversational book, *A Pedagogy for Liberation* (1986):

"There is a lot of pressure to teach this traditional way, first because it is familiar and already worked out, even if it doesn't work in class. Second, by deviating from the standard syllabus you can get known as a rebel or radical or flake, and be subjected to anything from petty harassment to firing" (p. 7).

John Keating, the teacher in the film *Dead Poets Society*, is a fictional example of what happens when liberatory education opposes deeply ensconced traditional ideology. Keating's pedagogy had a powerful influence over his students (and, in the case of the character Neil, had traumatic repercussions). Yet, regardless of the support Keating received from the majority of his students, he was fired — supporting Shor's warning about the risks involved in breaking from tradition. Keating's fate is always a possibility for any teacher who challenges the status quo; and alienation — as Neil and Heather experienced — is always possible for those challenged by their learning.

Every hour I am in my classroom I learn more about my students, myself, and our learning. Every time I read the works of educators on the role of education, I listen and ask questions. When, I made a commitment to the philosophy of progressive education, there was no going back. John Goodlad (1983) writes:

There is in the gap between our highly idealistic goals for schooling in our society and differentiated opportunities condoned and supported in schools a monstrous hypocrisy....We will only begin to get evidence of the potential power of pedagogy when we dare to risk and support markedly deviant classroom procedures (1983).

Too many students suffer from society's leading them to believe they cannot learn. Heather was one of these. To the extent that I could show her she could reverse this by responding to her needs, I freed her from her feelings of failure. That this freedom is a double-edged sword does not lessen, but adds to, its worth. Harman and Edelsky (1989) suggest that there is no progress without pain. The consciousness of learners can lead to alienation, but also to examination and action.

> [S]haring a common responsibility for effecting change...[and] the liberation of learners from the confines of the either-home-or-mainstream discourse dilemma into active struggle with the issues of literacy, community, identity, and social change [are] most likely to come from the power of the critical thinking and democracy learned and practiced in whole language classrooms. (p. 404)

As teachers, we need to see the possibilities for change in a system that is oppressive. We mustn't be paralyzed into inaction by a sense of failure. Rather, as Shannon (1990) says, we need a sense of history and hope. Taking up this challenge exposes teachers to risks. But the risks are much greater if student's voices aren't heard.

Addendum

Almost two years have passed since Heather's experience with her research. She is now in grade six, and I am in my second year of teaching grade fives in another school within the district.

My major concerns continue to be with students whose parents try to remain supportive of a school system that has disempowered them intellectually and politically. My belief that students learn best with and from one another in collaborative, purposeful work is not always understood by parents who are not familiar with the process. Parents often feel threatened by the independence their children develop as they become aware of their own power to change situations. They are often uncomfortable with children taking part in decision making and having a voice in what affects them.

To counteract this, I have tried to open up my classroom to parents, inviting them to take part in the learning process. Parent volunteers who work with my students not only serve to give students the support and feedback they require, but strengthen my link with the community. These parents become aware of the processes of learning in the classroom and the larger school environs while building a trust in me and what I am trying to achieve for their children.

It takes continual dialogue and demonstration to allay fears of failure that keep parents on edge with me, the person they see as being "in charge." It means holding conversations in nonthreatening settings, with each side appreciating what the other has to say. I continue to invite parents to participate in classroom enterprises, to be active participants in their children's learning. I try to keep in mind the importance of sharing control with one's students in the classroom and with their parents beyond it.

References

Dead Poets' Society, 1989. Film directed by Peter Weir; produced by Stephen Haft, Paul Junger-Witt, and Tony Thomas. Touchstone.

Gaskell, J., & A. McLaren. 1987. *Women and Education: A Canadian Perspective*. Calgary: Detselig Enterprises.

Goodlad, John I. 1983. *A Place Called School*. New York: McGraw-Hill.

Harman, S., & C. Edelsky. 1989. "The Risks of Whole Language Literacy." *Language Arts 66*(4) 392–406.

Labov, W. 1969. "The Logic of Nonstandard English." *Georgetown University Roundtable Monographs on Language and Linguistics* 22.

Little, J. 1972. *From Anna*. New York: Harper and Row.

Ogbu, J. 1987. "Variability in Minority School Performance: A Problem in Search of an Explanation." *Anthropology and Education Quarterly* 18: 312–34.

Province of Nova Scotia, Department of Education. 1986. *The Education Act and The School Boards Membership Act*, Halifax, 36.

———. 1989–90. *Public School Programs*, Nova Scotia: Published by Authority of the Minister of Education. 11.

Rockhill, K. 1987. "Literacy as Threat/Desire: Longing to Be Somebody." In J. Gaskell and A. McLaren, eds., *Women and Education: A Canadian Perspective*, p. 315 Calgary: Detselig.

Shannon, P. 1990. *The Struggle to Continue: Progressive Reading Instruction in the United States*. Portsmouth, NH: Heinemann.

Shor, I., and P. Freire. 1986. *A Pedagogy for Liberation*. Granby, MA: Bergin and Garvey.

Smith, D.E. 1972. "An Analysis of Ideological Structures and How Women are Excluded: Consideration for Academic Women." Reprinted in J. Gaskell and A. McLaren, eds., *Women and Education: A Canadian Perspective*, Calgary: Detselig. 1987.

INDEX